Partnering

A Guide to Co-owning Anything from Homes to Home Computers

• • •

Lois Rosenthal

Writer's Digest Books

Cincinnati, Ohio

The "Partnership Questionnaire" in Chapter Four used by permission. © 1982 by Edward Lahniers.

Partnering. Copyright 1983 by Lois Rosenthal. Printed and bound in the United States of America. All rights reserved. No part of this book may be reproduced in any form or by any electronic or mechanical means including information storage and retrieval systems without permission in writing from the publisher, except by a reviewer who may quote brief passages in a review. Published by Writer's Digest Books, 9933 Alliance Road, Cincinnati, Ohio 45242. First edition.

Library of Congress Cataloging in Publication Data

Rosenthal, Lois.
  Partnering.

  Includes index.
  1. Joint tenancy—United States—Popular works.
2. Joint ownership of personal property—United States—
Popular works. I. Title.
KF619.Z9R67 1983   346.7304'2   83-16687
ISBN 0-89879-127-8   347.30642
ISBN 0-89879-111-1 (pbk.)

Design by Alice Mauro

To the memory,
evergreen,
of Toni A. Lowenthal
and for
Barbara S. Marcus—
the essence of sharing.

In Appreciation

It would be impossible to thank every person who pointed me to a partner, shared knowledge, or lent their skills to this book. But I would at least like to mention the following:

Dick Asimus, who brought this idea to me with insight and generosity, is the ultimate sharer. I will be forever grateful to him for unlocking the door to the world of people who partner.

Many who sat over cups of coffee, under a tree, in front of a warm fire, and told me in enthusiastic and patient detail how they made their partnerships work, wished to remain anonymous—so be it. I have changed names and fictionalized some facts to protect their privacy. But publicly, I want to thank them for giving so much of themselves with such kindness.

Experts played a big part in putting *Partnering* together.

I checked with a bevy of attorneys to keep the information in this book on the right side of the law. I must have called Gloria Haffer twice a week to ask, "Is it legal to . . .?" Her answers went beyond the bounds of friendship. Attorney Mark Berliant laid a firm foundation for house partners with elan; Barbara G. Watts advised how to draw up agreements and keep partners honest with each other; Lynne Skilken taught me the basics of bank loans and mortgages and how to translate legalese; Ed Diller gave me the good advice not to give legal advice and stick to showing how to bring people together, and introduced me to a whole network of partners.

Psychologists were essential to this book, too: Stuart Scheingarten helped shape partnering ideas in the very beginning and was giving of himself and his expertise throughout; Jane Engeman and Daniel Langmeyer provided how-to-make-partnerships-work-and-keep-them-working directions; Edward Lahniers provided an invaluable tool in the form of his well-conceived partnering test.

Wayne Haupert of State Farm Insurance proved he *is* a good neighbor. He fielded dozens of phone calls that made other insurance agents shudder. ("You're talking about co-owning . . . *what*? And then *insuring* it?!") He never failed to come up with solid recommendations.

The Shared Housing Resource Center in Philadelphia was just that: a rich source they freely let me tap. I hope I have done justice to the bright, caring staff of this information hub, especially director Dennis Day-Lower and educational director Leah Dobkin.

Jim and Linda Nunes-Schrag with The Movement for a New Society in Philadelphia show, by example, how lives should be shared. They gave much to this book and to me.

Residents of The Boston Shared Living House, and especially Kay Thomas, the house facilitator, who answered a zillion questions, added greatly. Gwen Rono of Unihab and Mardi Rose of Cambridge Living Options for Elders explained how older adults can benefit from living together while we tromped through Cambridge and saw it in action.

Huzzahs to Robert H. Springer for maritime pearls of wisdom; Rob Root and Mel Williams of the Caesar's Creek Soaring Club for sailplane lore; Karen Bess of The Civic Garden Center of Greater Cincinnati for community gardens know-how; Toni Birckhead for art partnering possibilities; Susan J. Hickenlooper for unraveling the mysteries of business partnering; Adele Lipman and Jean Doyle for searching out apartment sharers; Winifred Kessler of Womonways for helping track down partners at the start; Howard I. Wells III, a kindred soul at Writer's Digest Books, who not only let me zing along on his electric alternative wavelength, but allowed me to pepper him mercilessly with questions he miraculously answered.

This book was a true joint venture between my editor, Carol Cartaino, and me. Without her bounteous ideas, without her nourishing and nudging mine, there would have been a hard lonely road. Partnering with her was grand and joyful.

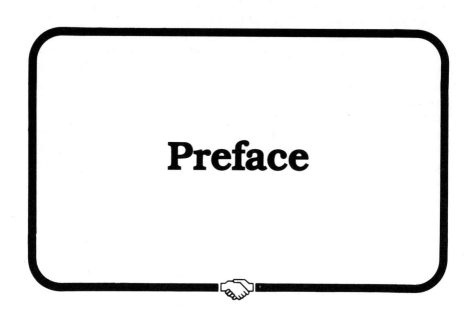

Preface

A letter in the mail. A man who reads my newspaper column tells me he and his wife share a home with another couple. It goes on to say that people all over the country are doubling up on home purchases. He thought this would be interesting for me to write about—it might even be a book.

I'm intrigued. I phone this letter writer, Dick Asimus, and we arrange to meet. The quiet summer evening we talked for hours changed my life. Ideas he planted in my mind took me all over the country interviewing people who share homes, sure, but everything else under the sun.

I tracked what I thought was a trickle of sharing and found it to be a rushing young stream. After six months I knew there *was* a book. A book about how people buy things together because they can't afford to buy them on their own—or don't want to. I discovered not only a kaleidoscope of bright, innovative ideas new to most of us, but a new economy, a whole new way of living.

Because I wanted to concentrate on this, *Partnering* stays away from business-type partnerships—partnerships for profit. There are libraries full of tomes that tell you how to strike it rich, if that's what you're after.

The partners in this book join forces to buy the things they want and need to enrich their own lives, not their corporate coffers. They are closely involved in their joint ventures. Belonging to a condominium association, time sharing—in those arrangements you have a monetary investment, but not much of your soul. The partners in this book oil the engines, weed the gardens, pick out the wallpaper—themselves. And they have to agree on how "it" should be done and what "it" will be.

I've avoided romantic partnerships, too. Since there is an overwhelming amount of material that will tell you how to live together successfully, married or otherwise, I circumvented the soulful subject of pairing up for love.

Though you will find sample agreements in this book, clip-and-use contracts are not what I had in mind. I've included agreements actual partners have drawn up to serve as models for you, to give you an idea of what you'll need to do for your partnership. You can build on what's here—with or without an attorney—according to what is appropriate for your joint venture.

A word about style: This book is written in the masculine gender because I think "he/she," "s/he," "he or she," "him or her," in sentences are eye-stoppers. And even "she" used throughout a book still jars many people, especially when "she" is operating a jackhammer. (Yes, we all know some women *do.*) I wanted to make ideas come alive with no distractions, so I reluctantly bowed to tradition for the sake of readability. I know God in Her Heaven will understand.

Contents

·1·
Partnering: What Is It?

You've been faithfully putting money aside ever since you started working. You can't wait to own your own home. Your rent has risen until it seems downright absurd—and it's all money in someone else's pocket. You wonder if now is the time to buy. Your accountant says you can deduct mortgage interest payments from your income tax and actually save while building equity. It all sounds sensible, so you begin to scour the classified ads each morning.

The listings are appealing, as are a number of the houses you go to see. But no matter which way you try financing, your nest egg can't buy anything you really like. You consider the alternatives. You can stay in your apartment and keep saving money while houses become more expensive, or you can buy a compromise house in a neighborhood an hour's drive from your job.

Or you can turn to an alternative many people are finding sensible—doubling up. Throwing in together for business, not romance, is the order of the day, as hard-pressed buyers help one another purchase homes.

You may already own a home, in which case the above example doesn't apply to you. But with the kids needing braces and the car making gasping noises again, you know you can't squeeze the new lawn mower you also need out of your budget. So you think of something you never thought of before—splitting the cost of a new lawn mower with a neighbor. Why does everyone on the block need a lawn mower anyway?

Joint ownership is possible on a great many levels. For those who live alone and want to keep it that way, but have always dreamed of owning a boat, divvying the cost with a co-worker may make that dream a reality. And if every appliance that hums, whirs, or wheezes is gobbling up dollars you'd rather spend on theater tickets or dinner and a movie on the weekends, buying the appliances in partnership with others is a good solution. Wouldn't you rather have a few extra dollars to slip a nice bottle of wine on the grocery list once in a while than be the proud, full owner of an extension ladder you use once each fall to clean the leaves out of your roof gutters?

Sharing

Sharing has not traditionally been a middle-class phenomenon. But those who thought joint ownership is only for "those communal types" are learning otherwise—and fast. The values of people with social commitments as well as material possessions in common are being adopted by those who realize that sole ownership—of everything—just isn't possible and isn't really necessary. So-called fringe ideas are hitting home to Middle America because people who were taught they had to make it alone to be successful simply can't. They're beginning to realize they can pool resources and gain strength from each other.

Partnering can be as versatile as you make it and as ingenious as the individuals who decide what and how they are going to share. It can be an integral part of your life, such as dual homeownership, or a lagniappe that reinstates the small (and not so small) luxuries more pressing expenses preclude.

This book will show you a world of partnering. Then it will explain, step-by-step, how to do it successfully. You will learn from the experiences of those who have joined forces to afford "dream-only" luxuries and those who partner nitty-gritty, day-to-day necessities. From those who share a love of adventure, as well as the soaring expenses of owning an airplane, you will learn how you can fly too. Down-to-earth homeowners who split the cost of an industrial-size polisher to whip their floors into shape in lieu of each buying a smaller model will explain how you can do the same with any appliance. Young professionals who solved their business problems on a jointly owned computer demonstrate how you can give yourself the high-tech advantage too. Antique aficionados who bought a mid-1800s weathervane—together—show how art bought in partnership is a movable feast.

Bulldozers to trampolines, suits to snake drain cleaners—anything you can imagine—can be jointly owned if you put your mind to it. In this book I hope to inspire you to make partnering a part of your life. I have tried to include everything you need to start a partnership, make it work, and keep it happy. Two heads, two hearts, and two pocketbooks *are* better than one.

·2·
What Partnering Can Do for You

Your new boat is pretty spiffy if you do say so yourself. Why, just compare the shape it was in when you bought it to how it looks now. It was worth the hundreds of hours you logged over the winter getting it ready for summer. It was worth giving up your spring vacation so you could buy a new engine. So you gave up seeing friends on the weekends to squeeze boat-rebuilding hours into your schedule—look at what you've accomplished, and you've done it alone.

Most of us think that way. But let's think again. If we share the purchase of a boat, the initial cost is immediately cut in half or however many slices there are partners. People buying together can buy a better boat than they could afford on their own. And few boat owners, no matter how enthusiastic, are actually on the water every weekend. As the novelty and initial pride in ownership wear thin, they often find they are using the boat (plane, vacation home, recreational vehicle, whatever) less than they envisioned. The dream purchase becomes a burden as they tire of sacrificing vacations and other extras for its income-draining upkeep.

The hours of working on your boat shrink as more people share them. Partners who do those jobs together share each other's company as well. There is group pride in making that boat something really special. "It's seaworthy! We did it!" And when it comes time to celebrate—it's just never as exciting to celebrate alone.

Think about it. Anything jointly held for recreation, from vehicles to homes, can be enjoyed separately as well as together by partners who work on it, plan for it, grow close while doing so, and come out ahead financially.

Neighbors who share home-related appliances, from electric sanders to snow plows, free their individual incomes as they bond as friends. The sharp edges of side-by-side but still isolated living soften as people share the burdens of homeownership creatively. Glorious storage space becomes available. Your jointly owned appliances spend at least half their time in someone else's house. You can actually get from the basement stairs to the washing machine without picking your way through a labyrinth of rarely used tools. Bliss! You can park your car in your own garage.

Spread the Fun and the Cost

Just sitting down and deciding what items are needed and then which can be bought together is often the first step in drawing closer as neighbors. Poring over classified ads, scouting the stores, and reporting good deals to each other build camaraderie.

A group of friends who buy paintings together meets monthly to keep abreast of what's new in the art world. They visit galleries, talk to the owners, discuss the books and magazines they read to increase their knowledge. Their twice-a-year purchase is the end product of an enlightened group-learning experience.

Car poolers who own vehicles in common might discuss job-related problems on the way to work or use the time to read the newspaper while someone else drives. They can pick up advice on which dry cleaner does the best job on drapes and who is the best dentist in their part of town. Four people in a carpool know there are always three people to push and one to steer when the car gets stuck on snowy days. All that and not having to buy a second car too?

Dual vegetable gardeners don't have to envision their tomatoes rotting on the vine or their peas shriveling in the pod when one of them takes a three-week vacation. Watering and weeding chores can be split or done in unison.

Home sharing offers as many pluses as the reasons people choose to live together. One man who shared a home with two others said, "It's great coming home to a dinner I didn't have to cook. But it's not just the convenience of having a meal ready that is important, it's sharing it with people who care about many of the same things I do.

It's having people to talk to at the end of the day. It's being part of a supportive atmosphere where I am accepted."

For beginning career singles who must live on their own for the first time, for the just-divorced, or for anyone who has been emotionally or physically uprooted, teaming up quells loneliness. It helps having someone around when you are navigating one of life's rough spots.

Older adults can share a home to keep each other out of institutions by providing the assistance each might need when they are no longer able to live alone. People who never had children can share a home with those who do to produce an extended family atmosphere. Single parents give each other moral and emotional support in the job of raising children alone even as they help each other heal the wounds divorce leaves in its wake.

Shared living provides security. And shared houses mean shared chores: not always having to make sure there are eggs in the refrigerator (when it's not your turn to shop) and being able to rotate hauling out the garbage cans. Stopping to split a pizza and a quart of beer with someone while you spend the weekend removing a dozen layers of wallpaper. Apprenticing yourself to a master as your partner introduces you to the fine art of hanging kitchen cabinets.

Individuals who share ownership of any object learn skills from each other. Whether it's finding out that patching a tent isn't such a mystery or that the knob you forget to turn is the key to getting a good close-up with your camera, you get hands-on know-how from partners. And if each partner has a different skill to contribute to the group (or each other), it is so much the richer.

Some dual homeowners share a special commitment. It may be a political cause; it may be to bring about social change; it may be a religious belief. It helps having other people around for reinforcement, especially if what you think isn't popular.

Co-owning gives you the chance to take chances. You always wanted to gaze at the stars but you know you'll never be a serious astronomer. You want to try river running but aren't sure you'll want to shoot the rapids every weekend. You'd like to make your own ice cream with natural ingredients, and that magnificent machine will make the best, but is a perfect strawberry worth that much?

Partnering allows you to be adventuresome. If you discover that you didn't *really* want to own your own rubber raft or that Saturn is not as exciting as the Saturday night movie on TV, your partners can buy out your share. You've spared yourself the fear and remorse of spending too much money on something you wind up not using. But you've allowed yourself to experiment without feeling guilty about what you've spent.

"Do it all yourself." "Own it entirely." Why? Just because we've grown up with these values doesn't make them true, especially in a world that makes it increasingly harder to put them in practice.

The tangible benefits of partnering are clear. By sharing expenses, people can own what they otherwise cannot afford and they can buy better quality—an unbeatable combination. The intangibles are as myriad as the facets of a well-cut diamond, whose luster changes with the light in which it is viewed.

•3•
Can I
Partner *That?*

Partnering, huh? It sounds pretty good; even exciting. But how do I know what I can comfortably share—what candidates for joint ownership might be right for me?

Let me think about it. One of the best ways for me to relax at the end of the day is to go down to the basement where all my lapidary equipment is.

That hobby has been a godsend to me. I love puttering with all the tools I bought. I love finding rocks and polishing them up to bring out their beauty. The stones I've collected mean a lot to me. To me, they're works of art.

My next-door neighbor, Bill, saw some of my stones and thought they were beautiful, too. He went fossil collecting with me one day and even brought over some stones he found for me to polish.

He's becoming more interested in the hobby and has talked about buying his own polishing machine. It seems silly for us to own duplicates; together we could trade up and buy a better one.

But I love being in my basement alone—when *I* want to be there. I don't want to make appointments to relax. I worry about schedules all day at the office. I don't want to find Bill using the diamond-bladed saw when I'm ready to open the most exciting geode I've ever found. I

9

don't want to find a burr on the pliers when I'm setting the most perfect peridot I've ever had my hands on. I don't want the tumbler tied up when I get back from a collector's tour of Idaho with a bagful of treasures. Sharing my lapidary equipment just wouldn't work.

But wasn't it just last week Bill was grumbling about the flab he's accumulated around his middle? In fact, we were both complaining about not getting enough exercise.

I told him about the stationary exercise bicycle my cousin Stan bought. Every morning he watches a half-hour of the *Today* show while he pedals away his excess pounds. Those things can cost a few hundred dollars or more. More than I'd like to spend, anyway. Maybe Bill and I could chip in and buy one together.

We could keep it at his house or mine. Our homes are so close it really doesn't make any difference. We each have an out-of-the-way place to store the bicycle and a portable TV to pass the time while we ride.

He could use it in the morning since he gets up earlier than I do. I could exercise during the six o'clock news before dinner. We could change schedules whenever we please.

A bicycle like that would never matter as much to me as my stone polisher. What could either of us do to it, anyway? But it sure would be nice to have. I bet Bill would be interested in half ownership of an easy way to keep in shape. I'll talk to him about it.

In deciding what you can partner comfortably, have a conversation with yourself similar to the one you've just read.

How much does the item you are thinking about sharing mean to you? How personally involved with it are you?

If you think you'd flinch every time someone else touched it, if you know you'd have nightmares over a scratch, bump, or chip on it, buy it on your own. If you can't afford it, do without until you can. It's not worth fighting over.

How flexible are you? If someone folds the dishrag over the faucet instead of draping it over the rack on the wall after wiping out the kitchen sink, do you go off the deep end? Does everything have to be done "your way," especially with your possessions, for you to feel comfortable?

In house partnering, of course, people must learn the fine art of give and take. House partners who *must* double up to survive learn to be lenient—whether they like it or not. But house partnering has some special requirements we'll deal with in those specific chapters. Here we're trying to identify the basics of a sharing attitude.

What's Mine Is Yours?

What you buy says a lot about you—how you feel and think. Is your car a sensible brown sedan or a sleek sports model? Did you pick it because you wanted steady transportation and good gas mileage or because climbing behind the wheel of that road-hugging beauty makes people's heads turn when you drive by?

Can you share something that close to your heart? Could you partner a Porsche if the person you bought it with lovingly waxed and vacuumed it the same way you do, felt the same exhilaration driving it that you do?

Could you co-own it then? Think about that. Only you can decide.

Right now, if you think your Sony Walkman radio is the most incredible invention since sliced bread, keep it for yourself, especially if you find yourself wincing every time your roommate borrows it. You run after work and your roommate jogs before breakfast, so the radio you both like to plug into could easily be split. But gut feelings play a big part in whether your partner should invest in his own way to jazz up his morning workouts.

It's like the first scratch you get on a new car. It hurts, but you know it's unavoidable. It is just as inevitable that objects owned in partnership will not always be used exactly as you would use them—all the time. Sure, you can look for partners who will treat possessions as you do, and many will. You can write agreements that make it clear how an object should be used—later I'm going to show you how.

Think deeply about how you feel when you visualize someone else using that $600 professional slicer you want to buy from the Hammacher Schlemmer catalog. You've been pining for one. Bulk cheeses and meats are cheaper and you can slice them to the exact thickness you desire. Trying to explain what you want at the neighborhood supermarket is frustrating. Prepackaged sliced cheese and meat are awful. It sure would be easy to share a slicer with someone else, or even a few people, because it's portable and no one would use it daily.

How often you use an object and how far you live from your partners are other factors to consider in sharing. If every time you reach for your jointly owned item, it's at your partner's house—and he lives across town—you're going to get aggravated. It's hard to partner something that's crucial to your daily life. You need to be able to set up a use schedule that doesn't impose real hardship or inconvenience on anyone. This is especially important when the partnered object is stationary, like a hot tub or a vegetable garden. It must be convenient and accessible to all.

The slicer would be an important purchase to you, but you could live without it. It won't be one of the ways you really express yourself. It won't make any subtle contribution to your self-concept. So wouldn't sharing make sense?

Think about all the items you've bought you have despised spending money on. They should move to the top of your list of "partnerables" when you need to replace them. Maybe a portable sewing machine falls into that category.

Some people love to sew and take pride in making their own clothes. You hate it, loathe mending, but have a basket filled with jeans waiting to be patched, shirts that could have a second life if seams were machine-stitched, and other stuff you'd like to forget about.

You don't want a fancy sewing machine. You really don't want one at all. But you do need one to attack the stack of Linda's clothes waiting to be made into the right size for Sally.

Suzanne, who works at your office, is not wild about sewing either. Neither is Jean. Who has time? At lunch the three of you complain about your pressed schedules when you compare notes on how hard it is to keep a career, a home, husband, and kids together.

"Maybe we could all buy a portable sewing machine—together.

"When anyone needs to use it, the one who has the machine at her house could bring it to the office. We don't need to get an expensive model—just one that does the basics.

"I'll talk to Suzanne and Jean at lunch today. If everyone agrees it's a good idea, we can start shopping for the sewing machine after work."

By now, a pattern of self-searching should be clear. If what you want to buy is too close to your heart to let anyone else use it, you'll just have to get it on your own. But passion can also make it easier to partner. You want or need it so much you *can* bring yourself to be flexible and generous with the people with whom you buy it. Even if your passion runs to hating (to shell out for it), it may be a sign of a prime partnerable. Find a few people who feel the same way and go for a joint purchase.

·4·
How to Find the Right Partner for You

If you've lived next door to someone for years and borrowed tools from each other without problems, odds are good that you can handle a partnership in the welding equipment you've both talked about buying. You know what the inside of your neighbor's garage looks like. You know how he maintains his tools and the condition in which he's returned yours. You know he's financially responsible—at least he's lived in the same house for years and his standard of living is on a par with yours. You've never had a major falling-out. Because you've known each other for so long, you'd probably feel comfortable asking him to be your partner, and if he agrees (you think he might because you bumped into him at Sears one day looking at a torch kit that caught your eye), a joint venture will be based on a pretty stable foundation.

Success rates in partnering soar when the principals have known each other for a period of time. But need can supersede the time it takes to build a long-term relationship.

You need a lawn mower, a home to share, a tractor—now. You need a partner you feel you can trust and rely on. So where do you begin your search? In your own backyard, if possible.

13

If the Shoe Fits, Share It

Ask a neighbor you feel at ease with (even if you aren't that close) how he'd feel about joining forces on a purchase you must make. He might need the very same thing and may have thought of partnering himself but was reluctant to ask you. Muster the courage to ask.

Here is a way that might make it easier. Let's use a prospective lawn mower partnership as an example.

You see Joe, your neighbor, working out in the yard. Walk over and strike up a conversation. Tell him you've been thinking about the two of you buying a mower together, since you know yours is heading into its sunset season and you've noticed him having trouble with his lately. Give him a few facts about the one you have in mind. Talk about what it would cost and how you think the two of you could arrange to take care of it and use it. Then ask him what he thinks about the plan. But don't rush him, and make it clear that pressuring him is the last thing you want to do. Say that you know he'll want a few days to think it over, since you're hitting him with a slew of new ideas cold. You realize he's going to have questions about the whole arrangement, and you probably will too.

Give people time—not only to think about what you've proposed, but also to show that you're not trying to push them into making a decision on the spot. They may feel uneasy with your proposal, but if you bring all the facts out into the open, present your bright idea as just that—a bright idea—and then back off, you won't look like you're trying to put anything over on anybody. People are wary of new schemes—sometimes rightly so.

Perhaps Joe hasn't responded in a few days. Get back to him, and try to steer the conversation this way.

You: "Since I hadn't heard from you, I wondered if you were having second thoughts about my grand lawn mower plan. You seem reluctant. What are you thinking about?"

Joe: "Well, we seem to be getting along fine as neighbors. We don't know each other all that well, but everything is swell as it is. Even though I do need a mower and the plan sounds good, I don't want to risk making a good relationship turn sour. If we buy something together, maybe we'll fight."

You: "What do you think we'll fight about? Whether I'll break it or you'll break it? That certainly can happen, and either you'll fix it or I'll fix it or we'll get someone else to fix it. Why don't we talk about how we'll manage it once we've bought it."

This is when you must plan—in detail—how you would share the mower. Write down your strategy to make sure what you both intend to do is clear. Be specific. (The ingredients of a successful partnership agreement and how to draw one up will be described in Chapter Five and in the chapters dealing with specific partnerships.) By going through this process, you and Joe talk away fears, provide for all the emergencies that may arise, make a sound managing plan, become partners, and remain friends.

Broaching the subject of partnering with an acquaintance can be hard. The whole idea of sharing possessions may be something he's never thought about. Partnering? Does that have something to do with living together? Setting up a business? Getting married? You may have quite a bit of explaining to do. You don't relish the thought of being turned down, and putting someone in the position of turning you down isn't too appealing either. By being open and honest in stating your plans and by not pushing the person for an instant answer, you can adapt the previous conversation to anyone you have in mind for a joint venture on anything.

Seek and Ye Shall Find

But maybe you don't know anyone who would love to be half owner of a kayak or a home computer or a condominium only 10 minutes from downtown. Now what? You tack up notices in places likely to draw the interest of the kind of person you are looking for and put notices in newsletters or bulletins that go to people with whom you have something in common.

According to Dennis Day-Lower, director of the Shared Housing Resource Center in Philadelphia, a national clearinghouse for information on shared living, safety is the biggest reason to be selective about where you advertise your needs. The more public the exposure, the more risk involved. This is why many people avoid using the classified sections of the newspaper or posting signs in supermarkets. People who have done this receive strange, not to mention obscene, phone calls from people they definitely do not want to hear from.

Choose a place to stick a notice whose frequenters are likely the kind of people you want to attract. Do some careful screening now to narrow the field before making your final selection.

Dennis thinks church or synagogue bulletin boards and newsletters are good places to put notices, since you'll draw replies from people whose commitments and values are similar to yours. He also recommends any association or bulletin that parallels the work you do. For example, if you're an architect, a notice in the local AIA newsletter will draw like-minded respondents. If you're a female reporter who belongs to Women in Communications, their local newsletter might be a good place to state your needs. Check to see if newsletters like these accept classified ads of this kind.

Your workplace is a fine place to find partners, too. At lunch, people are likely to talk about their backlog of bills, upcoming expenses, and dreams of what they'd like to be able to afford. Listen to the conversation with partnering in mind. You can also use company newsletters and bulletin boards to draw interested people.

As an example, four men who were transferred from one city to another by a large corporation commiserated at work that the homes they bought all had trees that needed drastic pruning. After figuring the rental cost of a chain saw for each of them, they discovered it would be more convenient and much cheaper to purchase one together.

Many places of business are fertile ground for car poolers. Some large companies even encourage this by providing computer printouts of employees' addresses to make it easy to find others who live nearby who also want to share a ride.

One joint car owner/car pooler felt he didn't need to ask his partners for credit references, since they all worked for the same company. Before hiring anyone, this corporation does such extensive checking, its stamp of approval was assurance enough for him. They all had steady paychecks; they even knew approximately what each one was earning, so they felt confident all partners could afford their share. Whether it's home sharing, car pooling, or any other kind of partnering you have in mind, co-workers are good prospects, and company personnel departments may help you in your choice.

What are your hobbies? Do you play tennis or golf? Notices where you play—if there is some definable membership (not just open-to-the-city-at-large recreation centers where you have no idea who will come and read your notice)—are good places to find partners.

Airports where private planes are kept can be hotbeds of gossip *and* hard facts. Talk to the manager or a mechanic for the scoop on who is buying what or who wants to but can't afford it. Leave your name if you want to partner on a plane and ask to have anyone considered a good prospect phone you. Don't expect that one visit will take care of it. Call periodically and ask if anyone has come to mind. Don't be a pest, but don't be passive either. And ask if you can leave your name tacked up on a wall along with what you want.

The same is true of marinas for potential boat partners, or stables for horse co-owners. The people in charge always know what's go-

16

ing on and will generally be glad to put you in touch with someone who may need a partner. They may be able to furnish a name on the spot.

You can also use these tactics at home computer centers or places where recreational vehicles are sold. Ask a salesperson or the sales manager to watch for customers who come in often to ogle a model they can't afford—alone. You may be one of the frequent oglers yourself and have a good relationship with someone on the staff. Make the most of it—ask if he'll put you in touch with prospective partners. Some of the people whose names he can give you may already own less sophisticated models bought at the same store. Ask if they have established a responsible track record.

Also check with the managers of apartment complexes where you may want to live but whose rent you can't afford. Other people in the same situation leave their names in the rental office, as well as apartment dwellers who have lost a roommate and are seeking another—often desperately. The manager can help in your evaluation of who would be reliable.

Be creative about where you leave your name. How about the small appliance repair shop near your house? The owner is sure to know whose food processor has sliced its last onion and who has mentioned he would like to upgrade to a Cuisinart. These people might be receptive to joint ownership. The owner also knows who is prompt in paying bills and how customers maintain machinery. Make him part of your screening process.

Another possible place to post a notice is a neighborhood association headquarters where everyone who belongs works for the betterment of the community. Better yet, is there a newsletter? This is a good way to tap into a congenial network of people.

Health food store walls are often plastered with partnering notices, and food co-ops were ranked as one of the most popular places for gathering partners by many of the people I interviewed. Generally both are patronized by people who share the same values and who are open to alternative ideas.

If you belong to a single-parent support group, this would be a natural place to try to find a house partner. Do you frequent a senior citizen center, swim a few times a week at the local YMCA, or play duplicate bridge?

Pipe your needs into any grapevine, network, or newsletter that would seem likely to draw responses from people with whom you would welcome sharing. Use ingenuity, persistence, and—always—caution.

Pin-Ups

A good notice that clearly states your needs will draw the kind of attention you want from the people you wish to interest. It should also discourage replies from people you would not be thrilled to hear from.

Keep the notice or the classified advertisement short—big blocks of copy are too much trouble to read. You may have to pay by the word for an ad, so make as few words as possible work for you. And make it inviting. You want to interest people, not put them to sleep.

At the same time, be as specific as you can so those responding will know exactly what you expect. Read the ad or notice you write as dispassionately as you can or try it out on friends. Are you (or they) really interested in what you propose? Do they understand it?

If you can think of a catchy headline, especially on a notice you will pin up somewhere, use it prominently to attract attention. Why not show how clever you are? You may just attract clever people to share.

Also, protect yourself. Use only your first name if you are giving your phone number, or use a post office box for replies.

Here are some examples to spark your imagination.

This classified advertisement appeared in a West Coast co-op newsletter:

> Vegetarian, nonsmoking, co-op-oriented person in the _____ area who has young children and dogs wants to share her spacious home. Rent negotiable. Send letter describing self and background to _____.

> [This would definitely weed out allergic loners who thrive on Big Macs.]

Another ad from the same publication:

> Recently returned from years abroad as a concert opera singer, voice teacher-therapist seeks home-sharing arrangement in minimum smog area. Speaks fluent French and Spanish. Write or call _____.

> [Grateful Dead fans living in the San Fernando Valley need not reply.]

Still another from a Midwest suburban church newsletter:

> Organic orchardist in _____ county needs help, advice, guidance, moral support, or just plain hard work from any or all who wish to

participate in and share in the development of an orchard. Please write and let us learn together. Reply to P.O. Box _____.

[Those who want to pluck their apples from supermarket shelves won't rush to respond.]

Off the wall of a private airport office in a northeastern city:

COME FLY WITH ME

My partner moved out of town (flew the coop, so to speak) and left me and my Beechcraft Bonanza with a bank loan that needs to be shared. If you're interested in half ownership of a three-year-old plane in tip-top condition, phone _____. Ask for Bob.

[A poetic pilot, I'd say.]

A notice noticed in an urban neighborhood association office in a southern metropolis:

REHABBING BLUES

Anyone living in the vicinity of _____ and _____ who is interested in swapping use of an electric sander for a paint sprayer and drop cloths, please call Nan at _____ after 6 p.m. weekdays. Let's talk about sharing other tools we might have. I'm not picky.

[If you are, stay away.]

HOWDY, PARTNER

You receive a phone call in response to the ad you placed in your neighborhood association newsletter. Someone who lives just three blocks from you wants to share—to stay with our example—a lawn mower. You're happy with the response; the person sounds like someone you could get along with. But don't just chat casually—make the first phone call count. During the conversation, be sure you clarify exactly what it is you want to buy and how much you want to spend so you are sure you are both interested in the same kind of mower. One of you isn't talking about a power-propelled job for $300 and the other a $1000 ride-on model, right? There's no point in setting up a meeting if you're on different tracks from the start. If you do agree on your prospective purchase, arrange a meeting, but say that its purpose is to see if you can work out a partnership. This gives you a goal to work toward when you get together. The meeting place can be at your house or his house—wherever seems convenient.

Go to the meeting with a list of questions prepared. (Could you make it mental, rather than written—which might look forbidding? But if you have a bad memory, write away and explain you didn't want to forget to discuss important points so you jotted them down.) A list will make clear what you are looking for in the partnership and establish parameters by which to judge whether this will be a good one. That way, you won't be too quick and make a decision based on need. You won't partner with someone instinct tells you you can't rely on or simply don't like.

You are meticulous, and the person whose home you visit to discuss the lawn mower is obviously a slob. It's easy to say, "Oh well, it will be all right. We'll work it out." You reason you can bend a little, but how much? Never enough to match up with the person you are meeting. You want a lawn mower partner. Don't want it that bad! You don't want a disaster.

"Tune in to your first impressions of the person you are meeting," says psychologist Stuart Scheingarten, director of the Center of Improved Productivity and stress management consultant for large national corporations. "They are incredibly valuable. How relaxed do you feel with the person? Can you say what you need to say to him? Do you like him?

"A good technique to use to put someone at ease in a first meeting is to talk about how you like to treat equipment, how you like to do things, maybe even how you like to cut grass. Then ask the other person what his preferences and methods are. That way he won't feel grilled and be immediately on guard. You've offered information—openly—first."

For instance, you might say, "I try to clean the grass out of the blades every time I use the mower, but sometimes I'm just too tired to bother. What do you do?"

He might say, "I'm a real stickler for keeping a mower in perfect shape," which may or may not sit well with you. He may say, "I try to keep it in good shape, too, but I'm not always on top of maintenance either. I don't care who does what each time we use it as long as we keep it running." That may please you more; it shows flexibility.

What do this person's house and garage look like? (He should come to your house and feel good about how you keep your things, too.) What is the present condition of his lawn mower? Has he ever shared anything with someone else?

When you own something in common, you'll have to talk to your partner periodically about its maintenance, scheduling its use, or anything else that may come up. If you don't like him, dealing with him will be difficult. The chemistry between you is important. You may not need the degree of compatibility house partnering demands, but if your partner swears all the time that might bother you. Or if he says, "The Lord will provide" every time the lawn mower conks out though it's clear you two have to provide as well as the Lord, you're going to hate to deal with him.

Some personality traits can be overlooked if you feel your prospective partner is going to take good care of the mower and is honest and dependable. That's basically what you're after. But if something about him makes your blood boil, back off. Pay attention to the little things you think (and hope) aren't going to matter. They may not. On the other hand, it's the little things that sometimes pile up and are destructive to partnerships. Be honest with yourself at the beginning to develop a long-term positive partnership.

Financial responsibility is extremely important. A good way to determine this, again, is to be open about your own finances and reveal your state of affairs first. Begin by saying how long you've lived in your house, that you have a steady job (give him the name of someone to call to verify this), and that you pay your bills. Bring a batch of current statements with you. If bills aren't paid promptly, balances from the previous months are carried over. Utility bills are often stamped as such if they are in arrears. Show that your mortgage payments are up to date. If you have partnered before, give those partners' names as references. Exchanging credit information will build confidence.

"If you act in good faith at the beginning, your prospective partner will trust you more than if you give him the third degree," says Stuart. You wouldn't like that if he did it to you.

"In addition to showing that you are trustworthy, ask yourself if you trust him. Trust is probably one of the most important ingredients in a partnership. If you don't feel, without doubt, the person would act in your best interests, partnering with him should be out of the question."

Talk about who, besides the two of you, would use the lawn mower. Where would it be kept? Who would maintain it, fill it with gas, fix it if it broke down? Do you both value the lawn mower in the same way? If, to you, a lawn mower is just something you need to cut a lawn and your prospective partner is going to treat it as a prized possession, you're in trouble.

21

All this leads to making an agreement—which is an important part of seeing if your partnership will work. At this point, you should bring up all the issues that are important to both of you. If you can't agree on what is to be in the agreement, or you are doing so with great difficulty, consider yourself lucky that you found out you're a bad match before you make the purchase. And *always* work out an agreement before you make the purchase. It's the acid test. (Ways to work out an agreement and specific lawn mower agreements can be found in the appliance chapter and in Chapter Five.)

It is generally better to think about all you've discussed and meet again rather than settle everything the first time you get together. How many meetings are needed before you make a joint purchase varies with the size and nature of the purchase—and with how rapidly you and your prospective partner make up your minds about anything. If the amount of money involved is considerable, if you need a bank loan, if a good chunk of your income is involved, you will probably proceed more slowly. If the amount of money you are investing will make only a small dent in your budget, you can afford to be less cautious.

In between meetings, go shopping for a mower together. Does your prospective partner want to drive all over the city to save a dime? Does he say, "Anything you want is OK with me?" This may be a glimpse into a future of him dumping all decisions (and maintenance headaches) on you. At the other extreme, is he too overbearing? Does he insist that what he wants to buy is best despite your objections? You go shopping not just to find what you want to buy, but to get to know your prospective partner. The expeditions can be revealing.

If you feel you're going to get along but find you have difficulty deciding which brand or model to buy, check out reports and ratings from consumer magazines to help in making your decision.

Remember that compromise is an important ingredient in partnering. You may feel a couple of the features your partner considers important in a lawn mower aren't quite so necessary. But he has been generous and has said he'd go along with the brand you favor.

The two types you're considering cost about the same. He prefers one model and you prefer another, but both do just about the same things. It doesn't make much of a difference, does it? Think about this.

Does the give and take feel right? Are you both happy with what you're gaining and what you're giving up?

However long it takes you to feel secure with the idea of the partnership, the timing and pace have to be right for both parties. One should not feel rushed and pushed into a decision by the other. Take your time to make it work.

This lawn mower scenario can be applied (with adjustments) to other types of partnerships as well. If you've tacked up a sign at the marina advertising the fact that a half-interest in your boat (your previous partner moved out of town) is available, an appropriate place to meet an interested person would be on your boat. Go through the same routine as just described, but bear in mind that the more money involved in a partnership, the more careful you must be in your choice.

Take the boat out together. Does one of you throw the rope in a pile while the other coils it neatly? If one person doesn't already own a boat and two people are starting out fresh, rent one together to make sure you operate the boat with equal safety. Your experience with boats should match to the point you feel confident the other person would take care of it. How often does each of you want to use the boat? Will there be time conflicts, or do you feel you can work it out? Again, specific step-by-step instructions on how to work out boat agreements and samples of them will be found in the chapter dealing with boats, but in your meetings with your prospective boat partner, it's your job to make sure you both want the same things out of the partnership and that you can get along.

Prospective airplane partners should definitely fly separately as well as together to see in what condition each leaves the plane. Operational experience is important—but so is whether one leaves soda cans and candy wrappers under the seat to irritate the other. Horse partners should have the same expectations for the horse. Does one want to make the animal into a champion jumper while the other is satisfied with trail rides?

Partners must not only want the same object, but want it for the same reasons. If one recreational vehicle partner considers it a dream come true he can use almost any time he pleases while the other wants to rent it to make money, there's going to be trouble. If one car-owner loves to tinker on the weekends to keep his old pal in shape while the other treats it as a necessary means of transportation and hates to even spend a few dollars on new windshield wipers, there are going to be disagreements.

Does the purchase burn the same hole in the pockets of all partners? If it's more dear to one than another, there may be problems.

Even if everyone hates the joint purchase to the same degree—if it was bought because no one wanted to buy it on his own and the up-keep style is definitely nonchalant—your partnership will still be consistent.

If one partner says, "I'll meet you at 9 p.m. sharp," and means it while the other says, "See you some time next week" and forgets it, it will never work. Fretting over missed meetings and tardiness can drive a partner crazy. Try to find out beforehand if you both have the same concept of time.

If one partner says, "Let's meet at Ray's Bar and Grill over a boiler-maker to discuss our buying a sailboat" while the other would rather meet at the Ritz for lobster salad, that's something to think about, too. You're going to have to meet in the course of your partnership to talk about it, so if your tastes are that far apart, pay attention.

The larger the purchase, the more partners must have in common. Partnering with a friend or a co-worker is much easier because many facets of his personality have been revealed in the course of your relationship. You may not have to ask for references, pose as many probing questions, notice how he behaves so closely—because you're just plain going to know what kind of person you are joining up with. If you don't, it's imperative to find out.

To Halve or Halve Not

We've covered a lot of territory in the search for a successful partner so far. To bring this very important business into crystal-clear focus, here's a summary of the most important criteria to look for:

(1) *Trust.* This is the primary consideration. If you have even an inkling the person you're going to partner with is trying to benefit at your expense—run. You must have confidence that you're going to do right by each other.

(2) *Financial Responsibility.* You must be sure your partner can pay his share of the bills. While we're talking about money, do you agree with how he handles it? Is he a penny-pincher, always a week late and a few cents short in coming up with the cash, or generous?

(3) *Do You Like Him?* How much you must care for a prospective partner has a lot to do with how close your shared arrangement will be. Obviously, those who will be living together should go for maximum amicability. You and your portable typewriter partner probably aren't going to spend many hours together. Still, you

should be able to deal in partnering matters with someone you enjoy rather than dread talking to. Look for someone you can get along with and make arrangements with easily, without feeling pressured, dominated, put upon, or whined at.

(4) *How Will He Take Care of "Our Property"?* Is he as fastidious as you are, or as easygoing? Does what you are buying mean as much to him as to you? Are you satisfied with his skill in using it? Will he be dependable about owning up to accidents and getting damaged property repaired?

(5) *Do Your Partnership Goals Match?* Do you want to co-own for the same reason as your partner? Is it for pleasure or for profit, for a short time or forever? Make sure that your reason for wanting to buy a condo in Colorado is your partner's reason too. You both want a place to relax, not a money-making rental property, right?

(6) *Location of Sharer and Portability of Shared Property.* If the co-owned property can fit snugly in the trunk of a car and joint owners of it don't mind driving, they can live scattered in all corners of a city and be fine partners. Not so with a ride-on tractor. Partners must live close to each other or own a pickup truck for hauling. Generally, if access to the jointly owned property is a hassle, the partnership begins to falter.

(7) *Will You All Get to Use It Enough to Make You Happy?* All partners must be able to use their shared property often enough to feel they are getting their money's worth. If one needs to use it more than another, does anyone care? Especially if use is not to be equal, everyone needs to feel satisfied on this issue at the outset.

Rejection

Sooner or later you may have to tell someone you don't want to share with him. It's easier to do this early in the getting-together process; harder after you have met with someone a few times. If you know in your heart at any point that a partnership between the two of you simply won't work—but your prospective partner is still eager to share—you're going to have to give him the bad news.

Perhaps the gentlest way to put someone off is to say, "There are a few other people I still have to talk to, so I'll phone you afterward." This would work with someone you've talked to on the phone or someone with whom you've spent only a brief period of time. But make sure you do phone rather than just leave the person hanging.

What should you say?

You can tell him the truth. But if the truth is you don't want to be his partner because he seems like a real stinker, you may want to say you ran across an old friend who is eager to share, a brother, a cousin; you'd rather share with a woman (if he's a man)—anything kind. Rejection hurts. Remember the last time *you* were rejected? It's easy to take it too personally, so choose your words carefully.

No Sin of Omission

No, we haven't skirted the subject of how to find just the right person to share living space with. We're going to cover it—in full detail, in Chapter 13.

All you've read about "the search" up to now applies to finding a compatible person you'd like to live with too. But for home sharing, each step in the process is magnified.

Actually *living* with another person is an intense kind of partnership. It takes a great deal of commitment. To make it work, you must ask more questions and be more cautious in the initial stages because there is so much more at stake—financially and emotionally.

Do you really care if your 50-cup coffee maker partner is a chain smoker? What about your housemate, if you can't stand the smell of cigarette smoke? See the difference?

Smoking is rarely an issue in commonly owned, separately used property partnerships. It can be an enormous problem in home sharing. The closeness and the amount of time you spend together make the difference.

Shared living space partnerships are exciting but take more time to put together. We'll show you how later.

Now we're going to consider a subject that is critical to every kind of partnership. We're going to find out what kind of partner you'd be, and what sort of person you should match up with, whether the joint property being considered is a moped or a mansion.

How flexible and cooperative are you? It's an issue you must grapple with to build a firm foundation—in any partnership. Ready? Let's find out.

Owning Up

One of the most important things you must be, to be a good partner, is *cooperative.* You must also be able to face changing situations and deal with them flexibly. All of life is unpredictable, and it is fair to assume the same holds true of a partnership. No matter how you plan in advance, no matter how you have decided to spend your money, no matter what you have written on paper, who knew there would be a storm to flood your basement and drown your budget? Who knew you'd be transferred out of town? Who knew you'd break your arm and be unable to do your share of gardening in the patch you and your partner own? Who knew a stray dog would make your front porch his headquarters and your partner couldn't bear to send him away, despite your initial agreement that there would be no pets? But can you really banish that skinny, brown-eyed mutt who follows you everywhere—to the SPCA?

When people are in love, their mutual affection seals and enhances the relationship. A couple can disagree, but they can smooth out the disagreement with a kiss and a hug. In a business partnership this doesn't happen. The partners have to know they can get along before they unite, and they have to know they will be able to deal with issues by talking reasonably with each other. So they have to make sure they speak the same language.

Some people are very direct and say exactly what is on their minds. Others are more subtle, hesitant, sensitive to nuances—or simply dodge the issue. If these two types become partners, the person who is hesitant might feel dominated by the more direct person. The more direct person might feel frustrated by someone he perceives as never making up his mind.

Two overly direct people might wind up punching each other out, but at least they'd know exactly why. It might even be their way to clear the air and go on with a positive (if somewhat explosive) partnership.

Two more indirect-acting people might play games with each other instead of tackling a problem head-on. One may leave an overflowing ashtray and muddy floor mats in their jointly owned car to irritate the other and let him know he is displeased about something. The other may not change the oil as he said he would, as a counterattack. Then after awhile one may make a conciliatory gesture. No words are exchanged, but they understand each other perfectly. They might be able to get along fine for years on this basis.

How partners express themselves is as important as what they feel.

Partnering calls for cooperation in the strictest sense—harmonious interaction, *compromise* between possibly differing points of view. If you know what your own style of communicating and approaching problems is, and that of your prospective partner, you will be able to tell if the two (or more) of you will be able to develop an interaction that works for you, one that communicates your concerns clearly and moves both (or all) of you to a positive solution. This is why the following test will be extremely helpful in your search for a compatible partner. It will illuminate what sort of partner you would be, what you can expect from the person you're considering pairing up with, and what kind of chemistry there would be to solidify or dissolve the match.

But please understand—if you don't seem to be good partnership material it doesn't mean you're not a good person. You may be better off going it alone. And if you're not in tune—according to this test—with the person you are considering as a partner, don't consider your explorations a failure. This test is designed to arm you with facts about yourself and those you intend to share with so you can make knowledgeable choices. Use it with that in mind.

Also note that you may not like some of the questions you will be asked to answer. You may consider some of them off-the-wall and maybe even slightly offensive. Some choices, you may say, will be very hard to make, because given how you generally behave, you might not choose either. But you must choose the answer *closest* to what you'd probably do in the situation presented to make the test valid. The results will undoubtedly be revealing.

Dr. Edward Lahniers, who conceived this questionnaire, is a clinical psychologist. The validity of this questionnaire has been tested, and it continues to be used in his private practice in conjunction with marital therapy and consultation to business and industry. If you wish validation information, write to Dr. Edward Lahniers, 1247 Ida Street, Cincinnati, OH 45202.

So, before you take one more step forward, sit down with a pencil and paper and take this test. Then give it to your prospective partner. Compare results and decide if you want to continue discussions.

LAHNIERS' PARTNERSHIP QUESTIONNAIRE

This questionnaire is designed to determine basic styles of interaction that affect how an individual handles situations of potential conflict. An effective means of conflict resolution is essential to a successful and enduring partner relationship.

After you have filled out this questionnaire on a separate piece of paper, making a list from 1 to 24, turn to pages 33 and 34 to tabulate your score. Ask your partner or potential partner to do the same.

Directions: This is a forced-choice test. In other words, for each set of statements choose the one alternative that best describes your personal style, the way you would react to the situation. You must make a choice. If this is difficult, then choose the *most acceptable* or *least offensive* statement. Respond to every question. The test cannot be scored unless all questions are answered.

1. You and your partner were planning to attend a social event together, such as a cocktail party, and had agreed to meet at a certain hour. But your partner is 45 minutes late. You would:
   a) go alone.
   b) assume your partner had a good reason, and wait another half hour.

2. You and your partner own a lawn mower together. The partner never cleans it after using it. You would:
   a) suggest that one of you buy out the other partner's interest.
   b) stop cleaning it yourself.

3. Your partner repeatedly plays the stereo too loudly. You would:
   a) do something equally annoying.
   b) tell your partner that you will turn it off unless he turns it down.

4. A prospective partner loves pets and you don't, and the partner wants to bring a pet into the house you both are thinking of buying. You:
   a) say "Sorry, no pets."
   b) ask what kind of pet they have in mind, and how they intend to take care of it.

5. If there was a repeated depletion of the pile of loose change on your dresser, you would:
   a) break up the partnership.
   b) decide it wasn't worth arguing about—the stakes are too low.

6. Which of the following statements best represents your viewpoint?
   a) Good manners and diplomacy are essential to any successful partnership.
   b) Honesty and directness are essential to any successful partnership.

7. You have one bathroom, and your partner abuses privileges. You:
   a) post a notice on the bathroom door stating when you must use the facilities for bathing and grooming.
   b) get in there first and monopolize it daily for a week or so to get your point across.

8. Your partner likes to set the thermostat lower in the winter, and you like it set higher. You:
   a) withdraw from your partner until you're asked what's wrong.
   b) buy a portable space heater and carry it with you from room to room.

9. You arrive at the cabin which you and a partner purchased for alternate weekend retreats. You invariably clean it scrupulously when you leave,

but your partner has left it a mess, as usual. You:
a) review your partner's good points, decide the good outweighs the bad, and start cleaning.
b) immediately write your partner outlining the problem and suggest the hiring of a local cleaning service.

10. You have been partners for years. When there is a conflict between you, your usual reaction is:
a) to tell your partner bluntly what's on your mind in order to clear the air immediately.
b) to figure out how to tell your partner based on the situation, and how you think your partner would respond.

11. Which of the following statements best represents your viewpoint?
a) Jobs and chores relating to the partnership should be evenly divided, with specific responsibilities assigned to each partner.
b) The work of a partnership will usually get done without having to assign specific responsibilities.

12. You and your partner have opened a small gourmet food shop. You find that the invoices have been tampered with and that some of the merchandise is being diverted for your partner's personal use. You:
a) rip up the invoices, throw them on your partner's desk, and walk out.
b) mention to your partner that you think you might have lost some merchandise, then suggest doing an inventory.

13. Your partner sometimes leaves dirty dishes around. You, as a fastidious person, would:
a) complain about it.
b) spend the few minutes cleaning up, while reminding yourself of your partner's positive points.

14. You don't mind a bit of a mess because your mind is on other things, and your partner complains. You:
a) explain why cleaning is sometimes at the bottom of your list of priorities; let your partner know that's just the way you are.
b) work out a tradeoff of chores or responsibilities, such that each partner feels satisfied.

15. Your partner, who is usually in good health, suddenly doubles up with pain. You would:
a) call the life squad to transport the partner to the hospital, since this seems to be a real emergency.
b) ask your partner to tell you what to do. If this is impossible, then call a doctor.

16. You and another person are considering purchasing a used airplane, with a deadline on the deal. You differ considerably on the price to offer.

You:

a) avoid all calls from the potential partner while you wait for the deadline to pass.

b) tell your potential partner that you agree with his or her price, and then "create" a last-minute emergency which prevents your showing up for the closing.

17. The electric bills for your shared office are excessive. Your partner frequently leaves the lights on all night, saying that he or she forgets to turn them off. You:

a) explain the importance of keeping the bills down and offer to have the business purchase timers for the lamps.

b) refuse to perform some task you usually do which your partner will notice. When asked about it, you say that you forgot.

18. Your partner informs you that your cigarette smoke in the office is nauseating. You:

a) suggest that an air filtration system be installed to remove the offending smoke.

b) refrain from smoking in the office after you become aware of your partner's feelings.

19. You want to set up a new business. You need capital investment from a partner. You:

a) flatter a fairly well-to-do associate by throwing a dinner in his or her honor. Later on you reveal your intentions.

b) contact an associate who has extra capital. Explain your proposal, outlining the risks and advantages.

20. Your co-owned vacation cottage has burned down. You discover your partner set the fire to collect the insurance. After you recover from your shock, you:

a) figure out a way to get all the insurance money for yourself.

b) confront your partner with the evidence, then terminate this unsavory relationship.

21. You discover that your partner has gone through one of your very private drawers. You:

a) move the contents to a more private place.

b) tell your partner you know what has happened. Make it an embarrassing confrontation.

22. If your favorite color is X and your partner's is Y, and you are in the midst of redecorating, you would:

a) argue for the color of your choice because you know you have to live with it.

b) suggest contacting a decorator who is an expert in designing color schemes.

23. Your partner's income jumps dramatically and she or he begins talking about putting more money into the partnership, but you can't afford to. You would:

a) arrange a celebration dinner to honor your partner's success and at the time explain your financial situation.

b) discuss with your partner how you feel about not having more money to invest. Openly reveal your emotions.

24. If your partner should lie to you, your first concern would be:

a) figuring out a way of humiliating and teaching the partner a lesson.

b) confronting the partner with the evidence of lying and telling him or her how this affects the relationship.

HOW TO SCORE THIS QUESTIONNAIRE

The test you have taken will be scored along two dimensions or scales. Thus, you will end up with two scores, the interpretation of which will be explained later. The scales are named the Cooperation Scale and the Expression Scale.

To find your score on the Cooperation Scale, look at the scoring sheet. There is an alternative (a or b) for each question (1 to 24). Next to alternative a or b in the far right hand column is a number. On your answer sheet record the number from the scoring sheet which matches your answer.

For example, your answer to question 13 is (b). The scoring sheet for question 13 reads:

13. a. 2

b. 3

Your match to (b) is 3. Place a 3 next to your answer. Record a number for all 24 answers, then total the score.

Next follow the same procedure for the Expression Scale, using the scoring sheet for that scale. Total your answers and record the score.

You now have two scores, one for the Cooperation Scale, the other for the Expression Scale.

SCORING SHEETS
Cooperation Scale

1.	a.	1		13.	a.	2
	b.	3			b.	3
2.	a.	2		14.	a.	2
	b.	1			b.	4
3.	a.	1		15.	a.	3
	b.	2			b.	4
4.	a.	2		16.	a.	1
	b.	4			b.	2
5.	a.	1		17.	a.	4
	b.	3			b.	1
6.	a.	3		18.	a.	4
	b.	2			b.	3
7.	a.	2		19.	a.	1
	b.	1			b.	4
8.	a.	1		20.	a.	1
	b.	3			b.	4
9.	a.	3		21.	a.	3
	b.	4			b.	2
10.	a.	2		22.	a.	2
	b.	4			b.	3
11.	a.	4		23.	a.	4
	b.	3			b.	2
12.	a.	1		24.	a.	1
	b.	3			b.	4

Expression Scale

1.	a.	1		6.	a.	2
	b.	2			b.	3
2.	a.	3		7.	a.	3
	b.	1			b.	1
3.	a.	1		8.	a.	1
	b.	3			b.	2
4.	a.	3		9.	a.	2
	b.	4			b.	4
5.	a.	1		10.	a.	3
	b.	2			b.	4

11.	a.	4		18.	a.	4
	b.	2			b.	2
12.	a.	1		19.	a.	1
	b.	2			b.	4
13.	a.	3		20.	a.	1
	b.	2			b.	4
14.	a.	3		21.	a.	2
	b.	4			b.	3
15.	a.	2		22.	a.	3
	b.	4			b.	2
16.	a.	1		23.	a.	4
	b.	3			b.	3
17.	a.	4		24.	a.	1
	b.	1			b.	4

INTERPRETING YOUR SCORES

Now that you have two scale scores, let's find out what they mean and how they are related. Bear in mind that the test has been designed to rate the feasibility of either same-sex or opposite-sex partnership.

The first Scale, Cooperation, is a measure of the degree to which you seek harmony in relationships. This scale ranges from a maximum score of 80 to a minimum score of 40. Put a dot on your score on the Cooperation Scale. The higher the score, the more emphasis you place on smoothness in relationships.

COOPERATION SCALE

| 40 | 50 | 60 | 70 | 80 |

If you scored between 75 and 80, you place almost total emphasis on cooperation, to the extent that many times your own needs are sacrificed. You can be taken advantage of because of your desire to please others. Your opinion of yourself may be low. You answer in a self-effacing way when there is no reason to do so. For example, question 21 described a situation when you *know* your privacy/trust has been violated. If you answered (a), then you can expect to be taken advantage of again.

A score in the range of 65 to 74 suggests that, while your major commitment is to cooperation in a partnership, you also are clear about your own needs, and attempt to integrate your wishes into partnership decisions. This score range would be considered best for entering into partnership agreements because such a person is likely to have a strong desire to make the relationship work; realize that compromise is an essential ingredient of partnership success; and be capable of expressing his or her own needs clearly. This person would probably be a practical person. For example, they would not be likely to hire the fox to guard the hen house.

People sometimes *do* take advantage of you. But if you are in this range, when someone is operating to your disadvantage, you can and will protect yourself. In question 9 you know you're being repeatedly taken advantage of. Why should you ". . . review your partner's good points"? You would be quite right to be upset and try to remedy the situation by suggesting a cleaning service.

If you scored in the range of 55 to 64, you are likely to be more content working alone. You have developed some distinct ideas about what is right for you, and you are not at all shy about showing how you feel one way or the other. This may result in conflict and disagreements with others, whether expressed openly or not. You may indicate an interest in sharing in a partnership, but you basically feel that others are not all that trustworthy. You tend to expect others to conform to your standards, and can get testy when they don't. You are also the kind of person who has trouble apologizing, or admitting you're wrong.

If you scored below 55, you definitely are suspicious of others' motives. You will not make a good partner unless, perhaps, you are working for the CIA. Your energies are self-absorbed, and you have little interest in others except as you perceive them infringing on your rights. An individual who scores in this range is more or less looking for trouble with others. Take, for example, question 13. Nobody is perfect. All of us are sometimes careless. The person who complains about dirty dishes that are "sometimes" left around is not very tolerant.

So, the Cooperation Scale measures the internal needs and drives of the individual—from complete self-preoccupation and suspiciousness to total altruism and the resulting vulnerability.

Now let's move on to the next scale, the Expression Scale, which shows the style in which an individual expresses his needs. Again, this scale has a maximum score of 80 and a minimum of 40. Place a dot on the scale corresponding to your score.

EXPRESSION SCALE

| 40 | 50 | 60 | 70 | 80 |

We express ourselves in a variety of ways, and this scale measures that expression along several dimensions. On the extreme right end of the scale, in the range from 70 to 80, is the individual who is direct and forthright in expressing himself. This person speaks directly, and others almost always know what is on his mind. This is the individual who when faced with a partner who forgets to turn out the lights (question 17), will tell the partner his concerns directly and offer possible solutions. This high degree of articulation is especially effective in bringing conflicts into the open in a partnership. One disadvantage with this direct, verbal style is that there are certain situations that can be just as effectively (or *more* effectively) dealt with by refraining from discussion, at least temporarily. Consider the effect of one partner trying to force the other to make a decision about something when the other's mind is *not* made up. The usual result is resistance. If the verbal partner had not been so direct, there might have been an easier resolution.

If your score is within the 55 to 69 range, your style tends to be an equal mixture of direct and less direct behavior. You are a person who will take action in a conflict situation; will confront or compromise according to the situation; you know the value of the deed as well as the word. Effective politicians usually fall within this range—people such as Lyndon Johnson, who almost always got his way because he was able to put to good use a wide variety of talking and action skills. You are the person who, in question 6, will answer that honesty and directness are basic to a relationship, but who also believes that diplomatic, less obvious means of handling conflict are valuable. In question 18, the case of the offensive cigarette smoke, if you answered (a) you would take the verbal, direct approach, by suggesting an air filtration system. But if this didn't work, you would take the behavioral approach and stop smoking in the office. Your style will depend on your internal needs. The more cooperative you are, the more you will adapt yourself to the demands of a relationship.

A score within the range of 40 to 54 indicates that you are uncomfortable with direct expression in a conflict situation. You seldom confront a partner in a direct, verbal fashion. Instead, you rely on actions to express yourself. This can be a plus and a minus. Your actions are sometimes seen as hostile, particularly if you are self-oriented, such as monopolizing the bathroom in question 9. A more cooperative person would be able to express himself more directly, if all else failed.

Now that you see where you score on each scale, draw a line between the two points. After your partner has done the same, you will be able to determine how closely your profiles correspond.

In general, if one or both of you falls within the range of 40 to 54 on the Cooperation Scale, you should not be in a partnership. If you are, you now understand why there are problems. If either of you scores from 55 to 65, there are no major problems—so long as one of you scores higher than 64, since one partner needs to initiate the compromise. The optimal range for a partnership is within the 65 to 74 spread. If you both score within these limits, consider yourselves fortunate. If one or both of you scores above 75, there is either a liar in your midst, or someone who can easily be taken advantage of. The way you score on the Cooperation Scale, then, is a basic measure of the underpinnings of a partnership.

How you express yourself is another matter. In general, if both of you score in a nondirect action-oriented direction, you can expect harmony—provided you are both very cooperative. Conflicts will seem to resolve themselves. Such people would answer (a) to question 6. They value good manners and diplomacy as a means of working out differences. They are attuned to each other's needs and behave in subtle yet beneficial ways to ensure that the partnership endures. If one or both is more self-oriented, friction can be expected in the form of indirect conflict. Withdrawal is a favored technique of this type. And this can make the going very heavy. In question 8 regarding the thermostat level, for example, both choices are nondirect. But the first choice—withdrawal from the partner—is self-oriented. The second—buying a space heater—is cooperative.

If both of you are verbal and direct and high on the Cooperation Scale, you will easily talk out problems as they arise. Yet you will not confront each other unnecessarily with "truths" that don't bear upon the problem at hand. As you score lower on the Cooperation Scale you can expect impasses. But at least you will both be clear as to what the bottlenecks are.

If you and your partner are at opposite ends of the Expression Scale, the action-oriented partner may feel that the other is too straightforward and lacks sensitivity, while the verbal partner will be frustrated because he or she doesn't know exactly what's on the other's mind.

One view might be that they don't understand each other's games. But if there is a cooperative basis for the relationship, these differences in style of expression will get worked out. On the other hand, if either partner scores toward self-centeredness, you can expect an environment that is uneasy, at times paralyzing, for the partnership.

·5·
Making
an Agreement

Working out an agreement is the final stage in making sure you've chosen the right partner. Putting your understandings on record is the last thing you do before actually making the purchase.

The partners I interviewed who failed most often were usually good friends who understood each other so well they felt agreements were unnecessary. Often they considered having to write down such things as who pays for what and who uses it when an insult to their long-standing relationship. They just *knew* everything would be fine. Unspoken conceptions that were in fact misconceptions caught up with them, and they not only failed in their partnership but often lost the friendship they valued. It's not worth it. A sound and thoughtfully conceived agreement is the best means of keeping your friendship and your partnership healthy.

Use Your Imagination

You and your partner should try to turn drawing up an agreement into a creative brainstorming session by dreaming up everything that could possibly go wrong. Think of any issue that could make you disagree, write it down and put your energies into solving those disagreements on paper.

Barbara G. Watts, assistant dean of the College of Law at the University of Cincinnati, says, "Try to visualize in microscopic detail all the motions you go through with what you will co-own. See it all happening in your head. It will help you identify all the special aspects of this particular partnership that should be covered.

"This technique was taught to me in my legal drafting course when I was a student. I have passed it along to those I teach how to write partnership agreements."

For instance, you and your partner have invested in a fancy new set of skis. You strap them to your car (securely enough that they won't fall off), drive to the mountains, and park your car in front of the lodge while you go in to register.

Is that safe? Could they be stolen? Do we need insurance, or does the insurance each of us already has cover theft? Are the skis worth bothering to insure? We better check.

Out on the slopes, you take a spill. Never mind what you've done to yourself—what have you done to the skis? If you've damaged them, what have you and your partner agreed to do about that? And during your three months in traction, can your partner lend the skis to others? Before he stores them, will he wax them like he knows he should? Will he put them in the hall closet, or in the basement too close to the furnace?

"This technique takes imagination," says Barbara. "Imagine as many risks as possible. In trying to think of everything that could happen, you can have a great deal of fun." (Coming up with an agreement that is thorough without covering 600 pages is the challenge.)

A meeting like this can be a remarkably unifying experience as people join together to make a germinating idea a flourishing reality. It can also be the kiss of death. If it becomes abundantly clear partners simply can't agree, they'll never breathe life into their plans—and shouldn't.

SOME VITAL TOPICS FOR ANY AGREEMENT

You will find examples of specific agreements and detailed suggestions on how to draw up yours in the chapters dealing with particular kinds of partnerships. The following general topics, however, are important to include in any partnership discussion.

Ownership—In and Out

1. Will all partners have equal ownership? Will ownership be in one person's name, or in the name of all? Will ownership be pri-

vately held, or will you establish a corporation? If ownership shares will not be equal, how will ownership be set up so everyone is satisfied? An idea to consider, if one partner cannot afford to put up as much money as another, is "sweat equity." This means one person can agree to do more maintenance, or bookkeeping, or provide storage space for the property, or even manage the partnership property in exchange for paying less at the outset and/or a smaller percentage of monthly charges.

2. Can others buy into your partnership, and how will you decide who?

3. What if one person wants to get out? (Anyone should be able to end the partnership voluntarily, whether he is moving out of town or just doesn't want to share any longer.) What will your buy-sell agreement be? How much notice must the exiting partner give the others? How much time after notice is given do the remaining partners have to pay him off? Do the remaining partners have the first option to buy a leaving partner's share so no one gets stuck with a new partner he might not like to deal with?

4. How will you determine the value of the exiting partner's share so he will be fairly remunerated and remaining partners pay a fair price?

5. Will there be penalty for the partner who wishes to leave? Will he receive less money for his share if he causes refinancing woes to the remaining partners?

6. What happens in case of death, divorce, or disability?

7. What if one partner wants another out because he feels that partner has been willfully irresponsible? (I've saved this point for last because it's sticky.)

Barbara Watts says, "You just can't list all the ways a person could break the law or all the things he could possibly do to joint property that is irresponsible, and then enumerate all the consequences—in any agreement. But a termination clause can help you out of trouble."

It can state that if one partner acts negligently (drinking while driving, buzzing the tower before landing the airplane, keeping cocaine in the house—something you both have agreed not to do or is just plain onerous or against the law), the other partner or partners have the right to end the association.

The person whose behavior causes the grief is penalized according to whatever terms you specify—for example, he gets paid only half the value of his share because the rest of the partners suddenly have to become buyers under disagreeable circumstances. This clause can act as an incentive for partners to behave responsibly. It can also raise hairy legal issues.

You tell your partner he's no longer your partner because you suspect he's been stopping off for more than a few martinis before he picks you up after work in your jointly owned car.

He says, "You're telling me you're going to pay me only half my money and I won't have a car to boot? You're crazy. I'll see you in court!"

A termination clause is open to interpretation (which can get heated) and hard to enforce, but it's important to include nonetheless.

Goals

1. Is this a long-term or a short-term partnership? Are you in this to fix up what you are buying (an important issue to house partners) and resell it to turn a profit? Or do you want ownership for convenience and pleasure?

2. Are you buying the joint property for partners' use only, or also to rent for extra money?

Money

1. How will you pay for your purchase? Pay cash or get a loan?

2. If there is a loan involved, how will those monthly payments be handled? Will there be a partnership bank account? How much money will be put into it and at what intervals? How will repair and regular maintenance costs be handled? Will partners write personal checks and collect from each other, or pay out of the partnership bank account?

3. Who will handle the bills and keep the records? Will one partner be the manager, or will financial responsibility be rotated?

4. Will there be a penalty if a partner defaults on monthly payments? What will it be, and how will it be set up? How long will the rest carry a partner who can't pay—or will they?

Maintenance

1. Decide how you would like what you will jointly own to be maintained. List specific chores that must be done to keep it that way. Who will do them? Will the chores be permanent or will partners

rotate? Will a single person be in charge of maintenance?

2. How must each partner leave the common property after each use? Everybody's property tends to be nobody's responsibility. To avoid that, spell out what each person needs to do.

3. What yearly or other periodic maintenance do all agree on? Will the partners do the work, or will it be hired out? To whom?

Usage

1. You must provide fair use of your jointly owned property. Will your schedule be rigid or casual? Can partners switch with one another?

2. What if use isn't equitable? Say we buy a rug shampooer together. Though we each use it only once or twice a year, my house has wall-to-wall carpeting and is much bigger than yours. You have only a couple of rooms with carpets you need to clean. Must I compensate for my greater wear and tear on the machine by paying for more of the repair costs when they occur? Does any of this matter? If it does, how will we work it out so both of us are satisfied?

3. Where is the common property to be stored, and who is responsible for putting it there? The last person who uses it?

4. Who else may use the property besides the partners? Must unanimous permission be given for this?

5. Carefully decide what behavior you absolutely will not tolerate in your partnership. What acts would trigger the instant partnership termination clause we just discussed? This is especially important to consider in conjunction with moving vehicles—on land, sea, or in the air—and houses. Discuss the use of alcohol and drugs while using your joint property. What about run-ins with the law? A clearly illegal act is generally cause for termination. Every partner should know and agree how he is expected to behave. Write down the points you consider most important. But remember, it is impossible to think of *everything* that could happen. (That's where the termination clause will help.)

You also have to be careful not to be offensive, or your brainstorming session will go up in smoke. How would you feel if a prospective partner said to you, "I want it clear—there will be no dope smuggling done on our boat." "Huh?" you say. "Who do you think you're talking to? What kind of person do you think I am anyway? What kind of person are you to even think those things?" Goodbye partnership. Be cautious, not obnoxious.

Loss or Damage

1. Will we insure the property? In whose name?

2. Who pays if there is damage? Should each partner pay for any accident he causes from carelessness, or does the partnership assume responsibility because whatever happened could happen to anyone?

3. If there is insurance, does the partner who causes the damage pay the deductible, or do the partners split it?

4. If the insurance cost goes up because of the accident, does the partner who caused the problem pay the increment, or does the partnership divide the expense?

5. What if the property is a total loss? Do partners absorb the loss? Does insurance? Or does the partner who causes the calamity pay the rest? At what appraised value?

6. What do you consider negligent? Again, be careful here. It's one thing to have an accident because you are careless or absent-minded; it's another to be willfully irresponsible to the point of being dangerous, or to do something that's against the law.

Permission

1. What can partners do independently to jointly owned property without asking the others? Is there a certain amount of money they can spend without checking with the others? This provision avoids bad feelings that may arise if one partner gets something fixed and asks others for reimbursement. If partners feel the price is too high, they may resent it and even refuse to pay. Set a minimum dollar value partners can spend without partnership authorization, or at least think about it.

2. As noted earlier, do partners need permission to lend the property to others?

Decision Making

1. How will decisions about the partnership be made? Will there be formal meetings? If so, how often?

2. How will disagreements be handled? What system for "talking it out" will you set up? In voting, will majority rule settle a dispute? Will you use consensus? Will you go to an expert third party

if partners stalemate? Who will the third party be? Or will you just draw straws or flip a coin?

3. As circumstances change, so must agreements. How will you change yours?

• • •

(There is additional discussion of forming partnerships, especially for a large purchase such as a house, in Chapter 15 on buying a home with someone.)

Once you have tackled these questions and others that may occur to you and have written down answers that satisfy everyone, you will have your agreement.

"While you do want to be thorough in writing a contract," says Barbara Watts, "the complexity of the agreement you draw up should be in proportion to the size of your investment. [If there is a lot of money involved, more points need to be spelled out. If not so much money is involved, you don't need as much detail.]

"Remember, anything purchased to produce income of any kind or that involves borrowing money will have tax ramifications. They can either help or hurt you. Think of tax writeoffs, capital gains, income to declare, possible deductions for depreciation. I'd certainly advise anyone to consult an attorney for any of these issues.

"You don't have to figure out every minute detail that could affect your partnership up to and including if the world ends," Barbara concludes with a smile. "Just close to it."

Review Your Draft

Go over what you have written, point by point, to make sure it's clear and you're happy with it. But don't feel you have to translate everything you've put on paper into legalese.

Lynne Skilken, an attorney who specializes in labor law, says, "Many people are fooled by the mystery of this secret language. They think they need magic words like 'whereas,' 'heretofore,' and 'witness whereof' to make an agreement. It's intimidating to those who want to record what they think and don't know how to throw formal words like these around. I believe many attorneys today want to eliminate meaningless, ritualistic phrases.

"The clearer and plainer the language, the better and more effective your agreement will be. Everyone will be able to understand it."

After you've drawn up your agreement draft, one of the almost-partners should be responsible for typing it and making copies to distribute to the others so all may jot down more suggestions. You may even want to meet again to thrash out a final version. Each partner should have a copy of the finished agreement—which should, of course, be signed by all.

Depending on the magnitude of what you have at stake, decide whether an attorney should check it over (or even rewrite it for you) before you affix your signature.

Many people I interviewed never again referred to the written document once they had worked it out. The catharsis of getting goals, preferences, doubts, and fears into the open and dealing with them positively was assurance enough the partnership would work.

On the other hand, knowing a written document does exist for reference, should questions arise, is an undeniable source of comfort.

Bylaws

In addition to your agreement, you may also want to draw up a set of bylaws for the actual use of your jointly owned property. These may be too detailed and specific to be in the actual "contract," but things you'd like to have on record nonetheless.

This will probably be necessary only with larger or more complex items, such as houses and boats ("draw the shades during the day to conserve energy"), but then maybe you'd like to make sure that *our* diamond ring is taken off when anyone does the dishes.

Draw up your bylaws as thoughtfully as you did your agreement (there may be a few details repeated in your bylaws that were in your agreement). After everyone has approved them, bind them up in a little booklet or tack them somewhere they can't be missed.

LIST-MAKING

If this process still seems too formal for your needs, or for the purchase you are going to make, there is a less intimidating method you may find more appealing. And if you're still not convinced of the merit of agreements, you will find this a persuasive argument in their behalf. Learn from Linda and Jim Nunes-Schrag.

This couple has devoted many years to The Movement for a New Society, a Philadelphia-based organization devoted to nonviolent social change. A national network of members is involved in a wide variety of activities, from promoting disarmament and environmental protection to addressing issues of sexism and racism. Seventy people live collectively in 22 houses that make up the Life Center, the organization's residential support base in Philadelphia.

These people, with a commitment to change the world they live in, are skilled in living in community—by speaking honestly but with caring, and by making decisions through group discussion and consensus. Their method of problem solving leaves members feeling affirmed rather than furious.

You'll find examples of the way Life Center members operate sprinkled through this book. Jim and Linda Nunes-Schrag will pop up in several chapters.

Right now, they share the way they "talked things out" before they got married.

Both had enough experience in group dynamics to know that unspoken expectations and undiscussed assumptions can be fatal to cooperative ventures. Linda, who was born in Tanzania of Indian parentage, worried that since she and Jim were from such different cultural backgrounds (and because he was previously married), their visions of marriage would be different. They loved each other. They wanted to seal their love with marriage. But what did marriage mean to each of them?

They concluded it would be a good idea to write, on separate pieces of paper, exactly what they thought their lives would be like and then compare ideas. Why not just talk it out?

Linda says, "If I put thoughts into writing, there is no way of saying later, 'I really didn't mean that. You misunderstood me.' Also, when you see something in writing you don't understand, you can question it. You can say, 'Wait a minute. I don't understand what you really mean by that. Tell me how you feel.' "

As an example of how their compared lists strengthened their relationship, Linda had always assumed Jim would want to join their last names. Jim's paper showed he assumed they would simply keep their separate ones. Talking it out, they agreed to a hyphenate, saving themselves a misunderstanding close to their wedding date.

On Linda's list were her strong feelings on how she wanted both of them to be active in social struggles, especially against racism. She said, "In marriage, if I continue to live in this country, I expect and need support from Jim on my convictions." He agreed completely. She felt affirmed.

Though Linda and Jim both agreed they would live in America most of the time (this was Jim's strong desire), Jim agreed to spend one year at some point in Linda's home. And to visit relatives in either

India or Africa every 3-5 years for 4-6 weeks so he could grow close to Linda's family. This was important to her.

"People generally write agreements about possessions," Linda says. "Possessions are not important to us, so we dealt with that in one sentence. We were more interested in things of the heart."

So we have just clearly seen, agreements can address aesthetic or spiritual issues—anything people who want to join together need to clarify before they make their partnership final.

If you want to crystalize partnering expectations the way Linda and Jim smoothed preparation for their marriage, try it. But it is very important to understand before you begin that this way will work only if partners are willing to *give to* each other, not just give in.

Those writing their expectations must be as specific and frank as they possibly can. Like ideas that show up on both lists strengthen the partnership. Inconsistent issues on the separate lists must be discussed honestly, but gently. Then a modified mutual statement should be drawn up and accepted by both parties.

The result? A new "statement of promises to each other," as Linda calls them, that reflect the partners' understanding. This pledge enables them to move ahead with confidence.

MAKING THE PURCHASE

Finally you're ready to buy. It's time to come up with the money—all of you. Each partner should put his share of the cash in the kitty to make the purchase—up front.

"You put it on your credit card. I'll pay you next month," one of your just-about-to-be partners says.

Don't do it unless you know the person well and that's how the two of you have operated in the past successfully. Otherwise you may wind up becoming a one-man collection agency—or worse, strapped with an expense you can't afford on your own.

If your partner can't come up with his part of the money at the beginning of your joint venture, or does so with hemming and hawing, or with a degree of difficulty that makes you queasy, forget it—especially if you are getting a bank loan and will have to depend on him for regular payments later.

"I've gotten this far, and now I should call it quits because my partner says he's a little short of money?" you moan. *Without doubt*— for your own good. We've done a lot of "talking it out" up to now, but at this point (as the old saying goes), it's time to put your money where your mouth is. And that means everyone.

·6·
How to Keep Your Partnership Happy

You've formed your partnership. Now how do you keep it vital? By keeping in mind all you've gained by sharing with someone else. By remembering the house you own with a friend gives you double the space you had in your apartment, or the snowplow you cleared your driveway with last winter beats shoveling hands down, or the airplane you fly would have remained a wish if you hadn't divided the cost with co-workers.

Concentrate on the big picture. Build on the positives of your partnership because if you focus on small disagreements and minor inconveniences, that's all you're going to see. Every little problem grows into a big one and your partnership drowns in a sea of negatives.

Did it tax you terribly to use the electric hedge trimmer on Sunday afternoon instead of in the morning because Fred got to it first? Mike usually forgets to readjust the seat when he finishes riding the expensive Italian touring bike you bought in partnership, so you do it, grumbling every time. Doesn't he always lubricate the wheel bearings when they start to squeak? You never even think about it.

Sure, there are going to be disagreements in the course of a partnership, and in this chapter we will show you how to deal with them—creatively. But if you keep benefits foremost in your mind, such as your vacation in the Bahamas last Christmas, made possible by the money you were able to put aside sharing mortgage payments, you're going to relegate petty problems to the back seat—where they belong.

It Is Better to Give . . .

Being generous counts a great deal in being a good partner—generous in your attitude toward other people. How much do you really expect from them? University of Cincinnati professor and clinical psychologist Daniel Langmeyer is often called in as a partnership consultant. His right-to-the-core-of-the-matter advice is this: "If each partner enters into the deal willing to give sixty percent and get forty, it will be a happy relationship. If one expects to give forty-eight percent and do better for himself at someone else's expense, chances are the partnership won't make it."

This doesn't mean that being a good partner is synonymous with being taken advantage of. But does it really matter that when you went grocery shopping, the bill came to 87¢ over the amount you and your partner put into the weekly food kitty and you paid for it out of your own pocket? Are you really going to ask your partner for 43½¢?

If grocery overages crop up constantly and it begins to bother you, maybe it is something to talk about. But on the other hand, your partner usually picks up a bag of donuts for Sunday brunch and never asks for money. And wasn't that his sweater you wore on your date last Thursday night?

The partners I interviewed who were most successful didn't "nickel and dime" each other and their partnership to death. They felt strongly about equal responsibility, but they also had faith that the money and energy they put into the partnership evened out in the long run. It's the long run that's important. They were happy they were able to own (in common) what they now possessed. Packages of Oreos bought by one and eaten by two just weren't worthy of mention.

One man who shares at least half a dozen home-related appliances with neighbors had this story to tell. A phone call in the middle of the night jolted him awake with the kind of nocturnal news we all dread. His mother-in-law had just suffered a heart attack and he and his wife were told to come to the hospital immediately, several hundred miles away. They threw clothes into a suitcase and left within the hour.

Just a few miles from home, their car began to conk out, and the desperate couple phoned one of their appliance partners for help. The friend drove to the gas station where the couple waited, gave them his car to continue the trip, and took the limping car to be serviced. Happy ending? Not yet.

The mother-in-law's condition stabilized and her prognosis looked good, so after a few days, the couple could return home. Again, they were plagued with car trouble. It was never determined if, when the automobile's engine locked up on the highway, the warning light that shows the oil is at a dangerously low level failed to come on. Maybe it did come on, but the couple driving a car unfamiliar to them just didn't notice it. In any case, the car had to be towed to a repair shop and the engine rebuilt to the tune of $500.

Although the events that led to the frozen engine were unclear, the couple paid the repair cost and gave the car back to the friend, grateful that he had been willing to lend it at midnight notice. The question of whether the trouble occurred because of their own negligence or because of their friend's poor maintenance of the car was brought up by the friend—not them. The couple felt responsible and lived up to it without question. They appreciated their friend's generosity and showed it.

The friend was not comfortable benefiting from a rebuilt engine, though he could have easily accepted it and come out ahead. He paid the couple back for most of the cost of the engine. They protested, but he insisted.

This story may sound exceptionally altruistic, but it's one to keep in mind because in this instance friendship was valued more than money, and trust was implicit. The spirit of caring, pulling together to whip what fate dishes out, triumphed. Isn't that what we're all really after?

The Only Thing You Can Count On Is Change

As I mentioned in the previous chapter, it isn't practical to write life plans in stone. Unpredictability is so much a part of what we face daily that a person who isn't able to roll with the punches is probably going to get a knockout blow.

You have your house partnership agreement. You thought of all the contingencies you could and provided for them on paper. Chores were worked out, too. You wanted to do all the cooking, so your partner agreed to take care of the yard. The arrangement felt good to both of you and you were happy because the solution was equitable and pleasing.

Six months later, your boss suggests you take a few courses in personnel management and offers you a better-paying job if you do.

The most convenient classes you can find are from 6:00 to 8:00 in the evenings. Your plans to take care of the cooking just got zapped, and in all probability other jobs will have to be reassigned because of your new schedule. And if one of the reasons for your partnership was sharing meals, that preference will have to be sidelined temporarily.

Needs change and so must partners, if what they have built together is going to last. While the ex-chef takes a semester of courses, meals can be catch-as-catch-can during the week, with maybe a special dinner planned together on Friday night. Partners will have to work out a new deal that will still respect each other's needs.

"But you said you would cook."

"Yes, I did, but I didn't know I'd be going to school."

"But we agreed you would cook" . . . and so on and on, is a useless, destructive conversation.

Negotiate might sound like a harsh or too-businesslike term, but it is exactly the skill good partners must have or acquire. Call it "give and take," flexibility, adaptability if it pleases you more—but Stuart Scheingarten says, "Partners must anticipate change. It is the one sure thing. When change does occur, partners must sit down and work out solutions to new situations in good faith. What they come up with must satisfy—be as comfortable as possible for both. The partners *must want it to be that way.*"

I Believe

This brings us back to the core issue of trust. You have to believe that since your partner can no longer make dinner because he's going to evening classes, he'll shoulder the house load some other way. You should feel he's not the type of person to dump everything on you and walk away without caring or without trying to work out a new system that doesn't overburden you.

Say you and a friend bought a motorcycle together. You have to trust that the price to replace the muffler is the best one your partner could get, if you agreed he would be the one to take charge of it. If you have a twinge of suspicion that he's pocketing money somewhere along the line, asking you to pay more than you think you should, it will be difficult for you to continue the partnership with confidence.

The feeling must prevail that "we're all doing the best we can for each other." You must have faith that your partner will always act in your best interest and that of your common property.

Though all of us have accidents and make mistakes and wrong

choices, distrust will have little chance to germinate if transactions are made openly and honestly by all partners. Muffs and misjudgments will not be blown into unscrupulous acts.

When someone senses something is amiss but can't quite put his finger on it, he begins to feel uneasy. Murky doubts set in that can't be banished. When these suspicions build to the point that one partner feels he is being ripped off, the partnership is devastated.

Set Aside Time to Meet

A good way for partners to air grievances and keep the atmosphere clear is to establish regular meetings. This is when day-to-day business can be discussed and long-range planning accommodated. People get together to say, "We're doing a fine job, aren't we?" or "Maybe we can do these four things better."

Most appliance or "noncrucial possession" partnership business can be handled informally, on the phone or in a meeting called whenever issues arise that require discussion. Many boat, plane, and car partners do the same, though some like to meet once a year (or more often) to go over the property and decide such things as whether it needs a new engine, a paint job, a different storage place, or a better mechanic to service it. These kinds of meetings turn into productive planning sessions.

Partners who see each other infrequently have a good excuse to have dinner together and share a few laughs about their common property—it's headaches and rewards. The problem becomes easier to handle and everyone is reminded why they embarked on the partnership in the first place.

No matter how frequent your meetings, try to begin with a few kudos before you hit the sticky points and air the gripes. It helps to affirm what you are all doing right together before you tackle what is wrong. (More details on procedure later in this chapter.)

"Periodic assessment of the partnership itself should be built into your meeting time schedule," says Stuart Scheingarten. "Review your partnership termination clause every year. Even if you intend to keep on partnering, discuss how you would end things if you had to today. It may be different from what you said a year ago. It's hard to talk about endings, so make it an integral part of your meeting structure. Deal with the issue and put it away."

Regular meetings are essential for people who share living space. How to set up house meetings and how they should be structured will be discussed in detail in the chapter on home sharing.

Talk to Me

When you talk to your partner, in a meeting or in passing, saying what is really on your mind is essential. But that's a tall order, when most of us don't like to have anyone think badly of us because we say something that might offend. Daniel Langmeyer says, "People who have to deal with each other sometimes do not raise key issues, because in our culture we are taught to avoid open conflicts. We fear them. So partners get together and talk about everything but the real issue at hand. Partners must learn to stop Mickey Mousing around because it's the small incidents which are not discussed that build up to destroy partnerships."

You didn't say anything when you went to use the fishing pole you and a friend bought together and found the line in a tangled mess—again. You untangled it, silently fuming.

You bought the dozen new lures you both decided you needed and he still hasn't paid you. And he's the one who loses most of them. He says he'll give you the money, but he doesn't—says he keeps forgetting. It's making you furious.

Then you go fishing and hook the biggest bass anyone has seen all season. Incredibly, you lose him because when he heads for open water you find you don't have enough line on the reel. Incredulous, you stare down at your snapped line.

Your partner lost half the line and didn't even mention it to you. Why the hell didn't he replace it?

That does it! You blow!

Backlashes, lost line, lost lures, a rank-smelling tackle box—you've been feeling taken advantage of for a long time and are ripe for a fight. Whatever produced the fight is only the tip of an iceberg of stifled emotions. Seemingly insignificant incidents become angry issues. A dirty filet knife, not a life or death matter, pops up in partnerships to sever them.

But we don't like fights. We shy away from confrontations. We simply don't like to say anything that may hurt someone else's feelings. So how can we begin to deal with what bothers us if we don't have the nerve or the skill? Though not speaking up hurts us, we remain silent—and upset.

"Get the skill," Langmeyer advises. Courses and workshops designed to improve interpersonal interaction, assertiveness training workshops, and encounter groups are flourishing everywhere from

YMCAs to universities. Choose the one you think will help you get in touch with your feelings and enable you to communicate them without being offensive or negative."

Books abound—newly published or classic standbys—to help you explore your feelings, be responsible for them, and let other people know about them in a positive fashion. Ask someone you consider knowledgeable to help you make a good choice.

In your search for communication help, steer clear of "taking care of Number One" workshops or books. Do not use models that teach you how to climb the ladder to success in a hostile world. Those tactics won't work in partnering because intimidation is the most destructive approach you can take. Your partnership should be supportive, not competitive.

CONFLICT-SOLVING

What we're after is an open atmosphere where people can say what is on their minds without fear, one in which conflict is accepted as part of life and dealt with creatively. No one has all the truth all the time; no one can always agree. But think of disagreement as a means of exchanging ideas and opinions—new thoughts for each side that, when thrashed out, can forge exciting solutions for everyone involved.

But Linda Nunes-Schrag says that people have to be reminded constantly that it's all right not to agree; it's perfectly acceptable to have differences. The trick is to get differences to work for you, to come up with an answer that betters the situation. This makes conflict productive. To do this you must agree to ground rules about how you are going to handle problems so that no one becomes angry and hostile.

If two people discuss a problem, each thinking he has to win the negotiation to be successful, both will only get madder. If one person must win and one must lose, usually both lose. You must be sure that both people get something out of the process; both should win and come away feeling good. If you solve differences with concern for your partner's welfare as well as your important mutual interest, you are more likely to come up with a good solution.

Let's go back to the fishing pole partners and invent a dialogue to illustrate how their differences over "proper maintenance" could be resolved reasonably.

Jim: We both want the fishing equipment to be put away so that it is always ready for the next person to use, but we don't seem to be able to agree on what is a satisfactory standard. Let's find out what "ready to use" means to each of us.

John: What I mean by "the equipment should be maintained properly" is that the line should be untangled if necessary and any lost lures replaced.

Jim: I can't stand opening a smelly tackle box. It turns my stomach. Also, the wading boots should be thoroughly air-dried before they're put away.

John: You know, that means neither of us has to second-guess the other—we really have to focus on only certain areas. We'll make sure the fishing line is properly rewound and that the lures are placed in perfect order in a thoroughly cleaned tackle box. The boots will be aired before they're hung in the closet. I won't wash the tackle pack vest each time I wear it because you don't really care. I thought you did. You won't have to sharpen the cleaning knives every time you put them away because you thought I would be furious if you didn't. Neither of us has to work so hard trying to do all the things he thought the other wanted. We know—now—what's really important to both of us. And that's what we'll pay attention to.

Why should we be pleased with this dialogue and its resolution? Because both partners expressed their needs clearly. Specifics were brought up and each person knew exactly what was important to the other. The solution satisfied both. Each came away feeling good—and best of all, neither had to worry about what he felt might be upsetting the other. Each knew exactly what he had to do to please his partner—and himself—and was willing to do it.

How do we generate dialogue like this when we're not used to doing it? Psychologist Jane Engeman shares a productive problem-solving technique she uses to cool tempers in her marital and job-related conflict practice. Though most psychologists view win-win problem solving as the best kind, and there are many strategies that are similar to the following one, Jane has adapted her step-by-step approach to the problems joint owners face. It should be of great help in settling yours, in creating the positive conversation and clear atmosphere that are so important.

Step One: Pick the Right Time to Talk

Your boyfriend comes to town to see you and you have planned a Saturday afternoon sail as one of the highlights of the weekend. When you drive to the garage where your boat and trailer are kept, you discover the trailer has a flat tire. Your partner knew it was going bad the last time he used it. He said he was going to have the tire taken care of when you spoke to him on Tuesday. Obviously, he didn't. Your weekend has just begun to fizzle and you're furious.

Do you call your partner in the middle of his lunch date and yell at him? If you do, chances are you're going to get yelled at right back and you'll accomplish nothing but making you both upset. Even though it seems hard to keep control sometimes, you must pick the right time to talk about a problem to get the best results.

A better way to handle your fury in the instance above is to phone your partner and say, "I'm really upset about something. Is this a good time to talk?"

If your partner says, "No," then ask, "When can we get together? I need to talk to you no later than tomorrow."

Sensing your urgency, your partner should be able to meet you on short notice, barring some genuine disaster. If he says, putting off the heat he knows is coming, "Can it wait till next week?" you should say, "This is really important to me. I want to get together with you soon." Then set a definite time. "Soon" is too nebulous. Say, "Exactly *when* can we meet?"

It's best to state what the problem is you'd like to talk about. Don't just say you're upset about something. Tell your movie projector partner you're angry because the last time he used it he broke the rewind apparatus and didn't tell you. Beth's Brownie troop went berserk when the Donald Duck film you were trying to entertain them with wound up all over the floor instead of on the reel. Tell him you need to get together to work out some kind of understanding.

"O.K. How does Saturday look?"

You say, "No. I'm pretty bothered about all this. I'd like to talk tomorrow or before the weekend—whichever is best for you."

You must give your partner the right not to be ready to discuss problems when you are. Don't tell someone how you feel regardless of whether he is exhausted, ill, or in a terrible temper.

"You may want to set up a system ahead of time that defines what kinds of problems need to be discussed immediately," says Jan Engeman. "Some schools have a list of the seven major rules that, if broken, cause immediate suspension. Emulating this, sit down with your partner and discuss what *your* danger zones would be. That way, each of you will respond quickly to the other's concern about a particular issue because it has been earmarked, in advance, as important. Less urgent issues can be discussed at regular meetings or on whatever more casual basis you choose. Setting up this way of dealing with problems in advance eliminates arguments about what is important and what isn't."

But no matter what orderly system you establish, expect the unexpected—as I have said so many times before. Something will always come up to confound you and you must deal with it on the spot.

Say your housemate brought her boyfriend home Friday night and they haven't come out of her bedroom for three days except for short forays to the kitchen. You both agreed in the beginning that men would not be welcome longer than overnight. You both know weekend guests should be cleared with each other. This is supposed to be important to both of us, you think angrily. How do you handle a red-hot situation like this? You want to do something about it right away. How do you control your temper so you can deal with the situation with some grace and reach a constructive solution?

Jane suggests trying humor to get you out of sticky situations. Rather than banging on the door and screaming, "Get out of there! You're driving me crazy!", try something funny.

Ring a bell. Bang a spoon on a pot. Use two lids as cymbals. Say, "O.K., you two. Take a break. Time out! You need a breather and I need to talk to you before you go into round fifteen."

Slip a note under the door that says, "Since I have heard no sound or seen either of you for the last 24 hours, I will call the life squad unless you both come out of there within 10 minutes."

"Some way or another," says Jane, "I'd let her know she is breaking a Code Red rule and this situation is something we have to talk about immediately."

Step Two: Define the Problem

When you get together with your partner, if you haven't already told him specifically what the problem is, do it now—clearly. If you're upset with how he treats the portable electric typewriter you bought in partnership, don't say, "I'm sick and tired of you ruining our typewriter." Do say, "When you spilled your coffee on the motor and shorted it out—for the second time—it really made me mad. We agreed not to sip drinks while we were using the machine. Even though you paid for the damage, I think having the same accident twice is inexcusable. How much can one typewriter take?"

If your partner has something on his mind he'd like to discuss, rather than interrupt each other and have a fragmented conversation, make an agenda. Talk about one thing at a time.

When you sit down together, you say, "Well, the two main things that are bothering me are your dropping drinks on the typewriter and leaving it on and forgetting about it for hours."

Your partner can then say, "What's really bothering me is the way you insist on using that old eraser and let the rubber flakes fall between the key bars making them stick. Either pull the carriage over to the side before you erase anything or—and this is the last time I'm going to tell you—switch to correction fluid."

Rather than talking about all three things at once, give your attention to each issue separately to come up with a more direct dialogue and better solutions.

Step Three: Listen

Partners must be sure they are talking about the same thing—are on the same wave length—so one can really understand what is bothering the other. When a person states a problem, it is important that the listener paraphrase it and then ask, "Do I understand this the way you mean it?"

For instance, your partner says, "You're not taking care of the typewriter according to our rules."

You say, "I want to be sure I know exactly what's on your mind. Are you bothered because I keep forgetting to change the ribbon and sometimes put it in the wrong way?"

It's important that you understand exactly what irritates your partner and that you say something kind and conciliatory such as, "I don't always notice the ribbon. But now I see how aggravating it would be to have your paper inserted, margins set, be ready to type, and then have to mess with the ribbon—especially when you're in a hurry."

You must let your partner know you *care* about what is annoying him.

Jane Engeman says, "This is a very important step and most people move through it much too quickly. They discuss the problems but they don't really understand why the other person is provoked. They should pay attention not only to what he is saying, but also to where all that feeling is coming from. Ask why the person is so upset; why it bothers him so much. If one person tries to understand why the other person is angry, the tone is immediately altered. Tempers cool."

Step Four: Propose Alternative Solutions

Next comes brainstorming. Partners should come up with as many ways to solve a particular problem as they can, no matter how wild. All sorts of ideas—even crazy ones—can lighten the situation and make everyone laugh. The main ground rule, at this preliminary, free-swinging stage, is: No one is allowed to criticize any idea.

Set aside a specific amount of time for brainstorming. This will depend on the complexity of the problem that has arisen from your joint purchase. However long your session, one person should be appointed to write down all the ideas.

If your particular problem does not demand a full brainstorming session, try at least to come up with two or three alternative solutions. The more accepting, nonjudgmental the atmosphere, the freer people will feel to say anything that comes to mind. That's just what you want—creative and innovative ideas.

And when people feel their input is important to everyone in the group, they'll feel immensely satisfied.

Step Five: Establish Criteria to Judge Your Solutions

How are partners to know they've come up with the right solution? When everyone is happy about it. This is why partners must discuss what they want the outcome to do for them, so they can judge whether the solution will fill those needs.

Let's say one partner finds the gas tank empty every time he goes to use the tractor. His partner always forgets to fill it with gas. They will know they have a good solution when they come up with a way to keep the gas tank filled without having to make a half-dozen phone calls back and forth to each other.

One criterion is, "I don't want to have to call you to tell you the tractor is out of gas again." Another is, "I want it to always be ready to use." A third is, "We don't want the solution to be expensive—every time we run down to the corner gas station it costs a lot more to buy gas than at the discount station near the office where we work." The fourth criterion is, "We want a solution that doesn't mean any person has to do more work than another."

At this point, don't get into solving the problem; stick to establishing the criteria by which you will judge the solution. Make sure your formula includes the elements to satisfy everyone and that no partner feels put upon.

Step Six: Test the Solutions

Test the solutions you've come up with during the brainstorming session, one by one or in combinations, to see which would most likely solve your problem. What are the advantages of each solution? The disadvantages? What new problems does it pose? What has been overlooked? Does it solve only half the problem? Would it be possible to put into action? Can everybody live with it?

By the time you have finished your process of elimination, you should have four or five likely ways to proceed.

Step Seven: Try Out *the* Solution

The solution you decide is the best should be tried for a period of time to see if it's going to work. *Do not regard it as final.*

This way, if one partner is sure the solution is a great one but the other is more hesitant, the unsure partner can feel good about going ahead with the choice because it's an experiment—it doesn't have to be permanent. He can say, "O.K., let's try it for awhile and if it's not working out, I'll tell you about it. Then maybe we can try our second-choice solution. It seems to have a lot of advantages, too." Set a definite period of time during which you will try the solution—and then decide if you want to go with it, or switch.

The following is an example of a solution that, put to the test, didn't make it.

My house partner, Jeff, and his ex-wife, Helen, were both friends of mine when they were married. Now that they're divorced and even though I currently share a home with Jeff, Helen is still my friend—though definitely not his. She likes to drop over on the weekends to visit my daughter, who is with me only on Saturdays and Sundays, but we are always careful to arrange her visits so Jeff will not be there.

Jeff and I thought that would be a good solution. He didn't want to stand in the way of Helen's and my friendship, but he made it clear he didn't want to see her. I respected that, so we thought this system would work out fine.

How could we anticipate that every time Jeff comes home after Helen visits and smells her perfume, he literally gets sick. Rational or not, he just can't live with our solution. Helen and I are going to have to meet somewhere else.

Back to the drawing board.

Step Eight: Evaluate Your Problem-Solving Process

"How do you think we did in that meeting? What do you think of the way discussions went?" Talk about whether you were working at cross purposes or whether you were able to follow the rules and go through a reasonable problem-solving process.

If tempers have gotten out of hand and the atmosphere is tense, you may have to discuss at another time how your meeting went. Ideally, though, you should do an evaluation immediately afterward.

Some common difficulties people run into during the problem-solving process are blaming each other for the problem, getting off the topic, overgeneralizing, mind-reading, making personal attacks, and bringing up the past rather than dealing with the current predicament.

"We did pretty well getting that problem worked out, don't you think?"

"I thought so, but it did bug me when you kept changing the subject and going to the second problem on the agenda before we finished the first one."

"When you said you knew I was just trying to get out of doing my share of the work, that really bothered me. I know we got it straightened out, but don't speak for me or try to read my mind. Let me speak for myself."

"That wasn't fair when you brought up a problem we had five months ago. We haven't had that trouble since, so why did you mention it? It just made things worse, so I'd appreciate it if you wouldn't do that in the future."

"I really liked the way we brainstormed. That was a good idea we came up with."

"It helped a lot when you tried to get me to tell you what that means to me."

Give yourself some "strokes"—don't just say what went wrong. All of the comments, positive or negative, will help you be more effective problem solvers the next time.

Step Nine: What to Do If You Still Can't Agree

Sometimes, even when you do everything right, you still can't resolve a problem. This is the time to call in a third party. But who you choose is extremely important. Follow these criteria when selecting a mediator.

1. Don't pick someone who will just come in and tell you what is right. You want a person who will help you and your partners work it out together—especially if it's a big problem. Part of your goal should be to learn to solve the next problem better so you don't encounter the same difficulty time and again.

Pick someone who understands how people interact. He may

have experience from serving on committees or be a social worker or psychologist.

Some partners build an arbitration process into their agreement. For instance, one person on the block may not have wanted to be a car partner, but those who are joint owners agreed that if they had any problems, they'd consult him. He's smart and fair. So they consented that he would make the decision and the rest would accept it. That may work. But Jane Engeman believes that, "In general, people can't agree to accept someone else's decision. They need to be part of the process that comes to the resolution. It's better to have a third party help you work it out than just make pronouncements you follow."

2. Don't choose someone who has power over you—like your boss. You might be embarrassed to reveal personal things about yourself to him, so how can he be effective? If you are having house problems, don't consult your banker—he might get nervous about your loan. Pick someone you feel free with.

3. The person to whom you give the power to help you sets the ground rules for the problem-solving process. He may consult you, but he has the final say. The arbitrator must take charge at this point rather than allow already warring partners to fight about how they will go about solving a problem. This is one fight that must be eliminated.

He decides where the meeting will be. It's generally in a neutral place rather than any one of the disputant's homes, so no one feels at a disadvantage. He also controls the agenda. He may say, "I'm going to give each of you 10 minutes to tell your side of the story; then I want each of you to tell the person what you understand about his story. Then I'll tell you how I see it. Then we'll find out how everyone feels about it."

4. The conciliator should know something about the backgrounds of the people who are at odds and have some knowledge of the issues in contest. For instance, if you are having a fight about the upkeep of your home, it's better to have an arbitrator who has owned a home rather than one who has always lived in an apartment. If you are squabbling over who is responsible for ruining the boat engine, it is better to choose a boat-oriented arbitrator or one who is mechanically minded as opposed to someone who has no skill in this area at all.

5. Ideally, the conciliatory person who has been called in should not know more about one of the disputing partners than another. Neutrality and balance are what you're after.

A SHORTCUT

This shortcut process can help you solve problems, too. It is somewhat more casual than the formal arbitration process just explored and may be more in line with the way you like to operate. It's also an excellent formula to employ when you're having trouble saying what's on your mind, especially if you must tell your partner something unpleasant. These pointers are taken from the *Clearness Manual*, a how-to booklet conceived at the Philadelphia Life Center to help individuals and groups support one another in decision making. Its concepts and concrete advice will be useful to anyone interested in group participation. Peter Woodrow did the actual writing; the ideas and processes were contributed by a number of people in this group.

The following is a summary of their main points.

1. Speak in a direct and firm manner. Be clear and specific. Relate the particular incident you feel objectionable, not everything they ever did that hurt your feelings or made you upset.

2. Say what *you* think. Do not say, "I understand that a lot of people don't like what you're doing." According to the *Clearness Manual*, the conversation formula should be, "When you do _____, I feel _____ about it because _____."

3. Acknowledge any feelings or actions of yours that have contributed to the problem.

4. Affirm the person if you possibly can. Think of the ways you like or appreciate him and *say so.*

5. Now listen to what he has to say. Listen without responding at this point; give him time to express himself fully. But at the same time, try to separate actual issues from his feelings about them. When you've heard enough, say so.

6. Be specific about what you are and are not willing to negotiate.

7. If you are afraid of your partner's reaction to what you have to say, practice it a few times with someone you trust. Have him tell you how it sounds—if what you are saying makes sense. Is it forceful enough? Is it too hostile?

8. You may want to reach out to your partner physically at this time. A handshake, a bear hug, a pat on the back to show you care helps. If touching is not part of how you relate to one another, this is not the time to start.

9. If you see real trouble on the horizon, ask a conciliatory person to join you—one you both agree should be there. This person will help you keep listening to each other and clarify what is being said. Do not call in this person as the doctor who will come up with a cure.

The *Clearness Manual* ($1.75 plus postage and handling) may be obtained by writing to Movement for a New Society, 4722 Baltimore Avenue, Philadelphia, PA 19143.

Throwing in the Towel

That a partnership ends—sometimes badly despite your best efforts—is a reality that cannot be ignored. It's a sad note on which to end this chapter. It's even sadder when people end a joint venture with bitterness and animosity. But it does happen, and you have to be prepared for its eventuality.

Stuart Scheingarten says, "Most people know a partnership isn't working long before they act. But they are resistant to change. They don't want to deal with the unknown—what happens after the partnership is over. It may be scary. People don't want to admit failure and they don't like to hurt someone else."

Stuart emphasizes, "End the partnership before everyone winds up hating each other's guts. If you wait till no one can stand each other, there is such adversarial tension that negotiating becomes impossible. Start talking about cutting ties as soon as you start thinking about it in a serious way.

"If you are the rejecting party, even though you may feel guilty, you must act in your own best interests as soon as possible. Basically, it's you or your partner. And you must save yourself. To assuage guilt, go out of your way to be financially fair. Then you will know in your heart you have made a move to minimize bad feelings."

If your agreement is a good one, most of the machinery for finalizing the ending will have been set up. But putting the machinery in motion is always painful.

THEY TOLD YOU SO

One last terrible topic to consider: What if your partner has out and out ripped you off? You have an agreement—a good one. You both saw to that. But the man you've played golf with for the last five years and who you bought an expensive set of clubs with six months ago got transferred out of town. When he moved, he took the golf clubs with him.

You agreed he would pay you for your share before he left, but he didn't. You thought he might have forgotten to mail the check in the flurry of packing. So you wrote to him and asked for the money—three times—and he wrote back saying it was on the way. You haven't received a dime and feel you've been had. What are you going to do about it?

"Agreements are only as good as the people who make them," says attorney Gloria Haffer, who advises many partners. "That's why I encourage people to be careful who they join up with at the very beginning. You can draw up a wonderful agreement, but it is binding only when it is enforced."

You have to decide whether your loss is worth the expense, the time, and the heartache it will take to bring legal action against your partner. Sure, you've been wronged—you can show that six points in your agreement have been violated. You have to prove it in court, and that can be expensive—possibly more expensive than your share of your jointly owned property.

Gloria says, "A good agreement is a clarification of intentions. If a person questions whether his partner is acting improperly, he can go back to the written document and check his rights. He can take the agreement to an attorney to verify whether he's being taken advantage of.

"Sometimes the agreement itself can inhibit legal action among the warring partners. If the point they are disputing is clearly spelled out and the wrongdoing partner is advised he would not fare successfully in court, the matter may be able to be settled more amicably, or the partnership can be dissolved in a somewhat civil atmosphere." (Another good reason for making strong, clear agreements!)

What you must do is ask the attorney you consult how much it would cost to recoup your loss. If you don't know an attorney, check with the Bar Association in your city to see if there is a legal reference service. Small claims court may be the best recourse.

Check with the clerk of courts in your county for the procedure you must follow to file in small claims court, and ask the limit of the amount of claim that may be brought before the court. It varies from state to state. Filing in small claims court does not require an attorney, and the filing fee is minimal. But it is a time-consuming process. You will probably miss a day of work on the date you are scheduled to appear, so that's an expense you must tally up, too. And even winning doesn't guarantee you get your money. Sure, the judgment is in your favor, but maybe your partner still doesn't pay up. No court automatically forces a debtor to pay. To collect, you will have to return to the clerk's office, fill out more forms, and pay more fees. Eventually you may get your money, but only after a lot of time and trouble. In the end, only you can decide how far you want to go and whether it's worth it in dollars and mental anguish.

"It's sad," says Gloria. "Even when I know a client has been hurt, I sometimes have to advise him to weigh the situation carefully.

"Sometimes clients decide the expense can't justify legal action. They walk away from a sobering, hard-knocks learning experience."

In that case, wherever your partner is with *his and your* $500 set of golf clubs, you may decide to do nothing more than pray it rains every Sunday.

·7·
Teaming Up with Tools and Appliances

Your first spring in your first home! Trees bud. Forsythia blooms. The air is ripe with the aromas of a fresh season. It's exciting to have your own house at last. You're sure it was the right decision, even though you went through more budget juggling than you ever imagined. You love waking in the morning to hear birds chirp. Having a green place to sit at the end of the day brings you the peace you've been yearning for. You're happy and satisfied.

Another look at the yard shows you the grass is sparse in a couple of places. Guess you'll need to put down some seed. Hmm, what kind do you buy when there's so much shade? How often, you wonder, do you have to water it, once it's spread? Apartment dwelling wasn't the greatest lawn care prep school, you chuckle, as you get out a pencil and paper to make a list of the tools you need for yard work.

Let's see. You could use a grass seed spreader (can you use it to spread fertilizer, too—or do you need another tool?), a hose, a mower to cut the grass once it has sprouted, a shovel, a rake, an edger, clippers for the bushes, an extension ladder—your list grows, and so does your consternation. It was winter when you moved into the house and spring chores seemed far away. You dealt with plumbers, carpenters, upholsterers, and carpet cleaners. You're still paying their bills to prove it. Now a new onslaught of expenses. How can you manage it?

71

Buying a home is one thing. Keeping it up is another. The expense of all the things you must acquire to do those maintenance jobs mounts up to shock many homeowners.

One way of cutting the amazing cost of this equipment is to buy it in partnership with others. You might love to have a shiny new ride-on mower with all the trimmings but not be able to fit such an expensive piece of machinery into your budget. Finding someone else who also wants to invest in first-class equipment and share the expense would be ideal.

It's also a dandy arrangement for people who know they need tools to keep their houses in shape but resent buying them. Blue-ribbon wheelbarrows do not make their hearts beat faster, nor does holding the latest and most expensive electric hedge clippers in their arms. They'd much rather spend their money on a good book to curl up with on the patio, or going to dinner at that new French restaurant they've been hearing so much about. Partnering tools to keep down expenses is ideal for these grudging gardeners.

So whether you'd like to buy appliances in partnership so you can afford the premium quality you can't afford alone, or so you can join the Book-of-the-Month Club rather than be sole owner of 200 feet of garden hose, doubling up is the best answer.

APPLIANCES

The most popularly partnered home appliance I came across is a lawn mower. Three very different types of lawn mower partnerships are included in this chapter to give you a range of examples you might find appealing. I have paid so much attention to these grass-gobbling devices because so much energy was given to their partnership by the people I interviewed.

Runners-up in the appliance partnership hit parade are others that are blue-jeans basic. Chain saws, Rototillers, and extension ladders may not be your idea of exciting, but these items and their close cousins are most needed and most partnered.

This does not preclude co-owning more glamorous appliances. Let me explain that my definition of an appliance in this chapter is anything—from blenders to snow blowers—that helps you do a job you have to do—better.

Thumb through a Sears, Montgomery Ward, Brookstone, or any catalog you fancy. Walk through any hardware store. Partnerships can be worked out for almost anything you see.

Think about sharing power lawn edgers, snow and leaf blowers, long-reach window-washing brushes, water brooms, grass thatchers, leaf catchers, posthole diggers, garden carts, even lowly standbys like rakes, hoes, shovels, pitchforks, and pruning shears. You name it. If you need it, you can share it.

In the first part of this chapter I'm going to cover workhorse-type outdoor-related appliance partnerships. Then we'll move on to all kinds of tools and kitchen aids. But first—lawn mowers!

A Lawn Mower in Every Two Garages

Two next-door neighbors I talked to fell into the "couldn't care less about lawn mowers" category. They considered them a necessity, not a status symbol. They shopped for a mower and finally bought a used, self-propelled, double-bladed Toro at an auction for $150.

The agreement they made with each other was that whoever used it last would fill it with gas and oil and also store it. They decided to share all maintenance costs equally.

"Since there usually is no way of knowing who caused what to go wrong, if the lawn mower went on the blink, we decided it wasn't even worth discussing," Ron told me. "We decided to share maintenance equally—period. But if one person was truly negligent, we knew that person would be responsible for the expense. We never formalized this, but there was enough trust between us that we knew that was how we would behave."

These partners were so successful in their lawn mower venture that they made new joint acquisitions and included more neighbors in the purchases. With a third friend they bought a used grinder for $65 to shred leaves for their individual compost piles.

"Where is it stored?" I asked Ron. Grinders are fairly large.

"In my garage," he said, "because mine's the biggest. But all partners have access to the garage at all times, so no one has to ask permission to come over to get it or make sure I'm home. That is an inconvenience partners should avoid."

The trio enlarged to a quartet to buy a Rototiller. Ron was going to an auction to bid on a used one and the other three told him to go as high as $100. He got it for $95.

"What if it was a dud after you got it home?" I asked him. "Would the others have blamed you and perhaps not have paid?"

"They trusted me to do the best I could," he said. "No one would have blamed me if it went sour after we used it a few times. That could happen to anyone. They also would have paid me extra if I had to bid as high as $115 to get it."

Even more appliances were jointly purchased—most of them second-hand.

"We ran them until they died," Ron told me. "None of us wanted to invest in fancy equipment and no one wanted to own all of these things solo."

A lawn sweeper was procured for $45, a fertilizer and grass seed spreader for $10, and a new chain saw for $70.

Clouds on the horizon. Ron's next-door neighbor had to move out of town. The person who bought his home also picked up his partnership shares in his appliance holdings.

"It worked out fine," Ron said, "because all of us knew the person who was moving in and we liked him. Otherwise we would have exercised our right to buy out the exiting partner's shares so we could choose a new one. We were such a congenial group, a new person none of us got along with could have destroyed the partnership."

Two members of the group splurged on one last purchase, an open trailer with sides 2 feet high and a 4x8-foot bed. Ron found a man to build it to his specifications for $300 instead of the $700 he saw a comparable one selling for at the store. The same man custommade a hitch for Ron's venerable Volvo for $27 and his friend's car as well.

The rationale for owning a trailer was that Ron heated his home with wood and found it much cheaper to pick up a winter's supply and bring it home than to have it delivered. Loads of manure for the garden could be hauled in the trailer, too. The lawn mower and the grinder could be moved from house to house in it (some appliance partners lived a couple of streets apart), and with Ron's penchant for finding great buys at auctions, he could use the trailer to ferry them home.

The two partners decided they could accept four more people in the group if they found interested parties. They wound up with three. The last one who joined caused a problem the four men had to solve. They had decided the last person to use the trailer would always store it. No one really wanted the clunker in his garage, but that was the rule to protect it from rust. The fifth partner had no garage. Group consensus okayed his leaving the trailer exposed to the elements. Since one partner had welding equipment, he volunteered to patch it if the trailer succumbed to rust.

This casual partnership arrangement has continued for years. More appliances are added to the stockpile as they are needed. Someone who buys a new piece of equipment checks by phone to see if the rest wish to be included. They have no set schedule for using anything. When someone needs something, he simply phones around to see who has it and then goes to pick it up.

The key to success: No one piece of equipment means enough to anyone to cause a fight. No one cares so much about a clogged seed spreader to make it an issue—someone just unclogs it. The group is homogeneous in lifestyle; all live in a small college town and are professionals. They like each other better than they like their tools. This laid-back partnership style works—for them!

• • •

Two brothers-in-law built homes on the same street. Though their new homes were dreams come true, cutting grass wasn't. Kurt said, "I definitely don't consider a new lawn mower the greatest thing to happen in my life." Both knew they *had* to cut the grass; they wanted to do it the easiest way possible. They decided to get a good, sturdy, ride-on model, a better one than either would have bought individually, at the nearby discount store.

Kurt had a friend in the lawn mower business and felt the price he was quoted on the agreed-on model would save them about $100. He relayed this to his brother-in-law, John, and told him to go see if he liked it. John looked at the mower and checked the price at a few other stores as well. He wanted to be satisfied it was worth $800.

"It was," he said, so Kurt made the purchase. To keep family relations amicable, the following points were discussed and agreed on:

1. After eight hours of use, the oil should be changed. Whoever is using the lawn mower at the time is responsible for the chore. (The hours the lawn mower is run are logged in a notebook kept where the appliance is stored. This way, each partner will know when it is time to do this job.)

2. Each time the mower is used, the gas tank should be refilled.

3. Whoever uses the last of the gas in the five-gallon can (kept to fill the mower) will buy more. (If one of them felt he was buying gas more often than the other, he would simply say, "Hey, you get the gas this time. I bought it the last few times." The cost is always divided evenly.)

4. After each use, grass should be cleaned out of the blades, especially if a lawn is cut when wet. Whatever other maintenance the lawn mower needs after it is used should be done conscientiously, so that it is always ready for use by the next person.

5. The lawn mower must be kept inside. (This means it has to be stored at John's house because his garage is bigger. Kurt simply

walks a few houses down the street and rides the mower back to his house.)

Note—This is an important consideration for partners of ride-on mowers as well as those who partner other large appliances. Keep the implement within riding (or easy hauling) range of the partners' homes to keep it convenient. The option is to buy a trailer, as Ron's group did, or own a pickup truck. Otherwise the system will be unwieldy and the partnership can become a nuisance.

6. All maintenance costs are to be split evenly.

7. Neither partner will lend the mower to a neighbor without checking with the other.

8. In case one of them is transferred to another city, the partner who stays in town will buy out the other's ownership. The value of his share will be decided by procuring a resale price for the mower and halving it.

• • •

The third lawn mower partnership included here is an example of how you can get your grass cut in style, set up a business for your children, and have a piece of equipment you can depreciate to create a tax shelter. It was appropriately conceived by two busy, energetic couples: a husband and wife who are both stockbrokers, and a husband and wife who are executives with large corporations. Both couples bought gracious homes with adjacent yards. Each had acres of lawn to deal with.

At a party, the discussion turned to how all of them with so little time to spend on yard care would get it done. Still, they wanted to do the work themselves rather than hire it out. Nancy, the stockbroker, told the rest she knew of a neighbor who wanted to get rid of a jumbo John Deere tractor that could do most of the jobs they were bemoaning. It had a 48-inch mower blade, a snow blower, a leaf vacuum, and leaf shredder attachment, as well as a wagon that could be hooked on the back. The price of a new model with all these extras would be close to $9,000. The neighbor was asking $5,000 for this one.

Neither couple alone wanted to lay out the full amount, so splitting the cost seemed ideal. All sorts of needs fit together perfectly. The tractor would be used by one couple's teenage children and the other couple's teenage relatives (the husband's brothers). Yard work needed doing; teenagers wanted to be in charge of doing it because they needed money. Besides, they loved driving the tractor!

Then the partnership took on a new dimension. A neighborhood grass cutting-snow removal service was conceived so that the kids could cut their own lawns and those of neighbors to earn even more cash.

Here's how Nancy and the rest of the group set up this ingenious arrangement:

1. The Internal Revenue Service requires that a business be a valid one in order to take depreciation. Therefore, the partners had to show they were in business in earnest to make a profit.

2. Legal partnership documents had to be filed with state and county authorities. An attorney was consulted to make sure everything was handled correctly.

3. Depreciation was allowed on a straight-line basis for five years. This means the purchase price of the tractor was divided by five (still a tidy sum) and each couple could deduct half of it from their income taxes for those years.

4. Personal liability insurance was purchased to protect the partners in case damage was done to a client's property with their tractor. (Insurance for possible damage to the tractor by the teenagers was not purchased. They felt the business could assume those expenses.)

The business became a two-family venture. Nancy and her husband took charge of finances; they were to keep the books. The corporate couple would do the marketing, since that was their area of expertise. They would create snappy flyers to distribute throughout the neighborhood to drum up business. They would also act as job estimators.

The partners decided customers would be limited to the four surrounding streets (this would encompass about 100 houses), so the tractor could be driven from lawn to lawn or on the sidewalk. It was not to be taken on city streets.

Money collected would be deposited into a business bank account. Mower maintenance and teenagers' salaries would be paid out of this account; minimum wage was decided as the scale.

Maintenance was to be done by a service that picked up and delivered the tractor. The couples alternated arranging for spring checkups. If the tractor broke down between checkups, the person who was using it at the time was responsible for scheduling repairs—speedily. The business would pay for repair costs. However, if negligence was clearly the cause for the breakdown, the erring individual would be held financially responsible. The cost of the repair would be paid by the individual into the company checking account.

The maintenance chores to be performed after each use were clearly established and were expected to be done as specified by the group.

Besides feeling responsible to each other, both couples felt responsible to customers who expected prompt lawn or snow attention. They decided that if the tractor was out of order and jobs were scheduled, they would let the teenagers use each family's individual, smaller lawn mowers to carry on.

Another responsible, and perhaps merciful provision: Lawn care training sessions were performed on the partners' yards before customers were lined up. Parents wanted to make sure no one's grass would get a military-style haircut and that shrubs, flower beds, and hedges would still be intact after the job was done. There were many preliminary run-throughs and safety technique drills before they actually went into business, so that adults and teenagers felt confident with their expertise.

This system worked for these neighbors, and for their children and teenage relatives, too. If you are as intrigued by the idea as they were, consult an attorney to make sure all legal angles have been covered before you proceed full speed ahead.

• • •

If you think about it, just about any equipment you own or are considering purchasing can be used to make money. But remember that if it's tax writeoffs you're after, the business you set up must be a serious, for-profit concern.

The business possibilities of partnering are certainly something to look into. But for-profit partnering will not be treated in any depth in this book. Volumes abound that show you how to make money in the world of commerce, if that's what you want to do.

Making money is not the driving force in the majority of our partnerships; *saving* it is.

Co-owner and Operator

Chain saws are an easily shared appliance because they are not in constant use by any one person but are handy to have at your disposal. Hourly rental costs add up. Joint ownership brings the cost down. Many chain saws are jointly owned by neighbors or friends, and co-owners do not have to live in close proximity. Chain saws can be easily transported in the trunk of a car—impossible to do with a snowplow.

I mentioned in an earlier chapter that four executives of the same company—transferred from one city to another—bought a chain saw in partnership to clear out dead branches of trees in their yards. They all lived in different parts of the city. To solve the inconvenience of driving to each other's homes to pick up the saw or deliver it, they used the office as the central pickup point.

After each finished his scheduled weekend use, he brought it to the office on Monday morning so the next scheduled partner could claim it. The saw was clean, oiled, and empty of gas. Driving a chain saw around with a full gas tank isn't safe. Each person kept his own gas supply. All maintenance costs were split; any breakdowns were considered due to normal wear and tear.

"It's hard to tell what makes a chain saw go kerflooey anyway," one of the partners said. "We trusted each other. We were also on our good behavior with each other. We all worked in the same office and we had to work well together. No one wanted to cause problems by splitting hairs."

• • •

Three men in one neighborhood bought an aluminum extension ladder for about $70. "It wasn't only the money we wanted to save," said Ben, a vocal partner. "It was just one more thing all of us didn't want to have to buy for once in-a-while use. No one likes cluttering up the garage with all this stuff anyway."

To make life simpler, the group decided that whoever used the ladder last, kept it. To find out its current location, they just called around.

"No one really cares if it is lent to other people," said Ben. "We don't ask each other's permission to lend it to friends. How often can a ladder be used? What can you really do to hurt it anyway? No one is going to fight over that amount of money, and if one of us lends it to someone who lends it to someone and we can't track it down, he'll replace it. We know that."

• • •

Though owning your own bulldozer may seem mind-boggling, it made perfect sense to two farmers who owned large spreads and needed one to clear trees, close ditches, and move earth. The $12,000 used model they purchased together fit the bill. "We each had liability insurance but purchased none for the bulldozer itself," Bob told me. "If we smashed into someone's barn, we were covered for the damage. If it busted up the bulldozer, we would swallow hard."

Maintenance costs were split 50-50, and each person gave the bulldozer to the other after using it with a full tank of gas and as clean as possible.

"But," Bob said, "if I was out till dark working in mud and my friend needs it at 6:00 a.m. the next day, it's not going to be as clean as he would like it to be. There has to be a lot of give and take in a partnership like this. We understood each other's way of life and needs. Also, if I put in a new oil filter one time and Joe replaced a few bolts, we're not going to go after each other for payment. On a piece of equipment this expensive, getting hung up on small expenses doesn't make sense."

They also bought two manure spreaders, so that, in tandem, work was done twice as fast.

"How come each of you didn't own one apiece?" I asked.

"We needed two working together to get the job done efficiently," Bob said. "We set it up so that each of us owned half of each manure spreader so that if one broke down no one could say, yours is in bad shape, mine is fine. Both of us were responsible for both machines. Also, in case one of the manure spreaders went bad, neither guy is hit quite so hard. Each person only needed to put up half the money to fix it or replace it. Since they cost about $8,000 apiece, that can be overwhelming."

HOW TO MAKE AN APPLIANCE AGREEMENT

Based on the positive and negative experiences of the partners we've looked at so far, the following simple ownership and usage agreement can be used as a model for your appliance agreement. We have chosen a tractor as our example. You can substitute whatever you wish and it will still apply, with some minor modifications.

When you read the agreement, please be sure to note the explanations following each contract clause. These contain some alternate choices to the working in the sample agreement so you can pick the ones that suit your particular needs. Between this model and your own requirements you should come up with the ideal arrangement for you.

TRACTOR OWNERSHIP AND USAGE AGREEMENT

The following Ownership and Usage Agreement is made on this _____ day of _____ , 19 _____ between Jack Maple, Margaret Maple, Carol Birch, and Stanley Birch, hereafter referred to as the Owners. It is agreed that:

1. *Ownership*

The Owners will have the following interest in the 1970 John Deere 400 Tractor (serial number 7CA079116) and equipment purchased by the Owners on March 12, 1983:

Jack and Margaret Maple 50%
Carol and Stanley Birch 50%

[This clause is standard and simple. It clearly states who owns what percentage of the property.]

2. *Obligations*

Owners will split payments on the following items in accordance with the ownership interests.

    a. Initial purchase of tractor and accessories.
    b. Miscellaneous expenses incurred in general maintenance and use of the tractor.

[This says that monetary obligations are in a direct ratio to ownership shares. If you own half of the tractor, half of the purchase price and the maintenance expenses will be yours also.]

3. *Withdrawal from Ownership*

    a. Existing Owners have the first option to buy each other's shares, if one party should choose to withdraw from ownership.
    b. No other party may buy shares without unanimous approval of all Owners.
    c. Any new Owner is bound by this agreement unless a new agreement is drawn.
    d. The value of shares sold to existing Owners is to be based on current book value as determined by a reputable John Deere dealer.

[This clause provides for the ins and outs; in other words, who can buy in and how partners can get out. To eliminate fights over the value of the tractor and who pays how much to a partner when he wants to leave the partnership, the buyout price has been established—simply.

Some partners may want to obtain three estimates and either average the estimates or take the middle figure.]

4. *Damage*

    a. Repair of any damage that is not the result of normal wear will be the responsibility of the user of the tractor at the time of its damage. User will have repairs made as expeditiously as possible.

    b. The Owner must make sure repairs will be made so that the aesthetic and structural integrity of the tractor is affected as little as possible.

    c. The Owner who causes the damage must notify the others.

[In this clause the partners have dealt with the fine points many partners choose to ignore. They have agreed that damage due to negligence will be paid for by the responsible partner. Now they have the responsibility (headache) of defining negligence versus normal wear and tear. The two often overlap.

If you look the other way and wave to a friend while you are driving the tractor and run into a tree, that's clearly negligence. On the other hand, if you run over a root and damage a blade, is that negligence or something every tractor driver will probably do sometime?

If you decide that you want partners to be financially responsible for negligence, make sure everyone involved understands what constitutes "negligence." This is difficult to do and is why many partners take the attitude, "Why bother to find out?" Many just divide all expenses evenly, saying whatever happens while their partner uses the tractor could happen to them, and call it a day. Decide what feels right for you. (One way to alleviate the negligence problem is to have great partners. If your agreement states all repairs are to be split, no matter what, and the partner who runs the tractor into a tree pays for the damage just because he feels responsible, problems dissolve immediately.)

The second paragraph of this clause means, "If you get it fixed, buy the same quality parts that were there in the first place." Don't substitute cheap labor for professional work. Keep it in the same shape as you first found it. It's not a bad idea to put this in writing, though many partners operate this way as a matter of course.]

5. *Usage*

    a. Owners will schedule use of the tractor by telephone as needed.

    b. Tractor will not be used by non-Owners without unanimous agreement of all Owners.

[These partners decided to schedule use by telephone, which is fine for appliances and probably most appropriate. If you wish to establish a more formal arrangement, you can attach a calendar with partners' names written on alternating weeks, or weekends—however you want to do it. Then you must deal with whether a nonscheduled partner may use the property with the agreement of the scheduled party. In other words, can partners switch days, or is that a pain? Can one use the mower, with permission, when it's not his turn if the person whose turn it is—isn't? Whew!

In this clause, the issue of lending has also been firmly dealt with. This point can be powerfully disruptive to some partnerships or not matter at all to others. Shape this clause to suit you.]

6. *Maintenance*

    a. After each use the user is responsible to (1) fill gas tank and cans, and (2) empty wagon of grass clippings and leaves.

    b. In April and November tractor should have maintenance check at reputable mower repair operation as agreed upon by all Owners. Owners will rotate the responsibility of arranging for this to be done.

[This is the "odd couple" clause and one that causes many headaches. If you're the partner who always has to soak and clean the petrified brushes, you'll probably end up telling your partner off one day.

To prevent that from happening, write down what you would like done each time your joint property is used. Whether it is filling a tank with gas after each use or changing the needle in a sewing machine if it dulls, spell it out so all understand exactly what they must do to keep others (and themselves) happy.

Decide what yearly, semiannual, or other periodic maintenance has to be done and who is responsible for seeing to it.]

7. Storage

    a. When the tractor is not in use, Owners must store it in either Maple's or Birch's garage.

    b. All Owners will have keys and access to garages.

[Your joint property should be kept in a place acceptable to all partners. If you specify where the property is to be kept, everyone can find it easily and the equipment will be protected. No one has to call to find out where it is—now. If this doesn't matter to you and your partnership is a casual one, you can ignore this stipulation altogether.

It is important that all partners have equal access to the storage space so no one feels inconvenienced by having to ask permission to pick up the item. It is a bother to make sure a partner is at home to let you in, and vice versa. An easy way to solve this is to make sure everyone has keys to the place or places the joint property is housed.]

  8. *Decision-Making*

      a. Decisions arising in following this agreement or when new conditions arise will be made in accordance with shares of ownership, with majority being required for a decision.

      b. If a tie vote occurs on any decision, Owners will seek more information in order to attempt to gain consensus. If consensus is not possible, the decision will be made by the flip of a coin.

      c. Amendments to this Agreement shall be made only by the written approval of all Owners.

[In this agreement, voting rights are in line with shares of ownership. Majority rules, but in case of an impasse, consensus will be sought.

You may want to insert, at this point, that you will seek arbitration by a third party and who that arbitrator will be.

In this example, a stalemated decision is to be settled by the flip of a coin. If you are fighting about a food mixer, this is a simple solution. A bulldozer may be a different story. The details of the decision-making process should be appropriate to the value of the property in question.]

In Witness Whereof, the undersigned have set their names on the day and year first set forth above.

_____	_____
Jack Maple	Carol Birch
_____	_____
Margaret Maple	Stanley Birch

TOOLS

How many times have you needed to do a special repair job and haven't had the right tool to get it done? Who can afford every tool to fix anything that could conceivably break or do everything you want to do?

The cost of professional service calls is climbing so rapidly that tools could pay for themselves in the long run. But really, how often are you going to need a snake drain cleaner, though you sure wished you had one when the drain backed up and flooded the laundry room? (The plumber you called to bail you out that Sunday cost a fortune.)

Neighbors can go in together to buy tools they'd like to have handy but don't use regularly enough to justify the expense. Or great tools everyone needs more often but may be reluctant to spend so much money on can fall into the realm of affordability.

Tool Pools

Tool pools. They make sense and they're simple to set up. The group can buy tools and split their cost, or each person can buy one and agree to exchange it.

The most important common denominator in the group (or between two people, if that's the size pool you feel most comfortable with) is that everyone treats their tools the same way. What does "taking good care of" something mean? It should be clearly spelled out.

If one group member thinks that good care of a saw means always making sure the blade is sharp for the next guy who uses it and his partner throws it on a jumbled shelf somewhere after he's finished with it, there's going to be a problem.

Some people love tools, love the way they feel in their hands, love to work with them. Others use them grudgingly to get nasty jobs done. They concede you need them, "but they're a nuisance."

You must take pains to find people who value tools the same way you do. If you don't mind waiting until the snow melts in spring to find the hammer your partner left out in the backyard somewhere, he'd be a good match for you. Someone else might want to murder him.

You will have to anticipate the maintenance needed on each tool you purchase and specify exactly who does it and when. If someone breaks it, is he responsible for getting it fixed promptly? (You'll find more about this subject in the chapter on Work Sharing.)

Also, make sure every joint owner has convenient access to the tools. Will they be kept at the partner's house who happens to have the most room, or will the last person who uses the tool store it until the next partner needs it? Everyone should have keys to "the place," wherever it is. It's a pain to have to ask to come get it or wonder if anyone will be home.

Hand tools in your collection can include all the sizes and types of pliers, wrench sets, screwdrivers, hammers, and clamps you'd like to have but would never buy yourself. How about axes, hatchets, scrapers, chisels, sawhorses? Think about those extravaganza tool sets with hundreds of pieces. They also cost hundreds of dollars. Wouldn't it be nice to have all those gismos whenever you need them? You could—if you split their cost.

The same goes for small hardware. You always have plenty of the kind you're not looking for. Those nail and screw and bolt sets with dozens of drawers packed with all sizes and shapes would be wonderful to own, but you'd probably never use them all in three lifetimes. Split the cost and everybody should be well covered.

A torch outfit would be nice to have to fix leaky pipes and for cutting and welding. Paint rollers and drop cloths, a paint sprayer, an electric sander, an electric drill complete with a set of bits of all sizes, electric staplers, brad nailers, soldering and glue guns. A whetstone grinder could keep tools and kitchen cutlery sharp. With the pickup power of a wet-dry vacuum, you and your partners can tackle big clean-up jobs from wood shavings to draining a flooded garage.

Woodworking tools . . . partnering paradise. Router tables, band saws to cut curves and contours, scroll saws for tricky cuts or patterns, rasps, lathes, planes, miter boxes—anything you and your partners decide to acquire together.

Do-it-yourself auto repairers can join forces to buy the equipment they need for at-home tinkering. Heavy-duty jacks and ramps, auto battery rechargers, air compressors to inflate tires (or your basketball), engine analyzers, tachometers for tuneups, ignition timing lights, even an auto vacuum are wise co-ownables.

Homework

Any piece of home-related business equipment could make sense to share.

As home computers become more popular, joint ownerships in this kind of high-tech equipment can make acquisitions easier. This is the arrangement four enterprising young professionals agreed to.

Since all of the men were good friends and all of them were interested in an Apple personal computer priced at about $2,000, the choice of the machine was easy. They each wanted the use of it, but none wanted to spend the whole amount. At this particular time in their lives, all of them were up to their ears in the expenses of renovating first homes.

Mark is in the building business and is studying solar-designed architecture. He wanted to use the machine to plug in solar design equations rather than write out pages of them. This way, he could have the variables at his fingertips whenever he needed them.

Paul is a chemist and sells testing devices to laboratories. He does his own research at night and wanted to punch chemical equations into the machine.

Gene, a journalist, wanted to use the word processor for his freelance projects. Walt, an engineer by day and a history buff in the evenings, also wanted the word processor and diskettes to store his writing.

That specific model was chosen because it had the storage capacity all the men needed. But each of them is individually responsible for the cost of the programs he uses, and for the diskettes he requires to store his personal information.

"That saves a lot of hassle," Mark told me. "The computer is kept at one person's house for three months at a time, because unhooking it, packing it up, and moving it around more often than that is a pain. We have worked out a 'reasonable right of usage' agreement so everyone can still use the computer even though it isn't at his house.

"We all have an extra bedroom—a guest room—away from the mainstream of the house. This is where we all keep the computer. If a partner wants to use the machine, he checks to see if it is free, and if it is, he comes right over. He is not disturbed by anyone in the house, and he doesn't bother anyone either. We all live within a twenty-minute drive of each other, so it's convenient.

"If the person who has the computer is out for the evening and someone wants to use it, he arranges to leave his house key somewhere accessible. If he is out of town, all partners have a key to his home. There is a lot of trust between us."

All maintenance is split evenly; negligence is a personal responsibility. Since Mark built the carrying case the computer is moved in, he deducted the cost of the materials from his first maintenance bill. The labor was free.

"The computer uses about as much electricity as a 60-watt bulb," Mark estimated. "Each of us absorbs the cost of it during the computer's stay at our house."

As for who fixes the machine, the rule is: "No tinkering with it." If it breaks at one person's home, he is responsible for getting it fixed by a reputable dealer. At the same time, though, each is to leave the machine ready for the next person's use.

The partners decided other people in the family could use the computer, but figured that the increased use might mean more maintenance costs. To handle that, they decided to tack on hourly use charges agreeable to all of them. The money is placed in the maintenance kitty.

"Our main interest was not to inconvenience or take advantage of anyone," Mark emphasized.

Finally, if one partner should wish to sell his shares, the three remaining have the first option to buy him out and then decide if they want to take in a new partner. It is important that they feel comfortable with each other and that they live close enough to one another for fast access to the computer.

"The buyout cost would be decided by a dealer," Mark said, "plus, we'd all probably look in the newspaper to see what machines of that age are selling for.

"Trading up for a better machine is a possibility, too. Majority would rule in a decision like that, but if there was a 50-50 split, we'd probably just argue it out until we came to some conclusion or other. Remember, we're all good friends, and we want to keep it that way."

• • •

The home computer partnership opens up a whole world of related equipment you can co-own if you work out the rules as carefully as Mark, Paul, Gene, and Walt did.

Tape recorders are simple to co-own if everyone is careful not to leave a partner with a dead battery. An interview you thought you had on tape, but find you don't, can be irreplaceable. And a loss like that can cause enough hard feelings to destroy a partnership.

Two college students who don't have to produce papers at the same time during the semester would be happy to get rid of half the expense of a typewriter. A portable model would be easy to move around. Anyone who finds someone else who needs one, but not constantly, can share a typewriter.

Desk-top copiers, dictaphones, even home photocopying machines—think about cutting the cost of the equipment you need to get work done at home by buying it with others who face the same chores and the same expenses.

A Piece of the Pie

Move on to the kitchen. Are those sharp and shiny things you need to get jobs done tools or appliances? You decide. But whatever you want to call them, think about splitting their use and their cost.

Two neighboring women who each had backyard vegetable gardens pooled food processors for mammoth kitchen chores. Louise told me, "When you are facing three bushels of tomatoes you are going to turn into tomato sauce, using one food processor would take hours. I use mine and my neighbor's at the same time to speed things up and she does the same when she makes gallons of minestrone soup."

When both women had to make new equipment purchases for canning vegetables and making preserves and jellies, they were careful to survey what they needed and split the purchases both agreed on. Louise bought a fruit and vegetable juicer-strainer; her neighbor bought a pressure cooker for about the same amount. Though they are kept in the respective owner's home, they are traded whenever needed.

• • •

Here's how two neighboring families devised a way to share a large deep freeze.

Since one of the wives was physically disabled, it was placed on her back porch so she could get to it conveniently. Here it was convenient for the other couple, too. They would never have to tromp through their partner's house or have to ask to use what they owned.

The lower shelves were easier for the handicapped woman to use, so dividing shelf space was easy. Utility bills were monitored before the freezer was purchased and after it was installed. The two couples determined what the extra electrical cost was each month and split it.

For those who want to cut grocery bills by buying in bulk but don't want to turn around and sink those savings into freezer payments, partnering is a sure way to stock up and save.

These partnerships are only a first course of culinary sharables. I mentioned a partnered meat slicer and a deluxe ice cream machine earlier. What about a pasta maker, a blender, a food dehydrator, a smoker, a fruit and vegetable juicer to mix up healthy fresh drink combos, a convection oven that is so nice to have if you need extra oven space when you're cooking for company?

How often do you use hot trays? Confess—mostly when you have guests for dinner, right? Couldn't they as easily serve a neighbor or two besides yourself?

What about having a nice big stainless steel fish poacher at your disposal when you want to show off and prepare a lovely salmon?

A 50-cup coffee maker is nice for a crowd, but it would spend most of its life on a shelf if you bought it solo. The same would be true of giant salad bowls (they could double as punch bowls), and colossal stock pots you use to make hearty soup to serve the bunch you've invited over after the football game. What about a soup tureen big enough to serve your aromatic brew? Add cheese boards, large platters, a few dozen glass dessert plates and fruit bowls, soup or coffee mugs to your co-ownership list. Anything you use when company comes, but don't normally need in that size or quantity, is a grade A partnering possibility.

Waffle irons and popcorn poppers can be joint purchases—that is, if popcorn and waffles are sometime treats and not daily fare.

Get out your Williams-Sonoma catalog and drool over their copper casseroles and au gratin dishes. Beautiful, hmm? But the price knocks you out. Buy them in partnership—and enjoy cooking and serving in them. Maybe you couldn't use them every day if you only co-own them, but would you use them every day anyway? Isn't using them often better than not using them at all?

• • •

A sewing machine didn't thrill the partners I mentioned in a previous chapter, though they needed it for mending and remodeling children's clothes. They purchased a portable model to get a chore they loathed done faster.

The same held true for four women who invested in a floor polisher.

Sally was the ringleader in getting this partnership off the ground because she felt a top-notch industrial model would do the best job. She hated to spend the money for it on her own because she knew she wouldn't use it enough to justify the expense.

"I mean, how often are you going to really do a number on your floors?" she asked.

The alternative—buying a cheaper model—wasn't appealing. She had tried the kind made for home use before and wasn't satisfied with the performance.

Sally's solution? She recruited three other families to join her as buyers. And buy they did—the best floor polisher on the market.

Whenever one family used it, they made sure it was in good working order for the next family. If it broke, the person using it would get the polisher repaired so as not to inconvenience someone else. Everyone shared the maintenance expenses equally.

Whoever used it last stored it. That rule turns up again and again. Among the advantages is freedom—it's great to own a ladder, a floor polisher, a torch kit, a 50-cup coffee maker and have them all cluttering up someone else's house!

• • •

Just because I've mentioned partnerables in generic clumps such as outdoor appliances, kitchen appliances, and tools doesn't mean partnership duos or pools have to stay within these boundaries. Cross-pollinate!

Who says you can't swap wallpapering equipment for the use of a giant stock pot? Why can't a group own a meat grinder, specialized brake tools, and a car-top carrier in partnership? There are no boundaries. The only rules for partnering are the ones you create; ones that seem right to you.

Tool and Appliance Points to Ponder

By now, it should be apparent that you don't have to be in love with someone to share a Cuisinart. But you should feel certain you're dealing with someone who will do right by you.

Generally, there are no problems on how to finance the purchase. Would you and your partner really take out a loan on a drill press—no matter how much you lust for it? Probably not for a heavy-duty sand blaster either, though it would zip your rehabbing jobs along so much faster.

Appliance partners do not have to deal with as many issues as larger scale partnerships because less money is involved and partners do not use common property in proximity. But they still have to tackle some basic questions—and come up with answers before they become problems so that everyone is satisfied. Keep the following in mind.

Where will it be kept?

How will we schedule its use?

What are the absolute no-no's while using it?

How will we maintain it?

Who will be in charge of maintenance?

What do we do if it breaks?

What if we have to buy a new one?

Will we lend it to others?

What if one partner decides to get out of the partnership or others want him to?

What if we can't agree?

You may also want to check Barbara Watts' visualization technique in Chapter Five. Then, using the tractor agreement as your model, you can form your own appliance cartel at a cost that diminishes with each new partner you bring into the group.

·8·
Dare to Share: Just About Anything

This chapter, a hopscotch of partnerships, is designed to stir your fancy, maybe even tickle your funny bone and strike a chord that says, "Hey, I can do that, too." The deals on these pages are as diverse as the needs of the people who dreamed them up and then made them a reality. Large or small, serendipitous or serious, they can also be made by you.

Active Sports

Two couples who loved to go camping decided to buy a tent they would own jointly. Neither felt they would use it enough to justify a separate purchase, and since they like to camp together anyway, a dual purchase made sense. They also agreed that either couple could use the tent on their own.

They wanted a dome style that could sleep four to six people and followed newspaper ads for good buys until they found one that suited their specifications.

Ground rules? If either couple used the tent separately, they stored it until it was needed next. They understood they were not to put it away damp or leave the floor muddy.

Repairs were everyone's responsibility, but whoever first noticed the broken zipper or rip in the sidewall was expected to fix it or get it fixed. The tent, they agreed, would always be ready for the next person's use. Lending it to others would not be considered without everyone's approval.

One tent for two couples led to purchases of a lantern, a portable stove, and sundry other outdoor equipment.

"There's no reason to duplicate all these accessories," they told me.

Food costs were split. So were cooking and cleanup chores when the four camped together. There was no formal agreement; everyone just pitched in. They got their money's worth out of that tent the first year they owned it, they said with satisfaction.

• • •

I would bet that people who love to sleep under the stars, who know firsthand how the world looks from the top of a mountain they have climbed, have the contents of the L.L. Bean, Eddie Bauer, and REI Co-op catalogs memorized. They know how expensive sturdy, dependable equipment is.

Not merely a tent or a portable stove can be shared by campers, climbers, or hikers. Sleeping bags, pads to place under the bag for insulation and liners to keep it clean, backpacks (sharers must make sure the fit is right for each of them), tarps, all-weather flashlights and lanterns, portable potties and heaters, camp grills, jugs and coolers, utensils for over-the-coals cooking, rain parkas—the list of co-owned possibilities is endless.

Those who enjoy the outdoors can also enjoy the luxury of top-of-the-line equipment if they share the cost. They must discuss how it will be used by everyone in the partnership, and certainly how it must be cared for. A nonconflicting schedule would have to be devised satisfactory to all involved, because if July is the month everyone wants to go camping, forget it. Weekend rotations should be easy to set up. One thing that should help here is that the better bags and tents you can afford partnering make year-round or at least three-season camping easier to do with a smile.

Wait a minute. You love to go fishing when you camp out. Why not make fishing equipment part of your partnership too? Agree on whether the kind you want to share is trout-weight tackle for fishing brooks, streams, and small ponds or whether you want a power model for long-distance casts or muscling bass out of hiding.

All the accessories that go with a rod and reel can be included in the partnership as well. And those flies, lures, creels, tackle pack vests, and wading boots (size of the prospective partners is a consideration here), nets, tackle boxes, rod carrying cases, minnow seines, knives for cleaning and filleting fish better be cared for up to the standards of everyone.

You like a more suburban sport, maybe? Golf is invigorating. Walking the course is great exercise; whacking the ball solidly onto the green instead of into a sand trap is terrifically satisfying. You'd love to buy a really great set of clubs, but they're too expensive.

Though golf clubs are pretty personal property, they could be shared if the someone you decide to co-own them with plays at completely different times than you do—or you rotate prime times. And if your partner would treat them as carefully as you do.

He better not be someone who wraps a club around a tree when he misses a shot or, screaming profanities, slams the whole bag on the ground when he comes in last in a tournament.

Make sure your temperaments match as well as your expectations—how will the clubs be cared for and use scheduled? If you haven't already, play some rounds together before you make a joint purchase.

Skis, downhill as well as cross-country, and even ski suits are great candidates for partnering—if you double up with someone your size. But if your idea of skiing means skimming the water, why not share water skis with other boat owners who love the sport?

How about sleds and toboggans—a variety of cold weather pleasurables owned in partnership or traded back and forth by neighbors to pep up snowbound winters? Sharing a cup of hot chocolate after a fast run down a slick slope sounds just as inviting.

A pool or ping pong table could be co-owned by neighbors and placed wherever there is room for it with easy access.

Would only co-owners and their families be allowed to play, or could they bring guests? When? If the equipment is yours, you don't want to feel like an intruder in someone else's house, right? You'd have to provide for that.

• • •

You want a daily workout to keep in shape—at home. In Chapter Three, two next-door neighbors saw the possibilities of co-owning an Exercycle. Set up in the basement of the partner who has the most room, its cost and use could easily be shared.

So could a rowing machine. It is designed for people who want a workout but who don't have oceans of room. Consider also a set of weights or other body-building equipment.

How much do you want to invest in your home health center? If partners have ultimate trust in each other and in the one who donates the space, wouldn't a neighborhood sauna, Jacuzzi, or hot tub be nice to come home to?

Setting up your own health spa would require detailed planning. The cost of the equipment plus the expense of operating it would have to be determined and shared. Who will keep the space clean? How will safety concerns be met? The spa would have to be as accessible to all members as a pool or ping pong table. If partners felt they were invading someone's home when they wanted to get some exercise and relax, the purpose of the partnership would be defeated.

Hobbies

You have a camera that will do for taking photos on vacations—remembrances of the beach you visited last summer, memories of your children's birthday parties, graduations, family picnics. But you're beginning to be interested in some things beyond the capacity of the color instant camera you haul out for "occasions."

You might not use a camera enough to justify buying an expensive one, unless you bought it in partnership with friends.

Enter Barb, Sandy, and Mimi. The all-purpose model they chose to buy in partnership cost around $300. They did a lot of comparison shopping before they decided on the one they finally purchased. They read *Consumer Reports'* and the various photo magazines' yearly comparison of photographic equipment and discussed what they read.

"Salespeople are usually helpful when you're looking at cameras," said Sandy. "But we wanted to be somewhat knowledgeable before we went shopping so we wouldn't have to rely totally on what store personnel told us."

The trio decided they were getting a good deal on the camera they wanted at a particular store, so that's where they bought it. They spent time with the salesman, who explained how to operate it until they all felt confident.

The women, who all lived within a few blocks of each other, set up some "good care for the camera" rules.

Don't clean a dusty lens with your shirttail. Remember to use a lens paper or soft tissue and cleaner.

There is a leather case protecting the camera, but users still have to be careful not to bang it against something or—horror of horrors—drop it.

It was decided that each should keep the camera after she used it until the next person needed it, but in a place that did not get too hot or humid. No one wanted moisture to seep inside the camera and ruin it. Anyone who used it near the beach (salt water!) would be sure to follow the manufacturer's directions for care after such use.

All three trusted that anyone who really messed up the camera (like dropping it in a tidepool) would be responsible and pay for the damage. At the same time, they recognized malfunctions could also occur. Rather than try to assign blame for the scratched shutter curtain—though the repair bill was $100—they divided it in three parts.

"Our basic camera partnership was so successful," says Sandy, "we decided to buy some frills. Our next purchase was a telephoto lens so we could zero in on the animals and birds we spotted. We also spent some money for a tripod to keep the camera steady.

"We bought a flash attachment, a set of filters, and a waterproof case and we get great deals on film because we buy in quantity.

"Right now, we're playing with the idea of setting up a darkroom. Barb has a big walk-in closet in her apartment she says we can use. So now we're pricing black and white developing equipment—an enlarger, a timer, and the trays and chemicals we'll need."

Movie cameras are candidates for joint purchases, too. So are projectors and screens for showing off your skill. If you want to capture Johnny taking his first tentative step and Mary in her formal gown opening the door to greet her tuxedoed date for the senior prom, you can afford the luxury of producing your own home movies by sharing the expense. Slide presentations and projectors can also be put to good business and organization-related use.

Ceramicists can share a wheel to throw pots and a kiln, in one of their houses. Rock hounds can share stone polishers and even metal detectors to ferret out the things they like to search for. Ardent gardeners can absorb the cost of building a greenhouse, and use it to start seedlings to replant outdoors in spring, to grow vegetables year-round, or to nurture exotic flowers.

Bird watchers or those who want to have a closer look at those tricky plays at the other end of the field can make fine binocular partners, though the subjects they view are not at all alike.

Home astronomers can star-gaze through a co-owned telescope. A good telescope can cost hundreds or thousands of dollars. Joint owners can get more powerful equipment and more excitement from what they are able to see.

Aficionado partners share their love of the activity, pass along tips, commiserate over flubs. That can mean as much as the dollars they save—in the long run, even more.

Music, Music, Music

So Marsha says she wants to take piano lessons. You're delighted. But all your friends have warned you about investing in a serious piano right off the bat. Just as you make the last payment, the kid tells you practicing is a drag, "and besides, it interferes with soccer."

That's when the screamfests usually begin. Parents are rightfully angry about the money they've spent for an abandoned piano. Short of chaining the child to the bench, what can they do?

Buy a sturdy, used piano in partnership with other parents whose children are novice musicians. Although the parents who house the piano would have to have a perfect out-of-the-way place for it, or a good soundproof room, or be willing to wear earplugs, it's an idea to think about.

A piano split four ways (or more) takes the heat off the pocket-book—and off kids who no longer want to take lessons. Tuning and repair costs could also be divided.

A practice schedule to accommodate those who play and those who live in the house would have to be thoughtfully worked out.

An organ could be partnered in the same way. Guitars, banjos, mandolins, ukeleles, violins, cellos, dulcimers, tambourines, maracas—all kinds of small instruments could make the rounds of the neighborhood. Even music stands and electric amplifiers can join this partnering symphony.

Serious musicians would certainly want an instrument—of any kind—of their own. But until kids make that commitment, parents can put off making purchases—together. (Adults who want to make music can partner, too!)

You may have noticed I left a set of drums out of the stationary musical instrument department. We are talking about generous people who would welcome children practicing at their house. Generosity is one thing; candidacy for sainthood another.

Overflow

With the size of today's trunks, roof-top car carriers are great to stash overflow when you go on vacation. They're handy to have—but not all the time. That's why they'd be easy to share.

Partners have to decide on the best size for everyone and a model that has adapter bars or straps that fit all cars. Then they have to plan trips so that all the co-owners don't hit the road at the same time. And figure out a system for storage.

Pet carriers can be shared just as easily. Cargo kennels officially approved by the airlines—in German shepherd size—can cost $70 or more. Steel foldup carriers, commonly used in cars to transport pets on vacation or to shows, can be joint purchases, too.

• • •

A crowd for dinner! Too many for your dining room table. They'll have to sit on the floor, the steps, wherever they can.

Tray tables help guests who do a balancing act with the dishes they try to keep steady on their laps. You can invest—in partnership—in a set of handsome wooden ones that can cost $100 or more instead of the flimsy kind you'd rather keep hidden in the closet than bring out for company.

Instead of throwing guests' coats on your bed because you have no room to hang them in your hall closet, buy—with partners—a collapsible garment rack on wheels, the expandable kind that can save your guests from rooting through piles of rumpled coats at midnight.

Folding tables—card table or larger sizes—and chairs are more items you can add to your party partnering supplies.

Instead of turning to a rental service to help you out when guests are expected, turn to each other.

• • •

When guests arrive, sometimes they don't just stay for dinner, they stay overnight, for the weekend, or (sigh!) a week.

You don't have a lot of room to spare. You don't even have a spare room. A foldaway bed would be a lifesaver (and a backsaver) when your brother Tony phones to say he's coming to town on business and can't wait to see you. Of course you want him to stay with you. You insist on it. He protests. You say you absolutely will not have it any other way. He takes your bed. You sleep on the couch. You don't tell him the last time you spent three nights on that couch you thought you'd never be able to turn your head to the left again.

A foldaway bed that could travel to several owners' homes to accommodate overflow visitors would be terrific for hosts and guests.

Grandparents whose children and grandchildren are going to pay a weekend call may need high chairs and cribs.

A grandparent partnership of baby equipment—things like strollers, buggies, and playpens you forget you need when toddlers are around—would work out well as joint purchases. Add sheets for the crib, blankets, and a whole world of pint-size supplies that have full-size price tags.

Yes, you could tell your children to bring these things with them to save you the bother. But you don't want to. Having everything ready and welcome is half the fun of being a grandparent. Wouldn't you like to see the kids' faces light up when you bring out a new puzzle or a pull toy or a board game or a rocking horse? (Couldn't surprises like these be the icing on your partnership cake?)

Ease your storage problems and divide the expense of all these once-in-awhilables—with others.

To Your Health

Your 8-year-old has the flu. Keeping him in bed is a major production. Toys, board games, and books help pass the time, but the bed looks like a battlefield. The sheets have a bright new hue—chicken soup yellow.

Those wonderful adjustable tiltable tables that fit over a bed are such a help when you or your children feel down and out. Spread a puzzle on it; serve a meal. Pile up paperbacks, boxes of tissue, cough drops—whatever you need to have within reach. They're sure convenient to own when you or someone in your family is sick. But how often is that? You got it. Partner them.

Add to your sickroom supplies a vaporizer, a hand massager to work out neck and back aches and pains, a foot massager to coax tired tootsies back to life. How about angle heating pads you can wrap around your elbow or knee when you're at the office, to soothe muscles and joints protesting a weekend of too many hot games of handball.

If you really want to get serious with your traveling medicine show, you can invest in a combination blood pressure-pulse monitor, or the latest high-tech thermometer, or even an otoscope set to detect inflamed throat and ear passages.

Talk about being prepared. This is one way to manage it.

Hope Chest

With the cost of china, crystal, and silver at its present level, these niceties are not part of every newlyweds' (or oldyweds!) hope chest, as they once were. Many people consider polishing silver a nuisance anyway and goblets too expensive to worry about chipping in the dishwasher. In these hurry-up times, it can be a bother to own pieces you use rarely and have to wash carefully by hand. Many people, by choice, stick to simpler tableware.

Still, sitting down to a meal served on delicate Limoges plates, sipping wine from sparkling Baccarat goblets, and spearing an asparagus with a Buccellati fork lifts life a pleasurable notch above the ordinary. If that's how you want to set your table, but there's no way you can afford to, here's how.

Buy piece by piece in conjunction with others.

If you have friends (who are not disasters as dishwashers) and you can all agree on a set you would like to build, you can make purchases together.

If your goal is a dozen of everything and three friends split the cost, each could still throw a posh dinner for four anytime. If two could afford to take on the expense of a set, they'd be in fine shape most of the time unless they entertained more than a half dozen people in elegant style on a regular basis.

Partners are likely to need the entire set only for parties or special occasions anyway, so there shouldn't be much conflict. That is, unless everyone wanted everything on Christmas and Thanksgiving, which could cause problems. Who gets custody on holidays would have to be negotiated with generosity.

The beauty of buying crystal, china, and flatware with others is that you can opt for a smaller amount of the best or shoot for more moderately priced pieces and build variety and quantity. Instead of a dozen of everything, you could wind up with two dozen or three—all you'd need for a big bash.

Money can be accumulated in a kitty, with one person as treasurer, or partners can make individual purchases at regular intervals. Everyone should watch for sales.

Even if your tastes run to honest pottery and stainless steel flatware (which isn't cheap, either) you can afford on your own, isn't it smart to have twins in your best friend's cupboard? By design, you are each other's reserves when you must feed more people than you have dishes for. Of course, you must agree on what you would both be happy owning.

No matter how you want to work out a partnership of this kind, make provisions for chipping and breakage. Do you want to insist co-owned glasses and dishes and silver be washed by hand? Soapy goblets can still slip through someone's fingers. And the awful sound of silver or stainless steel taking a trip through the garbage disposal is a real possibility.

Be careful when you transport tableware to each other's homes. Glasses and dishes should be safely padded in boxes, not stacked on the floor of your car.

The easiest system might be the "you broke it, you replace it" policy. Then each partner would know what is expected of him and be extra careful. You also want to partner with someone who isn't going to say, "What crack?" when you phone him about the condition of a dish he brought over. Basic confidence in each other's honesty to own up is essential.

Note that if you are getting into big-time joint silver purchases, everyone should be fully insured. Make sure appraisals are up to date so that if one partner is robbed, all will not suffer.

Toy Pools

Suburban backyards: neatly trimmed hedges surrounding manicured lawns sprouting swing sets, wading pools, playhouses, a badminton or volleyball net, and whatever else homeowners pluck from the shelves of toy or sporting goods stores and set in their midst. Each "don't touch my teeter-totter" stands as a sentinel to the arsenal of equipment children and adults stockpile.

Just as tool pools can end needless duplication, toy sharing can cut down child amusement costs while teaching those being amused how to cooperate.

A teddy bear is likely to be found snugly tucked under the arm of the child who loves him—a "mine only" without question. But how close to a child's heart are the monkey bars out back? They're never as much fun when you hang on them alone. As trusting neighbors co-purchase equipment they can easily share, involved parents who involve their children can buy anything from slides to playhouses in partnership, to everyone's advantage. Even a whole convoy of ridables and pullables—from old standby red wagons to Big Wheels—kids can enjoy more together.

Two next-door neighbors who live on an urban street lined with rehabbed townhouses have postage-stamp-size backyards and toddlers who need an outdoor area for play. Rather than lay down lines of demarcation, they tore down barriers and planted grass, a communal sandbox, a swing set, and a jungle gym. The areas closest to the houses are mini-garden/patios, but the middle is where all the kids' action takes place. That way, the grass is trampled mostly under the swings in the center. Sand is the ground cover for the "commons." The areas nearest the houses are kept as orderly as yards that host romping children can be.

The cost of the equipment was amicably divided and any small maintenance costs (bags of sand in spring?) are equally divided.

• • •

Three neighboring families in suburban Denver have owned a trampoline jointly for about 10 years.

"Our backyards all run together," Janie, one of the adult partners says, "so it is easy to share. We bought the trampoline for about $350. The children helped pick it out.

"We felt it was very important for the kids to help make out a use schedule to avoid 'my turn-itis.' No one wanted any child who had visiting friends to monopolize the trampoline. We also didn't want one child to take longer turns than was fair while others waited."

The parents and children sat down and worked all this out together. After-school and weekend hours were considered prime time and apportioned to give everyone a fair share. So that life would be easier for parents who did not want to be trampoline policemen, written permission was required from parents whose children came to visit and inevitably wound up on the trampoline.

"Playing on a trampoline is fairly risky," Janie says, "and none of the adults wanted to spend their time watching kids jump up and down. We have our own work to do and most of us have jobs outside the home. Our children know the safety rules—they helped set them. Other parents are required to take responsibility for their own children."

[A trampoline falls into the "attractive nuisance" category of insurance copywriters, just as a swimming pool does. Homeowners who have these kinds of amusements on their property are liable if someone gets hurt while playing around.

A homeowner's insurance policy can cover the risk of having what is considered an attractive nuisance should a guest be injured and sue. It also wouldn't hurt to ask for a note from the parents of children who come to play indicating that they know about and consent to their children's playing on it—and assume any risks involved.

The host parents are smart to ask for written permission.]

"Disputes are handled at round table discussions with children doing most of the talking," says Janie. "Adults enter in to help smooth things over, when needed, but we try to take a background role.

"Maintenance is shared and so are the costs. Sometimes springs need to be replaced; sometimes a mat. Once in a while it must be painted to guard against rust. As children grow up and go off to college, the families who use it most now assume most of the cost and maintenance.

"We three couples live as neighbors who want to share. It was something we wanted to teach our children. By involving them, from the purchase to the rule setting, from the maintenance to handling disputes, we gave them a lot more than just a trampoline."

• • •

Think of indoor toys, too—ones that don't create strong emotional ties—such as blocks, board games, beads to string, and puzzles. These can be tiresome once their novelty wears off. Rotating amusing mind and hand games from one home to another keeps them fresh and more fun to play with for the children who have the joy of rediscovering them periodically.

Backyard Pleasures

Kids are not the only ones who need toys for amusement. Can't adult pleasurables be shared as well?

Why must grills be planted on every suburban patio and dot the balconies of apartment houses? Grills on wheels—as plain or as deluxe as you please—can roll from house to house or apartment to apartment as needed. Two used in unison could serve up chow for a big outing.

Several families could partner picnic tables as well as grills. The tables could be bought separately and pooled whenever they are needed, or several could be bought by a group—whatever suits.

Backyard games like volleyball, badminton, croquet, and horseshoes are needless duplications. If they are stored (i.e., dutifully put away after they are used) so that everyone knows where to find them, you can build up a well-stocked neighborhood recreation sports chest.

Use these games to have fun with just your family; use them for good-natured neighborhood tournaments. It's a way to draw people who happen to live near each other—together. Think about that.

Dressups

If outdoor activities leave you cold, here's a plan a quartet of women concocted to heat up big city nights. These four savvy New Yorkers needed a "little black dress." You know the kind—one so simple and so well made it has the aura of being expensive without having to shout it. Art gallery openings, parties where they wanted to wear something that made them feel special—and noticed—something none of them could afford.

Since each generally culled bargains from Loehmann's racks

rather than picking up gems at Bergdorf's, they decided to pool their money and buy one spectacular dress they all would share. The necessary criteria to make it possible: All wore the same size and had the same kind of dress in mind. They were friends and were familiar with (and approving of) each other's taste in clothes.

Shopping together turned into wacky expeditions as the four women crowded into dressing rooms to try on likely candidates, pointedly ignoring saleswomen's surprised (and unnerved) stares. They persevered and found a dress that fit the bill—and all of them. A ritzy designer label in the $400 price range was their unanimous choice.

"How did you avoid fights over the dress choice?" I asked Emily.

"By keeping a sense of humor," she said. "And by realizing this was an important decision for all of us, but also a lark."

The dress was kept in the closet of the last person who wore it. She was also responsible for having it cleaned and ready for its next night on the town. The dress was also checked to make sure it was in perfect condition—no drooping hems, no split seams. God forbid any of them get close to a free-flying cigarette at a party!

Scheduling its use was done by phone with a calendar handy. Whoever had an important date reserved the dress for the occasion. If two needed it on the same night, they drew straws to decide who got to wear it. The dress was important, but all had other clothes they could wear.

"This partnership could be an easy one to dissolve," one of the women giggled. "Too many parties and too many fattening dinners could eliminate partners left and right. Sole ownership could fall on the wallflower!"

• • •

Who wants to work in order to earn enough money to buy clothes for work?" asks Alice. "Suits are so expensive these days that if you need to wear them to look professional on the job, a good part of your paycheck is essentially being recycled. My daughter, who is a legal secretary, and a good friend of mine who is an executive secretary—like I am—used to get together all the time and complain about the cost of a working wardrobe. Then we decided to do something about it."

What they decided was to pick three suits from each of their wardrobes, make them common property, and rotate them weekly. All wear the same size, and all are within an inch or two in height. All have the same taste in clothes.

"Our goal is to look neat and well groomed at the office," says Alice, "not glamorous. We all wear classic styles that we can easily exchange. Our suit club—as we jokingly call it—has done so well over the last two years that we bought new suits together. We now own 15."

The inner workings of this successful combined clothes effort are as follows:

The 15 suits are divided into groupings of five. These are rotated weekly. Each partner only has to transport the suits from house to house every third weekend.

Each group of five suits contains a newer model and one of everyone's favorites.

"That way," says Alice, "no one feels like she has all the dogs one week. Each group must move as a whole, too. You can't say, 'Oh, I'd like to hang on to the camel one for another week.' The five suits stay together so no one gets confused."

Suit Yourselves

The women can wear a different suit every day or one as many times as they'd like during the week they have them. How many of us can go for fifteen straight work days without repeating an outfit?

"This can cause office problems," cautions Alice. "Co-workers get jealous. When your wardrobe suddenly triples, people start wondering where you're getting the money to buy all these clothes. I've heard some pretty snide comments, so having lots of great outfits has its down side, too. And if you want to keep your supply a secret, partners should work at different offices, and maybe even make sure they do not have overlapping circles of friends."

Suit rules:

1). When you put on a skirt, bring it over your head rather than pulling it on over your hips to keep from straining the seams.
2). No jewelry may be fastened to suits, to avoid holes and snags.
3). Perfume may be worn on your blouse (it's yours, anyway) or on your body—not on the suit.
4). Smoking while wearing communal suits is discouraged but tolerated. Alice smokes but airs out the suits before she passes them to the next partner. The two nonsmokers grumble but appreciate her gesture. If Alice burns a hole in the suit while smoking, she understands she will be responsible for having it rewoven.
5). All women are responsible for damage, such as rips and tears, while they wear the suits. It is up to them to have the clothes repaired at their own expense. That goes for stains, too. If a partner

spots a suit, she must have it cleaned before it is passed along. 6). Regular dry-cleaning is scheduled two times a season in winter, more often in warm months. (Suit partners can decide on any frequency they find palatable—after every use, weekly, monthly, whatever.) Partners rotate the responsibility of getting it done at cleaners approved by all; the expense is split evenly.

7). At the end of each week, each partner must inspect the suits to make sure skirts are not wrinkled; that the hem doesn't need a stitch or two. If anything needs touching up, she is responsible for seeing to it before they move on.

"We are very conscious of clothing sales," says Alice. "We all watch for them in the newspaper and visit discount stores whenever we can. When we think it's time to buy a new suit, we take inventory of what we have. We may decide to stay away from a certain color because we have enough in that category.

"We only buy conservative tones and patterns. Grey flannel, herringbone, glen plaids, blues, and browns are favorites.

"When shorter jackets came in style, we talked about whether they'd be in fashion long enough to be a good investment. We all looked good in those we tried on, so we bought a couple.

"We go shopping together and try the suits on separately. If the suit works for all of us, we buy it.

"We never spend more than $90 on anything. That's a $30 investment for each of us. But then we never pay full price for a suit either. We make purchases at the end of the season, when they've been reduced two or three times. It's generally less than half of its original cost by the time we get it. That way, we can get the most for our money." (High flyers who want to invest in big-name suits without paying such steep prices would also come out way ahead partnering. A designer collection split three ways falls within reach!)

The three partners buy their own blouses and sometimes extra skirts, slacks, and blazers they can wear with the jointly owned clothes. They are currently in search of a plaid skirt to go with a grey suit jacket whose matching skirt has a threadbare bottom.

"That's why we stick to suits," says Alice. "They're more versatile than dresses. If a dress wears out, there's not much you can do with it. It's usually the skirt in a suit that goes first, and we can renew the outfit with a fresh skirt. Or if the jacket wears out, we can buy a blazer that will blend with the skirt."

If a suit partner goes from the office to dinner and a movie instead of straight home, that's fine with everyone. Outfits can be worn on weekends as well, if a partner needs them.

"We all trust each other to take care of the clothes," says Alice. "We know how much they mean to all of us. That's why my daughter teases me when she sees me start one of my ice cream binges. She laughs that I'll snack my way right out of our suit club.

"It's hard, when you're in your fifties, to keep your weight the same as your 28-year-old daughter. After a weekend of self-indulgence, I stick to salads so I can still get into our wardrobe.

"We all see each other on a regular basis. We're really close. And we all agree on a point that keeps our clothes partnership going: We'd rather buy a share of stock than a suit to wear to work."

Though these partners thought of a great many considerations, there were a few questions I asked Alice that made her pause and say, "Hmm, we never talked about that."

Maybe *you* should, if you think pooling clothes would be a fine idea for you.

Does anyone care what kind of hangers are used? Thin wire ones don't do much for a suit jacket's shoulders.

What about an invasion of hungry moths? Partners should have some kind of discouragement to winged wool eaters in their closet. If a suit in someone's possession gets nibbled, she should be responsible for repair.

What if a stain is permanent or a rip irreparable? Should the woman responsible for the damage have to buy another suit to take its place? Or should she reimburse the others for their share? The owner of a clothing resale shop could appraise the suit so its value would not be in dispute.

When is a suit retired from the pool and what will be done with it? Can one partner buy it cheap to wear among friends, or does Goodwill get it and the group a tax deduction?

Who stores the out-of-season suits, and in what way to best preserve them?

What if a partner gets pregnant or moves out of town? Again, suits could be appraised by the owner of a resale shop and the exiting partner paid her share.

What if there is a fire in one of the partner's homes? Or water damage from a broken pipe? Is she responsible for paying the rest for the damaged clothes? At what price?

• • •

Though the clothing partnerships on the previous pages were put together by women, why couldn't men do the same?

You've just graduated from law school. You've landed a dream job with a prestigious firm.

You worked your way through school doing any job you could, from waiting tables to pumping gas. You barely scraped by. The suit you wore for your job interview is your one and only, and you know for this buttoned-down firm you need to visit Brooks Brothers fast with some cash in hand. But you don't have enough money to put together a decent wardrobe.

Your salary is going to be respectable, but you don't have a dollar of it yet. In addition to buying clothes, you need to find an apartment, get some furniture—your list is scary.

If you have a friend the same size as you who needs to look like you—and who is also short of money—match up.

Grey flannels, herringbones, glen plaids, classic blazers can be shared by men as easily as women.

Decide on the cut and style you find looks best on both of you and join forces. You're a lawyer—draw up a good agreement. You can even share ties, as long as you are careful to have the soup stains removed from the maroon paisley before your partner puts it on and discovers he's wearing your lunch in court.

Coverups

All dressed up with someplace to go . . . and the only coat you have that looks decent enough to put on with your new steel grey chiffon is three inches shorter than your dress. You feel tacky, but you wear it anyway. You have to—there's a foot of snow on the ground.

You hate going out with a coat that ruins your outfit. But how many coats can you afford? The good tweed you just invested in and your expensive all-purpose raincoat do yeoman service, and should last forever—you hope.

It's the same old story. And a nagging problem. Evening clothes of all lengths and colors demand a variety of coats to cover and match them. Why not share?

Think about those gorgeous antique piano shawls—the ones with the exquisite hand embroidery that have skyrocketed in price since women discovered how fantastic they looked draped over a shoulder instead of a baby grand. Buy one in partnership with a friend who is likewise taken with its beauty.

If you're lucky, you may spot one more reasonably priced in a secondhand clothing shop. Most likely you'll have to buy one at a full-fledged vintage clothing store, since antique wearable dealers sweep through the goods at less pricey stores regularly.

Contemporary shawls, beautifully handwoven wool, are lovely for evening wear (they're especially handy over all lengths of dresses) and have a more tailored look than fringed oldies.

How about a short jacket that fits like a hug? Or a long velvet cape for splashy events? If you share the cost of coats, you can trade up in quality and go for variety.

What about a purse? That big brown leather carryall you sling over your shoulder when you go to the office looks clunky with your new red cashmere dress. A little beige clutch would be just right. Or maybe a black beaded bag. Or a mock tortoise-shell purse that matches almost everything. Round robin handbags? Why not?

Look in your closet. What do you wear seldom but find you really need when you have to finish off an outfit (and, agonizingly, don't own)? Think silk scarves and good-looking belts, too!

Make a list. Talk to some friends you like and trust and ask them to take inventory of their clothing and make a list of what they'd like to buy. If your tastes, how much you want to spend, and what you need to purchase match, you can start a collection that will have you stepping out in style for any event.

Jewelry

The L.L. Bean catalog doesn't keep you awake nights. Brookstone's array leaves you cold. It's the soft blue cover of the Tiffany catalog that makes your eyes light up. But Tiffany's prices definitely do not fit into your budget.

A box full of jewelry is not what Grandma left you. She did pass along some ingenuity. Use it.

With a friend (or friends) you trust, whose homes or apartments are satisfactorily secure, who will invest in insurance, who want to buy the same strand of cultured pearls you do, or a similar gold pin to dress up suits, or diamond earrings—go shopping.

See if a joint purchase makes sense. See if you can think up provisions to make it work. With partners, you could build your own collection of crown jewels. Now that's something to think about seriously.

Fine Art

Elaine and Lisa have been close friends for 15 years. Elaine is a travel agent, Lisa a staff writer on a city magazine. Though both are accomplished and hardworking, neither depends exclusively on her job (or her husband) for money. Both are lucky enough to have healthy trust funds left to them as a family inheritance. They use the money often to purchase antiques—a passion for both.

Elaine's house is filled with English antiques. Lisa likes American country pieces better. Both appreciate what the other buys, though they seldom purchase anything similar in furniture. Some accessories they own are quite alike. But joint purchases? It was the last thing they considered—until they took off together one weekend to the fall antiques show in New York.

"Elaine and I were both looking for a weathervane," says Lisa. "She has a beautiful garden and wanted something wonderful for a spot she had in mind.

"I wanted one for a corner of our library that looked bare. We both spotted that mid-1800s rooster at the same time. We fell in love with him.

"The rooster is one of the rarest and most extraordinary weathervanes I've seen. It has so much character. It was mounted on a long pole—perfect for the places we both had in mind for him. The dealer's price (we both had bought from him at other times) was $10,000.

"Elaine felt that was a lot of money to plant in her garden. I loved the rooster, but not ten thousand dollars worth.

"All of a sudden, it was as if a light bulb went on in both our heads. It occurred to us that we could buy the weathervane together.

"Elaine wanted the rooster mainly in the summer, when it could be framed by greenery in her garden. In summer, I place tall vases filled with flowers and branches I bring in from our woods in the library corner. I wouldn't even have a good spot in the house for the rooster during the summer.

"It was a perfect deal. The rooster would soak up the sun in Elaine's garden for six temperate months; he would winter in our library.

"We each paid half his cost and brought him home. That was two years ago and it has been a wonderful partnership.

"Elaine and I trust each other implicitly. We both carry insurance to cover robbery or any damage; we have that for all of our antiques anyway. I think we enjoy the weathervane as much as we do because its joint purchase made so much sense. We're considering buying some pewter candlesticks in partnership, some Nantucket or Shaker baskets we'd love to use as table centerpieces to fill with fruit and flowers, some redware and burl bowls, maybe some tole trays and boxes.

"Our rooster could be the start of a blossoming antiques collection we can enjoy in rotation. Really, any antique that you don't depend on to furnish your house can be easily exchanged. We think we've come up with a terrific idea."

• • •

Antiques and art can be bought in partnership whether you are as wealthy as Elaine and Lisa or are beginning collectors with more appreciation than money. Toni Birckhead, whose Cincinnati art gallery is filled with the work of many young, innovative artists, says, "I think art partnerships would provide a tremendous amount of enrichment to the people involved—not just the ability to purchase paintings."

Going to galleries and studying art in order to buy it are exciting learning experiences.

Toni feels two people or a group must decide what they want to collect. There must be commonality of interest. Does the group want prints, watercolors, folk art, minimal art, or traditional pieces? Do the partners want a mix? Do they love only a few specific artists? Do they follow a particular movement? Toni suggests people go to galleries together, talk to owners, read magazines and books to make sure their tastes match and they want to buy the same kinds of things.

"Find a dealer to advise your group," says Toni. "Call a museum in your city and ask for a list of reputable ones. Ask the dealer you're considering if he is a member of the Art Dealers Association. You must be in business five years to belong. Check with the Better Business Bureau to make sure he's aboveboard.

"An art dealer (or an antiques dealer) can help you further the quality of your purchase, though I never suggest buying art as an investment—other than a Picasso or a Henry Moore or a Grandma Moses, someone in that category.

"I tell clients they should buy what they love. Buy a painting because it talks to you, touches you in some way. Buy what you want to live with, what will give you plesure whenever you see it—never what matches your couch."

A group of people interested in buying art should establish the amount they want to spend on a purchase and put money in a kitty or in a bank account once a month—or however often they decide—toward it. The group may want to appoint a treasurer to keep track of the cash.

"I think two people buying art together should begin with two pieces," says Toni. "That way each has something to enjoy. Then they can switch every six months. I wouldn't advise switching more than twice a year anyway—especially larger pieces—because of the wear and tear in hauling them around.

"Group size depends on how many people can be compatible. The more people in the group, the more levels of taste you have to contend with—but then, you can pool more money. You must decide the number of people that can work for you."

The following suggestions apply to any art object—or antique.

Not only must art partners trust each other, they must trust the dealer they buy from. Make sure you ask the gallery owner whether he will sell the piece for you should your group disband or one partner wish to sell his shares. You should trust the dealer's appraisal, too.

This is one partnership where a clear buy-sell agreement is mandatory. Especially if you buy something that may increase dramatically in value.

Art partners must also make provisions so they feel safe with how "their" art is cared for in their partners' homes. Is the painting hung in a place where the sun might damage it? Could a small child or a Doberman knock over a sculpture? Does everyone have insurance to cover calamities? Large or particularly valuable pieces should be reappraised every few years.

" 'I love this painting, but I can't afford it,' is something I hear all the time in my gallery," says Toni. "An art partnership is an innovative avenue for people who want to make significant purchases. They'll have something stimulating instead of just something to fill space on a wall. To look forward to having new things in your house periodically is even better."

Art partnering can take place on any level. Big-time collectors can split big-time pieces. Go for an Ellsworth Kelly or an Alexander Calder or a Jean Dubuffet if they're within your means—a piece of them, anyway. Your walls are certainly not bare if you're in that league. And if you could have the painting a few months a year to enjoy, you have an investment as well as a great deal of pleasure.

Performing Arts

Going to the symphony, an opera, the ballet, or the theater brings you so much pleasure. It's part of your life you consider important, even if tickets are expensive.

Season tickets ensure you a better choice of seats and generally mean a price break. With the cost of tickets so high, you want any break you can get.

But you really don't want to go to twenty symphonies a season and twelve operas and ten plays—lower cost or not. So divide the season tickets with friends.

Dora and Dan split season symphony tickets with two other couples.

"Each ticket has a number on it," says Dora, "so we put all the tickets in a hat. We pass it around and everyone picks without looking. This way, no one fights over performances they want to see.

"Sometimes people are really disappointed when they don't get their favorites. But once all the tickets are selected, we trade with each other to get the ones we do want. Everyone gets to go to most of the ones they really care about, though if Isaac Stern is one of the performers, he's generally not bargainable."

You can divvy up one set of tickets or several. Couples can attend six ballets, four plays, and five operas a season by buying smart—together.

Nourishing the soul with the help of others. A fine idea—no?

Books and Magazines

Don't stop now. Add books and magazines—even newsletters—to your sharable list! Whether you like *The New York Times* best sellers or paperback thrillers—buy them and pass them around to save money.

Regardless of the number of people in your group, each can buy one book simultaneously at whatever intervals you specify. Decide how long each person gets to keep a book and who gets final ownership. Or is there final ownership? Does everyone own all the books, even if they're kept at various partners' homes? Who will remember where?

Keep the partnership to a manageable number (four) unless you have exceptional recall.

Establish how you want books to be treated. Must readers use a bookmark instead of dog-earing pages? Should partners remove the dust jacket so it doesn't get raggedy, or keep it in place to protect the book? What about smudge marks on pages or broken spines?

If you care about how the books you buy are kept—and serious book buyers generally care—make your concerns clear. The group should then try its best to adhere to the adopted agreement to keep everyone happy.

Book-buying groups can get together to talk about new books they want to purchase and to discuss those they've read. There's a lot more to sharing here than being able to say you read it.

How about magazines? Subscriptions for a year or more are cheaper than single newsstand purchases, just as season tickets are less expensive per performance than buying tickets whenever the spirit moves you.

You buy *Newseek*; Joyce, who lives next door, buys *Mother Earth News*. Ed, who lives down the street, subscribes to *The New Yorker*; Hank, another neighbor, gets *Gourmet*.

You agree on who gets what and then you switch. You can subscribe to new magazines yearly or keep renewing ones you like. Pick diverse subjects or competing magazines that deal with the same ones—from a different point of view.

You cut costs. You boost the number of periodicals you receive. You lessen the chance that costly publications lie around unread in guilt-inducing piles.

Decide: How long may people keep each magazine before they must pass it along? Can kids cut out pictures for class projects after everyone is finished with the magazines and no one says they want to keep that particular issue? That you will try to be careful if you munch while you read?

And if your way of relaxing is reading in the tub, see that only you and not the bottom half of the magazine takes a bath.

Recordings and Video

Records and tapes could be partnered just as easily as books and magazines. First, though, you have to agree on the theme of the collection. Sex Pistol and Pavarotti fans may not make beautiful music together.

The people involved have to decide how long each partner keeps a record or tape, how often purchases are made, and, of course, which ones.

They have to agree to hold only the edges of a record between their fingers to avoid smearing the playing surface with fingerprints, not to scratch or chip the record (serious chips or scratches should be as much grounds for replacement as breaking it). They have to wipe off the lint and dust before playing with a record cleaner, not an old rag or their sleeve.

Records should be placed in their covers immediately after they are played, not left on the turntable. They should be stored vertically rather than stacked and in a dry, cool place to prevent warping.

Tapes are easier to take care of because they can't fall prey to as many disasters as records. Still, partners must make sure they don't record over what's already on the tape, expose it to extreme temperatures (or they'll ruin the sound), and leave it in the cassette deck after they play it. Tapes must be returned to their cases after playing.

While we're on the subject of tapes, video games on cartridges (a distant relation) are becoming a popular partnerable. Owners tire of their purchases after awhile, and rotating them revives interest.

You buy *Pac-Man* and *Asteroids,* Ricky picks up *Space Invaders* and *Star Raiders,* Moe gets *Smurf* and *Pitfall.* You exchange. It can go on and on. From challenge games to sports and space, partnering keeps video game freaks amused and the cost of their amusement down.

HORSEFEATHERS

Although the strong emotional attachments we develop to living things make furred and feathered partnerships tricky, they're still altogether possible. In this section you will find creature co-ownerships that worked, as well as an explosive one that didn't.

• • •

Though cowboys have been known to say, "Never lend your saddle, your horse, or your wife," two working mothers who juggled jobs, family responsibilities, and their love of riding turned that old saying around.

The women had known each other for years and taken riding lessons at the same stable. They rode with the same expertise and wanted desperately to own their own horse. Holding them back were finances, and the fact that neither could afford to carve the amount of time out of their schedules they knew owning a horse would demand.

They began talking about buying a horse together. Feeling good about their similarities, they decided to begin looking; the ceiling was set at about $1,500. They quickly found a horse agreeable to both.

Goal setting, in this kind of partnership, is imperative. And these women did this well. Both wanted to ride the horse in shows—little shows, not Madison Square Garden. They wanted to jump the horse—over small fences, not in a steeplechase. One didn't want a trail horse and the other a champion. Both women are about the same size and have the same riding style, and found a hunter they admired to fit all of these requirements.

They groomed the horse in the same manner because they were

trained by the same person. Their views on what was important for the health of the horse were the same, as were their standards of cleanliness for the stall. They agreed on what was too much of a workout and what was just right for their horse. Neither wanted to run it into the ground.

The horse was kept at a barn owned by a friend of both women. Feed, board, veterinary, and blacksmith bills were shared equally.

In the spring, time schedules became intense because the horse needed to be exercised almost every day so he would be in shape for shows.

Marge, one of the owners, said, "We worked out a schedule for who would exercise the horse on which days by backing into it. We both have such hectic lives we would call each other and say, 'I can't go on Thursday or Friday this week. Can you do it?' We'd take it a week at a time. We both needed flexibility but we cared enough for each other to work things out. Some weeks one did more than another, but it evened out."

On weekends, they rode together. One woman would ride; the other would set up the course and act as "teacher."

"We really helped each other a lot," said Marge, "besides enjoying the horse and our time together. If we directed the horse differently, we talked it out. One of us would say, 'I think the horse will respond better if you.' . . . We'd try it and see."

To transport the animal to shows, the two partners and the barn owner bought a used trailer together.

"It took three of us to handle it anyway," Marge said. "I had a hitch installed on the back of my car to pull the trailer; the insurance was in my name, too—though I had only personal liability which covered all of us. The trailer itself was not insured for damage.

"Though bridles were bought for the horse in partnership, we each had our own saddles and riding clothes. But we always traded clothes back and forth. If I discovered a rip in my jacket, I'd borrow Karen's. If she hadn't gotten around to ironing her shirt, she'd wear mine.

"Taking turns riding at shows was as important as trading off training sessions. One person riding while the other served as 'ground person' was extremely helpful. If one of us really wanted to ride at a particular show, we asked for it. Exactly who won the ribbons was never a problem for us, though it could be for some partners. This can really breed jealousy. It depends on what partners want—acclaim or just to have a good time.

"We're always careful to be up-front with each other. If one of us got to the point where we couldn't swing board expenses any longer, we'd say it. We'd give our partner the right to buy us out or search for a new partner who would. We've both wanted a horse for so long, we want to do everything we can to make it work."

• • •

The father of a 10-year-old was appalled when he found out how much monthly board for the horse his daughter wanted would cost. That would be in addition to at least $1,000 for the horse itself. Realizing that some adolescents fall out of love with horses when they discover the opposite sex, he decided to be cautious.

The owner of the stable where his daughter rode told him that a man who owned a gentle horse was going to be out of the country for a year. The man wanted to exchange riding privileges with someone who would pick up his monthly board and feed bills. A nurse who rode at the same stable was also interested in this offer, but neither really felt like undertaking alone the $110 charge per month. The stable owner got the two together and asked if they'd like to share.

They decided to give it a try, and split monthly costs as well as riding time. They alternated riding days during the week, and each took one day each weekend.

Even though the age difference between the two temporary partners was great, their riding skills were similar. So was the way they cared for the horse. But for the most part, the two partners saw little of each other.

"It was a wonderful way to hedge the purchase of a horse," the father told me. "I could see how serious my daughter was about having her own horse, without having to swallow such a large expense.

"My daughter felt like she owned her own horse without my having to buy one for her; the nurse felt good about having the same horse to ride whenever she wanted and being able to afford it, too."

• • •

Two families who firmly believed that raising chickens for eggs would give them a source of food independent of the "system" decided to do it together. They live only a few doors from each other, are close friends, and share the same political views and lifestyle. Joining forces seemed natural. One family already had a dilapidated coop in the backyard, so each invested about $100 in raw materials to refurbish it.

"Let's raise chickens," they said.

They all knew how and they all knew each other. But they forgot to ask each other some key questions.

Andy is from rural Virginia. His father always kept chickens. They ran around the yard and that is how he happily remembers them. He loved hunting for eggs each morning. Fencing in the yard around his chicken coop seemed like a compromise to him because he wanted to raise free-wheeling chickens like his father. But knowing neighborhood dogs would tear them apart, he settled for what he felt was second best.

Sam's mother also raised chickens—in cages, in a chicken house that was a production-line affair. Her chickens laid eggs until production tapered off—and bingo!—they went to market. She then bought a whole new flock. When Andy began to fence in a yard for the chickens, Sam thought he was not only extravagant, but crazy.

Sam said, "The chickens you got were worthless anyway—and now you're building them a play yard? I'm not going to spend money for that. Why didn't you talk to me before you brought in such a miserable flock? Out of the 20 we have, only 5 are decent."

Andy said, "A friend gave me these chickens. I think they're fine."

Sam sneered, "Scrawny roosters and those midget hens? You'll have small eggs, maybe every other day. Some of those hens are such pitiful producers, they should be slaughtered right away."

"What?" Andy countered. "Kill Mama Cass? She's given us so many eggs and just because she's tapering off, you want to kill her? A chicken that works all her life should retire gracefully. If a hen isn't laying, she can still hang around and be part of the flock. Besides, you know I'm a vegetarian."

"You mean you're going to have a house full of chickens that die of old age?" Sam asked incredulously. "What are you going to do with them?"

And so it went. Not only did they fail to talk about the specifics of how they would raise chickens, they also forgot to clarify who would own them.

Andy felt that the chickens as well as the coop were his. He considered himself sole owner. He felt Sam's investment of $100 and labor entitled him to only half the eggs produced as long as the coop was burgeoning. He thought Sam understood that.

Sam was furious because he was not included in any of the decision making. He couldn't understand why Andy didn't ask him about what kind of chickens to buy and how they should be kept. Considering himself a co-owner in the whole project, he became so angry that he told Andy he never wanted to see "those damned chickens" again and asked for his $100 back.

Andy told me, "The chicken-raising experience reminded me of an anti-war meeting I attended when everyone sat around a table saying, 'Let's stop war.' Everyone agreed, but no one talked about how he thought war should be stopped.

"One person went away from the meeting thinking the way to stop was to bomb the hell out of the Commies. No one said it wasn't, so wasn't that what everyone thought?

"The second person felt the only way to stop war was to be a pacifist.

"The third and fourth people had ideas that fell somewhere in between.

"We all agreed, war must be stopped, right? And we looked forward to the next meeting when we were to discuss what we'd done to put our ideas into action. That's when everything went haywire. No one's methods matched, because we never talked about what anybody had in mind."

If goal planning ever went astray, it was in this chicken partnership. A friendship was sorely tested and the people involved didn't speak for a long time.

"Ultimately," Andy said, "relationships were mended."

The chickens are all his, and, best of all, Mama Cass is still alive and well and not laying. As for making plans and clarifying them—all are believers now.

Movable Zoo

Though I think people generally become too personally attached to dogs and cats to share them (at least I do), some trainers I talked to said co-ownership could be successful. If two next-door neighbors provided bowls for food and water plus a special place for Tiger to curl up, the animal could mosey back and forth between two houses with ease.

Joint ownership would certainly be a plus for the dog or cat (he'd have twice as many people to love him) and the problem of what to do with the animal when people go out of town is already solved. Tiger wouldn't have to spend vacation weeks at a kennel. That's nice, all right, but could it really work?

Who would decide what the animal should be fed, and how many snacks, and what kind? Who'd keep track of who fed it what? Who would name it? Who would walk it? Should it be spayed or neutered, bred, or declawed? Where should it sleep? What happens if it gets sick—who takes it to the vet and then takes care of it? There's so much caring involved, feelings are likely to be explosive rather than rational.

But how about animals every kid wants at some time or another that don't evoke such deep emotions? I'm talking about gerbils, white mice, guinea pigs, hamsters, hermit crabs, turtles, lizards, snakes, and frogs—animals that can live happily in cages or aquariums that are transportable. (And manageable, for apartment dwellers.)

Our gerbil couple, King and Queenie, lived with us for three happy years (that's a ripe old age in gerbilville) producing litters every time we turned around. We were fond of them, all right. When they passed to the great beyond (Queenie went first—a stroke, we thought; King pined for her for three weeks and then went to sleep forever), my husband and children and I buried them under a maple tree in the side yard. We even sent a few words heavenward in their behalf.

But I wouldn't have minded sharing King and Queenie with friends or neighbors. Just as long as we agreed on how many toilet paper rolls a week the two would be allowed to shred to construct tunnels in their aquarium, who should freshen the wood shavings and how often, that kids shouldn't be allowed to turn them loose in the house, that they should be safe from cats and dogs and too much heat or draft—I think we could have made a partnership a success. Especially since finding a place for King and Queenie to stay when we went on vacation was a challenge. There are kennels for dogs and cats, but have you ever seen a hospice for gerbils?

When my children were in first grade, the class had a resident black snake, a pair of guinea pigs, and an obese hamster. Every weekend a different child got to take them home and care for them—a cherished responsibility.

The teacher never covered what would have happened if one of the class mascots had expired or gotten loose. How could a kid have faced his classmates and said "Monty Python" bit the dust at his house? I don't know how the teacher would have been prepared to handle it, either. I never asked. I was too glad to get Monty back to school after our weekend together to probe any further.

But what about a movable zoo in a partnership with classmates or neighboring children? Say there were four 8-year-old partners. Couldn't each own a different creature and rotate weeks or months they played host?

It could be a wonderful learning experience for parents and children to set up the rules for caring for the animals. Everyone would find out more about their behavior and habits—a biology lesson in living color. Kids would also learn, you hope, how to get along by setting up a structure to avoid disagreements.

Parents would have to have a vested interest in this partnership. With small children as partners, Mom and Dad would have to help with transporting animals and making sure—however in the background—that the animals were not mistreated.

The animals would always have a home when one of the partners went on vacation. Kids wouldn't get bored with an animal because new ones would arrive monthly (or weekly). Of course, visiting privileges to the near and dear would go without saying. If Matilda had babies, everybody would have to be allowed to celebrate the event and stop by to watch the cute little white mice grow. That has to be part of the deal.

If you can handle what happens with kids when an animal dies; if you can find people you feel would be as responsible for the pets as you are, who would care for them in a way that would make you feel secure; if you are happy not to have a houseful of animals and think one at a time (with occasional sabbaticals) would be a lifesaver—sharing would be something to think about.

A traveling menagerie could be a treat for everyone involved. And if you don't want to have an animal all the time, two, three, or four families could share one. Think of all those wonderful weeks in between the time you have the iguana at your house.

• • •

One last idea. If sharing pets is out of the question for you, what about co-owning grooming equipment? If you're fed up with the beauty shop bills for your poodle and want to invest in a good clipper, a variety of blades and brushes—maybe even a grooming table—so you can keep him looking good yourself, look around for someone with a shaggy sheepdog. You could be great partners.

Owning pets is unquestionably rewarding. It is also undeniably expensive. Grooming animals yourself is one area where you can cut the cost. Share the equipment and you've halved it again.

MAKING AN AGREEMENT

We've looked at dozens of partnerships in this chapter so far, for such different items that each could produce its own special set of joint ownership rules.

The best way to draw up agreements for all of these one-of-a-kind partnerships is to turn back to Chapter Five and go over the list of agreement topics and provisions and see which ones apply to what you are considering co-owning—and use them.

Put Barbara Watts' visualization idea to work. Whether it's a camera or a subscription to *National Geographic* you intend to partner, go through the motions of using it mentally.

Uh oh, you remember you usually put magazines in a basket next to the fireplace. Sometimes your 2-year-old daughter sits next to the basket, picks out a delectable selection and sucks on the corners. Better pick a better place for a neighborhood *National Geographic.* You'd write the following in your agreement: "Jointly owned magazines are to be placed out of reach of children and animals."

Sometimes when you're in the middle of an article, you fold back the magazine to that spot so you won't lose your place if you're interrupted. Better to use a marker so the magazine doesn't take on a permanent press. When you partner your magazines, remember that others would appreciate a clean copy.

Use your imagination and go through mental ownership motions. Write down what you're thinking with your partners as you go along, and you'll have your agreement.

Let's take the example of the cooperative little black dress and show how an agreement for its ownership and use could be drawn. This agreement, of course, is weighted to the concerns a clothing partner would have. Yours would reflect the matters important to you—whether it's the detergent your dishes are doused in or what you can use to restring the mandolin. The wording of the agreement can be light or serious—whatever you find fitting for what you own.

DESIGNER DRESS AGREEMENT

The following Ownership and Usage Agreement is made on this _____ day of _____ , 19 ____ between Ann Red, Sue Blue, Jean Green, and Betty Yellow, hereafter referred to as the Owners. It is agreed that:

1. The Owners will have the following interests in the black silk dress, size 10, purchased on September 15, 1982.

Ann Red	25%
Sue Blue	25%
Jean Green	25%
Betty Yellow	25%

2. Owners will split the cost of the dress in accordance with their ownership interests.

3. Usage

a. The dress will be scheduled by phone as the need arises. If conflicting schedules occur, who gets to wear the dress will be decided by gentle negotiation. If there is an impasse, Owners will draw straws.

b. No smoking when wearing the dress.

c. No jewelry may be pinned to the material of the dress.

d. Perfume should be applied to the body, not to the dress. For that matter, drenching *yourself* in Chanel No. 5 is discouraged because the fragrance lingers on.

4. Maintenance

After each use, the user is responsible for:

a. Having the dress drycleaned at one of the establishments on the list of acceptable dry cleaners drawn by all four Owners.

b. Checking the dress for imperfections and seeing that they are repaired.

c. Storing the dress in a cloth garment bag (an old clean pillow case dropped over a hanger will do).

5. Damage

a. Repair of any damage which is not the result of normal wear and tear will be the responsiblity of the wearer of the dress at the time of damage. This includes yawning seams and drooping hems, which must be promptly restored.

b. Repairs must be made so the aesthetic integrity of the dress is unaffected. This means if you can't sew, find someone who can.

c. If the damage is permanent, such as a cigarette burn, stain, or rip, the other Owners must be notified of the damage immediately. The Owners must decide whether professional reweaving or similar repair will bring the dress back to the wearable state. The wearer will have the agreed-upon work done and pay for it. If the dress is ruined, the wearer must reimburse her partners at the current market value.

6. Storage

a. The last person to wear the dress stores it. The next person who needs it phones when she wants to pick it up. If an Owner will not be home, she should arrange to leave her apartment key somewhere agreeable to both so access is not a problem. (If no one is home when an Owner picks up the dress, no fair going through closets for privately held alternative selections.)

b. In case of a catastrophe—like fire—in the apartment of the Owner who is storing the dress, she is responsible for reimbursing the other Owners for their loss at the current value of the garment.

7. Withdrawal from Ownership

a. Owners have the first option to buy the share of an Owner who chooses to withdraw from ownership.

b. No other party may buy shares without the unanimous approval of all the Owners, *and* she must be the same size.

c. If any Owner gains fifteen pounds or more over her original weight when the dress was purchased, she will be put on probation. During a period of time agreed upon by all, she is to diet seriously and may not wear the dress until she is back within five pounds of her purchase weight. This is to protect the seams of the dress from cruel and unusual wear and tear. If the Owner does not lose weight or does not wish to, she forfeits her interest in the dress. The other Owners will buy her share at the fair market value.

d. Any new Owner is bound by this Agreement unless a new agreement has been drawn.

e. The value of shares sold to present Owners by the exiting one is to be based on the current value of the dress as determined by a reputable clothing resale shop agreed upon by all.

8. Decisionmaking

a. Decisions (like buying a new dress) will be made in accordance with shares of ownership, with a majority being required for a decision.

b. If a tie vote occurs, more information will be sought to gain consensus. If consensus is not possible, the decision will be made by the flip of a coin.

c. Amendments to this Agreement shall be made only by the written approval of all Owners.

In Witness Whereof, the undersigned have set their names on the day and year first set forth above.

_____	_____
Ann Red	Jean Green
_____	_____
Sue Blue	Betty Yellow

By now you might think co-owning almost anything is possible. You're right. Hamsters to hothouses, pearls to pasta makers—if other people can come up with ideas like these, so can you. Because you know what you need and how far your cash will go.

Turn your imagination loose. Break down all the barriers in your mind. You can partner. Dare to share.

·9·
Work
Sharing

Buying a house and remodeling it yourself can be infinitely rewarding. You return rundown rooms to their once elegant state; you up-
date antiquated plumbing without sacrificing marble sinks and
claw-foot bathtubs. You shape where you live with your mind's eye
and your own hands.

But remodeling can also be draining. Raw materials siphon your
salary. The work itself takes any "free" out of your time. You have to
get the kitchen finished because hot-plate dining is wearing thin. You
spend every minute on the weekends plus as many evenings as possible feverishly replastering, painting, wiring, and installing plumbing.

Physical limits begin to enter the picture. Are you really strong
enough to install the wall ovens by yourself? Can you afford to hire
help?

People who buy homes that need work (reclamation of vintage urban townhouses is popular) may find the work they were itching to
get into overwhelming. (How do you know if you've never tried it before?) They become resentful of the time the house takes away from
favorite pastimes and friends. (What was the last movie you saw?
When was the last Sunday afternoon you spent taking a long walk in
the park?)

Rural folks know how to get a job done fast. Think about barn raisings. Banding together, they surely built a barn, and enjoyed each other's company while doing so. Everyone brought food, so a dinner break could be a festive way to exchange news and gossip. Friendships were strengthened by people pitching in together, not eroded by everyone working extra hard alone.

Urban remodelers are rediscovering the barn-raising technique. Instead of spending weekends by themselves tearing out moldy insulation, they get together to finish each others' houses. This system has worked well for many rehabbers, saving them money and providing support when all those unfinished projects loom like giants. Work sharing, however, can also have pitfalls—as a group of five homeowners found out.

"It's a question of standards," Alan said. "You must establish them in advance or you're going to have real problems. My father was a tool and die maker and his work had to be precise. That's how I was brought up. 'Close' doesn't count for me. Something is either exactly two inches long or nothing at all. I don't like approximations. I know my standards are higher than a lot of other people's—higher than many can put up with.

"The group was at my house and one of the jobs on my list was hanging a door. To me, a door must be plumb for it to be right. I admire perfect carpentry. To the person I was working with, a door is to keep out the wind. We sure had different points of view on how it should be accomplished.

"It's a terrible feeling to have a job done in your house that you're unhappy with. The whole time we were hanging the door, I was mad because Hal wasn't working the way I wanted him to. Hal was seething because he thought I was being too fussy. We kept going; we didn't say what was bothering us, but we were both doing a slow burn.

"I think it's a good idea to sit down and set standards, evaluate work sessions, and deal with issues directly. It's imperative to be clear about how you want the work to be done; how you need it to be done. On the other hand, if you don't care how something is going to look when it's finished, if you just want something to function and forget it, say so."

In addition to setting goals clearly before you start, people in the group should meet to talk out feelings—either after work or before— to build a feeling of community.

Work group members generally agree to meet one day a week at a member's home on a rotating basis. This way, people know when they can count on help at their house. Explicit work hours should be set (9:00 a.m. to 3:00 p.m. is popular) and everyone should try to be prompt. If being on time isn't an issue, members should still agree to put in the same number of hours to keep things fair.

Job lists are important so group members can pick those they prefer. This also prevents anyone from saying, "Every time we go to Fred's house, I get the dirtiest job to do." Having task choices also helps people at any skill level find something they feel they can accomplish, or at least have some desire to learn about. Remember, there are some jobs some people just don't like to do. A list of chores gives everyone leeway.

If no one in the group knows how to do a particular thing, it's best to be honest. Then if some members, or all of them, decide to take a whack at it, they can get a how-to book or directions from an expert and muddle through together. No one gets blamed because the paneling they put up is somewhat less than even.

Alan says, "Who really works hard and who doesn't can be an issue in groups. There can be a lot of underground grumbling about it. But there are considerations as important as elbow grease and skill. In our group, Hal could make jokes about unpleasant jobs until we all started laughing. And Deborah, who wasn't particularly strong or skillful, was such a bridge builder and peacemaker she kept up morale when people got discouraged. That's as important as knowing how to wire light fixtures."

It's the "urgent" jobs, surprisingly, that build solidarity and camaraderie among group members.

Alan says, "When we needed to clear rocks out of Hal's yard because he was having cement poured for his deck the next day, we all worked as hard as we could. When Deborah's basement flooded, we were up to our knees in muck helping her clear it out. No one likes 'make-work' jobs. Everyone wants to feel he has accomplished something important."

The way you assign chores can make a big difference. If you have a side yard overgrown with honeysuckle and weeds you want to turn into a garden, say to the person who chooses to clear it, "See if you can make a dent in that terrible mess." That way, any dent the person makes will give him a sense of accomplishment. If you just say, "Well, the yard needs clearing," and your co-worker feels you expect him to finish it in one afternoon, he'll be nothing but frustrated, even though he's tried.

How you communicate is important. Be specific about what you want someone to do—in an upbeat manner.

It's a good idea to phone work group members the day before they are to show up at your house to let them know what jobs need doing. Then they'll know what tools to bring with them. Work group members often use the host member's tools for jobs at his house but supplement with their own if the right ones are lacking. This is where the tool pool makes its usefulness apparent.

But using each other's tools can be a fiery issue.

Alan and Hal both believe they take very good care of their tools.

But Alan told me, "The way Hal takes care of his tools would be like me throwing them in the basement and letting them rust for six months."

What Hal feels is good care Alan considers abuse. They absolutely agreed to "take care" of each other's tools. Although they were using the same words, their meanings were miles apart.

When Alan broke the handle on Deborah's axe, he put on a new one before he returned it to her. When Hal used Alan's leaf shredder, he ran over some rubble and injured the blades. He returned it unrepaired, said he was sorry, and left.

Alan believes tools should be available to all group members but should be returned to the owner in their original condition. "It's the responsiblity of the user who breaks a tool to repair it."

Hal feels there should be no remuneration for broken tools unless serious neglect was the cause. "It's too much nitpicking to decide who is responsible for something that breaks."

Work group members must agree on who uses tools, how the tools are to be used, and the condition in which they must be returned to their owner. Standards should be set in detail, and everyone must take pains to abide by them.

"We had a problem with meals in our group, too," says Alan. "We decided whoever's house we were working on would fix lunch that day. Well, my wife and I made hearty meals—split pea soup, soy burgers, millet-stuffed peppers—things like that. Hal's wife didn't like what she considered 'strange,' and she never ate much at our house. But she never said anything about what she did like to eat. One day, after just picking at the lunch we served, she made an offhand remark that made us feel awful. It would have been so much better if she had joked about it at the meal, and asked for a cheese sandwich. We all could have laughed—and fixed her a cheese sandwich. People should say what's on their minds, or the issue of food will end up making stomachs churn."

Before You Roll Up Your Sleeves . . .

Work members I interviewed who had no written agreement felt it would be a good idea to write one. They blamed vague group intentions for individual hardships. Here are some points to consider and agree on before you begin.

1. What is the standard of finished work for your group? It may be a good idea to go to each other's homes and see how chores have been done so far to understand what will be expected of you in the future. Make sure you all know exactly what the "acceptable work code" is. Then write it down.

2. Decide what kinds of jobs your group will do. Will members do everything from cleaning house to plastering? Will you do any job the person needs you to do? Do you want to do only remodeling jobs? Some people hate nitty gritty chores that don't require skill. Some unskilled people like to work with those who know how to do a specific task so they can learn. Will you provide one job only for everyone to do? Will you have a list of options for everyone to choose from?

3. Does everyone use only his own tools? If tools are borrowed, how must they be returned? Who is responsible for fixing a broken tool? Who is responsible for paying for it? Should you define what is normal wear and tear versus what is neglect? (If you do, you'll have lots of talking to do.) How quickly must a broken tool be repaired? Even if you are a laissez-faire crowd, remember this can be a hot spot. Deal with it even if you write down, "Nobody cares how tools are used"—and mean it.

4. What do you consider "a good day's work"? If everyone in the group has the same skill level, chores get done faster and more easily. If everyone is not a master fix-it, does perseverance and pluck count? Make sure you talk about this matter so no one feels overburdened or unappreciated.

5. Set a specific time schedule. Agree to be punctual if that is important. If not, agree that everyone must work the same number of hours *on the same day,* even if hours overlap. Equal effort by every member is vital to group cohesiveness.

6. Decide what kind of meals you'd like. If there are vegetarians in the group, or people on special diets, or anyone who hates a particular kind of food, speak up.

7. Will there be music while you work or not? Does anyone care? If you do want music and you'll all be working in the same room, who gets to pick? If you're used to driving in nails singing along with Willie Nelson, can you also work up a sweat with Stravinsky? Talk about music.

8. Can you smoke while you work? Does the member whose house you are working on get to decide?

9. Besides a lunch break, are there coffee breaks? Does the host provide that, too? What about beer or wine? Can people bring it? Is it allowed?

10. Is profanity acceptable? When you drop a cinder block on your toe and creative swearing makes you feel better, will you be able to say, "Oh golly, gee, it hurts"?

11. What if someone spills paint on a newly sanded floor, or backs a ladder into a window and breaks it? He didn't mean to. It was an accident. In your group, are you going to consider this a possibility that could easily happen and all help fix what has inadvertently been messed up—or hold the well-meaning bumbler responsible? Who fixes the mistake, and who pays for it?

12. How is the work area to be left at the end of a day? What does "cleanup" mean to your group?

13. Make sure you have a regular meeting time scheduled—either before work, after work, or at a meal break. (Bear in mind that problem solving while eating does have its hazards. Members can go home with a good case of heartburn along with their calluses.) Try to create an atmosphere where people can freely say what is bothering them. Remember that you're not just working together to get jobs done you couldn't do alone—you're sharing the company of people you like. Do everything you can to make it a pleasant experience.

Raising the Roof

Whether a work group is formed to meet on a regular basis or is made up of people who band together to shoulder a single project, strength in numbers certainly holds true.

When a tornado blew through a small Ohio town, many residents needed to have their roofs repaired—those who were lucky enough to have roofs left to work on. Four men who lived in the neighborhood decided to patch their roofs cooperatively.

"Roofing is a terrible job," Bill told me. "We thought if we all banded together, we could have some fun. We sit all day in our jobs. Tackling something so energetic was appealing. There was no skill problem; we were all semi-handy. We banged our fingers with hammers, cursed, and laughed about it."

It was decided that the group would work equal amounts of time on each person's roof—roughly two to three days. The group would do the heavy work; individuals could do the finishing on their own time.

Bill described everyone's roof as "mildly dangerous." None were heart stoppers—the risk and the work involved were about the same for all.

Each person brought his own materials and all had their own tools. Whoever owned ladders carted them from place to place. Bill made an elevator out of his ladder to help ferry materials up to the roofs. One member picked up a mechanical pulley system everyone used.

"There was a frenzy of activity. It was exciting, and we accomplished our tasks with pride. We gained a lot from the experience," Bill said.

MEAL SHARING

You've had a terrible day at the office—nonstop meetings. The phone rang incessantly. You grabbed lunch from a vending machine and ate it at your desk.

You look at the clock. How did it get to be six o'clock? You stuff the papers on your desk into your briefcase as hope for a quiet evening fades. You'll be up till midnight finishing the report that's due tomorrow.

Driving home, you wonder whether your husband remembered to pick up Jenny's ballet costume. She'll need it for her dress rehearsal tomorrow. She's been excited about her first recital for weeks. The dry cleaning will have to wait; you don't have time to pick *that* up too. Damn, in your hurry this morning you forgot to take a package of ground round out of the freezer. You were going to have hamburgers and toss a salad for dinner. Fast and easy. Seems like that's all you do for meals these days anyway. Throw things together—or you and Jim take turns visiting the Colonel on the way home from work.

You and your husband both love your jobs; you love your children. But tending to the demands of a family as well as a career takes a great toll on leisurely dinners.

You want to hear the important events in your kids' day when you get home. You want to give them your full attention. But when you're rushing around the kitchen it's hard to listen attentively. There has to be a better way.

There is.

Three working women devised a meal-sharing system that takes the pressure off daily planning and preparation. They come home knowing a hot dinner is on the way. Sound good? Here's how you can do it.

Kate and Diana live next door to each other. Leigh lives across the street. Kate is a marketing director with an advertising agency; Diana teaches English at a nearby university; and Leigh is a high school physics instructor. All have children born within six months of each other, now near the age of 3.

"Instead of each of us coming home to worry about what we're going to fix," says Kate, "we worked out a system to help each other. This is how we did it.

"Monday is Diana's light day at the university and usually my heaviest. That's the day she cooks dinner for her family and mine. When I get home, it's ready and waiting, and either my husband or I walk next door to get it.

"Tuesdays, I cook for Diana. On Wednesday, Leigh teaches late so I send a meal over to her. On Thursday, Leigh sends dinner to me.

"I cook for others two days a week, they cook two meals for me. Leigh and Diana also exchange meals with each other two times a week. Each of us cooks on the days our schedules allow us to spend time in the kitchen. That's how we worked it out.

"Each of us wanted to prepare meals for only one other family at a time, so we wouldn't have to cook gargantuan amounts. We figure each end up cooking for the same number of people, so the money we spend for food comes out even. I've watched our grocery bills since we started this system and there has been absolutely no increase."

The families made a list of food preferences at the outset. They all wanted to limit the amount of beef, salt, and refined sugar they consume and prefer food without heavy sauces or gravies. They enjoy meals made from scratch that are healthful and inviting.

"I cook a lot of stews in a crock pot over the weekend," Kate says, "when I have the most time. Stews are better when they age for a day, so it's fine for Tuesday. We all have microwave ovens, so if we're late in picking up meals, we can warm them in a minute.

"Diana generally roasts two chickens instead of one when she gets home early from the university. I look forward to her chicken once a week. Leigh may make a tuna and rice casserole. I may make pork chops with teriyaki sauce and onions. We all love homemade soups and chili. We vary our meals so no one gets bored.

"We only make entrees for each other; salads and vegetables are prepared by the individual families. And while wives generally do the cooking, husbands tend children, set the table, make food deliveries, and act as backups. Everyone pitches in.

"No one has ever forgotten to prepare a meal. If we have a work conflict, we arrange to switch days or provide food some way or another. In an emergency, we stop at a restaurant and buy a meal for the person we are responsible to. We don't let each other down.

"On the other hand, if one of us is going to have a terrible week, or we're going to be away, we call and ask if we can cancel. Everyone always agrees, since it happens so rarely."

How do they keep track of whose dishes are at whose house? "Easy," Kate explains. "When I send a meal to Leigh in my casserole dish, she sends it back the next day filled with hers. That way we don't forget whose pots and pans belong to whom. They're continuously recycled.

"It means a lot to all of us to come home to a home-cooked meal. In the summer, sometimes we'll eat outside together on a picnic table in someone's yard while the children play. We talk over what's happened that day, chat about the children, just relax. It really helps when you lead a hectic life to have people around who understand."

To make this system work, Kate advises everyone involved to get together and write down all the things they love and hate to eat. No one should be on restricted diets or they all should. They must generally buy the same-quality products so money spent for groceries comes out even. They must make up a schedule and stick to it. Proximity is extremely important to meal sharers. Members must live close by—driving hot food across town is just one more chore busy people don't need at the end of the day.

These women have decided to cook for just one other family several times a week, but you can make any arrangement that suits your situation. One family could cook for four others one night a week so everyone is covered every weekday. Set up a system that feeds not only your family but also your sense of well-being.

GARDEN SHARING

Vegetable gardens are springing up in record numbers because people want to cut food costs and eat fresher vegetables they know haven't been doused with an alphabet of chemicals. At the same time, busy people who juggle jobs and family responsibilities may not be able to weed and water as diligently as they should. The answer? You guessed it. Share the work; share the bounty. Besides, isn't it nice to leave for your vacation knowing your zucchini is in capable hands instead of worrying that it's rotting on the vine in the August sun?

Gardening is often a very personal process; a creative extension of yourself. You dig in the earth; you plant seeds lovingly. Watching them flourish is a warm reward. That's why joint gardeners must have common aims. Do you plant just for food, or is this a passion? How much of yourself are you sowing?

Gardeners who decide to reap what they sow—together—have some talking to do before they begin.

Karen Bess is coordinator of the Neighborhood Garden Program of the Civic Garden Center of Greater Cincinnati. The center encourages city gardeners to cultivate plots set aside for them on park property and in some neighborhood locations.

Karen helps groups in the formative stages, then keeps them moving. From her experience with group gardens, she offers this advice.

"People must agree on growing methods, such as organic versus chemical. Can you imagine an organic believer seeing his almost-ripe strawberries being sprayed with pesticides by a well-meaning partner? Are you going to use compost to enrich the soil, or store-bought fertilizers? How will you weed, prune, harvest?

"Make a list of all the essentials—from stakes to mulch—you feel you need for your garden. Are they essentials to everyone? Will you split the cost evenly? Make sure that when you say, 'Let's plant a garden,' you state your goals and agree on techniques.

"Find out what each plant you intend to cultivate would yield, so if you have limited space, you can make the best use of it. You will also know in advance how much of a crop you will each wind up with, to eat and to preserve. Sometimes the overabundance is overwhelming; sometimes the pickings are slim indeed."

• • •

Connie, a member of an enthusiastic group, says, "All of my partners were 'literary gardeners.' We read reams of material, quoted every popular expert, and had not a lick of hands-on experience. No one agreed on which expert's advice we were going to follow, but we exuberantly planted a garden together anyway.

"The result was so many tomatoes we couldn't see straight. We canned for days. We made ketchup, tomato sauce—anything. We hated those tomatoes. We blamed each other for their overpopulation. The next year, each of us became responsible for one vegetable and concentrated on that."

• • •

Deciding where the communal plot will be located can be tricky. Some joint gardeners simply put it in the yard where they think it will thrive best. It can overlap several yards if the people involved are next-door neighbors. If the garden is on one person's property, make provisions for watering costs. You can review past bills before the garden is planted and have partners split the increase in the water bill. If that seems like too much trouble, have the host partner pay for the water and others assume equivalent expenses of seeds, fertilizer, or tools. Perhaps the host garden partner should get a larger share of the bounty for donating the land. Decide what seems fair to everyone.

Make watering hours convenient to the person who owns the property. If he's a late sleeper, you won't want to wake him at 6:00a.m. dragging hoses around. Do the same with other plot-tending chores. Work out a schedule convenient to everyone.

Again, according to Karen Bess: "It is often easier to have captains responsible for specific jobs than to have everyone do everything. It's better for one person to know he is supposed to water once a week than have five people tramping through a garden watering it five times a week or not at all. Appoint one partner to be in charge of pest management, one in charge of weeding, one in charge of watering, and so on. People can choose jobs they like or have most experience with."

Discuss vacation schedules so that someone is always in town to care for the vegetables. Decide in advance whether the person or people left in charge are to harvest what ripens for their own use during that period or whether they are expected to can or freeze a portion of the produce for the vacationers.

Talk about tools. Are individually owned tools to be shared by everyone, or must each gardener provide his own? In what condition should implements be kept? If one gets broken, who is responsible for the cost of repair or replacement?

Tools should ideally be kept close to the garden site. No matter who owns what, if they are stored in the garage or shed of the person on whose property the garden is located, everyone should have access to them at all times.

Pre-planting tasks and after-harvest chores should be discussed and designated. Who will rent the Rototiller to plow the land in the spring? Will you mulch the garden—and with what—to avoid weeding? Decide who will clear the garden of stakes, strings, and vines in the fall. Will a cover crop, such as rye or winter wheat, be sown to hold the soil in place during the winter? If this is agreed on, in early spring this crop must be cut and plowed under. Who will be in charge of this?

Karen says, "Gardeners must plan for nature's cycles. Agree on the method you wish to use to replenish the soil, and follow it."

Besides her work with the Garden Center, Karen is an active participant in a garden she shares with friends.

"Rather than everyone tending all the vegetables, we decided to make a list of the crops we wanted to grow," she explains. "If only one person liked parsnips, we gave them a small space. If everyone wanted carrots, we put more effort into growing them. We divided the list of crops by the number of people in our group. As it turned out, each of us was responsible for three vegetables which we chose from the list. If we didn't have much spare time, we picked ones we were experienced with; often we wanted to tend those we were interested in learning about. By each of us concentrating on three vegetables, we came to know the needs of the plants. We learned which crops were easier to grow, which crops had small yields. It helped us make an intelligent choice next season.

"We all took turns watering and weeding, but our group had a great deal of sensitivity to each other's feelings. If one person wasn't putting enough effort into his crops, we all suffered."

Karen advises people who want to tend individual plots within a large communal area, rather than grow one common garden, to be acutely aware of each other's needs. If an organic and chemical gardener have spaces next to each other, make sure the organic plot is upwind.

"Also," says Karen, "use common courtesy. Don't spray your vegetables with chemicals on a windy day and destroy your neighbor's setting for ladybugs and praying mantises."

"Don't have a radio blaring with rock music if you know your adjacent partner wants quiet along with his cabbages. Divide plots with stakes and strings, and avoid conflicts over who gets which plot by drawing straws. Establish paths through the garden so no one tramples another's vegetables.

"Sadly, you may have to think about a sentry system to protect your vegetables. Joint gardeners arrange to drive by the garden at odd intervals—especially at harvest time, if no one is home for long periods during the day. If you have serious pilferage problems, or think you will have, this is something you must plan for to protect your hard labor from becoming the prey of outsiders other than rabbits."

●　●　●

Sylvia had a simple gardening system in her neighborhood. Her yard was too small and sloping for planting; her next-door neighbors, a couple too elderly to keep their garden active, had 300 flat, open, sunny feet of space.

"They used to talk about how beautiful their garden was," says Sylvia, "and during the course of one of our conversations they offered to let me cultivate their space. They wanted to see the land used.

"Since the garden was at the back of their lot, we never disturbed them by being on their property. They enjoyed seeing our small son help with the planting. They loved to come out and offer advice."

Sylvia offered her neighbors vegetables from the garden in return, those she knew met the requirements of their diets. It was not a planned exchange, only her expression of appreciation.

"I'd bring them home-baked bread and cakes from time to time," Sylvia remembers. "We were also careful to clear the patch when the harvest was over so when they looked out at their yard, there would be no ugliness or trash left on the ground.

"It was a positive exchange between an older couple and a young one, a bonding experience between neighbors."

Co-Composting

If you can share a garden, why not a compost pile? Many people who grow their own vegetables wouldn't think of enriching the soil with anything other than organic overflow from their yard and kitchen.

Those who are involved in growing vegetables together can contribute leaves, grass cuttings, and food fallout to an extravaganza group compost pile. It could be a heap on the ground or in a bin near the co-tended garden.

Just remember, there are as many theories about composting as there are about growing vegetables. Some people are nonchalant and just dump things in a pile. Once in awhile they kick the top layer around. Others are more scientific and turn the compost periodically, keep it damp, and may even want to layer in high-nitrogen fertilizer so that the bacteria that break down natural materials will do so faster.

It's not only possums and raccoons who come to munch on compost delectables. Rats are among the furry foragers scrounging for a meal. Whoever hosts the compost pile must also expect visits from hungry critters—not all of them desirable. That could put a decided strain on your partnership.

Think about throwing in together, because if the pile is placed so as not to cause serious problems to any partner, you can cut down on waste, create your own garden nutrients, and ultimately bring down the cost of growing food.

GARDENERS' AGREEMENT

The following gardener's agreement (with modifications) is used by the Civic Garden Center of Greater Cincinnati when individuals sign up for garden plots. Their system is to provide land within the city, portions of which citizens rent for a nominal fee for the growing season. The points listed below will give you the foundation for an agreement if you follow the large common area-individual gardens system. If you prefer the one-garden, "we're all in this together" plan, the points discussed at the beginning of this section will apply to you when you write your contract.

1. I will help keep the community garden site clean by keeping trash in the garbage cans on the site.

2. I will keep my garden weeded, since weeds can creep into my neighbor's garden and provide shelter for bugs that are harmful to the garden. If my garden becomes a nuisance, and I am notified of this by others, I will have one week to clean up the mess. If not, I will give up my spot to the next person on the garden waiting list, if there is one, or to a person the remaining gardeners appoint to take my place. I give up any rights to my garden crop and expect no remuneration.

3. If I am out of town or unable to tend my garden for a period of time, I will make some arrangement to have it taken care of.

4. If I have more produce than I can use or give away during harvest time, I will notify my fellow gardeners so it will not go to waste.

5. I promise to clean my plot of all stakes, string, rocks, and other debris in the fall, so that it can be plowed again and a cover crop put in for the winter.

6. I will attend the meeting of gardeners at the beginning and end of the season.

7. I will contribute work on the pre-planting and after-harvest chores and assume my share of the cost of materials or machine rental to accomplish these jobs.

·10·
Deals on Wheels: Vehicle Sharing

Next to a house, a car is probably the most expensive necessary purchase you make. Two cars? A double gulp. That's why carpools have become so popular.

They're a help to working couples who head in different directions each day, as well as spouses (especially suburban ones) who stay home to care for small children. They would be stranded without a car if their husbands or wives drove it to work. If people who live and work near each other can arrange to commute together, it saves everyone money on gas and parking fees, cuts down on wear and tear on individual cars, and helps all of us breathe cleaner air.

If the commuting member of the family joins a carpool, it eases the strain, but then one person could still be without transportation on those days of the week the car is in use. An answer: Carpoolers can buy an auto in partnership to use expressly for commuting. This way there is even another benefit—the driver of the week (carpools generally rotate drivers weekly) gets the use of the carpool car during the evenings and on the weekend he is in charge. Additional horsepower is added for minimal cost.

People are sharing stripped-down cars, luxury vans, and vehicles that fall everywhere in between. Though buying a car in partnership is serious business, it can be done successfully with careful planning.

Financial responsibility and good driving skills are the basic ingredients.

Co-Owned Carpool Cars

Tim, a chemist with a large national manufacturing company, juggled car use with his wife constantly. So did a number of other men in his neighborhood who worked for the same firm. Since most of them were on the first rung of the upward mobility ladder, a second family car was out of the question.

Tim and his co-workers came up with such a triumphant solution (this was in the early 1970s) that he has partnered a succession of carpool cars ever since.

It all started when Tim needed to trade in his 1963 Buick for a station wagon. The dealer told Tim he could probably get $650 if he sold the car himself, but it was worth only $300 to the dealership.

Already a member of a carpool in which drivers rotated using their own autos, Tim mentioned his unwanted Buick one morning on the way to work:

"They told me it was worth more to me than it was to them, because it needs so much body work, plus new tires," he told them.

It was in good enough shape to get everyone dependably back and forth to work—even though it didn't look like it—so the men thought it would be perfect to use as a full-time carpool vehicle. It would sure put an end to the one-car two-step most of them and their wives danced so often!

A partnership purchase of $400, midway between market value and what the dealer offered, seemed fair to all. Each of the three other drivers paid Tim $100, and Just Plain Bill—as the car was affectionately nicknamed—belonged to everybody.

"I kept the title in my name," Tim says, "but I called my insurance agent to make sure I wouldn't have anything to worry about if anyone had an accident. He had never worked out a deal like this one before but offered to check into it and call me back.

"He told me to get maximum liability insurance for the car, which we did. We also bought a comprehensive policy to cover costs such as the windshield getting broken or the tires stolen. The car wasn't worth enough to bother with collision insurance. The agent said the only way we'd get into any serious trouble with this arrangement was if one of the drivers got drunk and plowed through somebody's front door.

"We're all reputable drivers. Basically the car was to be used for transportation to and from work, when no drinking was involved. I felt we were all responsible people. Though I knew I was hanging out there with my name on everything, the insurance followed the car so everyone who drove it was covered. I trusted my carpool partners to pay me if anything happened, so I felt comfortable with the arrangement." (If this sounds risky to you, it is. Car co-owners generally take chances and are comfortable with that because they choose partners carefully.)

The rules Tim's group set up covered a lot of contingencies. They agreed that all insurance and maintenance costs were to be divided equally.

"I can afford a $50 maintenance bill any day of the week," Tim says. "But $200? I'd think twice about that. It was beautiful. Splitting everything by four made driving a second car affordable.

"Each member put $1 a week into the car kitty so that at the end of the month we had $16. Since gas was only 59¢ a gallon then, we had more than enough to pay for it. We were able to build up a fund with the excess to absorb maintenance costs without having to dig into our own resources."

It was decided that amortization would be set at $33 a year for three years. If a driver left the carpool after the first year, he was to be paid $66 by the others (plus one-fourth of any money accumulated in the kitty). This was also the value set for the share a new carpool partner would have to pay to enter the group. After three years, the car was free and clear.

Just Plain Bill could accommodate six riders but had only four regulars.

"People called us all the time to ask for rides," Tim remembers. "We charged them a dollar each way and put that money in the repair kitty. This was how we were able to take care of most of our maintenance costs."

All members agreed that a no-frills car suited them just fine. They never wanted to worry about someone denting the doors while it was parked in the company lot or wrecking it in bad weather, as they would have with their personal cars. They decided they would do only basic maintenance, paying for problems as they arose. So it was rusty. No one wanted to pay to have it painted. But a new clutch when the old one wore out, safe tires, oil changes, and grease jobs at the right intervals were important.

"One day a woman banged into the back of our car in the company lot," Tim laughs. "We kidded the woman that she knocked the rust and dust loose. Her insurance company estimated the damage at $275 and that's what they paid us. We spent $25 to unjam the trunk release and split the rest of the money. It wasn't worth repairing the body."

Tim's carpool rotated drivers weekly. When it was his turn, a member drove the car home on Friday evening, had Just Plain Bill at his disposal all weekend, and then began carpool driving duties on Monday morning. Though the car insurance would have covered family members, their use of the car was discouraged. Any family member under the age of 25 was simply not allowed to drive the car.

"We would have had to pay a lot more insurance," Tim emphasizes. "We didn't even take anybody under 25 years old into the carpool as a partner. We didn't want to assume the additional expense."

Weekend drivers were expected to pay a mileage charge for the use of the car—the same amount the company paid for business driving. This was the reason:

"If we charged each other 10¢ a mile to drive Just Plain Bill for personal use and the company paid 20¢ for business use, this could be a problem," Tim explains. "We never wanted to suspect someone of reporting business mileage as personal and pocketing the difference. Making the charge 20¢ a mile and having the driver pay the money into the maintenance kitty kept things straight.

"One year I drove 1000 miles back and forth to the airport and I used the carpool car. I wouldn't have wanted to load the packing crates I had to take with me into our family car. No one in the carpool minded. Though I paid the company mileage costs into Bill's slush fund, it was worth it to keep my own car from getting messed up. Besides, whatever amount I donated, I'd get one-fourth back anyway."

Any of the partners were also allowed to use the carpool car for personal errands during the working day.

"This was another way to save money," says Tim. "If I had to go to the dentist, the round trip was 17 miles. It cost me $3.40 to drive Just Plain Bill. If I had to drive my own car, I would have had to drive 20 miles round trip to work plus 17 miles to the dentist for a total of 37 miles at $7.40. I couldn't drive my own car as cheaply as Just Plain Bill."

While partners benefited from Bill for personal use, they were also held responsible for any damage they might cause. If they wrecked the car, they knew they had to pay off their partners' shares at the previously established value.

"We decided to take it on the chin, if anyone wrecked the car," Tim sighs. "The person who totaled it would not have to use his own car or provide a rental car for the rest of us. We couldn't afford that. We'd just look around for a new automobile.

"If someone had an accident while using it for personal errands,

144

though, and the damage was worth fixing, we expected the driver to have the car repaired and pay for it himself."

Drivers were also held responsible for any injury they did to the car if they were at fault while driving the carpool—that is, unless they asked for dispensation.

Tim says, "This mostly happened when there was a lot of snow on the ground, or icy roads. The driver would simply say, 'Hey you guys, today is a bad day. I'm willing to drive, but if the car skids into something, I don't want to be held responsible.' Any one of us could be in that position. So the rest of us would say, 'O.K., if the car gets wrecked, it's gone. And it's nobody's fault.'

"Unless we asked for dispensation, if any of us wrecked the car, we would lose our equity in Just Plain Bill, besides having to pay half of everyone else's equity. That was the rule we worked out as an incentive for everyone to drive safely. If we collected money for someone else damaging the car, we split it. If we caused the problem, we had to pay for it. If we demolished the car, we had to pay off everyone else."

Smoking was discouraged in the carpool, and so was eating. If the driver's music selection offended the rest, someone would speak up. If the driver woke up to an uncooperative car that made noises but didn't start, he was responsible for using his own car to get people to work, or else call around to get someone else to drive.

"Generally everyone was ready in the morning when we picked them up," says Tim, "but if we waited at someone's house for a few minutes, the driver would knock on the door. If the guy showed up in his pajamas, we'd leave without him. If he made us wait often, he'd be met with an uncomfortable silence when he got in the car."

All carpool members finished work at 4:10. To encourage one member, who usually trailed out at 4:30 while others waited in a freezing auto, to be more prompt, they instituted a system of fines.

"Whoever got to the car first became the official timer," says Tim. "We started the clock at 4:10 even if it was 4:20. It was still 4:10 to us. We gave everyone five minutes to get to the car. After 4:15, we docked everyone one point per minute. After 4:30, it was two points per minute. At 4:45 we left.

"We had a small notebook on the dashboard we used as a trip ticket. People signed in and out so we knew who to pick up. We also used it to keep track of fines.

"At the end of the month we multiplied the number of times each of us was late by the number of tardy points each had accumulated. This way, if one partner was five minutes late 15 times he would not accumulate as many points as a person who was 15 minutes late twice and 20 minutes late three times. The latter was penalized more because he was the bigger nuisance.

"On the way home from work, the day we settled up fines, we'd stop for a couple of beers. The guy who had the highest number of points bought the drinks. It soothed our souls to see the guy pay up who made us wait the longest."

The reason this carpool decided to wait for members rather than leave immediately without them, as many do, is because of the hardship it would have imposed on wives who had to pile babies in cars to pick up their husbands stranded at work.

"If any of us was in a meeting and the boss decided to extend it an extra ten minutes, none of us would have walked out to be on time for the carpool," Tim says. "We all understood that. There was no way we could contact each other. That's why we decided it would be all right to wait. It was chronic lack of consideration we wanted to discourage, and fining was the way we did it.

"When Just Plain Bill's odometer hit the 125,000-mile mark, we didn't want to push our luck any further.

"We sold him for $50, then I acquired another clunker—a 1968 Chevy which my mother- and father-in-law gave to my wife and me because they no longer wanted to drive. It was a perfect carpool car. The rest bought ownership for a $100 apiece and we were back in the carpool business—this time with The Lame Duck. This carpool has been chugging along for five years and is still healthy.

"Most of the same rules applied to the new car—except keeping large amounts of money in the kitty. We were all in better financial shape to meet maintenance costs, so we didn't have to set a weekly charge to build a slush fund."

The driver of the week is responsible for keeping track of gas, which is usually bought on the way home from work. A tankful, which Tim estimates costs $28, is split four ways and paid on the spot. Any other expenses that arise are also evenly shouldered.

"Sometimes, someone will be a month behind in paying his share of a bill," Tim says. "We all know he's good for the money so we carry him along. We do get a little anxious after six weeks. Though it's never happened, we would probably ask someone to leave the carpool if he was two months behind. This would be especially important to people who had to make monthly payments on a car loan.

"We talk over a lot of our partnership problems on the way to and from work. We decide who will get the muffler fixed, who will be responsible for the transmission. I do most of the keeping track of money, so the others do maintenance chores. It's a good idea to switch jobs periodically.

"We have one rule that makes us laugh. If The Lame Duck dies, we will divide the money we get for her by four. But the carpool member whose personal car has the oldest battery gets the Duck's.

"We try to handle small problems that arise diplomatically. If one guy turns around to talk to people in the back seat, we teasingly tell him to keep his eyes on the road. Another guy began swearing a lot. One day we told an extra passenger, 'Don't mind Al. He teaches Cussing 201.' Al didn't say a word on the way home and after that stopped using as much profanity. If we have a real problem, though, like tardiness, we confront someone directly."

This carpool not only has rules to keep problems from arising, it has rules to buoy spirits.

"We're not big drinkers," says Tim, "but we like to celebrate our auto adventures. For instance, if the mileage reads 88,888.8 as we drive up to a partner's house on the way home, we honk the horn and go inside and have a beer.

"We all work in the research department of our company and we're not supposed to talk about what we are doing on the job, so we talk about other things. You're likely to hear someone ask, 'Who knows how to repair a toaster?' Or someone may say his car has been backfiring—does anyone know a good garage? It beats the boredom of driving alone."

Reminiscing about the year a blizzard hit the city, Tim says, "The Lame Duck made it to work anyway. We all piled out of the car to move other cars stuck in front of us. Meanwhile the driver of the Duck crept along until he got to the spot where we were waiting for him. We learned to climb aboard while the car was moving so he wouldn't lose momentum. Extra manpower is easy to come by in bad weather.

"Some people felt the streets were so dangerous, they didn't want to drive by themselves. My boss rode with us for three weeks during that winter because he was afraid to drive alone. We always make it— together."

Vanpools

George never paid much attention to the expense of driving his car to and from work, but he began paying attention when the corporation he worked for began sending out literature encouraging employees to form carpools. Adding up parking, gas, and maintenance costs as the company suggested, he found that his expenses were $248 a month.

"I could use $3,000 a year in many better ways than driving to work," he says, "so I began to research the idea of putting together a vanpool."

"I called car dealerships to get prices on vans; I called insurance companies and banks to get figures on a loan. I put together a pro forma balance sheet which broke down everything in terms of three, four, five, or six partners and how many years we took to pay it off. Then I sent a letter to eight people who live in the same suburb I do and also work downtown, inviting them to a meeting to discuss vanpooling.

"I thought carefully about the people I invited. Social position was not a criterion. Social responsibility was. I wanted people I felt would be financially reliable and who would respect each other's privacy. No one worked for the same company because I didn't want riding to and from work to be an extension of my business day. We were all managers and had top-level corporate positions. There was never any question whether the people I invited could afford the proposal.

"I prepared carefully for the meeting. I wanted to get people to accept or reject the idea and also to clarify the rules. I had done a lot of research so I knew what vanpooling was all about. My purpose in meeting was to bring everyone up to speed with me, and present them with facts so they could make a decision. I even prepared handouts so that each person could have the information in front of him in writing.

"Before the meeting, I asked one of the people I invited to work as a facilitator for me. I wanted someone else to say, 'Let's make a decision—now.' It's a technique we all use in business meetings. It's not manipulative; it just gets people to move ahead. This person did his job very well."

Six of the eight invited prospects showed up at Paul's meeting and they all said, "yes." A definite decision to form a vanpool was made.

Although all of them could afford to drive a second car to work, each felt a social responsibility to lessen their individual gas consumption and ease air pollution. Besides, all were delighted with $3,000 in "found money." Some decided to get rid of their second car. Some decided to add the van to the cars they already owned.

George was charged with selecting the van and assured that whatever he picked out would be all right with everyone else. His choice was a standard model with a radio and air conditioning for $9,000.

The van was to be financed over 48 months (a minimum down payment was considered favorable, since the interest part of loan payments is tax-deductible). As it worked out, each person put down $250. Figuring loan payments, gas, oil, insurance, and other costs, the monthly fee for each of the six would be $67. This would not only cover routine costs but also build a cash fund to pay the insurance deductible in case of accidents.

A checking account for the van was established—in the van's name—and George became the first treasurer. (This job was to rotate yearly.) His name was on the title and the insurance policy.

"It took a little time to get the insurance we needed," George says, "because most companies aren't geared for our kind of arrangement. But we did get insurance for everyone who drove the van, including wives and anyone else we wanted to lend it to. Though my name was on everything, there was no question about my trusting my partners to bear financial responsibility for any damage they might cause."

The partners then set up some very clear rules. One person was to drive each week and have the van over the weekend. Before Monday morning, the interior of the van was to be cleaned. It was to be fueled, and the oil and water checked.

"We all have small children who love to ride in the van," says Phil. "But we agreed that it's a piece of equipment and has to be maintained in good order."

The weekly driver of the van was considered the captain of the ship. Music, air conditioning, heat, whether the windows were opened or closed, were his choice. He parked the van wherever was most convenient to him, though the fee was deducted from his monthly payment, as was gas. There was to be no smoking, drinking, or eating in the van anytime (coffee got spilled on other people, so it was outlawed).

A weekly schedule was attached to a clipboard on the dash so partners could sign in or out and the driver would know who and who not to pick up. If you forgot to sign out and the van arrived at your house, you were met with icy stares the next time you rode. Responsibility was encouraged.

Pickup started at 7:30 each morning and everyone was expected to be ready. Riders were dropped off at intersections close to their offices; generally no one walked farther than a couple of blocks. Partners were to board the van at an appointed downtown location at 5:30. At 5:35 the van left. It waited for no one, and no one asked why it left without him. How the late partner got home was entirely up to him.

Weekend use cost partners 20¢ per mile, and it was sometimes taken on vacations with everyone's consent. The vacationer simply left his personal car for carpool use (this was generally done at Christmas, when the average number of riders fell to three) so no one would be inconvenienced.

There was no question about personal responsibility. If a partner damaged the van over the weekend, he would not only arrange to have it repaired in a manner acceptable to the vanpool, but would also supply an alternative means of transportation while it was out of commission. Whether he rented a van or a car, or simply used his own car, was up to him.

Lending to others outside the pool was all right—with everyone's permission—but each was careful who he lent it to. Partners were responsible if there was damage, so they were very clear in giving directions about how it could and could not be used.

"This was how we operated in our jobs," George explains. "You don't let people down. You say you are going to perform in a specific way. You make an agreement to do so. You fulfill the agreement.

"At the end of the month, the treasurer summarizes each partner's expenses and credits and comes up with the net amount he owes, but we are casual about our monthly payments. When the insurance bill is about to come due, everyone gets up to date so our bank account isn't depleted. It's the responsibility of the person who's keeping the books to let everyone know the bank account is short so that everyone pays up."

The buy-sell agreement is simple. The person who leaves the vanpool sells his shares to the remaining members.

"Since our partnership is based on trust, it could be a disaster if a member sold his share to someone we may not approve of. We all want to choose a new partner to make sure he is compatible."

Partners will establish the fair market value of the van by having it appraised by the dealer who sold it to them. (They trust him and don't want to take the time to go to several places.) If the van has depreciated more than the partner's original out-of-pocket investment, that amount is divided by the number of partners. The resulting figure is what the departing partner has to pay.

Why? Because the loan balance will generally be more than the value of the van. The partner who leaves must share that cost so as not to burden the rest.

Here's an example of how this system would work. Let's say that after two years, one van partner is transferred out of town and must sell his share. The van is now worth $6,000; what's left on the loan is $6,600. The difference is divided evenly among the six partners, so the exiting partner owes $100.

(Another buyout method would simply be to have the new partner pick up the exiting partner's equity and payments. No cash would change hands unless the leaving partner was owed money.)

After two years, four of the partners decided they wanted to buy a more deluxe model.

"The air conditioning didn't cool the back half of the van and the seats were hard. We decided we wanted to ride together, but in a more comfortable manner," says George. "We looked at stretch limousines, but they weren't big enough. We tried out other vans, but aesthetically they were offensive.

"When you look at more expensive vans that you can enjoy riding in, you wind up with a lot of junky extras none of us wanted. After rejecting most we looked at, we got together and decided we wouldn't just say we hated all the vans we saw, we would specifically list what bothered us.

"One partner said the big wheels on the fancier vans made them look like hot rods. He didn't want them. One disliked the running boards. Others didn't like loud paint schemes on the outside and rug art on the inside.

"Finally, we took our list back to the van dealer we were negotiating with and asked whether he could accommodate all of our requests. He shook his head in disbelief but agreed to try.

"We settled on a $15,000 model that had soft upholstered seats and individual lights overhead so everyone could read. It also had a stereo that wouldn't quit and a bench in back that folded out into a bed, but we laughingly agreed we would have to live with these 'amenities.'

"Some of the partners were afraid we were getting too far away from our original utilitarian purpose. The rest of us said that we understood how they felt, but why should we flagellate ourselves every time we drive to work? We decided to go ahead.

"We formed a corporation this time which assumed the title and the liability. Monthly payments rose to $100 a month. Again, we wanted the maximum amount of financing for tax benefits."

Complete with an orange and purple Sierra sunset interior no amount of wheeling and dealing could eliminate, this vanpool is still on the road and running smoothly.

VEHICLE POOL POINTS TO REMEMBER

One of the most troublesome aspects of car partnering is obtaining insurance. You'll find some insurance agents and companies do not want the headaches of a multiple-ownership arrangement, which they consider unusual.

The best advice from joint owners who have gone through the insurance-finding process is to shop around until you find someone to accommodate you with the kind of insurance that makes you feel secure.

According to insurance agents I spoke to, some of whom readily insure partnerships and some of whom were aghast at the prospect, these are important points to consider.

● Before you commit yourself to a partnership, make sure everyone involved is legally licensed to drive. Carefully consider everyone's driving record as well. Insurance premiums will be based on all of your driving histories. This is true whether the insurance is in one partner's name and the rest of the partners are covered by it, or whether all partners are listed as owners of the policy. The age of your partners makes a difference in the price of the insurance, too.

One way partners can assure each other their driving slates are clean is to write to the Department of Motor Vehicles in their state and ask for a copy of the transcript of their record. Then all partners should show their records to each other. (Because of privacy laws, you cannot obtain someone else's records.)

Generally, the last three years of your driving history is kept in an active file, which you can easily obtain. Most insurance companies aren't concerned with your driving record prior to the last three years, so if your prospective partner can prove he has been careful for that period of time, this should be sufficient evidence of his stability for you, too. Going back ad infinitum may turn up more information, but everyone has made a mistake at some time or another.

Car partners should, without hesitation, produce written evidence to reassure the group (or each other) they are safe drivers.

● Some insurance companies will allow all partners to be named as policy owners. Some do not favor this. Ask the agent who may insure you which is the best method for your group and which his company will write.

● Who will be listed on the title? One partner, or all? Corporations may be formed to buy vehicles. This spreads the liability (the corporation is liable, not the partners), which makes partners feel safer. However, incorporation can be costly if you run up a batch of legal fees. You must decide whether your vehicle is worth it.

● There must be trust among partners if one person is the listed insured. If catastrophe strikes, he must feel his partners will do right by him financially, especially if the title is in his name. Consult your attorney to see whether a written agreement making each partner responsible for his own liability, even though only one owns the policy, is legally binding.

● If you have a co-owned car that warrants collision coverage and one partner causes an accident, will he pay the deductible amount of the insurance? Or will the partnership split the deductible? If the negligent partner causes the cost of the insurance policy to go up, will he pay the increased amount, or will the partnership absorb it?

• If you are jointly buying an older car and feel only liability insurance is necessary (not collision, etc.), insurance agents generally advise partners to take out the maximum amount for safety. Increased coverage does not mean increased costs on the same scale. In other words, a lot of insurance won't cost that much more money and will give you peace of mind.

Every vehicle partnership presents its own unique insurance problems. Get clear in your mind what kind you would like to co-own, how it is to be used and by whom, and seek advice on the best way to set it up from an insurance agent. (If it makes you feel better, consult an attorney as well.)

Keep looking until you obtain insurance coverage that satisfies you. And don't get discouraged. There *are* people who will help you make your partnership work.

After you settle the question of insurance, also consider these issues in setting up your agreement.

1. How will the vehicle be financed?

2. What will the monthly charges for each partner be?

3. Who will be the treasurer? How will the money be kept?

4. Who will be in charge of maintenance? Will these chores be split among partners, or rotated? What safety checks are de rigueur? How often must they be done?

5. What are *your* safe driving standards going to be? Think of everything from seat belts and back seat driving to how fast is too fast to your group. Deal with drinking, drugs, and driving. What if the group considers a partner reckless, or he begins chalking up traffic tickets? What behavior would trigger instant ousting from the group? Would the ejected partner be penalized by receiving less than his share in the car's worth?

Be sure you draw up safety rules that encourage everyone to be on their best driving behavior.

6. Can members of a partner's family use the car? Can the car be loaned to others outside the partnership? What permission is needed?

7. If this is a carpool car, how often will you rotate drivers—by the week, every two weeks? What will be the morning and after-work pickup times? How flexible will you be in waiting? Create a sign in, sign out system so that the driver will know who and who not to pick up.

8. If this is a carpool car, what will your weekend use system be? Will you charge mileage for weekend use? If damage is caused during weekend use, is that member required to provide an alternate vehicle at his expense until the joint vehicle is repaired? Who pays for the damage? For that matter, what is each partner's dollar responsibility for accidents incurred any time?

9. If this is not a carpool car you are sharing, but one to serve multiple people in a multitude of ways, how will you schedule its use?

10. What are your rules for the kind of music to be played? Who decides about air conditioning, heat, open windows, eating or drinking in the car? Will the driver decide, or the partnership majority? Will you allow business discussions or ban them?

11. Where will the vehicle be parked while everyone is at work? Must it be parked in a garage or carport at night, or is out in the open all right with everyone?

12. What is your cleanliness standard for the vehicle? Be specific.

13. What will your buy-sell agreement be? Can an exiting partner sell his share to a new one, or do existing partners buy shares and reserve the right to pick a new partner? How much notice must the leaving partner give the rest?

14. How are you going to deal with problems that arise? When will you have discussions—on the way to work, or in regularly set meetings?

In setting up the finances—especially on an expensive vehicle—legal advice is something to consider strongly. It's easy to create smoking, music, and scheduling rules; harder to know in advance what to do if a partner defaults on his monthly loan payments.

Pay attention to this because if you take out a loan to buy an expensive vehicle, chances are you'll be in a bind if your partner can't swing his share. You can lose it. Work out a default provision with an expert so that you will have, in writing, how many months of nonpayment by one partner will cause the others to mobilize any of the following options:

1. Buy out his interest at fair market value and split the cost less any costs incurred by his default.

2. Find a new partner to replace the defaulting partner. The new partner can buy his interest at the fair market value as set forth in your contract.

3. The partnership can be liquidated and proceeds distributed to

154

all partners after the costs of liquidation have been deducted from the defaulting partner's share.

If you think through how you will handle any complication that may arise—and its ramifications—you will feel more confident as a partner.

The Indomitable Dart

Rides to and from work are not the only purpose of joint vehicle ventures. Dual (or more) ownerships of vehicles to be able just to get from here to there are popular, too. A mind-boggling example of auto sharing is the system set up by the Life Center, related to the Movement for a New Society. In this group, 30 or 40 people smoothly share a 1969 Dodge Dart. Their careful setup should be a fine model for any partnership you may be planning. If they can make it work with 40 people, think how easy it will be for you with four.

Pick and choose from the guidelines they've established; not all will apply to what you have in mind. They are, however, guaranteed to get you thinking.

The venerable Dart, complete with automatic transmission and six cylinders, was a gift from the parent of one of the Life Center members. It arrived in January 1979, in good condition, a veteran of 33,000 miles. In 1982, after it had logged an additional 38,000 miles, Life Center members expected it to deliver two more years of good service. It's still delivering.

The basic goals of this partnership are the following:

1. To make a car regularly available to members of the community.

2. To keep the car safe, running well, and inexpensive.

3. To provide a nonprofit service.

At the time of this writing, the car was owned by co-custodian Jim Nunes-Schrag and covered by his private insurance. That insurance was relatively inexpensive (approximately $325 per year) and permits him to loan "his" car to anyone he chooses and the insurance still holds. *Inexpensive insurance that permits all drivers to operate the auto is critical to the objectives of this partnership.*

One way car costs are kept down is by having most maintenance work done by the appointed car custodian, who is paid $4 per hour for all nonmechanical work, and $5 per hour for work on the car itself.

Members call the custodian to reserve the time they want to use the vehicle. The car may be scheduled for an hour or a week. But if you schedule the car and don't use it, you pay a penalty for inconveniencing others. (In your partnership, you may want to consider limiting the number of uses by any individual per week or whatever.)

Jim and Linda Nunes-Schrag, who acted as joint car custodians for several years, caution others who are in charge of keeping auto schedules to allow at least an hour leeway between uses. Too-tight schedules cause tempers to flare. One person, waiting for the car to be returned, fumes over a missed appointment while another driver is stuck in traffic.

Besides a per-mile charge, users of the car also pay a 50¢ flat fee whose purpose is to fatten the car's disaster fund and hopefully build up money to replace the car with another when the time comes.

Payment is expected immediately after using the car, though leniency is the rule. However, if any member uses the car twice without paying, he is denied use until he coughs up.

Occasionally, Life Center members who own small cars exchange theirs for the use of the Dart, which holds six people. This transaction is done directly between the person who has scheduled the use of the Dart and the person who wants to use it. The custodian is involved only to the extent that he knows who has what car where.

The custodian has complete authority in all matters relating to the car. In fact, the custodian's job is immaculately spelled out in the Life Center's job description. (This responsibility is rotated by members; the chores stay the same.)

The custodian is responsible for the following:

1. Short- and long-term maintenance, keeping the car clean and in reasonable running order. If the car breaks down, it must be fixed promptly. This includes:

   a. keeping the car supplied with gas, oil, and coolant;

   b. taking care of any damage to the car arising from breakdowns that are not the borrower's fault (e.g., failure of pumps, fan belt, radiator leaks);

   c. taking care of insurance, inspection, registration, financial and repair records, keeping costs down;

   d. informing borrowers of important pecularities or problems to be aware of. An example of a "state of the vehicle" message is this cheery note Jim wrote to members:

A few more points on the car's condition: it needs a front-end alignment soon and four new tires. It won't be able to afford these things for at least six weeks. I've fixed several of the leaks in the trunk, but still need to fix one more. The gas tank gauge doesn't always indicate the amount of gas actually in the tank, especially when it's close to empty. Lastly, the switch on the defrost and/or heat fan doesn't always turn the fan on.

Happy trails,

Jim Nunes-Schrag

2. Scheduling the use of the car. This includes:

    a. Arranging the practical details of where people borrow the car; how they return it if no one is home when they've finished; exactly how they pay for it. Providing a logbook, use agreement forms, scheduling calendar, extra sets of keys, tarp for covering seat, etc.

    b. Setting guidelines for the car's use: who can borrow it; what happens if it's returned late; how many days it can be reserved; restrictions on use; deciding which request for the car at any given time gets priority.

If you think looking after all these details is endless work, Jim and Linda estimate the car custodian's job takes not more than 12 hours a month, and usually around 8.

Jim and Linda not only detailed what the custodian's job should entail; they also drew up the agreement/instructions for borrowers, with the Life Center's approval. Procedures were updated as everyone gained experience. These people are skilled at anticipating issues that can cause unhappiness in joint ventures. They circumvent them by dealing with problems head on. (Also remember this venture works because of enormous group caring and support.) Use their agreement to build yours.

BORROWER'S AGREEMENT AND INSTRUCTIONS

I. The borrower is responsible for:

1. Reading this agreement carefully and agreeing to abide by it.

2. Returning car and keys to the custodian at *agreed upon time,* unless newer arrangements have been made with him.

3. Paying bills within 24 hours of car's return, unless otherwise arranged, without custodian having to remind borrower and pursue payments.

4. Returning car as clean as you received it; if it comes back really dirty, the custodian will probably ask last borrower to clean it up!

5. Avoid putting dirty, wet, or sticky things, or inadequately sealed food containers on seats. Use a tarp or blanket on seat for dirty loads.

6. Use a van or truck rather than the Dart for loads like lumber, heavy furniture, large cases of food, many boxes of books, lots of bricks or cinder blocks.

7. Check with custodian before using it to tow anything, or to jumpstart another car.

8. Record all gas purchases, mechanical happenings, and other occurrences in the log book, preferably tell Jim what happened, and where car is parked.

9. On long-distance trips, check oil when gas is purchased.

10. Pay 25¢ per mile for in-city travel, and 18¢ per mile for out-of-city travel.

11. Make sure that only people who have been approved drive the car.

12. Promptly arrange and pay for repair of any damage to vehicle or contents due to (1) borrower's negligence (e.g., not watching gauges, leaving lights on, not checking oil, hitting or breaking things, leaving it unlocked and vulnerable to theft or vandalism) or (2) outside causes (e.g., hit-and-run accidents, vandalism).

13. In case of a substantial accident involving another vehicle or someone else's property:

   a. If other vehicle is at fault, borrower is responsible for arranging for repairs to Dart, and getting payment from other party.

   b. If borrower is at fault, and there are no personal injuries and neither vehicle is "totaled" or nearly totaled, borrower is responsible for arranging and paying for (perhaps requesting the help of the Life Center community) damages to Dart and other vehicle.

   c. If borrower is at fault, and there is personal injury or substantial damage to another vehicle or building, etc., custodian's insurance will apply, but borrower is responsible for arranging and paying for damages to the Dart, and for paying for any increase in custodian's insurance premium caused by the accident.

14. In case of a substantial accident involving only the Dart, borrower is responsible for arranging and paying for repairs to it. In case of personal injury, custodian's insurance will apply, but borrower is responsible for same conditions vis-à-vis insurance as in point 13.c above.

An Easy Exchange

Ready for a simple solution to car problems? These two neighboring families made an easy exchange that benefits everyone.

They live in houses next to each other that are quite similar. The big difference is that one has a garage and one doesn't. Wouldn't you know—the family that owns a car is the one without a garage while the family that swore off driving has a garage out back that once was a big, roomy barn.

Sarah says, "We made a conscious decision to give up driving. My husband and I no longer wanted to own a car for social as well as economic reasons. When our neighbors asked if they could keep their car in our garage, we thought it was a fine idea.

"In Maine, the snow can bury a car left outside in winter. The car pays a heavy toll in wear and tear when it is left to the elements. We were happy to help our neighbors out. In exchange, they offered us the use of the car whenever we wanted it. They even gave us a key. They also keep the driveway plowed in winter."

Though the neighbors offer the use of the car whenever Sarah and her husband might need it, they are careful to use it only once or twice a month for large grocery shopping expeditions. They know it is there if they really need it.

"If we used the car more often, we might as well own one," Sarah says. "We don't want to slide into easy car use again. Whenever we do use the car, we only drive two or three miles since this is such a small community. But even so, we put gas in the car after we use it. There is something about the exchange of money that makes using the car a business arrangement instead of a favor.

"We never use our neighbor's car without notifying them first even though we have the key. And every time we tell them we want to use the car, they tidy it up for us.

"If the car conked out while we drove it to the grocery, I'd call my neighbors and ask what they want me to do with it. Since my husband and I use it so little, we really don't feel responsible for general repairs. But we would pay for any damage we caused through an accident or negligence. As for insurance, their policy covers our driving the car.

"Good manners have a lot to do with how well this arrangement works," Sarah stresses. "I think what we are doing is nice for all of us."

How About . . .

The possible combinations of people who can jointly own cars are infinite. Big-city dwellers who use public transportation or taxis during the week often wish for a car on weekends. It's hard enough to pay the rent these days without adding garage fees on top of it. Sharing a car and the cost makes sense.

Families who own small cars to save on gasoline are in a bind when they need to haul a couch home they've picked up at a yard sale, take a big old desk to be refinished, or cart six kids to the circus. Neighbors can buy a jumbo station wagon in partnership. It doesn't have to be in great condition—as long as it serves as the workhorse everyone seems to need on occasion, it will be fine. Who wants (or really needs) a heap like that sitting in the driveway all the time? This is when the favorite rule, "whoever used it last has to store it," comes into play. (If a small pickup truck would be handier than a station wagon, couldn't it be shared just as easily?)

How about communal wheels for stay-at-home spouses who take care of small children? While the family car is at work, why don't the home-bound spouses invest in an "errand car" together? For grocery shopping, nursery school pickups, trips to the pediatrician—with scheduling, a neighborhood "runabout" is a great possibility.

I know—teenagers and driving is a hot topic. But I haven't met a teenager yet who doesn't count the days until he gets his license and his hands on a car to call his own.

A resurrected auto reclaimed by a group of teenagers would be a positive project. Parents could kick in as much money (or none) as they wanted. Teenagers could earn money for parts. Work on the car could be done by the group, if they're handy, or under the watchful eye of experts. Do-it-yourself auto fixeries abound from coast to coast, where you rent a bay at an auto shop which entitles you to the use of their tools and some advice from the expert-in-residence.

Earning cash for the car is a goal to get kids moving. Splitting the work and ultimately the use of the car teaches sharing.

Though this setup could prove to be an insurance nightmare, and while parents must make sure car and driver safety is a prerequisite, isn't junior co-ownership something to think about?

No matter who or how many people own a vehicle in tandem, they have to sit down and thrash out the goals they have in mind for it and how they are going to solve problems. What if someone forgets to pry the half-eaten peanut butter and jelly sandwich off the back seat? Who pays the increased insurance cost if one of the partners has an accident? Who is supposed to put in the antifreeze or get the car washed and waxed?

By now, you should have a pretty good idea of what to expect from vehicle partnering and some basic knowledge to help you handle the difficulties that could arise. In any event, consult professional help (insurance agents and attorneys) to make sure you understand exactly what your legal responsibilities will be and what your liabilities could be. With all that in order, hit the road!

We and Our RV

Since a car is sharable, wouldn't rules for joint ownership of a recreational vehicle be the same?

"Wrong," declares Tom. One of four partners of a mobile home bought in 1977 for $32,000, he says, "A recreational vehicle is not like a car. It has all the headaches of owning a home—only worse because these roll around on wheels.

"When we drove ours, it vibrated all the time. Everything in it was shaken loose at one time or another, or broken. There was constant maintenance.

"If one person forgets and leaves water in the lines, they can freeze. If a partner forgets to empty the toilets after he uses it, and another partner goes to use the RV, the thing smells like an outhouse.

"When I drove around a sharp turn one time, the television set went flying through the window. It's a nightmare."

All partners are friends who had rented recreational vehicles before they decided to purchase one together. One wanted to use it for camping. Another wanted it for his yearly family vacation. Two liked to travel to football games in neighboring states. No one really wanted to take care of it.

The mobile home was financed so that monthly payments were $400. Split four ways, that amount seemed fine to all partners. It was stocked with dishes, pots and pans, and other essentials. The cost was equally divided. Liquor, food, and linens were supplied by individual partners for their own use.

Since three of the partners wanted no maintenance headaches, the fourth partner offered to serve as the manager. In return, he paid only $25 per month; the rest paid $125. It was his job to get anything that broke fixed and to clean the vehicle after each use. Since no one wanted to keep the thing in his driveway, either, the manager got lucky, and got to keep it in his.

"We didn't have scheduling problems," Tom said, "because no one used it that much. The managing partner did schedule it, though, for our use and for the people we rented it to.

"We all paid to use the recreational vehicle. We looked in the newspaper to see what the going rental rates were, and we charged ourselves and others we rented to 60% of that amount. We paid the manager 10% of the money as an incentive to rent the RV, and the rest was put back in the pot to pay our maintenance bills. But we were always running short. We always had to kick in extra money. We began to hate that thing."

The problems escalated when three partners wanted to get out of the deal. "We didn't have anything on paper, so we had fights over the market value of the mobile home! It was then worth $8,000 but we still had a loan of $15,000. We didn't realize it would depreciate so much so fast. It wasn't fair for the rest to walk out and leave one person with so much debt.

"We finally worked it out and those who wanted to leave the partnership paid the difference between the RV's value and what was left on the loan.

"I'd advise anyone who gets into this kind of deal to have an agreement in writing," Tom stresses, "especially spelling out what appraisals are needed to determine the value of the vehicle."

In this case, the partnership road was bumpy. It doesn't have to be. Those who are interested in buying a recreational vehicle in partnership have to be sure they really *do* want one—along with all the maintenance that goes with it.

Given the wide spectrum of on-the-road vacation vehicles to choose from, partners should take care to pick one that fits all of their needs, so it will remain a valuable possession instead of becoming a pain in the neck.

Why should you be saddled with a mobile penthouse on wheels when all you really want is a roof over your head when you travel? Take care not to get swept up in group excitement and wind up with a giant motorized albatross instead of something you are happy to own and care for.

Think about how you like to vacation—rent a few RVs and see which you like best—and then pick a mobile home that fits your style.

Then join forces with partners who want what you want.

In the partnership we just looked at, joint owners grew tired of the RV not only because maintenance was a problem but because the novelty wore off. They just didn't want it as much as they thought. That should serve as a warning. "Let's get it" fever can cause terrible problems later. Will you really use it enough to justify owning it? If not, pass up buying one—even a piece of one.

In a recreational vehicle partnership, everyone must squarely face all the maintenance jobs that must be done and either divide them or pay someone else to do them. Either method circumvents hard feelings.

Insurance, finances, accessories, and buy-sell agreements must be worked out impeccably. That way, all those dream vacations and weekend excursions you've wanted to make are possible— partnering.

Two-Wheelers

Before ending this chapter with a fitting finale—a granddaddy on wheels (I'll keep it a secret for a page or so)—there's no overlooking two-wheeled vehicles. Bicycles, trail bikes, those giant tricycles grown people pedal around, mopeds, and even motorcycles can be owned in partnership.

As long as the bicycle, motorized or people-powered, isn't used as a daily means of transportation, why couldn't it be shared?

You want to save gas, so you ride a moped to do close-by errands. Couldn't your neighbor do the same with one you buy in partnership?

Touring—even racing—bikes could be shared as long as their use can be scheduled easily. Bicycles for pleasure can be jointly owned as long as the co-owners are pleasured by the same bike.

Let's be exotic. Tandem bicycles—the racing and touring kind— can cost a couple of thousand dollars. A bicyclist who would love one of these would need a partner to ride it, right? That is, if he's not half of a couple already. A bicycle-built-for-two partnership? Why not?

What kind of maintenance should be performed, at what intervals, and who sees to it would have to be worked out for any two-wheeled partnership. Also how the cost of upkeep is to be split.

How partners will treat the cycle in question should be talked over so both (or all) are satisfied. Should you leave your bike chained to a street sign while you pop into the drugstore? Should you hose it off if you drive through mud puddles so your partner doesn't find it dirty?

How safe a rider is your partner? Is the bike's safety equipment up to snuff? You don't want to have to worry whether your bike (and your partner) is taking a beating.

If cars can be co-owned successfully, a bicycle or motorcycle should be a cinch. For increasing your getting-around capabilities, it's sure cheaper than buying an additional car.

All Aboard

An ambitious partnership on wheels: a jointly owned, late-1940s railroad car.

"Trains get in your blood," Mike says. "I've always loved them. So when I noticed a Pullman car advertised in a southwestern newspaper, I just couldn't pass up the chance to buy it."

"When World War II ended, there was a backlog of demand for rail equipment that couldn't be built during the war. In the late 1940s and '50s, industry began turning out the passenger cars everyone had been waiting for. Then people started taking the plane.

"Rail cars built to last 40 years were used for maybe 10. Some were never used at all. In 1971, when Amtrak took over the passenger business from all the railroads, 95% of the existing passenger cars were sold for scrap."

In 1973, Mike and his friend Burt bought a mint-condition Pullman car containing 14 roomettes (one-person sleeping rooms), 4 bedrooms (two-person sleeping rooms), and 19 toilets (!) for $2,500, which was its scrap value.

"People thought we were crazy," says Mike. "I guess it was a nutty thing to do. But other people spend thousands of dollars on extravagances. This was ours. Neither of us could spend $2,500 on something like this, but we could swing it together."

Mike became the managing partner while Burt took a back seat. That was fine with both of them because there was long-standing trust between them and a good relationship.

They quickly learned how expensive it is to run a train.

"Hooking a car on Amtrak trains, you can travel all over the country—if you're a millionaire," says Mike. "They charge so much a mile on a decreasing scale according to the number of miles you cover. We found out that we would have to invite other people to share our trips with us, for a fee, in order to afford to use the train. And the train must be used to keep it in good running condition. We needed a solution to our quandary.

"We had to do most of the work on the train ourselves because we couldn't afford to hire help. With 19 toilets you know something is always going to go wrong!

"We became associated with a local historical train society and promoted trips under their auspices. This way, it was easier to sell trips and be able to cover our expenses. If we made extra money, we used it to maintain the train. We also donated a percentage of what was earned on each trip to the historical society. It was a break-even situation, and it was perfect.

"I'll never forget the excitement of taking a cross-country trip in that train—a 6,000-mile, two-week trek that everyone on the train enjoyed. That's when I decided to buy another car."

A rare one became available: a glass-top, double-decker dome car. He and Jake, whom he had come to know through the train society, snapped it up for $8,000. They estimated it would take about $20,000 to fix it up. It wasn't until it was too late that Mike realized he didn't know Jake as well as he thought.

"We had the same interest in trains," Mike says. "We didn't have the same goals for ours. We didn't discuss any of this in advance or put anything in writing. We just thought we understood each other.

"I only care about breaking even on a trip or having enough money left over to put back into the train. Jake wanted to make a profit. When I advertise a trip, I believe in first-class service for the people who pay a fare. Jake wasn't as concerned with providing extras.

"For example, some of the sheets on the train were getting raggedy. I wanted to replace them. He thought they were fine. I bought two dozen new ones and paid for them myself.

"We had different opinions on how clean the car should be when a trip went out. Though we paid someone to clean the car after each use, I didn't always like the job he did. I did extra work. Maybe I was too fussy.

"I want to run trains because I love them. Jake wanted publicity. He wanted to make a name for himself.

"We had different ideas about how the train should be restored. He and the historical group were purists. They didn't want anything done to alter the car's original condition. Out of necessity, so that we could run the train and afford to keep it, I took out the porter's area and put in a shower to accommodate paying guests. They didn't like that a bit."

Problems were settled when Mike donated his half-ownership in the train (he got a healthy tax deduction out of it) to the historical group. He bailed out of the partnership after three years because the problems were just too great. But it's nice to know that the dome car is still around and it's being well cared for (it's also 10 times its original value). The sleeping car is still his and Burt's and is now worth $50,000.

"I've learned a lot from my two partnerships," Mike says. "This is what I would advise anyone buying anything of historical value to do—in a *written* agreement."

1. Define goals for what you own and agree on them. Are you in it for fun or profit?

2. Decide how authentic you want the structure and furnishings to stay.

3. Decide how money is going to be spent for renovation. Make a list of priorities. Put in order of importance these three ways your money will surely be spent: (a) structural problems, (b) creature comforts such as plumbing and heat, (c) aesthetics. Make sure you agree on the standards for the work to be done.

4. Designate maintenance jobs so partners know who is responsible for what.

5. What does "keep the property in good condition" mean? Be specific.

6. Who pays for damage? For instance, if damage occurs when a group is on the train, Mike feels the repair bill should be evenly split between partners because group damage can happen to either partner and is part of the risk of selling trips on the train.

7. Have a clear buy-sell agreement and a definite system to decide market value. Anything historic (cars, ships, structures, whatever) can shoot up in value. This is vital. If one partner loves the object and wants to keep it no matter what price he's offered and the other finds it hard to turn down ten times his original investment, there is going to be grief.

• • •

Although having your own railroad car is out of the ordinary, most of the problems that arose from its joint ownership weren't. Who does what jobs, how money is spent, and how much it is worth when one partner wants to get out, turn up whenever people decide to buy anything of value—together.

·11·
How to
Launch a
Boat Partnership

Lying on the deck watching the gulls overhead, lulled by the steady lapping of water against the sides, smelling the salt air, slipping the throttle into high gear to cut through the waves . . . you forget everything else in the world exists when you take a boat out on the water. And you try to take one out whenever you can.

But the ones you enjoy are never yours. Either you rent a boat from a marina or go out with a friend on his.

You've always wanted the freedom of owning your own boat. But wishing doesn't make it happen. The ones you'd love to captain are far out of your price range; the kinds you can afford aren't very exciting.

Don't just mutter, "Well, some people are lucky *and* rich and I guess I'm neither." Open your eyes and ears the next time you go to the marina to the possibility of partnering. Ask the marina owner if anyone else is interested in part ownership of the kind of boat you like or if anyone wants to sell a share in his. Chances are he'll be able to reel off a list of names of people who enjoy their crafts in partnership with others. Ask your boat-loving friends if they'd consider partnering with you. In nautical circles, this has been going on for ages.

Why? Because many people are in the same fix you are. They simply can't buy the boat they want on their own. The initial purchase price is not only too steep, the ongoing expenses are out of their range. So are bank payments if they have to finance it.

But many people who choose to divide ownership *can* afford it solo. Why do they share? Because they don't want to spend that much money on a boat they wouldn't use often enough to justify the expense.

It's not good for any craft to go unused for long periods of time. It also plays havoc with a boat owner's conscience. (Why did I pay all that money for something I used three times this season? I knew I needed to have the kitchen remodeled. But no, I had to have this boat. Well, now I'm stuck with it. *Three times* I used it!)

Boat maintenance goes hand in hand with boating pleasures. If you can spare the time it takes to do the chores yourself, or you can afford to pay to have them done for you, you're in ship shape. If you can't, the effort it takes to keep your craft seaworthy can sorely strain your work and family schedule. Partnering takes care of that problem, too.

Smooth Sailing

Judy, an actress, and Larry, an artist, bought a sailboat together for the combination of reasons just mentioned. They're good friends who lunch together, usually once a week. They both love to sail.

Though the $1,500 price of a Laser sailboat both were interested in owning would not have strapped either of them, neither could justify the purchase alone.

"I just wouldn't have used it enough to feel good about spending the money," says Judy. "Larry felt the same way."

"We made phone calls, followed up newspaper ads, and shopped for a boat until we found one we both liked. It's a simple day sailor that suits our needs, since we can easily trailer it to nearby lakes. We decided to store it in Larry's or my garage.

"Later, my son, who is nineteen, bought half of my interest in the boat. Though I can see how this would have complicated some partnerships, Jay isn't a problem. He's the best sailor in the group."

Though Larry and Judy are such good friends that trust is implicit, they wrote an agreement that covered all their needs.

"We brainstormed one evening and wrote it ourselves," says Judy. "We put everything on paper we felt could cause problems. For instance, Larry was concerned that repairs be made so that the beauty of the boat and its basic structure be affected as little as possible.

That was fine with me, but we wrote down that provision so he'd feel good about it.

"We made up a use schedule, though we rarely refer to it. Often one partner takes the boat out in the morning and another uses it the same afternoon. We're very casual. Sometimes one of us takes the boat away for a week at a time on vacations—with the other's permission.

"Once a year, we have work parties to paint and patch the boat. At Christmas, we all get together and give each other gifts—for the boat. Things like a good cooler to bring aboard, a set of unbreakable glasses, and a picnic basket are nice extras to have.

"We each have trailer hitches so we don't have to borrow each other's cars to haul the boat. We also buy our own life preservers. We do lend these back and forth so that when we have guests aboard we don't have to buy extra ones. We split maintenance expenses.

"I guess a couple of times I didn't clean the boat as well as I should have after I used it and Larry gave me some grief about it. But neither of us would ever violate our understanding to the degree that our partnership or our friendship would be threatened.

"I think our partnership is still working so well because we respect and trust each other. We value our friendship more than the boat. That's why we were so careful to put everything in writing."

Judy, Larry, and Jay's agreement is beautifully simple. It covers all the issues important to them and is adaptable for your use. Whether you pare it down or add clauses, you will find it a valuable springboard of ideas for your maritime contract.

SAILBOAT OWNERSHIP AND USAGE AGREEMENT

The following Ownership and Usage Agreement is made on this 10th day of April, 1980 between Larry Walker, Judy Jasper, and Jay Jasper, hereafter referred to as the Owners. It is agreed that:

1. Ownership

The Owners will have the following interests in the 1980 Laser sailboat and trailer, purchased by Larry Walker and Judy Jasper on November 30, 1979:

Larry Walker	50%
Judy Jasper	25%
Jay Jasper	25%

2. Obligations

Payment on the following items is to be divided in accordance with the ownership interests.

   a. Initial purchase of boat, trailer, and related accessories.

   b. Insurance premiums, licensing fees, and relevant miscellaneous expenses related to general maintenance and usage of the boat.

3. Usage

   a. Owners will meet at the beginning of each sailing season to schedule the boat for full days in accordance with a calendar to be attached to the Agreement. The basic principle of usage will be time in accordance with ownership, with Judy and Jay, and Larry using the boat every other day except as otherwise agreed. An Owner who does not attend the meeting gets last choice.

   b. The boat may be used by a nonscheduled Owner with the agreement of the scheduled Owners.

   c. The boat will not be used by guests without at least one of the Owners being on board, except by unanimous agreement of all Owners.

4. Maintenance

   a. After each use the user is responsible for:

      (1) wiping down deck,

      (2) folding sails (sails are not to be folded wet),

      (3) storing the boat and trailer safely.

   b. Owners are responsible for completely washing and waxing the boat at the beginning of each season, middle of the season, and end of the season, unless there is unanimous agreement that this is not needed. The Owners will divide these chores at the Owners' meeting at the beginning of the sailing season.

5. Damage

   a. Repair of any damage which is not the result of normal wear will be the responsiblity of the user of the boat at the time of its damage. User will pay the insurance deductible and have repairs made as expeditiously as possible.

   b. Owners must see that repairs are made so that the aesthetic and structural integrity of the boat are affected as little as possible.

   c. The Owner who causes the damage must notify all other partners of the incident.

6. Storage
   a. The Owner who has used the boat must store it in either Judy's or Larry's locked garage when it is not in use.
   b. All Owners will have keys and access to garages.

7. Decisionmaking
   a. Decisions that arise from the provisions of this Agreement or when new conditions arise will be made in accordance with shares of ownership, with a majority being required for a decision.
   b. If a tie vote occurs on any decision, the Owners will seek more information in order to attempt to gain consensus. If consensus is not possible, the Owners will flip a coin to make a decision.
   c. Amendments to this Agreement can be made only with the written approval of all Owners.

8. Withdrawal from Ownership
   a. Larry and Judy will have the first option to buy each other's shares, if one should choose to withdraw from ownership.
   b. If none of the existing Owners wishes to buy shares which are available by virtue of one of the Owners reducing or withdrawing from ownership, shares may be offered to other parties. No other party may buy shares without unanimous approval of all parties.
   c. Any new Owner is to be bound by this Agreement unless a new Agreement is drawn.
   d. The value of shares sold to existing Owners is to be based on the appraisal of the proprietor of Sailboats International. If the final price of shares is not acceptable to either buyer or seller, either has the option of soliciting estimations from two other Laser dealers. The average of all three estimations will then be used.

In Witness Whereof, the undersigned have set their names on the day and year first set forth above.

_____   _____
Larry Walker   Judy Jasper

                                     _____
                                          Jay Jasper

An Unsinkable Partnership

Holden's first experience with owning a boat was in partnership with his best friend—the man, in fact, who had been best man at his wedding. "We just fell into a boat partnership since we were together so often," Holden says. "We talked a lot about how much fun it would be to have a runabout powerful enough to pull water skis on the river nearby.

"We knew how much money each of us had to spend; we were both in the same financial ballpark. We watched newspaper ads and finally found a well-used 15-foot wooden Lyman with a 25-horsepower outboard engine we thought would be fine. The engine motor and trailer cost $800." (This was in the early 1960s.)

The partners quickly discovered the engine wasn't strong enough to pull water skiers, so they jointly bought a 40-horsepower engine for about $500. They also found that trailering the boat to the launch each time they wanted to use it was a pain, so they decided to dock the boat at a harbor on the river. So far, they agreed on everything.

Holden and his wife and Dirk and his dates spent many happy weekends together on the river. There were no scheduling problems because the foursome generally used the boat together. But they used it separately without conflict, too.

"On those occasions, we always tried to leave the gas tank full for the next person," says Holden. "But if Dirk came home at three o'clock in the morning and there was no place open to buy gas, he'd stick a five-dollar bill under the handle of the gas tank. That was OK with me.

"Maintenance wasn't a problem either—in the beginning—even though I wound up doing most of it. I enjoyed it so much, I didn't mind.

"I'd say to Dirk, it's time to clean up the boat and paint it," Holden remembers. "Dirk was still single and running around on the weekends and would want to put it off. I'd just go ahead and do the work myself.

"I love to putter around on boats—so much that my wife often teased me about enjoying fixing ours up more than I liked taking it out on the river. But doing all the work while Dirk did none of it finally got to me. I was too fond of him to tell him how angry I was. I kept swallowing feelings and grumbling.

"I heard about an 18-foot inboard I wanted to buy. Dirk didn't. My interest in trading up for a bigger boat was a good excuse to end the partnership. We sold the boat and split the money."

Some years later, Holden and two friends, Luke and Brad, heard that a 40-foot houseboat was for sale. Though Holden had never thought of owning a boat that large, the deal was too good to pass up.

"It was brand new," Holden says. "The fellow who owned it was building it himself. He had a fair amount of work done, but a lot was still unfinished. He had lost his job and was pressed for money. We paid $6,000 for the boat. He threw in all the parts he had accumulated—a plumbing system and all sorts of odds and ends he hadn't had time to install.

"The three of us felt we could make a $20,000 boat out of what was there. (Today, the boat is worth about $70,000.) None of us wanted to own it alone because we knew one family could never use it enough for it to be practical. No one wanted the responsibility or the cost. It was perfect for the three of us."

Luke was a good plumber. Holden was a pretty fair electrician. They had skills they needed to finish the work on the houseboat. But Brad said he was awfully busy in his business and didn't think he'd have as much time to work on the boat as the others.

That statement set off an alarm in Holden. Drawing from his past partnering experience, he instituted a system to circumvent the "I'm doing all the work" blues.

"I said, 'Let's stop right now and talk this out,' " Holden says. "We set up a work-credit system. We made the pay $2 an hour, which is nothing for people who make $20 or $30 an hour in their jobs. Still, we felt token compensation would be fine as long as credit was given for work performed. The work credits would be applied against the cost of maintaining the boat. Brad paid all the harbor and insurance bills every year because he knew he would always be short on work credits. It's a good system."

A notebook was kept on the boat so people could keep track of the hours they worked. Help from family members was recorded, too, and everyone received $2 an hour.

Receipts for boat-building materials purchased by partners were kept in an envelope in the notebook. At the end of the year, they did a grand total and settled up credits and expenses.

Fixed expenses, such as insurance, winter storage, summer harbor, and major mechanical or physical repairs or improvements, are shared equally. Partners pay for operating expenses according to how much they use the houseboat. The fee is so much an hour, depending on the current cost of running the boat.

A log is kept on board. When a partner takes the boat out, he enters the hours he uses it. He also keeps track of gas and oil and any other costs incurred using the boat because these will be credited against the money he pays to operate it at the end of the year.

Not just expenses are entered in the log. A partner is expected to write down how many guests he has aboard, what time the boat went out and returned, and where it went. If there is an accident or something breaks, he makes note of that, too.

If an accident occurs, marine insurance takes care of the cost. However, the partner who is piloting the boat when the accident happens is expected to arrange for repairs.

"It's mandatory to have good insurance for boats," Holden says. "Partners should find out exactly what amount they need to be safe. That's why we agreed never to let anyone other than the three partners operate our boat. We don't allow our children to take it out because we don't want insurance problems. One of our kids could steer the boat if we're right there with him. But the partners always have to be completely responsible."

To share the boat equitably, the trio sits down with a calendar every spring to divide up summer months.

"We begin on June first," says Holden, "and give each partner a week at a time throughout the season. But we're flexible in letting another partner use the boat on a week it's assigned to us if we don't have plans for it on the particular day he asks for it. We also switch weeks with each other, and weekends, which are considered prime time. We always try to accommodate one another."

Personal supplies on board a multiple-ownership vessel can cause problems. To avoid hard feelings over one person using what belongs to someone else, the group came up with a simple solution.

"We thought of this when we built the boat," says Holden. "We constructed four large lockers under the front dashboard. They're each about 24 inches deep and 36 inches wide. We each keep liquor, cigarettes—whatever personal things we don't want others to use—in our own locked locker. We store things like a good set of tools, binoculars, and a hibachi in the communal locker to which we all have keys. It works out fine. We're all good friends, so we respect each other's belongings. We rarely keep track of everything everyone uses down to the last nickel.

"If I want to buy new towels for the boat, I buy them. If I think about listing them as an expense at the end of the year, I will. Otherwise I just contribute them and forget about it. If the supply of paper plates we keep on board gets low, someone replaces them. No one keeps count of who bought them last. If I bring six beers on board and only use four, I'd probably leave the two cans in the refrigerator on the boat rather than drag them home. When it's my turn to use the houseboat, someone has usually left something for me.

"I suppose there could be a problem among partners if one person always used supplies and never replaced them, but that just doesn't happen in our group."

How a boat is furnished can be an issue.

"We all live in the same neighborhood," says Holden. "We've been to one another's houses hundreds of times. We're familiar, and approving, of each other's tastes. We were lucky, because we had absolutely no trouble in picking out tables, chairs, sofa beds, drapes—whatever we needed—for our boat.

"Leave the boat in the shape that someone else could walk aboard and use it," was the cleanliness standard these partners set.

"The boat is like a motel room," says Holden. "If it's dirty, it's downright distasteful. No one wants that.

"Partners should decide—and feel comfortable with—the way the boat is going to be used. I know married men who use their boats as floating bedrooms when they meet other women. Other couples give parties on their boats some people definitely wouldn't want to attend. Word gets around the marina where the boat is docked; it gets a certain reputation. Partners have to make sure they like each other, each other's friends, and what they do while on board." Partners should talk about this issue and maybe even write it into their agreement if they feel strongly about it.

Another point Holden feels is important to a boat partnership is mutual knowledge and skill in running it. Partners should always feel confident the boat is in good hands. They should trust that it is going to be well taken care of, that unnecessary risks aren't going to be taken. Safety standards are vital.

A meeting is always scheduled at the end of the season so partners can go over the ship. After inspection, they decide what maintenance should be performed before the boat can go back in the water the next season. They all have to agree.

"Generally, it's a good idea to have a managing partner," Holden says. "It's a job that can be rotated yearly if people wish. The partner in charge should be able to spend a specified amount of money to keep the boat in good running condition without checking with the others. It's simpler than having to phone each other to ask permission to buy a piece of equipment every time someone feels it's necessary. Of course, the manager must also be able to justify those expenses, too.

"We have a lot of trust in our group. If I think the boat needs a new radio, I'd call my partners and tell them that. I'd say I'd looked around for a good one and come up with a price. They'd tell me to go ahead and get it. I'd pay for it and then get a credit at the end of the year. We're comfortable working this way, but a managing partner and another who takes care of the expenses is a good idea for many partnerships."

This partnership has a buy-sell agreement that no one has looked at for 15 years. Still, simply stating that if anyone wants out of the partnership, the rest would have first right to buy him out, reassures everyone. If a "fair price" couldn't be agreed on by the partners, a neutral expert would set the price. If the boat was to be sold by all three, the proceeds would be split equally.

"Though we don't have a provision in our agreement that one partner has to give notice to the rest if he wants to sell his shares, it's a good idea," says Holden. "On an expensive boat, partners should have a decent amount of time to come up with the cash to buy each other out."

SWEAT EQUITY

The sweat equity system this partnership created is a popular one. To illustrate how it all works, I have concocted a boat partnership among four imaginary people as an example. (Please note the expenses listed here are not realistic. Expenses vary with the type of boat shared. Use this example only to get the picture of sweat equity on paper.)

Here is what their year-end balance sheet might look like.

Fixed expenses for the year 1983:

Insurance	$500
Summer harbor	$1,000
Winter storage	$500
License	$100
	$2,100

Operating expenses for the boat are computed at $10 per hour. Each partner records the hours he uses the boat, as well as out-of-pocket money spent for gas and oil, on the log kept aboard. Work credits paid at $5 per hour and gas charges are deducted from each partner's share of the operating and fixed expenses.

Repair and maintenance charges for the year come to $2,500. Deducted from $3,375, this leaves $875 in the boat bank account toward repair charges for the next year. Often expenses total more than the amount stashed away, so partners wind up paying additional money at the end of the year.

DOUG	ROGER	STAN	MAX
Used 100 hours @ $10 an hour = $1,000	Used 50 hours @ $10 an hour = $500	Used 150 hours @ $10 an hour = $1,500	Used 25 hours @ $10 an hour = $250
Gas slips = 300	Gas slips = 150	Gas slips = 450	Gas slips = 75
Worked 50 hours @ $5 an hour = 250	Worked 50 hours @ $5 an hour = 250	Worked 50 hours @ $5 an hour = 500	Worked 0 hours @ $5 an hour =
Doug owes	**Roger owes**	**Stan owes**	**Max owes**
$ 525 fixed expenses	$ 525 fixed expenses	$ 525 fixed expenses	$525 fixed expenses
$1,000 use	$ 500 use	$1,500 use	$250 use
$1,525 -300 for gas -250 for work	$1,025 -150 for gas -250 for work	$2,025 -450 for gas -500 for work	$775 -75 for gas
$ 975	$ 625	$1,075	$700

Storm Warnings

Two architects, one of whom lives on the East Coast, the other in the Midwest, have sailed together for 25 years. They chartered boats or used the 60-foot sailboat one of them owned. Twice they sailed across the Atlantic—trips that lasted over a month. They never quarreled.

They were such good friends and had such similar tastes, incomes, and lifestyles that they bought a 34-foot sloop-rigged aft cockpit sailboat in partnership. It almost ended their longstanding relationship.

Reflecting, Ray says, "Before we bought our boat, we usually sailed in Eric's. We did things his way. His crew cleaned up for him. We knew we were such good friends, buying a sailboat together would be wonderful. We never discussed how the boat would be maintained. In fact, we didn't discuss much at all. We never felt we had to."

They did agree in advance on a buy-sell agreement, but it was verbal. If either partner wanted to get out, he would state the price for which he had to be willing to sell his half or buy the other's half. The price would be based on the current value of the boat, plus its improvements.

This time-honored method is considered fair because if one partner states a figure that is too high, the other would be likely to want to sell at that figure. If the partner who wanted to dissolve the relationship offered too little money, his partner could turn around and buy him out at a bargain. It behooved both to set a fair figure.

Boat usage alternated each month, as did dock charges. If a partner didn't use the boat, he still had to pay the harbor bills.

It was agreed that expenses would be split 50-50. Damage that partners were not directly accountable for would be paid by their insurance company and the deductible divided. Individual partners were responsible for damage due to negligence.

Everything else the partners thought they were in agreement about was hazy. And because it was, there was a lot of anguish that culminated in a letter from one partner to the other I have included here, though it is lengthy. In eloquent anger it exemplifies everything that can go wrong in a boat partnership.

Dear Eric:

You're right about one thing—I'm getting disenchanted with your one-sided and self-serving views of our mutual obligations.

To begin with, you know damn well I was counting on you to bring *Callisto* to Norfolk. That was our understanding last fall and I reiterated that in my note to you of 3-31-81 (left aboard) and at no time did you ever hint there might be a change of plan. As I've explained somewhat by phone, your casual decision to end your cruise early, in Charleston, almost totally destroyed the careful plans I'd made for the month of May, including a day-by-day itinerary, air reservations for myself and others, week-by-week crew arrangements, plans for visiting friends along the way, plans for seeing my brother in Connecticut, plans for visiting Anne who had found a summer job in Newport, plans for sailing in a Memorial Day race from Hyannis to Nantucket and back, etc.

You complain about my failures to communicate—and yet you not only failed to inform me of your intention to leave *Callisto* in Charleston, you didn't even bother to call me for four or five days after you returned to Boston, thus impacting my mislaid plans even further.

And on top of all this (in your letter of 4-29-81 found on my return) you have the effrontery to demand that I get the boat to New York or pay a professional delivery fee for any distance short of that. I find it incomprehensible that, after screwing up my plans for an entire month and leaving me with a boat severely impaired for travel, you could then presume to penalize me for not reaching a destination dictated by you! Is this your idea of cooperative boat ownership?

When I left *Callisto* for you in Nassau, I tried very conscientious-ly to leave her in good condition. She was clean, shipshape, and functionally fit. The teak was bleached, recaulked, and refinished and the hull was cleaned with Poco to remove the brown waterway stains. The dinghy looked like new, was inflated and, I thought, air-tight. I'm sorry if you had problems with the anti-stall device, but if you had heeded my caution about it and followed my recommenda-tions, you'd have had no trouble. Instead, you ignored the whole thing until it failed entirely, and then made a half-assed string and baling wire repair for me to cope with later, vowing meanwhile (ap-parently) to make me pay for your misfortunes by demanding reim-bursement for the fuel you lost!

Your troubles with the water pump were also exasperating, I'm sure, but I can't imagine what makes you feel that I'm in any way re-sponsible—financially or otherwise. Over a year ago, I had the same problem, caused by the same situation (a clogged intake—as you noted in the log). I fixed it myself, made sure that the necessary items (spare impeller and grease) were aboard in case of future fail-ure and wrote up a description of the problem for future reference by others. All you've done under similar circumstances is send me bills for the hit-or-miss efforts of various "mechanics" you hired and give me a hard time about not waiting long enough for the spare impeller which you agreed, grudgingly, to send. Well I waited til the 5th—damn near a week—which may also have some bearing on how far I got up the coast, but still no impeller—only your bill for it.

Aside from this, I found the boat with a grimy brown hull. She was closed up tight, musty and smelly below, the carpet oily and sog-gy. Rotten vegetables in the quarterbirth hammock were dripping down the hull liner. The icebox was putrid with moldy leftovers and it took a week to get rid of the stench. The dinghy was carelessly dumped in the forward cabin—dirty floorboards, sand and all, along with the dirty laundry. Also left for me to cope with was our engine running wild at idle speed, the fuel drip and a propeller shaft bearing rattling loudly against the hull.

I cleaned up your messes, did your wash, patched and cleaned the dinghy (again), fixed the fuel leak (exactly as I'd urged you to do it—and with $2 worth of glue, not $200 worth of mechanics' bills), adjusted the idle speed, replaced and reseated the bearing (with the help of a diver), re-oiled the teak, and again left *Callisto* in good con-dition for you. Granted, I didn't Poco the hull again, feeling that it was finally your turn, but I did leave you the material to do it with. I also, among other things, compensated the compass, replaced the icebox's weather stripping, cleaned and chalk-proofed the rub rail, installed a new fuel filter and restored the engine, cleaned and oiled all of the tools and washed the sleeping bags.

Beyond this, I felt obligated only to leave *Callisto* in a safe place, pay mooring fees through the 31st, and inform you of her location—all of which I did. There was nothing "garbled" about the message I left with your secretary. If she or you subsequently garbled it, that's your concern, not mine.

As for our finances, we've been unable to agree on a bottom-line figure since last October, largely because of your insistence that I owe you the full value of the old jib. You are mistaken about this. I owe you half of its value. If Carol and Jim Cross agree with you, it doesn't make you right, it simply makes all three of you wrong.

What if (God forbid) we were uninsured and one of us lost *Callisto* entirely. Say she was a total loss (like the sail) and that I was responsible. I assume then, that you (and Carol and Jim) would insist that I owe you her full value—something in the order of ±$40,000. But what if you were responsible—is that what you'd owe me, or would you (et al.) come up with another figure more to your liking?

For the reasons I've already given, I'm unwilling to share in any of your expenses for fuel, water pump repairs, or delivery to New York. I also decline the opportunity to be half-owner of the mask (we already have one), flippers, and spear.

As for your arbitrary assessment of $30 for small items you claim you've magnanimously donated, I'll accept that (half) not because I've *ever* charged you for dish detergent, coffee filters, toilet paper, or the like but because you feel, apparently, that I've taken unfair advantage of you by keeping careful records. Actually, the list of small items you complain about is an indication that maintenance work is being done and improvements are being made. The labor is free—do you want this also to stop, or just your share of the costs?

One point I think we're both missing is that, as we're nickel and diming one another and getting uptight about toilet paper or lube oil, we're destroying a situation which *saves* each of us over $4,000 each year (the income from $20,000 invested at 15% plus half the costs of maintaining and docking *Callisto*).

The partnership also furnishes more opportunity to sail than either of us really wants or needs and yet, for some reason, it is producing more anger and frustration than either of us can bear. I doubt, though, that poor communications is our major problem (as this letter may help to prove). I think the problem is that we've each presumed that, being good friends who've happily sailed together for 25 years, we could:

1. Dispense with formal written agreements.

2. Duck responsibilities (postpone them, really, and make it up later).

3. Leave the tank a "little" less than full ("the fuel dock was closed when we came in").

4. Leave things a "little" less than clean and shipshape ("I had a plane to catch").

5. Squeeze an extra day (or two) out of the month ("we only had this one week together—and after all, remember last year when . . .?").

6. Make unilateral decisions ("surely he'll understand that it's really in his best interest").

7. Get by with primitive accounting procedures . . . and so on.

We even thought we could maintain a joint checking account. Well, obviously, friendships (ours at least) can't take that much stress—which leaves us then with about two alternatives: End the partnership (along with its many advantages—and perhaps along with the friendship as well) or try to end (or at least minimize) the friction.

Maybe now, in retrospect, we know enough to draw up a joint venture agreement which anticipates and defuses conflicts. I'd be willing to give it a try if you are.

Sincerely,
Ray

What happened after the letter from Ray reached Eric? The partners arranged to have lunch together in Boston.

During the meal, Eric said, "I was telling someone about you at a cocktail party the other night. About how we sailed across the Atlantic through a big storm. Everyone's morale was at rock bottom, and you baked an apple pie. The friend asked if you were the same guy I was having so much trouble with now. I thought a lot about that. This seems a terrible way to end 25 years of sailing together. How much do you figure I owe you?"

COVER THE WATERFRONT

From the varied experiences of the boat partners in this chapter, some things to consider before closing the deal are clear. Though small boat agreements would certainly be less complicated than those for yachts, it is important for partners to think of everything that could make waves, even such things as what you will name your boat. By dealing with them in advance—in writing—their partnership will have a better chance of staying afloat.

1. Are you going to pay for the boat outright, or finance it? Loan payments introduce a whole set of problems partners must face. If one partner falls on hard times and can't make his monthly payments, the other partner or partners may lose the boat. This must be taken into consideration and worked out with an attorney. (See the vehicle chapter for more on default.)

2. How will you split routine expenses? This means everything from yearly license fees to life jackets. Think of anything that may cost you money and decide how you will pay for it.

3. How will the bills be paid? Will there be a boat bank account, or will partners write personal checks and reimburse each other?

Will there be monthly assessments, or a charge per mile to run the craft?

4. What do you want yearly maintenance to include? Be specific. Who will do the maintenance—partners or professionals?

5. Think about sweat equity. If one partner does more work on the boat, should he pay less of the bills? Should the person who keeps the books do less maintenance? Talk about what jobs must be done, who should do them, and how partners should be compensated for their toil, or if they should.

6. What are your safety standards? Be specific. Also list what safety equipment should be aboard the boat at all times. Who is responsible for checking?

7. What skill level in operating the boat (or trailering it, if that's what you'll be doing) will you expect partners to have in order to feel your property will always be in capable hands?

8. What are your rules of behavior on board the boat? Include the use of drugs, alcohol and the kinds of partying you will allow. What actions would you consider a breach of partnership trust that could trigger termination and possibly a penalty to the wrongdoer? What will that penalty be?

9. How will you handle accidents that cause damage? Who pays for repair? Will you divide the deductible amount if you have insurance, or make the negligent partner absorb the cost? How will you decide what constitutes negligence? Will you share "ordinary breakdown" expenses evenly?

10. Must repairs be done by professional mechanics? Will you accept "patch-up jobs"? What are the repair standards aesthetically acceptable to your partnership?

11. Insurance is important and will often dictate where the boat can travel and who besides the owners will be allowed to use it. Make sure partners agree on the kind of insurance they feel comfortable with. What are the operation restrictions (distance, open sea vs. inland waterways, etc.) for your boat?

12. Can the boat be used by anyone other than the partners? Can it be rented?

13. Can anyone else on board with the partner "captain" the ship? Who captains the ship if the partners use it together? Do they take turns? Does anyone care?

14. Can the boat be used for racing, fishing, deep sea diving?

What ancillary activities are all right with everyone? What are not?

15. How will you schedule use of the boat?

16. In what condition should the boat be left after each use? Remember everything, from cleaning food out of the refrigerator to what should be done to the engine. Write it down.

17. Will your boat be trailered, or will you keep it at a marina? Which marina? Where will the boat be stored out of season?

18. What happens if a partner does not return the boat at the time or place he promised? Will you impose a penalty? Must he pay a professional to get the boat to the agreed-upon location?

19. How will the ship's log be kept?

20. What kind of furnishings do you intend to buy? How much money would you like to spend? If a partner breaks a dish or a lamp, must he buy one of like value? If he burns a hole in the upholstery, can he patch it, buy whatever cushion he happens to pick up, or must he replace it with an identical cushion?

21. How will you make decisions about the boat? What if you can't agree? Will you flip a coin, or seek a third party to help you gain consensus? Who will the third party be?

22. What is your buy-sell agreement? On an expensive vessel, specify a period of grace during which partners can come up with the money to pay each other off. How will the value of the boat be determined so there will be no fighting over the cost of the shares? Write it into your agreement. Will there be a penalty for the partner who wishes to leave?

23. The advice of an attorney—especially on the joint purchase of expensive boats—is a good idea. A binding agreement should be drawn, one you feel will cover all the points important to all of you.

A handy book to consult to set up a boat partnership is *Yachtsman's Legal Guide to Co-Ownership* by Dexter and Paula Odin. It is published by John de Graff, Inc., Clinton Corners, New York, NY 12514.

Small Fry

Though we've explored the ins and outs of co-owning larger boats, I don't mean to ignore small ones—canoes, kayaks, rafts, or open boats

183

with an outboard (or inboard) motor favored by fishermen, not to mention the whole world of inflatables.

Their scheduling would not be difficult, and as long as partners trust each other and their skill in using and caring for the crafts, why not add them to your list of sharables? You don't have to paddle your own canoe.

·12·
Come Fly with Me: Airplane Partnering

Airplane partnerships are as popular as boat co-ownerships, for many of the same reasons.

Cost is one big incentive to partner. So is the question of whether one person will use the plane enough to justify a purchase of such sobering scale. Maintenance is not usually as large an issue here because most airplane owners leave such work to licensed mechanics. That way, the plane will be sure to meet federal aviation standards and pass the required periodic checks.

What chemistry makes joint airplane ownerships work? The love of flying and the thrill of owning your plane is the magic combination that binds many enthusiastic aviators. But to make a long-term partnership work, there must be absolute agreement on safety standards and the care of the aircraft; partners must have complete faith in each other's financial responsibility.

High Fliers

Todd, treasurer of a flying club that has been in existence over 25 years, thinks that buying an interest in a club is an excellent way to become part owner of a plane—a flock of planes, in fact.

Sundancers, Inc. is a group of 75 people who own six aircraft. Todd says, "This is the least expensive way people can have access to the most equipment. Some people in our club could well afford to own their own planes. But a membership gives them the chance to fly a variety of aircraft with no hassles about maintenance. We appoint specific members to take care of those jobs on a rotating basis."

It sounds great—and, indeed, there are flying clubs all over the country. Not all, however, are as successful or as long-lived as the Sundancers. The system this club has developed to ensure longevity can serve as a model when you put together your own airplane partnership. It can also suggest points to look for when you investigate existing flying clubs in your area, if that's the route you decide is best for you. Find out about them at any airport where private planes are kept. The manager or anyone who works there will be able to tell you whether there is a local club and can probably supply some hot leads on its members. You'll go home with the phone number of the right person to contact.

The Sundancers own an impressive group of airplanes to attract members who enjoy diversity. Their acquisitions range from small craft such as Piper Apaches to Beechcraft Bonanzas, which can make cross-country trips.

Who is eligible to join? Anyone who fills out the application form and is approved by two-thirds of the membership. Basically, a person must be financially responsible and a safe pilot. The form asks for a description of flying experience, past aircraft accidents or any Federal Aviation Agency (FAA) violations, an employment record, credit references, and whether the person ever violated any law—criminal, civil, or military. It also asks which of the club's aircraft a prospective member would like to use.

Todd says, "The last specification is often the most important because the needs of the club must be weighed against individual requirements. If one club plane is overbooked with pilots who want to fly it and a prospective member expresses most interest in that one, too, he may not come up for membership as quickly as a person who specifies he wants to fly a less frequently requested aircraft."

The capital contribution to join the club is $900; monthly dues, payable to the treasurer, are $30. To use planes, members pay an hourly fee, which can range from $25 to $60, depending on the plane. This fee includes gas; if a member refuels, he turns his gas bill in with his log so that the cost will be deducted.

"Hourly rates are adjusted at the end of each year," Todd adds, "so that the cost to run the planes reflects fuel and other expenses.

"Monthly dues are designed to take care of earthbound costs. If we have a streak of bad weather and planes can't take off, we still have to pay for insurance, tie-down costs, and maintenance not associated with flying."

You might wonder how the Sundancers are able to obtain insurance to satisfy the insuring company and all club members. Todd explains, "The club is incorporated, so no member bears personal liability. The policy we hold covers all planes and all members. There is a $1,000 deductible for any in-motion accident."

For instance, if a member causes $250 worth of damage while landing, the club decides whether the cost should be assessed to the pilot. The decision is made at the discretion of the board of directors. They may decide the pilot owes the full amount for the damage he caused or only a portion. If the accident could have happened to anyone, the club may absorb the cost entirely.

"Though this is the system we currently use," Todd says, "there is a push to change it. Basically, it's a pain in the neck. It would be better for members to know automatically they're responsible for *any* damage that happens while they have the planes, and understand they must pay for it. It would be simpler for the club to tell members when they didn't have to pay than to go after them to cough up accident money they may not assume they're responsible for."

Insurance also governs who flies the planes and for what purpose. Planes cannot be lent to anyone outside the club, nor can any member fly people and charge a fee. This would require a commercial license. Members may, however, use the planes freely for their personal business.

How do 75 members manage to schedule six aircraft? A loose-leaf notebook for each plane is kept at the airport and club members pencil in their names under the times and dates they desire. To control overscheduling, there is a $4 charge for each day blocked off more than a month ahead of time. The fee is $3 per day, a month in advance. If they decide not to use the plane, members must still pay the fee. If the trip goes as planned, the charge is turned in as a credit against the bill. Thus the planes are available on a first-come, first-served basis. But members know they must forfeit long-range reservation money if they change their plans.

"If we see a person consistently scheduling more than we think is fair to the rest of the group," Todd explains, "we'd talk to him about it and hope he responds in a reasonable manner. Most of the people in the club would feel comfortable speaking up in this way. We'd rather do that than concoct a batch of rules that limit what everyone can do. No one wants to live with that."

Not all 75 members are active, which helps prevent overscheduling. The club is even flexible enough to allow a member to take a plane for two weeks at a time, although most members sign up for only one day or just a few. There is a strict rule about weekends. Since they are considered priority time, members may not schedule more than four hours on a Saturday or Sunday without the operations officer's approval.

Though the Sundancers have refrained from creating unnecessary rules, the rules they do have are clear. They have a strong board of directors to enforce club policy and to decide the fate of members who act in a manner that might jeopardize the rest. Besides board members, other officers include the operations officer, who has control over how the club aircraft are scheduled (longer than normal trips must have his approval) and how club aircraft are operated; and the maintenance officer, who is charged with keeping all equipment in fine order, seeing that logs are properly filled out, and making sure all airworthiness licenses, certificates, and registrations are in order.

"A common problem," says Todd, "is getting members to be conscientious with equipment. They may spill something on the upholstery and not clean it up, or be careless with chewing gum.

"Members must enter on the log sheet anything they notice that is wrong functionally or otherwise while they're flying the plane. The next person who uses the plane is bound to note a discrepancy if something goes unreported. We know who does what and it is conveyed to the maintenance officer.

"If one member saw another doing something out of line, like flying recklessly, he'd speak to him or report it to the operations officer, who has the authority to ground him.

"Our first step would always be to talk to someone and tell him he's not acting in the best interests of the club. If this didn't work, we'd get stronger. If a member jeopardized someone's safety, he'd be asked to resign. There is no question about this when people's lives are on the line. Safety is always our first concern. Our rules are more stringent than many of those specified by the FAA."

In the same vein, if one member notices another flying in a way he thinks would endanger the careless person and the plane, he discreetly mentions it to the operations officer. The officer talks to the wrongdoer, notes the problem, and, if the officer feels it is necessary, asks the member to take some extra flying lessons before taking a plane out again. If the member refuses, he is grounded.

Maintenance on club planes is never done by members. To keep costs down and ensure compliance with FAA regulations, only authorized mechanics can work on club planes.

"We always remind members that the maintenance officer is just a phone call away," says Todd. "If a member is out of town and something needs to be repaired in order for him to get home, he is told to get an estimate and phone the maintenance officer. The maintenance officer will tell him whether to get the plane fixed or have a temporary repair made and then fly the plane back to home base where it can be fully repaired more economically. People can spend twice as much as they need to if a single person isn't in charge. The maintenance officer knows all the alternatives. He must be in control of everything that is done to the club's planes.

"At our monthly meetings, the operations and maintenance officers make reports. Members can bring up gripes and make suggestions. We vote on what should be carried out. There are just too many people involved for everyone to act on their own. In any group this size, specific people must be appointed to be in charge of specific areas of responsibility."

This doesn't mean there is nothing members are responsible for each time they use the plane. The log must be properly filled out, and if something is wrong enough with the plane that it should not be taken out by the next scheduled person, the maintenance officer must be contacted immediately.

Seeing that the plane has enough gas and oil for its scheduled flight as well as oil changes (when they're due) is the responsibility of the member scheduling the aircraft. When gas is not added after completion of a flight, a notation to that effect must be made by the member in the comments column of the aircraft flight time record sheet.

Before leaving the airport, members must make sure the aircraft is tied down or hangared, controls fastened with a lock or safety belt as is appropriate for the aircraft in question, doors and windows closed and locked, and the master switch turned off. Members should leave the interior as clean as they found it.

Specific rules for buying and selling memberships are described in detail in the club rules and regulations. Basically, members cannot sell their shares to outsiders; the membership reverts to the club so control over who is allowed to join can be maintained. If a member dies, his death is treated as a resignation. Any money owed him is paid to his designated beneficiary.

Nonpayment of monthly bills is dealt with in an orderly manner, too. Although the club may let a member having financial problems ride for awhile, if it is suspected he is just freeloading, he is approached by the person who keeps the books. If the delinquent amount totals 50% of his initial contribution, the member is ejected if he still doesn't pay up.

When the membership decides to buy a new plane, a committee is formed to scout out what is available in that category. They report back what they've found at the monthly meeting. Then the membership votes whether to make a purchase or not.

Capital contributions are requested to finance the purchase. For instance, ten members may put up $1,000 each, for which they get a document guaranteeing reimbursement, if the club is liquidated. Over a period of time, these investors are reimbursed by a portion of the club dues so no one member has a larger stake than another.

"We ask for capital investments from members," says Todd, "so we can keep dues at a minimum. We don't want to have to charge each member more on a regular basis in order to stockpile money."

One of the most positive things the Sundancers do is to give rudimentary flying instructions to spouses or children of members, or anyone who customarily rides with the pilot. That way, regular passengers would be able to operate the plane in case of an emergency.

They are taught what the gauges and dials mean and how to read them. They learn the emergency signal so they can call someone who will "talk them to safety." They even practice landing the plane.

"It would be awful for someone to just sit there and not know what's going on if, God forbid, the pilot had a heart attack," says Todd. "We're trying to ensure the safety of everyone."

As for the jobs some people assume in the club, Todd is philosophical about it. "Sure, some people are going to do more than others. It takes a lot of time to be treasurer or maintenance and operations officer, but no one gets paid for this or gets work credits.

"We know that some members are going to treat our planes like rental ones. We tolerate those people. But if this were the rule rather than the exception, our club wouldn't work.

"There's more to being a member than just paying bills. You have to be willing to be generous with your time."

The Sundancers' articles of incorporation state the purposes of the club—to encourage interest in private civil aviation, to educate and advance the aeronautical skills of its members, and to provide safe and convenient air transport for its members at economical rates. The liabilities and responsibilities of all members are clearly spelled out.

The regulations specify admission procedures, terms of withdrawal and reasons for membership termination, when meetings are to be held, voting procedures, how the board of directors shall be elected, and what duties the officers are charged with carrying out.

The operational rules of the club are based on those of the Federal Aviation Agency. Anyone who flies knows the FAA rules for operating a plane and must abide by them. Some people like to go a few steps further. The Sundancers have made some of their regulations even more strict.

So operating rules, as specified by the Sundancers and Uncle Sam, settle matters of safety, night flying rules, what documents must be aboard the plane during flight, how often members must be flight checked, and hundreds of others. When you and your partners write your agreement, one of the most important issues you will have to deal with is how rigorous your operational rules will be and the severity with which you will enforce them.

"The quality of the club is based on the quality of its members," Todd emphasizes. "Our club has high expectations and people live up to them. But there is a delicate balance. While we make every effort not to have an overload of rules, we still have all the safeguards we need so that if a member goes beyond responsible behavior, he can be immediately dealt with."

To draw up articles of incorporation, club rules, and operating regulations similar to the Sundancers, a group of pilots should seek an attorney with both feet firmly on the ground.

Terms such as scheduling and capital assessments can be easily molded to suit the people involved and the type of aircraft to be jointly held. But the FAA and the insurance company will have a great deal to say about how the club operates.

• • •

Gary and Nick were members of a flying club but hated the scheduling hassles. What they really wanted was a plane of their own. They got along so well they thought they'd be fine partners. Charlie, who flew with both of them as a passenger, wanted to be a partner in the deal, too, so he could own a piece of a plane and learn to fly it.

"I heard about a 1947 Aeronca Champ that was for sale, so I asked Nick and Charlie if they were interested in it," says Gary. "Both said they'd rely on my judgment. After I looked the plane over carefully, they looked at it, too. Then we decided to buy it.

"The aircraft cost $1,700 and we decided to finance it through a bank. I did all of the footwork on the deal and put the finances in a neat package. We each put up $200 and paid $40 a month on the loan.

"We wanted an economical means of transportation without scheduling problems. That's what we got."

Insurance was purchased to cover the pilot with the lowest rating. It was more costly for Gary and Nick, since Charlie was still a pilot in training, but both were content to pay the extra amount because they all got along so well. For congeniality and to have a third partner they would unquestionably trust, they figured the extra money was worth it.

All paid money into a plane bank account each month to cover expenses; each could write checks on the account, but Gary was the only one who did.

"I like to do the paperwork," says Gary. "I want to know where the partnership stands. I'm the kind of person who likes to make sure everything is done right, so I do it myself. If the others have the plane away from home base and it needs repair, they can write a check on the plane account to cover it. But this rarely happens. I maintain the flight log and do all the other paperwork, too."

After the three men spent close to $2,000 on plane maintenance in one year, they decided to tear the plane apart and rebuild it. They trailered it to Gary's mother's garage and worked on it for two years.

"Nick and I were there every Tuesday night," remembers Gary. "Charlie came whenever he could. His schedule was different than ours so he did work on the plane on his own. It was a real labor of love. We split the rebuilding costs three ways. Each of us paid $30 a month for parts—more, if we needed to.

"During this time, Nick was divorced. He had a hard time paying for a few months, so we carried him. I think that if you're scared a partner is going to stick you for money, you'd better not join up with him in the first place."

Two years after the plane was put in mint condition, Charlie "ground looped" it. The wing was caught in a cross wind—the damage amounted to $200. The insurance policy had a $250 deductible.

"Charlie wanted to pay for the damage, but the partnership paid for it," says Gary. "We divided the expense. That kind of accident could have happened to any of us.

"We don't get hung up on money in our partnership. I did the upholstery work and I didn't ask the others to pay for the materials. Nick usually buys oil for the plane and we've never paid him back for a single can. We try to fill the tank with gas after we fly as a courtesy to the next person. But if we've filled up before we land and we've flown 20 minutes into the next guy's tank of gas, we'll mark it in the log. Next time we see him, we'll tell him we owe him a lunch.

"If we have problems and we feel someone isn't pulling his weight, we'll sit down and talk it out. We don't want hard feelings to ruin our relationship. We don't want to annoy each other and be bothered with a lot of dumb little things, either."

Scheduling is done on the KISS (Keep It Simple, Stupid) principle, according to Gary.

"We start making out our schedule on the first day of January. We each have the use of the plane every three days. We mark our initials on the calendar and keep it simple. If we need the plane for several days or a week, we clear it with our partners and are free to take it."

The buy-sell agreement states partners have the first option to buy each other's shares. Partners would obtain three appraisals and average them for the fair sale price. One-third of the money plus one-third of any funds held in escrow for airplane maintenance would be paid to the exiting partner.

If a partner dies, his spouse takes over his shares, though the original partners retain first option to buy her out if she wants to sell.

In 1978, these high-flying partners decided to trade up. They bought a Cessna 172, which could fly cross-country, for $7,500. Monthly payments jumped to $75, but, according to Gary, "That's a fair price for all the pleasure we get.

"Everything has worked out fine for us. Our partnership is still going strong. In a couple of months, we're going to throw a burn-the-loan-papers party because the Cessna is just about all ours."

• • •

In his job as owner of a company that sells machine tools, Steve has a large territory to cover. He'd rather fly than drive to call on his big accounts. Currently he owns a $90,000 plane in partnership with a friend who also uses it for business. Its cost is depreciated for tax benefits because 90% of the time it is used as a business tool. For people who love airplanes, it's an exciting way to combine commerce and pleasure.

This is the third plane Steve has co-owned since 1970; each subsequent purchase has been more sophisticated and expensive. "We try to trade up each time we buy a new plane," says Steve.

"We charge ourselves so much an hour to use the aircraft. This money goes into a kitty to pay for hangar rent, insurance, maintenance, and other normally incurred expenses. If that amount isn't enough, we each add more. The manufacturer puts out a booklet that tells how to estimate operating costs. We use their figures to decide what our hourly charges will be for the plane.

"Good records are extremely important. That way there can be no misunderstandings."

A log sheet is kept in the airplane. Partners write down the date, time, and hours they fly. Once a month the sheet is taken from the plane; the hours are charged to each partner, who puts a check in the bank for that amount plus the money to cover the loan.

Steve is the banker in this partnership because he likes taking care of numbers. He keeps the maintenance invoices, writes all checks for airplane-related expenses, and then makes copies of everything, which he sends to his partner at the end of the year.

"Once a year we meet to review what has happened in the past months, to decide whether to increase the hourly charge or leave it alone," says Steve. "We give a report on the operation. I then arrange to have the work we decide on done. I guess I'm managing partner, but I enjoy the job and never feel it's a burden."

Scheduling is done according to who needs the plane for a business meeting. If there is a conflict—which is rare—the men have agreed to alternate taking a commercial flight. The plane is maintained and operated according to FAA standards and insurance provisions.

The buy-sell agreement is that one partner can buy out the other based on how much the plane is worth at the time.

These men manage their airplane partnership the way they run their offices. Each is respectful of the equipment, responsible in using it, financially impeccable, and mainly interested in being able to own and use an expensive aircraft.

There are no arguments over such issues as who put the last tank of gas in the plane or who left the cockpit a mess—that's not how these two airborne executives operate. And how they operate is an unquestionable success.

PLANE TALK

In setting up a plane partnership, the issues partners must settle—in advance—are quite like those boat partners must get clear, though the Federal Aviation Agency dictates a good percentage of the operational and maintenance procedures. Here are the main questions prospective co-owners must ask themselves:

1. How will the partnership be set up? Will shares be equal? If not, who will own how much? Will you consider incorporating?

2. How will you finance the plane?

3. How will bills be paid? Will there be a plane bank account, or will partners write personal checks to reimburse each other? Will there be monthly assessments, or will there be a charge per mile to fly the plane?

4. What standards will new members have to meet if you decide to expand your partnership? Will you admit student pilots, or must

prospective partners already have a private license? How much experience must they have to be accepted?

5. What will your safety standards be? Will you go beyond the rules and regulations required by the FAA? What operational behavior would be considered reckless by all? What actions would constitute a violation of the partnership trust and mean immediate expulsion from the group? What would the penalty be for this?

6. What kind of insurance does this group want to purchase? If hull insurance is agreed on, who pays the deductible in case of damage—the group or the person who causes the problem? How will you decide what is normal breakdown due to wear and tear versus negligence? Who is responsible for paying for what?

7. Can anyone besides partners fly the plane? If so, with whose permission? Can anyone else fly the plane while a partner is on board with him?

8. What are the distance and terrain limitations for your plane?

9. How will you schedule use of the plane—by the day, the week? What about weekends and holidays? How will you provide for a partner who wants to take the plane on vacation? For how long?

10. What happens if a partner does not bring the plane back as scheduled? Will he be penalized for inconveniencing his partners? What will the penalty be?

11. How shall the plane be maintained after each use? This includes everything from cleaning the interior to how the log book should be kept to when it should be washed and waxed.

12. Who will see that regular maintenance on the plane is performed by licensed mechanics? Who is responsible for keeping the books? Will the job be rotated? What about sweat equity—can the person who keeps the books pay less of the bills?

13. Where will the plane be kept? Will it be tied down on the field or hangared?

14. How will you make decisions about your plane? If you can't agree, will majority rule, or will you try for consensus? Will you flip a coin or seek out an arbitrator? Who will your arbitrator be?

15. What will your buy-sell agreement be? Who will appraise the fair market value of the plane to avoid fights over the dollar amount of the shares? Must a partner give due notice when he wants to get out of the partnership? How much time will be allowed for partners to come up with the money to pay him off? This

is important when bank payments must be kept up and partners must depend on each other for a steady flow of cash. Will the leaving partner be penalized for selling out and receive less than the value of his shares? What if someone can't shoulder his financial load and defaults? Will you carry him? For how long? Will there be a penalty for the hardship?

SAILPLANES

Sailplane enthusiasts say the sensation of soaring silently through the clouds is incomparable, indescribable. Floating along with the air currents without a motor is a heady experience.

So are the expenses of this sport—thus partnerships are the rule rather than the exception. These planes can cost upwards of $30,000—a lot of money for what is basically weekend excitement. Sailplanes are not used often enough for most people who wish to own one to justify the outlay.

Sailplanes are a different breed of bird from their motorized counterparts. Just getting one in the air demands a crew. A tow pilot must haul the glider up to the wild blue yonder and release it. Then, when the flight is over, the crew—which has stayed in radio contact wth the sailplane and followed it by car—arrives at the spot the pilot has landed the plane, dismantles it, places it on a trailer hooked to the car, and drives it and the pilot back to home base.

That's the way it works when there are no kinks in the operation. If the plane outflies the crew and radio contact is broken, or the crew car is not equipped with a radio, the pilot phones home base from wherever he lands and the crew members hop in a car with a glider trailer to fetch him.

Partners who own sailplanes in common crew for each other to cut down the considerable cost of having to hire people. There is a great deal of camaraderie among co-owners.

Partners can outfit their plane with more sophisticated communications equipment and instrumentation—a decided plus.

Because sailplane partnering demands more cooperation and togetherness than other airplane partnerships, is more sport than solid transportation, I'm treating it separately from motorized aircraft partnerships in this chapter.

Because the Caesar Creek Soaring Club in Waynesville, Ohio, is such a unique example, it's being examined in detail. Here sailplane aficionados actually bought land and set up their own private gliderport—in partnership. If having your own airport is a secret dream, you can certainly learn from this example.

But before we dive into how you can set up your own gliderport, let's first see how you can own a piece of your own sailplane.

Keep Your Feet on the Ground

Bob Root and Mel Williams are members of the Caesar Creek Soaring Club; both are veteran partners in sailplanes, though not with each other. In fact, there are only a couple of privately held planes in their whole club. Most are owned by at least four people. Based on Bob and Mel's long-standing experience with sailplane partnerships, the following are some co-ownership suggestions.

1. Partners must have the skills to fly the *specific* sailplane they will own in common. "Some are like driving a Ferrari," agree Bob and Mel. "If someone is more used to flying a Chevy, there is bound to be trouble. Partners must be familiar and comfortable with the equipment in question and with each other's flying prowess."

2. "It's a big help if partners have technical skills," says Bob. "There's painting, patching, instruments to install, tires to repair on sailplanes. Major repairs are generally performed by FAA-licensed mechanics, and work done to the plane must be inspected by them. But if partners are handy, they can save money.

"One of my partners can weld, so we put together our own trailer. We ended up with one worth about $1,000 for an investment of a couple of hundred."

3. Financial responsibility is important. Partners must be able to handle their share of expenses. If one hits hard times and has to sell his portion, it's a good idea for partners to have provided for this in advance. Enough notice should be given so partners can find another. And partners should have a decent amount of time to come up with money if they have to buy the troubled partner's shares.

A default clause should be considered (see the vehicle chapter).

4. Many sailplane owners incorporate their joint venture as protection against liability. Mel, a lawyer, helps many soaring pilots put together the necessary legal work for a ride in their plane. That is definitely a friendly price—all partners have to pay is an Ohio State filing fee of $25.

If a friendly price isn't available to you, investigate, with an attorney, how much it will cost to incorporate and if it is worth it.

5. Partners should decide how they are going to accept their collective risk. Liability insurance is mandatory. Hull insurance, which covers damage to the plane in flight, can run to 10% of the cost of the plane each year. "This is why," emphasize Bob and Mel, "many partnerships decide not to buy it. They simply make an agreement that if anyone demolishes the plane, everyone takes their lumps."

Another alternative to hull insurance is to agree on a figure a partner will pay—let's say it's the first few hundred dollars—in case there is damage to the plane; the partnership agrees to split the rest, no matter whose fault the accident is. No partner is stuck with a huge bill even if he caused the problem. (Of course, if he causes too many problems, too often, his partnership will be terminated.)

"The corporation or partnership can vote to sell the assets and start all over without the accident-prone aviator," says Bob. "A partnership can vote to share damage any way they wish. If there is hull insurance, partners can agree that the one who causes the damage pays the deductible. The cost of comprehensive insurance, which covers such things as wind or storm damage to planes tied down on the field, is shared by everyone."

6. Partners should decide whether they will accept students as new partners or only those who already have a pilot's license.

7. Personal compatibility is important. If partners are going to crew together, they must get along. Crewing is not only work, it's a social event for people who enjoy each other.

8. Scheduling should be equitable, since weekends are prime time. If the plane is taken by one partner with permission of the other partners to a contest in a distant city (this is a big part of the sport), he should give up prime time days equal to the number of prime time days the plane was away.

Bob remembers, "In one partnership, a man flew the plane from Cincinnati to Indianapolis and left it there. He got a ride home but not one for his sailplane. The next day, when it was another partner's turn to fly, the first partner told him, 'Well you can take the plane up today, but you'll have to go to Indianapolis to do it.' That didn't sit too well with any of us."

There is an excellent free booklet available that can help you put together a sailplane partnership. Recognizing the trend to co-ownership, *Shipmates: How to Spread the Fun and Costs of Owning a Sailplane through Group Ownership*, was drawn up by the Schweizer Aircraft Corporation, a respected maker of sailplanes. It is available by writing to P.O. Box 147, Elmira, NY 14902. Besides offering practical advice on creating a partnership, it contains a sample sailplane ownership partnership agreement you can use as an example in drawing up yours. It covers how to divide expenses, obtain insurance, handle expenses and how the plane should be operated, scheduled, and more.

Using this agreement as a base should cut attorney's fees, should you decide to consult one, since he won't have to start from scratch. The agreement can also be modified to suit members who wish to incorporate.

The Sky's the Limit

On to the Caesar's Creek Soaring Club and their private gliderport! Over 175 enthusiasts from the Cincinnati-Dayton and surrounding areas bought their own airport in partnership. The club first operated out of a municipal airport, but members wanted a gliderport of their own. To make it happen, the group formed a corporation in which they sold stock. In 1969, the Soaring Society of Dayton bought an 88-acre farm (subsequently more land was purchased; the current total is 146 acres), which they turned not only into a gliderport but also camping, fishing, and recreation facilities for their families.

For an initiation fee of $300, monthly dues of $8, and $1,200 for 12 shares of the stock (you can pay this in one fell swoop or $10 a month at 10% interest), you become an owner/member entitled to the full range of benefits. Members receive their $1,200 back when they sell their stock and leave the club. Members may buy a maximum of 20 shares to prevent any member from gaining control.

Active participation of club members makes it possible for people to operate gliders for much less than if they had to hire their own tow pilot and crew. Each member serves one day per month as a weekend crew member; crews consist of two tow pilots, two instructors, a radio operator, two or three handlers, and a crew chief.

Members pay for their flying based on a tow charge of $6 for a 2,000-foot tow and $2.50 for the use of the club glider, with no charge for instructions if they are needed. Members who own their own gliders pay only the tow fee and a tie-down charge for keeping their plane on club facilities.

Mel and Bob estimate the cost of getting a glider in the air through a commercial facility at about $30 to $50—quite a savings over $8.50 (at minimum) every time you want to fly.

If club partners cannot serve as crew members, their tow charge increases, but those who don't crew are not favorites in this association. Participation is the mainstay of the group.

Flight scheduling is pretty informal. When you get to the field on a given day, you put your name on the list and wait your turn for an hour's flying time. No reservations can be made in advance, so if you really want to fly on a particular day, you set your alarm clock and get there early.

"There is very little concern with people's social status in this club," Mel asserts. "We care about flying here. Members are accepted on the basis that they want to fly and can pay the charges. Student pilots make up a large percentage of new members because they join the club to learn."

The Caesar's Creek Soaring Club Board of Trustees, elected annually, handles club business and sets policy, subject to members' approval.

"We have very few arguments and people generally get along," says Mel. "Most of us feel like it is a privilege to belong. After all, who could afford to own their own gliderport?"

Flight instructors and crew chiefs have complete authority over members' flying methods. If a member makes a bad approach, a crew chief talks to him about it in a constructive manner. If someone was flying recklessly, a crew chief can, and will, ground him until he gets some friendly instruction on how things are done.

Rules and regulations are based on Federal Aviation Agency standards, but the club has made theirs even more stringent in many areas. This is why.

The club owns about $150,000 worth of gliders and airplanes on which they carry no hull insurance, just liability. Every member who joins must understand the philosophy: "If we lose a glider, we all share the loss. There is a great deal of peer pressure to fly right. There is a terrific amount of esprit de corps and pride in what the club stands for."

If a glider or anything else the club owns is damaged, the corporation pays for it. This includes diesel tractors for mowing grass, tractors to pull gliders around, the clubhouse, and campgrounds where members can bring trailers.

How do jobs get done? People who feel like doing them simply do them. Some members enjoy mowing, some like maintenance, some serve as crew members. Going out to the club and grounds on weekends to work is part of the whole soaring hobby.

But before members use any particular piece of equipment to do a job, they must be checked out in the operation of it. Someone who knows how to run a tractor in an expert fashion will make sure a newcomer knows what he is doing.

Bob says, chuckling, "If any member suggests to others how he'd like specific things to be done, that qualifies him for the committee—or at least, first in line to do it. It's the tremendous involvement of members that keeps the club successful."

Club members are justly proud of their accomplishments. They are also willing to share information, so if you would like to tap into the energy of this group to fuel yours, write to Caesar's Creek Soaring Club, 5385 Elbon Road, Waynesville, OH 45068.

·13·
How to Find a House Partner

Powerful forces draw people to share living space: loneliness; friendship; the death of someone close; divorce; a common social, political, or religious commitment; a financial squeeze.

The needs of people who join together shape the type of arrangement they create. And create they do—with wit and ingenuity—amazingly unique places to call home. Whether to salve, soothe, shore up, or cement, shared housing is flexible enough to embrace almost any imaginable circumstance.

This chapter will present a galaxy of bold, inventive people who have turned to partnering homes as a solution and a way of life. From their triumphs and their setbacks, you will learn how shared living can be a strong choice for you.

But first you will have to find the right partner. You learned a lot about search techniques, from where to pin up notices to making an agreement, in earlier chapters. All of that also applies to matching up with a house partner on the same wave length you are. But for this you need even more information.

Sharing living space brings people close together day in and day out. You're going to have to know more about your partner's values, lifestyle, habits, and friends because you're going to *live* with them. He has to hold up his end of the partnership financially—without question. You're going to have to like him, because if you don't, no matter how grand a place you are able to afford partnering, life will be miserable.

Look in any bookstore and you'll find shelves devoted to advice on the tricky business of romantic pairups. A whole literature has developed to help couples get along. A good book with no-nonsense legal advice is the *Living Together Kit,* written by attorneys Toni Ihara and Ralph Warner (Berkeley: Nolo Press, 1978, 1979).

Sharing a home for other reasons isn't as difficult as more passionate arrangements. But there *is* a lot to think about before you plunge in. Let's start with home-sharing counseling services.

HOME-SHARING COUNSELING SERVICES

As house sharing has grown in popularity, house sharing counseling services have mushroomed accordingly. For people who want to circumvent the process of placing notices and advertisements and interviewing prospective partners themselves, these agencies can be extremely helpful because this is exactly what they do for you. But in this field, as in most others, there are A-plus performers, those whose practices fall below acceptable standards, and some that hover somewhere in between. If you wish to employ an agency, the following will help you choose one intelligently, and understand what to expect from them.

Most home-sharing agencies match people who need to share residences on a temporary basis, generally when or until something changes in their lives. A newly divorced person needs a place to live, or a newly divorced person is left with a house and a mortgage he can't pay; a graduate student has to find a flat for a couple of years; young professionals want to share the rent until one of them is transferred or gets married—these are typical clients. The staff of matching agencies I spoke to do not bring together people who want to buy homes together; they match those who need a place to live to those who already have a home and want someone to share it. *How* they go about the process of matching is what you need to pay attention to.

Some matching agencies are run as commercial ventures and some are publicly funded. Private agencies have to turn a profit to stay in business and generally survive by matching self-sufficient, mobile people who want to share but who won't be devastated if the match doesn't survive. If things don't work out for them, they can move. Private agencies charge a flat fee or bill on a sliding scale in line with the rent charged and the rent to be paid, and the fee—according to every agency owner I interviewed—is nonrefundable. Most will provide the matching service for two or three months for the initial money paid, and if the first match doesn't work out within this time (guaranteed in the contract), they will help make another.

Public agencies generally wind up matching those people private agencies can't afford to spend time working with—the elderly, the handicapped, and those with low incomes who require more effort and often additional support services. Matches for the elderly or handicapped tend to be more permanent, so they take more energy to put together. Many of these agencies like to take an intergenerational approach with their clients, making arrangements for people of all ages to live together.

According to Dennis Day-Lower, it currently costs a public agency $150-$450 to match clients; the average is $200-$250. The higher figures mean more assistance in home interviews—even transporting clients to homes for face-to-face meetings. More straightforward referrals involve simpler interviews and reference checking and cost less.

These figures were arrived at by the Shared Housing Resource Center from studying operating budgets of matching agencies all over the country. Since most private agencies charge somewhere from $50 to $125 per match, you can see why they cannot afford to spend unlimited time tending to clients.

This is exactly why a number of private agencies appear on the scene with high hopes of making a healthy profit and fade quickly as they find they cannot produce matches fast enough to stay in business.

This does not mean that all public agencies are better than private ones; it does mean that public agencies generally have more time to be sensitive to the needs of the people they serve. But note that even public agencies have to show success in the number of people they match to be refunded. In any event, no matter what agency you choose, it is up to you to be a smart consumer. Make sure you consider the following carefully before you employ any of them.

Check It Out

1. Ask how long the agency has been in business. Then check to see if complaints have been lodged against them with the Better Business Bureau or your local consumer protection agency. This will help ensure that you don't pay a fee to a here-today, gone-today operator or one that has a poor business reputation.

2. Describe yourself to the person on the phone (for example, "I am in my mid-thirties, divorced, with a six-year-old child and want to share a house within a few blocks of a bus stop with a person who has no children of his own but who would be kind to mine. His age doesn't matter.") and ask how many people are on file who would be prospective matches. If the person answers quickly, "Oh dozens!" without checking, be wary.

To be really meticulous, invent a hard case. An example would be the following: "My lame great-grandmother with three dogs and two cats wants a housemate." If the reply you receive is in the line of: "We don't have people available right now, but we'd be willing to try even though the chances are slim," or "We may have a person in mind," or "I'm sorry, we just can't help you," you're getting a reasonable and responsible answer. If the person on the phone still insists he has many people in his files who would love to double up with your great-grandmother, stay away.

3. Does the person you are talking to seem concerned with your needs? Ask how much time he will spend interviewing you when you come to the office. (The average for many concerned agencies is 45 minutes to an hour.) Some agencies will ask you to come in, fill out a brief questionnaire asking your vital statistics, if you smoke, have a pet, maintain late hours, like to party—and call it a day. Some will want to take your photo to pin to the questionnaire as part of the matching process, though many private agencies and most public ones avoid this practice. Matching by photo can smack of being a dating service, and many agencies are afraid of being placed in that category. If you pick someone to live with according to how he looks, you're making a surface choice. Shouldn't you be concerned more with intangibles?

Find an agency that brings people together through extensive interviews rather than superficial questionnaires and photos of people they keep on file.

4. Ask what questions you will be presented with during your interview to see if they sound reasonable. You should be prepared to answer questions about your space requirements, living habits, and reliability—not more intimate preferences.

5. When you meet the interviewer in person, how does he strike you? What is your gut feeling? Is he the kind of person you think you can rely on? Most nonprofit agencies are staffed with social service personnel; some private agency personnel are former social workers now in private business; some have no training at all. But don't discount all matchmakers who are untrained in social

service. Some I talked to were just as professional and caring—they had been through the process of finding roommates themselves in the face of economic problems and were completely sympathetic to what their clients were going through. Some were in it for the fee only. You are placing yourself in someone's hands, so be sure you feel good about them.

6. Ask how long you think placement will take. Based on your expectations and preferences (you should be clear, specific, and not change your mind every two days, so the agency can help you expeditiously), a good agency should be able to give you a realistic idea of the period you must wait.

7. Ask how the agency checks references. Who do they call, and how thorough are they? Some check employers, at least two character references (be sure they aren't just good friends), the current landlord or roommate. Make sure you are satisfied with their screening process.

8. Ask if they will provide you with names of satisfied clients. Some will do this unhesitatingly; some will protest that they don't want to constantly bother past clients with this request. That can be a valid response, but does it *sound* like a dodge?

9. What services does the agency provide? These can range anywhere from visits to prospective home sharers to the offer to go along on first meetings to help smooth introductions. This may be more assistance than you require. You may simply want names of prospective housemates and are perfectly capable of taking it from there on your own. But if you do require more support, will it be there if you need it?

10. What follow-up is there? Make sure you understand the period of time the service is rendered for the fee involved (remember, it is generally nonrefundable) and if you can come back within that period for assistance if the match isn't working out. Some will help work out troubles; most will try to provide another roommate. Be sure you know what you can expect for your money.

11. Find out what your responsibilities will be. It is unrealistic to think the agency can do everything for you, because the process of finding a roommate is two-sided. Ask how many times a week you will be expected to check in to see if a prospective roommate has been located or whether they will phone you. Remember, matching agencies will provide you with names of prospective roommates; it is up to you to interview them and finalize the match.

12. Expect to sign an agreement that states the service you are

employing will furnish referrals for residence sharing but does not guarantee placement, that gives the service the right to reveal information you provide to persons it considers prospective roommates, and that the responsibility for the selection of the final roommate will be yours. Some agreements contain even more stipulations about the services to be rendered and who is liable for what. Make sure you understand completely what you sign and that you're happy with it.

First Meetings Through an Agency

When matching services come up with names of clients they feel would be compatible, they relay these to the prospective pair. The agency has already checked references, knows what type of person each client is seeking as a partner, where they live, and what accommodations are preferred. This information is also passed along so that clients have a feel for each other's needs before they even talk to each other. This helps immensely.

The clients then phone each other and decide whether they are interested enough to set up a meeting. To protect the privacy and safety of their clients, generally only first names and phone numbers are given out by agencies in case either party wants to avoid meeting the other.

Although there is comfort in knowing that an agency's reference-checking provides an element of security for prospective partners, many counselors encourage female clients not to interview males alone at the initial meeting. Women should take someone with them if they are going to a man's house, should have someone with them if a man is coming to their house, or meet in a restaurant or some other mutually agreeable public place. There is never a guarantee that any person you interview—even one screened by an agency—doesn't have a motive, not in your best interests, in mind. Even though most agencies feel disreputable people stay away from reference-checking interviewers—and you must have a trusting nature to be a good partner—that doesn't include being foolish. Man or woman: Don't take chances with your safety.

Agency personnel commonly recommend a minimum of two meetings before people decide to move in together. The first is generally to look at the residence, a general introductory meeting that helps the potential partners decide if they like each other. The second should be purposely informal. You may want to go out to dinner together, play tennis, do something active to break down barriers and relax you. Then you should be able to really talk about the issues that are important to you. Be frank and specific. Talk about everything from your love life to your eating habits. (A questionnaire to help you with this is coming up.) Based on this kind of conversation, you will be able to decide whether living together is a possibility.

HOW TO DO IT ON YOUR OWN

If you haven't used an agency to help you find a house partner, you must do more of your own screening and be even more careful. It's a good idea to conduct your first meeting someplace other than your home. Before you give the person who noticed your name posted at the food co-op your address and show him your home, be sure you want to show it to him. If the caller protests that this is too much bother—that he'd really like to come to your house to meet you and seems unreasonable or too impatient about your outside-the-home first meeting—I'd be wary of him as a partner. Don't feel pushed into accommodating someone else and compromise what you feel is best for you. That's a terrible beginning.

Another reason not to hold the initial meeting in the home or apartment to be shared, if one person already lives there, is to eliminate power plays. The person who wishes to move in with you (if you own the home) knows a lot about you immediately—your taste, what kind of housekeeper you are, your level of affluence are apparent. You know only what the visitor tells you—and he can tell you anything he thinks you'd like to hear based on what he sees. You do not want to dominate the person you are interviewing by setting yourself up as "the landlord," unless that is exactly what your role will be. (More about this later.) But if your intentions are to make "my house" "our house," get to know each other first on common ground.

When matching agency personnel go along on first meetings, it helps put everyone at ease. And when one person wants to partner with someone who doesn't want him, the agency interviewer can generally think up a face-saving excuse so the interested person won't feel rejected. Leah Dobkin, educational director of the Shared Housing Resource Center, puts it bluntly to clients. "If it's not right for both of you, it's going to be hell for you when you move in."

Ask the Right Questions—the Right Way

The first time you get together to discuss house sharing, ask questions that don't intimidate the person you are talking to but still provide answers that are revealing.

Linda Nunes-Schrag finds it relaxes the person she is interviewing for The Life Center to talk a little about herself first, but she
advises not overdoing this. "Otherwise," she says, "it can backfire.
The person begins to wonder why this other person is telling me all
this stuff about herself. Talk about yourself only as a means of making
it easy for your prospective partner to talk about himself."

Linda asks what the person likes to do in his spare time. This
question will usually be answered readily because it doesn't seem to
lead to any big issue. But it does. If the person barhops all night or is a
movie freak, that tells you a lot. Does he play chess or with pistols?

Talk about the kind of places you like to travel. Does the person
you are talking to love to camp in the mountains (as you do) or prefer
Disneyland?

Linda says a question she now includes in interviews is what the
person uses as an outlet for conflict. Does he do yoga, jog, bang his
head against the wall, or see a therapist? She just wants to make sure
the person she is talking to has some way to vent frustrations other
than on the person he is going to live with.

Linda also likes to ask whether she may ask a personal question.
She states up front that the person doesn't have to answer it, she
doesn't want to upset him, but asks it anyway. (You decide what question to ask based on the situation.) The way the person answers gives
Linda her answer. An edgy, reluctant response leads her to believe the
person is uptight. The more open the response, Linda feels, the more
open the person.

"Talk about how you live," many home-sharing counselors urge.
Say things like, "When I get up in the morning, I usually make my bed
because it bothers me to come home and see it unmade. But sometimes when I'm running late, I may not. What do you do?" You are giving your prospective partner permission to be imperfect. He will
express his own feelings more easily. Home sharers have to discuss
frankly as much as they can and agree on the rules of the house—together. Unilateral pronouncements such as, "I expect you to make
your bed every morning because I do" is an immediate turnoff.

One last tip from Linda Nunes-Schrag: If she is conducting the
interview in the home where the person will be living, she asks him
what he would like to change if he lived there. "Look around," she
says. "Imagine how you would relocate the furniture or redecorate, if
we decided to do that."

She wants to see if he will think for himself, have an opinion and
not be afraid to express it. If he says, "Oh everything is fine. I wouldn't
change anything," Linda wonders about that. "I don't want to live

with anyone who expects me to do all the thinking for him," she says.

Some Important Preliminaries

Home sharers have to be sure they are sharing for the same reasons, and these should be made clear in the initial meetings. A person who wants to have meals with someone, have somebody to go to the movies with on the spur of the moment—who is sharing for companionship—should say so. If another wants a purely "split the rent and let's go our separate ways" lifestyle, they should say so. If they don't, the partnership doesn't last long.

Matching values is as important as matching needs. If one partner looks at the oak floors of an old brownstone and says, "Wall-to-wall carpeting would make this place look terrific" and the other can't wait to refinish the floors because that's one of the reasons he loves the house, their radar should be picking up nonpartnering blips. Shopping together, especially for those who are buying homes, is essential.

So is checking out your partner's financial state of affairs. You don't want to be stuck with his half of the rent, let alone his half of the mortgage payments. Supply each other with credit information and references to prove that you can pay the bills.

Leah Dobkin urges potential home sharers to visit each other's homes or apartments, spend a few weekends or at least a week together. Take a trip. Take on a work project together. Even better, go camping.

When two people are pitching a tent in the rain, have to tote water to the campsite from a pump or a spring a quarter of a mile away, cook dinner over an open fire and discover half the ingredients have been forgotten, tempers can flare. You learn a lot about someone's true personality—more than you would by staying together at a hotel and getting piqued over slow room service.

One home sharer who did go camping with her prospective housemate and the woman's three children said it was this experience that convinced them they would be able to live together.

"I screamed at one of the kids when he knocked over the container filled with all of our drinking water," Kate remembers. "His mother knew I was a screamer and all the kids found that out, too. They later saw that I wouldn't stay mad long, so it bothered them less. They also knew they could climb up on my lap after dinner and I'd read them a story.

"We were all happy with each other. I don't have children of my own so it was important to me to find out what kind of kids I'd be living with and how I'd react to them. Going camping was a great partnering preliminary for us."

Many people who are in a rush to move in with each other don't bother with any of this, but they should. Most home placement counselors agree that the "honeymoon" period is three months. Leah says she can generally predict who will be on the phone with what problem three months after a placement. After this magic time, people generally stop tiptoeing around each other. Politeness falls by the wayside as irksome issues are no longer overlooked but met head on. True personalities become apparent.

Even after being told a three-month trial is better than a full-fledged commitment, people are in a hurry to get situated. They look at the things they clearly have in common (we like the same music, neither of us smoke, both of us are early risers) and double up. Doing it this way is dangerous.

OWNING UP

During this "getting to know your partner" period, you must ask each other candid questions about living habits and attitudes, difficult though this is. There is no way around it.

You have to know—before you move in together—whether your prospective partner intends to bring along a live-in lover, whether his idea of relaxing in the evening is getting stoned, and whether having a great-looking wardrobe means helping himself to your clothes.

In interviews with partners and partnering experts issues like these are the hot ones. They must be faced, talked over, decided on, and dispatched, because if you ignore them or gloss over their importance—so say veteran partners—your alliance may end up in smithereens.

To help you get all of these matters out into the open, I have made up a nonthreatening questionnaire that will shed good-natured light on how you and your partner feel and think about a great many things.

"But I like my partner," you say. "I know enough about him already. So I don't like some of his friends. I don't need to know the history of his life before we decide to buy a house together. I don't feel like bothering with another questionnaire."

Just remember, when his friends—the ones you're not so keen on, the ones you didn't know partied until 3:00 most mornings— have become permanent fixtures in the new house you bought with your friend, you'll wish you had spent more time learning about how he spends his leisure hours *before* you made the joint purchase.

Why wait until it's too late to learn you can't stand living with someone who thinks it's too hot indoors when the thermostat reads 60 degrees in February—in Nebraska? Before you invest in thermal underwear and fleece-lined slippers, fill in the following blanks, check the answers appropriate to you, or answer yes or no. Then compare your responses to your prospective partner's. This will help you measure yourself and each other.

You may agree on the points that are vital to both of you. The matters you disagree on may be of little importance and possibly won't affect how you feel about going forward. On the other hand, you two (or three or four) might find out you're just not *simpático.*

Honestly discuss how you feel about the replies to this questionnaire and decide whether a house will be big enough for both of you.

DOUBLE OR NOTHING MATCHUP QUESTIONNAIRE

Cleanliness

1. Thorough cleaning should be done _____.
   a) weekly b) monthly c) annually d) _____

   Develop your own definition of thorough cleaning. It can mean vacuuming and scrubbing on hands and knees to one person and an occasional, casual dusting to another. Be specific.

   _____
   _____
   _____
   _____
   _____
   _____
   _____

2. Dishes should be done _____.
   a) immediately after every meal
   b) once a day c) when you run out of clean dishes d) _____

3. Newspapers, magazines, record albums, books strewn on sofas, tables, and floors make me _____.
   a) crazy b) comfortable c) who cares? d) _____

4. The bathtub and sink should be cleaned out after _____ use(s).
   a) every b) every three c) you name it _____

5. The refrigerator and oven should be cleaned _____.
   a) once a week b) once a month
   c) when the Health Department declares them off limits d) _____

6. Unmade beds _____.
   a) bother me b) are all right as long as they're not in my room
   c) I haven't made my bed since 1962 d) _____

7. As long as the space used in common in the house is kept orderly _____ what the other person's private space is like.
   a) I don't care b) I do care

8. Wastebaskets and kitchen garbage must be emptied _____.
   a) daily b) whenever it overflows c) whenever I think about it

9. I don't want the responsibility of cleaning, and would like to share the cost of a maid or cleaning service which would clean once a week.
   a) agree _____ b) disagree _____

10. Each partner should be responsible for his own laundry.
    a) yes _____ b) no _____

11. Write out any other cleaning issues that are important to you. Think about everything from emptying ashtrays to cleaning out the garage.

    _____
    _____
    _____
    _____
    _____
    _____

Music

1. I like classical music only.
   a) yes _____ b) no _____

2. I like rock only.
   a) yes _____ b) no _____

3. I like _____ music.

4. I like anything that isn't blaring.
   a) yes _____ b) no _____

5. I like no music.
   a) yes _____ b) no _____

6. I want music confined to private spaces. Music played in common spaces is intrusive and the listener should use earphones.
   a) yes _____ b) no _____

7. I like music all the time to keep me company.
   a) yes _____ b) no _____

8. Music isn't an issue.
   a) yes _____ b) no _____

9. Whoops, I forgot to tell you. I'm taking trumpet lessons. I practice when the spirit moves me.
   a) yes _____ b) no _____

10. State any music instruments you play and when.
    _____
    _____

Television

1. Television sets in common living areas _____.
   a) are fine b) drive me wild if played when I want to read
   c) can be played if the viewer uses earphones so I can't hear it
   d) should be destroyed

2. I like to flake out on the living room couch after dinner and watch television until I go to bed.
   a) yes _____ b) no _____

3. Sunday sports on television with food spread out all over the living room is my idea of heaven.
   a) yes _____ b) no _____

4. _____ watching television with someone else.
   a) I like b) I hate

5. Watching late night television is _____.
   a) fine b) terrible
   c) doesn't bother me if it's in someone else's room, kept low

6. I _____ morning television.
   a) like b) hate

7. Television sets should be in private spaces and there should be two so there are no fights about shows.
   a) yes _____ b) no _____

8. If there is only one set, we should alternate _____ in deciding what to watch.
   a) days b) hours c) weeks

9. Guts and gore are what I like the best.
   a) yes _____ b) no _____
10. I only watch the educational stations.
    a) yes _____ b) no _____
11. I _____ to spend money on cable, ON TV, Beta Max, Home Box Office, video games, or anything else electronic.
    a) want b) do not want

Sex

1. I am _____ .
   a) heterosexual b) gay c) bisexual d) celibate
2. Sex without marriage is _____ .
   a) a sin b) great c) not an issue that concerns me
3. I believe in _____ .
   a) one relationship at a time
   b) the more men or women in your life the better
4. Promiscuity upsets me.
   a) yes _____ b) no _____
   What is your definition of promiscuity?

   _____

   _____

   _____

5. Finding someone strange in the kitchen or bathroom in the morning

   _____.
   a) doesn't bother me b) freaks me out
6. Overnight lovers _____.
   a) should be cleared with me first so I can be somewhere else
   b) don't bother me c) are not an issue
7. Overnight lovers are O.K. once in a while, but not every weekend.
   a) yes _____ b) no _____
   My definition of once in a while is:

   _____

8. If my partner had a permanent live-in friend on the premises, should a relationship develop, _____.
   a) I'd ask them both to leave b) I wouldn't mind
9. Discretion is my main concern. Sex is not the issue.
   a) yes _____ b) no _____

The Others in Your Life

1. I belong to Hell's Angels and on Saturday nights we meet at my place to tear it apart.
   a) yes _____ b) no _____

2. Prayer breakfasts, three times a week at my house, are the most important events in my life.
   a) yes _____ b) no _____

3. Seriously now, you'll probably fall somewhere in between these two examples. Please describe the people who are most likely to drop over, visit for a weekend, or be with you frequently at your home.
   _____
   _____
   _____
   _____

4. When people visit, I would probably _____ with them.
   a) talk b) have a drink c) watch television d) play cards
   e) blast the stereo f) get drunk g) you name it _____

5. I _____ my partner's relatives, friends, or children from a previous marriage visiting on a regular basis. We should agree in advance on how long they can stay and the extra money my partner should contribute to entertain them.
   a) don't mind b) do mind

6. If any homeless or in-trouble friend or relative turns up on the doorstep, they _____ stay until they get back on their feet.
   a) can b) cannot
   How long? _____
   _____

7. Halfway houses are not my responsibility. "Overnight and out" is my motto. Better yet, don't come at all.
   a) yes _____ b) no _____

8. I like to have people around all the time.
   a) yes _____ b) no _____

9. I need a good deal of time to be alone. Enjoying my home without people running in and out all the time is important to me.
   a) yes _____ b) no _____

10. I want to be included in my partner's parties.
    a) yes _____ b) no _____

11. I want my partner to disappear if I have guests for the evening.
    a) yes _____ b) no _____

12. Formal parties are how I like to entertain.
    a) yes _____ b) no _____
13. I like casual parties with lots of people all over the place.
    a) yes _____ b) no _____
14. A few people and serious conversation constitute my ideal evening.
    a) yes _____ b) no _____
15. Think through your other people-related preferences and write them below.

    _____
    _____
    _____
    _____

Children

1. I _____ partner with someone who has children.
   a) would like to b) would never
2. I have children and want to share with someone who _____.
   a) has children so we can help each other with child care chores
   b) doesn't have children but who would like to babysit for mine some evenings
   c) is tolerant of children
3. I don't have children but would share with someone who does as long as they are _____.
   a) under 10 b) teenagers c) past adolescence d) specify_____
4. When I am angry at my children, I _____.
   a) scream at them b) sit down and talk calmly, in a low voice
   c) run into my room and slam the door
5. I would partner with someone who has children as long as _____.
   a) they are not my responsibility
   b) I can share in their lives and discipline
6. Under what circumstances would you share with someone with children? Be specific. _____
   _____
   _____

7. If you have children, how involved should your housemate be with them? Be specific. _____
   _____
   _____
   _____

Money

1. I'd like to keep money for household expenses _____.
a) in a joint kitty b) in a house bank account
c) to myself and pay for everything separately

2. I want all expenses _____.
a) split down the middle. b) kept track of meticulously so we know who spent how much for what

3. I _____
a) always keep track of every penny I spend b) am always broke at the end of the week and never know where my money has gone.

4. I _____ keeping household accounts.
a) hate b) enjoy c) I've never balanced a checkbook in my life and don't intend to start now

5. Running a house costs money. That's one of the reasons you're sharing, right? What method do you see you and your housemate using to divvy expenses and keep accounts? _____

_____

_____

_____

_____

Booze, Dope, and Smoke

1. I don't drink and I will not have liquor in the house.
a) yes _____ b) no _____

2. Social drinking is fine with me and I like to have a drink before dinner.
a) yes _____ b) no _____

3. I don't drink but I don't care if anyone else does as long as it's not to excess.
a) yes _____ b) no _____

4. When I relax at night, my kind of relaxation includes scotch, gin, or bourbon.
a) yes _____ b) no _____

5. Getting drunk on Saturday night and coming home plowed and singing at 4 a.m. is my idea of a great time.
a) yes _____ b) no _____

6. Drugs—all kinds—are out.
a) yes _____ b) no _____

7. I don't want heavy drugs around, but marijuana and other "recreational

drugs" occasionally, are O.K.
a) yes _____ b) no _____

8. I don't care about drugs; it's the other person's business.
a) yes _____ b) no _____

9. I like to try all kinds of drugs and want to live with someone else who does, too.
a) yes _____ b) no _____

10. I like to have a joint now and then and would hate to have someone around to hassle me.
a) yes _____ b) no _____

11. No cigarette, pipe, or cigar smoking anywhere in the house.
a) yes _____ b) no _____

12. If guests come to the house, they may not smoke. Tell everyone beforehand to leave their cigarettes at home or smoke outside.
a) yes _____ b) no _____

13. I prefer to live with someone who doesn't smoke but would never offend a guest who did.
a) yes _____ b) no _____

14. I smoke and don't intend to quit. The person who lives with me should leave me alone about it.
a) yes _____ b) no _____

15. I would feel comfortable with a restricted smoking area in the house. Let's talk about it.
a) yes _____ b) no _____

Modesty

1. I walk around the house _____.
a) nude b) half-dressed c) always fully dressed

2. I think people who sit around all day in their robe _____.
a) are disgusting b) look comfortable

3. If anyone barges into the bathroom while I'm in there I _____.
a) don't appreciate it b) just keep brushing my teeth

4. Someone who undresses while they tell me the events of the day would _____.
a) embarrass me b) not bother me a bit

5. I believe in modesty at all costs.
a) yes _____ b) who cares? _____

Odors

1. Odors such as frying food, paint, glue, and perfume bother me. I either spray room freshener or open windows to eliminate them.
a) yes _____ b) no _____

2. Incense _____.
a) is something I like to use occasionally
b) is something I use frequently
c) makes me feel like throwing up

Schedules

1. I usually arise at _____ a.m. and _____ the early morning hours.
a) look forward to b) dread

2. I go to bed at _____ p.m. and am a _____ sleeper.
a) restless b) sound

3. I'm a night person and from midnight on is when I like to clean out the refrigerator or catch up on reading.
a) yes _____ b) no _____

4. I sleep until noon on the weekends and want peace and quiet.
a) yes _____ b) no _____

5. Weekends are times to do the errands and chores. Up and running is the way I look at it.
a) yes _____ b) no _____

6. I want my partner to have about the same job hours and sleeping patterns as I do so we will not disturb each other.
a) yes _____ b) no _____

7. I don't care about another person's schedule as long as he is careful not to disturb me.
a) yes _____ b) no _____

Punctuality

1. I am _____.
a) always late b) usually punctual c) generally unaware of the time

2. If I'm late _____.
a) I phone ahead to let people know when I can be expected
b) I forget to call because I'm tied up in a meeting

3. I _____ if I have to wait a short while (five or ten minutes) for some-one.
   a) get angry b) don't care

4. When a meeting is set _____.
   a) it bothers me if the time has to be constantly changed
   b) I am generally agreeable if the time has to be altered
   c) I get furious if someone doesn't show up

Temperament

1. When I come home from work, I need about an hour to myself before I want to talk to anyone. I'm not angry, I just need to decompress.
   a) yes _____ b) no _____

2. When I get home, I want someone to talk to.
   a) yes _____ b) no _____

3. I don't talk much and having someone constantly chatter at me would drive me up the wall.
   a) yes _____ b) no _____

4. I am quiet, so having someone lively around would cheer me up.
   a) yes _____ b) no _____

5. I am happy-go-lucky and want a live-and-let-live type to share with.
   a) yes _____ b) no _____

6. I live a quiet life and want to share with someone who does the same.
   a) yes _____ b) no _____

7. When I am angry, I become silent and sulk.
   a) yes _____ b) no _____

8. I get angry fast, say what I think right away, and forget about it five min-utes later.
   a) yes _____ b) no _____

9. If someone yells at me, I yell back, or if he makes me mad enough, I might just slap him around.
   a) yes _____ b) no _____

10. I'm a slow burner and try not to show my anger.
    a) yes _____ b) no _____

11. When someone crosses me, I hold a grudge forever.
    a) yes _____ b) no _____

Food

1. Food is _____.
   a) a very important part of my life b) not an issue

2. My favorite food tends to be _____.
   a) fresh fruits, vegetables and whole grains
   b) Fritos and Froot Loops   c) anything fried   d) specify _____
3. I am a vegetarian. Anyone preparing meat in the kitchen would

   _____.

   a) make me sick   b) make me angry
   c) not bother me as long as I don't have to eat it
4. I want to eat meals with a partner and split the cost of food and preparation duties.
   a) yes _____   b) no _____
5. Each partner should buy his own food and cook it when he pleases.
   a) yes _____   b) no _____
6. Cooking is a hobby and I spend weekends in the kitchen and don't
   want anyone to bother me.
   a) yes _____   b) no _____
7. I eat all meals out and if I'm at home reach for a can of Spaghettios.
   a) yes _____   b) no _____
8. The refrigerator and freezer space should be equally shared.
   a) yes _____   b) no _____
9. Anyone who attacks a drumstick with a knife and fork is too rich for my
   blood.
   a) yes _____   b) no _____
10. A good meal ends with a burp and a toothpick.
    a) right on _____   b) where are you going to eat?

Health

1. I feel _____.
   a) in tip-top shape   b) good for my age
   c) so-so, but I can still do most everything

2. Health problems _____.
   a) do not enter into the partnering picture
   b) are the reason I want a roommate. I need someone to help take care
   of me.

3. My _____ would prevent me from mopping, sweeping and scrubbing, let alone gardening and painting.
   a) back problems   b) allergies   c) heart trouble   d) specify _____

4. What health problems, if any, do you have? Fess up. Yes, everything.
   Even your trick knee, your asthma, and your eye problem that prevents

you from driving at night. _____

_____

_____

Possessions

1. If anyone touches my stereo _____.
   a) he dies b) I don't care as long as he uses it carefully
2. As long as he checks with me first, my partner can borrow anything.
   a) yes _____ b) no _____
3. Private possessions should not be shared—ever.
   a) yes _____ b) no _____
4. Some possessions can be shared. Let's talk about which.
   a) yes _____ b) no _____
5. I save rubber bands, empty jars, shopping bags, and gift paper from anything I receive.
   a) I do, too, as well as empty boxes, old Band-Aid tins and other things too numerous to mention.
   b) The less you have around, the better, is the way I look at it. I'd throw all that junk out.

Great Expectations

1. I'd like to go to the movies, have dinner out once in a while, share some weekend activities with my partner.
   a) yes _____ b) no _____
2. House sharing means splitting a place to live and its expenses. I don't want my partner to be a pal.
   a) yes _____ b) no _____
3. I'd like to share some space I own, in exchange for services such as driving, cooking, and gardening.
   a) yes _____ b) no _____
   If this is an arrangement you want to explore, be specific about what you expect and how much time per week these chores will require.

_____

_____

_____

_____

_____

4. How emotionally involved do you want to be? How much time do you

want to spend together? Explain:

_____

_____

_____

_____

5. I consider this shared arrangement permanent.
   a) yes _____ b) no _____

6. I want to share until _____.
   a) I get married b) I get my graduate degree
   c) I can afford a place of my own d) specify _____

7. I definitely consider our arrangement long-term, but if life-changes alter our situation, I want dissolution to be reasonable and without hostility.
   a) yes _____ b) no _____
   Try to explain your feelings on this subject:

_____

_____

_____

_____

Space

1. I need my own bedroom, bath, and an additional room to call my own, to feel comfortable sharing a house.
   a) yes _____ b) no _____

2. I need only my own bedroom to feel I have enough privacy.
   a) yes _____ b) no _____

3. Crowded? What's that? My eight sisters and brothers shared two bedrooms and one bath and we managed to survive.
   a) yes _____ b) no _____

4. How much "private space" versus "commonly shared space" do you need to feel comfortable?

_____

_____

_____

_____

5. There is a one-car garage/one parking space allotted to each apartment, who gets it?
   a) I get it _____ b) We'll alternate weeks _____
   c) Specify _____

House Beautiful

1. The decor of my home _____ to me.
   a) means a lot b) means very little c) is moderately important
2. My taste in furnishings runs to _____ .
   a) antiques b) modern c) Early Goodwill c) specify _____
3. My partner and I should agree on how the common areas of the house should be furnished. Private space can be anything we choose.
   a) yes _____ b) no _____
4. The house should be furnished with all the odds and ends we can put together from our previous places and that should do it. If one of us leaves, we take our own pieces with us. If we must buy any furniture together, it should be serviceable and inexpensive.
   a) yes _____ b) no _____
5. When you think of spending "some money" to decorate a house, what is the dollar figure that comes to mind? _____
6. Colors should be _____.
   a) neutral b) knockouts c) decided by a decorator
   c) decided on by both of us for the common area; anything each wants in private space
7. Clutter drives me bonkers.
   a) yes _____ b) no _____
8. Brandy snifters filled with matchbooks collected from favorite restaurants, my bowling trophies, and "I visited Niagara Falls" salt shakers should be on display.
   a) yes _____ b) no _____
9. _____ should be hung on the walls.
   a) my velvet painting of The Last Supper
   b) my blue ribbon collection of nude posters
   c) my Ku Klux Klan awards d) specify _____
10. Will there be room for my African violets, spider plants, fig tree? ____
    a) bring them all b) I only like silk flowers c) let's talk about it
11. Never mind this whole interior decorating bit, I don't want to look at a couch until the roof is fixed and new insulation is installed.
    a) yes _____ b) no _____

Comforts

1. Heat should be set _____ .
   a) low no matter how cold it is, to keep the utility bill down

b) should be between 65 and 70 degrees. I like to feel comfortable.
c) specify _____

2. Air conditioning _____ .
   a) is a necessity b) should be used sparingly
   c) is not part of my life; I use fans.

3. Windows should be open. I like ventilation.
   a) O.K., but how open? _____
   b) and let that lousy air in? Keep them shut. _____

4. I love microwaves, electric can openers, automatic garage door openers and anything else I can plug in.
   a) yes _____ b) no _____

5. Having my own washer and dryer is _____ .
   a) a must b) not necessary

6. Washers and dryers _____ .
   a) should be used at the convenience of the partners
   b) only when there is a full load, to save energy

7. What other major conveniences are important to you?
   _____
   _____
   _____
   _____

Politics and Religion

1. Politics is _____.
   a) boring to talk about b) my passion
   c) interesting, but I'd rather talk about baseball

2. _____ what my partner thinks politically.
   a) I do care b) I don't care

3. My partner could be a John Bircher or a Communist for all I care, as
   long as he keeps his politics to himself.
   a) yes _____ b) no _____

4. My religion is _____.

5. I want my partner to have similar religious beliefs.
   a) yes _____ b) no _____

6. Religion is a big part of my life and I want my partner to share the same
   commitment.
   a) yes _____ b) no _____

7. Religion is not an issue in my life and I don't want to live with someone who tries to convert me.
a) yes _____ b) no _____

Pets

1. I hate all animals. Yes, that includes birds, puppies, and gerbils. Don't even think about exotic pets.
a) yes _____ b) no _____

2. If my partner wants to have pets, that's fine as long as he takes care of them and they do not bother me, destroy my possessions, or wake me up.
a) yes _____ b) no _____

3. One pet is fine.
a) yes _____ b) no _____
What pet would be fine? _____

4. Love me, love my 150-pound Great Dane.
a) yes _____ b) no _____

5. List any animal you own that would be included in the house arrangement.
_____

6. I _____ to have my cats declawed or neutered, if my partner objects to the destruction of furniture or the odors they spray.
a) would be willing b) would be unwilling

7. I would like to buy a pet to take care of in partnership.
a) yes _____ b) Are you kidding _____
Please specify what pet. _____

Jobs

1. I love things like painting and wallpapering. I'm good at it, too.
a) yes _____ b) no _____

2. I am a klutz at fixing things, but I can _____
and _____ and am willing to trade skills.
a) yes _____ b) no _____

3. I expect all work to be done to perfection.
a) I agree _____ b) Are you serious? _____

4. I'm not skilled at specific jobs but I'm a fast learner and am energetic.
a) yes _____ b) no _____

5. Repairs around the house should be done by plumbers and electricians. I don't like to do the work and don't want to do it.
   a) yes _____ b) no _____

6. If my partner wants to do repairs, that's fine. I'll take on a larger share of the mortgage payments.
   a) yes _____ b) no _____

7. I'm a whiz at bookkeeping and would be willing to take on bill-paying and record-keeping. It's all that shoveling, sanding, and plastering I hate.
   a) yes _____ b) no _____

8. What jobs would you be willing to undertake?

   _____
   _____
   _____

9. List your strong points and skills in keeping a house in good shape.

   _____
   _____
   _____
   _____

10. Jobs should be rotated so no one gets stuck with something he hates doing forever.
    a) yes _____ b) no _____

11. Men should do all the heavy work and women should cook and clean.
    a) yes _____ b) no _____ c) HAH! _____

12. All jobs should be equally divided, regardless of sex.
    a) absolutely _____ b) no way_____

13. Serious rehabbers who intend to tear a place apart, discuss what talents and energies you can pool—honestly, so you don't get in over your heads and furious with each other.

    _____
    _____
    _____
    _____
    _____
    _____

As a finale, list anything else you can think of that might create problems for anyone living with you. Consider everything from your bad humor when you go on a diet to your habit of rearranging furniture on those nights you can't sleep. If you or your prospective partner say there are no such things, you're not being honest—or realistic.

There are always problems, even if they are small ones. But if you face them squarely, they can be handled. If you're so desperate to partner that you deny how things really are, you'll be setting up the biggest obstacle of all.

_____

_____

_____

_____

_____

_____

_____

_____

_____

_____

Nobody's Perfect—Not Even Me

This matchup exercise is not meant to be all-inclusive. While it does cover the major areas that have proved problematic if partners' expectations are not made clear, it should also stimulate your thinking so that other significant points come to mind.

The questionnaire was designed to make you chuckle together and make it easier to discuss important but sensitive subjects. "Love me, love my 150-pound Great Dane." Who would ever want to share with someone who has a dog that big? Not me.

But did I tell you about my 14-year-old cocker spaniel? He's such a love. He doesn't have many teeth left so I cook him soft food every day. Sometimes I have to feed it to him to get him to eat. Oh—and he has to sleep on the couch because the floor is just too hard for his old bones. I don't know what I'd do if anything happened to that dog.

Sleeps on the couch, eh? He cooks him special food. Though I've never been that crazy about animals, I wouldn't mind sharing with someone who is. But this guy goes way overboard for my taste. Do I really want to share my couch—let alone my house and my life—with a senile cocker spaniel?

See? This test just got you to think and talk about what you deeply care for and what doesn't concern you a bit. This is the way you'll decide whether you can become partners—not by any special grading system.

For instance, the person you are interested in sharing with is a great carpenter, doesn't drink, has a deep religious commitment, and seems very easygoing. You like him. But he likes to get up at 5:00 a.m. in the morning to jump rope and lift weights before work, loves to fry okra, and seems a little penny-pinching for your taste.

Do his good points outweigh his bad ones? It's up to you. Does a nice personality outshine waking up to someone jumping up and down before daylight—especially when you don't have to get up until 8:00 a.m.? Does his being handy around the house overcome the odor of frying food? After all, he wasn't so wild about your girlfriend spending weekends with you and the fact that you have a way of dropping dirty clothes all over the house. Can you work out a system to please both of you?

Watch for the red flags. (No, I couldn't share with someone who likes to walk around the house naked, even though he's terrific in every other way.) And note all the ways you agree. (Great! We both love to entertain and have friends over all the time.)

Talk all this out. In doing so, you'll be able to put issues in their proper perspectives—and, better yet, to rest.

Where Do You Go from Here?

Thought you were finished? Not so fast. Even though you've just sidestepped a slew of potential problems home sharers have to face, you still have to decide how you are going to handle money matters, draw up a contract that will provide for all the contingencies of your jointly held property, decide how often you are going to convene house meetings, and maybe even think about taking out disability insurance, so you can keep up mortgage payments should disaster fall. There's more, too. But every point won't apply to every kind of shared living arrangement we cover.

A person who rents space in the large home of another won't have to worry about his landlord's agreement with the bank; only his own rent and whatever the two of them have agreed each should do to keep the house running smoothly. Two people who share rented space don't have to deal with any mortgage problems, only their joint lease and each other.

This is why you will find explanations of how to handle the special problems of each type of shared living in the chapters that follow. That's less confusing than having to plow through pages of general paragraphs here that don't apply to your specific circumstances.

Your living arrangement will dictate much of the system you devise. And the best way for you to learn how to construct a good one is at the knee of someone who has experience. In how real-life house partners have managed, you will have concrete role models to follow— or not.

So, the next step is to plunge in and take a look at what partners have put together. We'll peer at their ground rules, some of their written agreements and contracts, and the reasons they have done what they have done.

·14·
How to Share a House or an Apartment

Shared homeownership is a wonderful goal to shoot for, but not the most common reality. As we pass through the stages of life (Shakespeare said there were seven, and who are we to argue?), our needs change. That influences how we live, where we live—and whom we live with. Doubling up is certainly an economic boost in a transitional or crisis period; it can also act as a shock absorber for people going through hard times.

One man was married for seven years and has a 3-year-old son. His marriage failed and he moved out of his house. Where? Through a shared housing counseling service, he learns that a divorced woman with a small daughter is offering space in her home to help meet mortgage payments. They meet and they get along. He moves in.

Their deal is business; romance between them is not in the picture. Financially, they are helping each other over a rough spot. But there's another ingredient in this arrangement, too.

Carl says, "I miss my son. I like living in a home with a small child. It makes me feel less isolated. After being married so long, I hated the thought of being alone.

"On the days I have my son with me, I have a place to bring him where we can be together. He is allowed to use the swings out back. He can play with Wendy's toys. It's awful dragging him to the movies or

233

the zoo every time I see him. This way, I have a home where we can do quiet things."

But Carl is not the only one who benefits. "I was afraid, just plain scared, of being in the house alone at night with Wendy," says Julie. "Every creak made me jump. Even when Carl's not home, just knowing he will be later is comforting. I feel so much safer with a man in the house."

Two nurses working different shifts don't need, don't want, and have arranged not to have much of each other's company. But they live in a better apartment, in tandem, than they could alone. They are also able to put aside money for a place of their own someday. They use each other to make it happen.

Divorcees often need housemates to help make the overwhelming mortgage payments on the homes they have been left with. Single parents seek each other for support—economic and mental. College students, older adults, and young professionals double up. From distress, for company, because they can't make it on their own momentarily, or they can but want to save—they share houses one owns and another rents or live together in rented space.

Accessory Apartments

Accessory apartments are becoming an increasingly popular alternative. Here is an example of why: A couple has lived in their gracious home for 40 years. Though it's been too large for just the two of them since their children married and had children of their own, they've loved having all that space. Until now.

They find they just can't keep up with the maintenance. A new roof and a furnace that gives up the ghost wreck their fixed income budget. They are hard-pressed to finance improvements and are getting tired of thinking about them. The house they love is becoming a physical and financial burden.

Many older people solve the problem by sharing their homes. Some do so keeping the existing structure intact; others carve out a separate apartment within the house.

According to Dennis Day-Lower, these accessory apartments are multiplying at a phenomenal pace. Some homeowners play by the rules and dutifully apply for the proper permits needed to make such improvements. Many don't and operate sub rosa. Going from a single- to a multifamily home can infuriate neighbors who foresee property values dropping and excess cars littering the neighborhood.

"Trying to circumvent the authorities is dangerous; it can be an expensive chance to take," says Dennis. "Neighbors can report you and inspectors can come to your home, slap you with a fine, and make you rip out improvements. Accessory apartments rarely cost under $5,000 to install (consider the price of putting in plumbing and kitchen facilities), and are often in the neighborhood of $15,000 or $20,000. It's best to go through the zoning board and present your plans."

Mardi Rose, vice chairman of the Cambridge Living Options for Elders, an organization founded to encourage and enable older people to live comfortably and independently, has an accessory apartment on the third floor of her suburban Boston home. Though her house is filled with her teenage children and husband at this time in her life, the accessory apartment brings in extra income. Looking toward a future when she is elderly and possibly alone, Mardi feels someone in the house at that point will be reassuring.

"I wrote letters to my neighbors explaining what I was doing, told them I'd be glad to speak to them about my plans. The objections were the same old ones; changing the exterior of the house, depreciating property values, parking problems. The city councilman who lives nearby wrote a letter supporting me, and when my plans were brought up at a council meeting, they met all their criteria. I abided by all the safety regulations and everyone was assured I was not turning my home into a boarding house. There was no kerfluffel. Everything went ahead."

All manner of people can benefit from putting in accessory apartments. Those buying first homes get a hand in making mortgage payments. So do newly divorced people with too-large homes and too little cash.

Older adults who do install accessory apartments can live in the smaller space and rent the rest of their homes if it's just too much for them to care for. They can rent the accessory apartment and stay put if they wish.

The key to all this is affordability. Older people who find it financially prohibitive to keep their homes, young people who can't afford a mortgage, renters who need a reasonable apartment—all gain by living under one roof, separately. Accessory housing serves those with houses too large as well as it serves those with none at all.

Granny Flats

Another phenomenon on the shared housing scene is a freestanding structure put up in the backyard of an existing residence—the "granny flat."

According to Dennis Day-Lower, "These units are constructed for Mom and Dad in the backyard of a grown son or daughter's home so their parents can be close enough to keep an eye on and separate enough so that everyone has independence and privacy.

"Granny flats usually contain about 600 to 800 square feet and are prefabricated buildings erected on a concrete slab. They're less expensive than accessory apartments since no remodeling is involved. So far, several companies in the United States are manufacturing them.

"Another point in their favor is that neighbors don't usually raise objections to children taking care of their parents, even if they do put up a building out back they're not too crazy about.

"Granny flats must be dismantled when the house is sold or when Mom and Dad pass away. Aunt Theresa and Uncle Marvin can't move in and take their place. Accessory apartments are permanent. You can rent them to anyone. The neighborhood can change, which makes neighbors nervous."

Mardi Rose says, "Granny flats don't work in Cambridge or in other densely populated cities because there is simply no room for them. Backyards are scarce and space is sky high." True. Granny flats are usually found in the suburbs or in more rural areas.

Both accessory apartments and granny flats are a growing trend. They are mentioned here so you can add them to your arsenal of housing alternatives. For more specific facts, advice, places where granny flats can be obtained, write to the Shared Housing Resource Center, 6344 Green Street, Philadelphia, PA 19144.

Check Your Zoning

Structural changes in homes wave a red flag in front of neighbors who race to check zoning ordinances. Doubling up in homes that remain intact can be just as incendiary.

Again, some people fear the neighborhood will change. If two people live there, will there be three or four or more? Will there be loud music, wild parties? Will this place turn into a rooming house?

If you are going to take in a housemate, you may not get complaints. But it's not a bad idea to investigate in advance how your neighborhood is zoned. Even many of the strictest ordinances provide for two or more unrelated people living together. If that's what you have in mind, you'll probably be fine. Just make sure. Because anything you do that annoys neighbors will send them running to the zoning board with complaints. They'll use those regulations as a battleground rather than the real issue at hand. Even if you gloss over the letter of the law (lots of people do) in sharing a house, know what the laws are when going in.

YOU DON'T HAVE TO GO IT ALONE

The next group of people we're going to become acquainted with have created, at various way stations in their lives, the housing alternatives I've been explaining. Some did so well that you may be encouraged to play follow the leader. Others have sloshed through puddles you know you'll want to jump over.

• • •

Marilyn, a professor of botany at a local college, was married to a prominent physician for over 25 years. Their large, charming home is filled with antiques and mementos of travels around the world.

Marilyn's husband fell in love with a graduating medical student and left the marriage; Marilyn was left in a state of shock. She had never lived on her own or managed her own finances. She was in total panic. She was terrified she wouldn't have enough money to keep up the house, and couldn't decide whether to sell it. She decided not to decide. By renting two rooms and a bath, she felt she could keep out of debt. The rooms were set off from the main part of the house and would make a nice apartment. The renter would have privacy. So would Marilyn. But she could also have company. She despised being alone.

To find a compatible person, Marilyn put up a notice in the church she attended. A 30-year-old woman who was looking for a place to live responded.

"Missy seemed awfully nice when we met," says Marilyn. "I told her the rent would be $200 a month and she decided to move in."

Missy moved in, but so did her boyfriend, who was there most of the time.

"She treated me like a landlady," says Marilyn. "I felt excluded. It made me feel even more lonely.

"Although her own rooms were entirely hers to keep up, she never cleaned the kitchen after she used it or pitched in with any jobs around the house. She used my washer and dryer—which I told her was fine with me—but to wash her boyfriend's clothes. That wasn't fine since it drove up electrical bills. To add insult to injury, she used my soap. He also raided the refrigerator and ate my food.

"I confronted her with all this and asked her to do more work around the house. After all, I wasn't her mother; I wasn't going to pick up after her. Finally, I asked her to move."

The next renter in Marilyn's home responded to an ad she ran in the university newspaper. Again, two rooms and bath plus kitchen privileges for $200 a month seemed fine to Matt, a 27-year-old engineering graduate student. Marilyn liked him and thought a man to help with heavy jobs around the house would be just what she needed.

"Matt's Saturday routine drove me nuts," says Marilyn. "He sat in front of the TV all day watching any sports event that would come on. I asked him to buy a television and put it in his own room. He was making enough money as a teaching assistant to afford it, but he never did. He was sullen and uncommunicative, and when I tried to have conversation with him, he just grunted."

Marilyn's hopes that Matt would shoulder odd jobs were also dashed.

"He never took the garbage out, he didn't shovel the snow when I asked, he cooked the worst-smelling food—all frozen patties of some sort he always fried. He didn't even like my dog.

"When I interviewed Matt he seemed outgoing and pleasant. He was the opposite after he moved in."

Reflecting over her two disasters, Marilyn feels they came about because she was not assertive enough.

"After my divorce, I wanted peace at any price," she says. "I didn't want confrontations. I hated asking probing questions. I never clarified responsibilities or expectations. I was willing to put up with anything just to have someone in the house. When I rent my rooms again, I'll have a long list of questions to ask."

• • •

Marilyn would have benefited from a conversation with Ruth, who has rented four rooms in her house in a small Midwest university town for ten years.

Interested renters respond to notices she tacks up in the college housing office, but those who do know exactly what's in store for them when they meet her. Ruth shows them around and one of her first stops is the spot in the kitchen where the following rules are posted.

Rules for Roomers at 111 Evergreen Avenue

1. Your rent is due on the first of each month.

2. No smoking in this house or on the porch. This goes for guests as well as roomers.

3. You may have a guest occasionally overnight; for anything regular or long-term, please talk with me.

4. The use of the kitchen and other parts of the house is extended as a privilege that may be revoked. In other words, you rent your room and that is *your* space. You have the right to use the bathroom. The rest of the house remains basically mine, and I am very happy to share it with you as long as you use it responsibly. If you abuse privileged areas such as the kitchen, or appliances you have permission to use, I will prohibit you from using them.

5. You are expected to clean up after yourself right after meals or snacks, regardless of who else hasn't, e.g., *me.* I do the general cleaning and don't think I should have to move other people's stuff to do it.

6. In general, please do not strew your belongings throughout the house. Keep them in your own room. You may use the kitchen coat closet. Please do not use the corner china cupboard or any of its contents without explicit permission.

7. You may use the downstairs refrigerator but label your designated shelf space clearly, or label your food.

8. Label your towel rack in the bathroom. I do not supply towels, though I'm usually able to lend them temporarily if you ask.

9. Use of space in basement, garage, or downstairs freezer is by arrangement with me only.

10. It is your responsibility to keep track of your pay phone calls. Add them up, add 5% for tax, and pay me soon after I put the bill on the kitchen table. See below about calls in the last month of your stay here.

11. I have an evening class that meets here once a week plus occasional workshops. Please avoid using the kitchen or passing through the living room at these times. You can go in the front door.

I hope you will feel free to talk with me about any problems you have about the house or your room (ex.: it is too cold, too hot, too ugly, inconvenient, etc.) and together we'll see what we can do about it.

Before You Leave:

1. In the last month of your stay here (i.e., after the 26th of the previous month, in which you have paid for all phone calls) please make *only collect phone calls.* With the best of intentions on your part, doing otherwise seems to leave me with extra expense and/or trouble.

2. Please leave a forwarding address card at the P.O. and leave a forwarding address with me. I do not feel responsible for forwarding mail, but I do it sometimes.

3. Please take all of your belongings and pay all of your bills.

"When I first put up these rules, I apologized for them," says Ruth, a plain-talking, lively woman who rents space because she needs the money. Divorced and not able to make enough to keep her roomy white Victorian running on her own, she decided to rent rooms. "I soon got over apologizing, because the rules helped weed out people who objected to them and decided not to live here. I wouldn't have wanted them anyway."

Asked how she deals with renters who don't play by her rules, Ruth says, "I am direct. I am factual rather than emotional and calmly confront the person with what is upsetting me. I keep my expectations clear so that people know what I expect. That helps head off problems. I also try to be flexible and accommodating.

"All of my rented rooms are furnished with thrift shop furniture. If there is nothing of value to worry about, there is nothing to get hysterical over.

"Renters can have a party downstairs with my permission. They have to clean up afterward. They can also use my television and stereo, but we have to work it out. The house is mine, and renters clearly know that. If I want to have people over for dinner in front of the fire in the living room, I tell people to avoid that area.

"Anyone who rents space in a house must figure out how much of it they want to keep for themselves and what part of it they are willing to share. They must make whatever is important to them clear in the beginning. They have to know what they want and give themselves permission to say it."

Ruth also keeps very good records so she knows who pays and who doesn't. "If you like a renter, it's easy to fall into the habit of being lenient with money." She cautions homeowners who rent rooms to guard against this.

"When I put the phone bill on the kitchen table, people initial their own long-distance calls and are responsible for paying me. If any are left uninitialed, I call the phone company to see where the calls were placed.

"I ask, who called Joe Blow in Des Moines? If I still get no answer, I feel some of the rent money I ask covers these kinds of expenses. But I'd feel just as comfortable prohibiting use of the phone if things got out of hand."

A look in the kitchen refrigerator shows renters' food clearly labeled, though there is a general shelf from which people are welcome to help themselves. Each has his own cupboard space for individual cooking equipment, although Ruth's appliances may be used by all. Only the blender is off limits. But anything of Ruth's that renters may use must be replaced if it is broken.

"I would expect anyone who burns up a pot to buy a new one," she says emphatically. "I let everyone use my washer and dryer, but they must supply their own detergent."

What Marilyn left to chance and hope, Ruth has worked out thoughtfully. Learning from early mistakes, Ruth got tough and found it enabled her to enjoy the people who shared her house more.

"If there are rules everyone understands," she says, "no one is apt to get angry. Everyone is much more relaxed. We even get to like each other."

Two Single Mothers' Solution

Now let's see how two women with young children merged their families in a small apartment with no privacy—and made it work. Against tough odds, they created a positive place to live.

"I met Susan through the LaLeche League," says Gloria, "when we were both living in separate apartments. Since we belonged to a group that fosters nurturing attitudes in rearing children, I knew we had the same philosophy about bringing them up.

"Susan was divorced and living in her own apartment with her year-old child (he's now almost 3). I knew my marriage was no good, and when I needed to leave quickly with my three children (their ages are 6, 4, and 2), I moved in with Susan just as a temporary measure. We had known each other for about a year at that time.

"Once I was there, we talked about sharing a place on a permanent basis, since both of us were short on money. It seemed like a good idea, so we moved into a six-room apartment in Queens."

Six rooms may seem large by New York standards, but not for two mothers and that many children. The families share the kitchen, dining room, and living room. Each mother sleeps in a bedroom with her children; the third bedroom has been turned into a playroom for all the kids.

Though bedrooms are decidedly cramped, loft beds make the best of the existing space. The women combined their furnishings to make the place livable. Both have had to accept welfare in order to stay home and raise their children. It was a hard decision, but one they have learned to live with.

"I was a latchkey kid," says Susan. "My mother always worked. I carried an apartment key around with me, let myself in after school, learned to cope with being alone so much. I didn't want that for my child so I'm developing a craft I can do at home."

Besides a craft, the two mothers have developed a system to help create a sense of independence in a place where people live on top of each other.

"We do not take care of each other's kids," says Gloria. "If I have an appointment and even if Susan is home, I arrange for a sitter. If I can't get one, I'll ask Susan for help. We do watch each other's children after nine o'clock, when they are asleep, if one of us has to go out. We're careful not to take advantage of each other with our kids.

"The same goes with disciplining each other's children. If a kid talks back to an adult, his own parent takes care of the problem.

"When kids fight, it's hard to think your own child is to blame," says Susan. "It can get emotional and touchy. We talk about our feelings and get them out in the open.

"We figured out that if we handle the children's fights in a way that's not good for them, it won't be good for us either. Sometimes I stand in the other room when I hear them bickering and wonder whether I should stop the fight or leave them alone. Sometimes I think it would be easier to give up and run away. But both of us stay and work it out. We have to."

Grocery shopping, cooking, and cleaning are shared by both women. No one ever says, "You do this or that" because there is so much to do; everyone pitches in. Each mother does laundry for her own children; kids are expected to make their own beds and clean up.

Both women signed the lease; each pays half the rent, utility, and food expenses. As for sharing, kids learn it by example.

"No one says, 'you can't sit in mommy's chair,' " says Gloria. "That's what I tell my kids when they're not generous with their possessions. The mommies in this house both share. You have to, too.

"Kids don't have to share all their toys, though. That would be a lot to ask. If they want to keep something exclusive, they put it on their bed or dresser. Everything else is up for grabs.

"We trust that if one of our children breaks another's toy, we'd replace it without questions.

"When we buy a new toy—for any child—we think of what none of them has and what they all might like."

Both women feel that combining households has been a source of support during and even after a divorce. They give each other help and advice and cheer each other when life seems overwhelming. But they are careful not to bog each other in the blues.

Gloria and Susan spend a great deal of time with their children. This is their choice and one they have made sacrifices for. But being alone so much with small children can be isolating. They find it comforting just knowing there is someone else—an adult—in the same house, even if she isn't there at the moment.

Susan and Gloria go out together but are also careful to maintain their own friends. If one wants to have a private conversation in the living room, the other discreetly disappears into the bedroom.

"You must understand," says Susan, "if there's a problem, we have to deal with it immediately. There is no spare corner for anyone to go off and sulk.

"Neither of us had the money to live on our own and we're making this situation work. We consider it a success. But sometimes I just wish the noise would stop."

OLDER AND WISER

For the elderly living alone, the pandemonium of Gloria and Susan's life is planets away. Maybe gratefully so. But many are lonely—and afraid.

In increasing numbers, older adults are seeking roommates for security. Sitting ducks for break-ins, unable to offer much resistance if a robbery does occur, doubling up offers them a measure of freedom from fear. Going out in pairs is also better protection against street crime than venturing out companionless.

The money crunch for those on fixed incomes can be devastating. At the mercy of inflation, social programs that may be cut or dispensed with, many find their spending money has been whittled away. Sharing living space enables them to afford a better lifestyle in upgraded surroundings.

When you're by yourself, the thought of a fall in the night scares you. Older adults with disabilities that warrant someone else nearby but not constant attention keep an eye on each other—out of nursing homes.

Most people eat better when they eat with someone else. Cooking for one and eating in front of a television set is not as appetizing as sharing food and news of the day.

Though this is the down side of sharing by older adults, one issue must be faced squarely before they form a joint household. What happens if one partner becomes incapacitated or no longer able to live without intense care? Will the other partner be able to care for him? For how long? If that is not possible, what steps need to be considered? Should they specify a person in advance to step in to help make decisions for the incapacitated partner? What happens to the remaining one? Can he make it on his own? What provisions will be made for that?

Matching agencies throughout the country are helping seniors in ever-increasing numbers find places to live together. Many encourage an intergenerational approach to sharing. It's lively living with people of all ages. Intergenerational group houses are popping up nationwide, and I'll take a look at some of them in a later chapter. Right now, let's probe the means by which these next three twosomes filled voids in their lives—with each other.

• • •

Janet and Irene have shared a three-bedroom first-floor apartment in a sprawling suburban apartment complex for four years. For six years before that, they lived in separate apartments in the same place. But their history goes back even further. For eighteen years, they lived four houses apart on the same street during the years their husbands were alive and they were raising children.

Janet's grown son died. So did her husband. Still active as an operating room nurse, she moved to an apartment.

Irene's 16-year-old son lived with her when she moved to a two-bedroom town house. When he went away to school and later married, as did her daughter, she knew her children would never live at home again. The apartment was getting expensive.

During the six years the women lived in separate apartments, they maintained their close friendship. Each had dogs they walked together several times a day, and it was during these walks that the idea of sharing an apartment was explored.

For each, the cost of a two-bedroom apartment was becoming prohibitive. Rent was hiked continually; so were utilities. Though they felt they'd get along, Janet and Irene didn't jump right into sharing a larger apartment. They took time and set up some rules to make them feel comfortable about it.

Each wanted to live separate lives though they would live together. If one woman was invited to dinner with friends, she would go. They would share each other's company but not consider themselves a matched pair people had to see together or not at all.

Janet likes to watch sports on television; Irene, who has emphysema and is more home-bound, is addicted to the soaps. However, since neither can stand the other's favorites, each has a television in her bedroom so they can view the programs they like. The television in the living room is for watching those programs they enjoy together.

Janet knew ahead of time that if there was cooking to be done, she would have to be the chef. Irene hated to fix meals and lived mostly on grilled cheese sandwiches and chocolate bars when she was alone.

"I hated cooking only for myself," says Janet, "so preparing simple meals for both of us was no big deal. Sharing them with someone makes the effort worthwhile."

Each woman does her own laundry. Both are easygoing about cleaning. To decide which furniture to use in the new apartment, they took stock of what they had and selected the best of the lot.

They also protected their household furnishings in their wills. If either woman died, her heirs could take her possessions from the remaining partner only after both were deceased.

This way, after giving away so much of their own things to join forces, if one woman was left alone, she would not be without resources. It's a smart provision to incorporate into an agreement.

The cost of new purchases (they bought themselves a microwave one Christmas, a freezer the next year) is split evenly. There is a joint account into which each woman deposits equal amounts of money to pay the rent, utilities, and telephone bills.

Into a coin purse they put equal amounts of cash for groceries.

When they eat out, they pay their own checks; each has a separate telephone line.

"My own telephone was a way to keep my identity," says Janet. "We both have listings in the phone book so our friends can find us. It's more expensive, but we feel it's worth it. We pay the phone bills out of our joint checking account and never add up who makes how many long-distance calls. We figure it will come out even in the long run."

Irene has children and grandchildren who are now Janet's family, too. Having no one, Janet feels this is an enormously satisfying part of sharing.

"We rented a three-bedroom apartment so Irene's grandchildren could come and spend the night," says Janet. "I always loved to stay with my grandmother when I was a young girl and I wanted Irene's grandchildren to feel welcome here. "The only problem when they visit is that Irene is a spoiler. When I see something I don't like, I say something about it."

Irene says, "I don't like Janet to criticize my grandchildren, but in my heart, I know she's usually right. Still, I tell her that I can correct my grandchildren; no one else can. She stops."

"If the grandchildren visited all the time, maybe there would be problems," says Janet. "But they don't. They're here often enough for us to enjoy them but not enough to be a nuisance."

"What if you had two sets of grandchildren who didn't get along when they visited?" I asked.

Both were thoughtful, but they answered in the same manner.

"They'd have to learn to get along," says Irene. "For the small amount of time children and grandchildren visit, I wouldn't want to sacrifice my relationship with Janet. We'd work out alternating visiting schedules—anything to preserve peace."

"If something happened to Irene, I'd have to move to a smaller place," says Janet.

"If anything happened to Janet," says Irene, "I'd have to go to a retirement center where I'd have nursing help because of my emphysema. One morning I went into pulmonary arrest and Janet called the life squad to get me to the hospital. I was there for two weeks. She took care of me when I returned home."

"Companionship overrides anything," says Janet, "even Irene's corny jokes in the morning. You can't worry about small things. You have to have faith everything will work out. For instance, if I know Irene's granddaughter is coming for the weekend, I'll buy extra treats I know she likes out of our grocery money. When I buy extra things for patients at the hospital where I volunteer, I offer to pay for them myself, but Irene thinks it's ridiculous. It all comes out of the same account—and it comes out right for both of us.

"We respect each other's privacy and try to avoid pettiness. When I sense Irene wants to talk privately with her daughter, I take the dogs for a walk. If my lawyer comes to discuss business matters with me, Irene goes to her room to watch television.

"People who share must be completely honest with each other or it won't work.

"But then, there is so much to gain. When my dog died, one of Irene's started coming into my bedroom to sleep with me. He must have known how much I needed him. Material possessions mean very little compared to the warmth that comes from a partnership like this."

● ● ●

Two sisters share an apartment. Will their lifetime of sharing ensure success? No. But they made it work by laying good ground rules.

Edna never married. She lived with her mother until her mother died, then moved to an apartment where she lived alone.

Sophie was married 41 years and has three married children. Her husband died six months ago.

So Edna and Sophie decided to live together. Sophie had never lived alone. Edna was nine years older, the older sister who always took care of the younger ones. It was a natural move.

Edna and Sophie looked for a two-bedroom apartment in the same complex Edna was renting a one-bedroom. First floor space was important to minimize steps.

"It took months for me to realize this was my home," says Sophie. "I had always come here to visit Edna. It took a while to sink in that now I lived here, too."

"I had to adjust also," says Edna. "I moved from my one-bedroom apartment to a bigger place. It's good that we both had adjusting to do. Neither of us felt we were moving in with the other."

Edna, now 74, retired from her sales job in a department store nine years ago. Sophie still works—in the same store.

Edna plays cards, does volunteer work, goes off with her own friends. Sophie, busy five days a week and still in mourning for her husband, sees her children on her days off or shops for groceries with Edna.

"I was used to cooking for myself," says Edna. "Now all of a sudden, I felt like I had company coming for dinner every night.

"Sophie is still a working woman. I felt like I had to have dinner ready for her when she came home."

"I told her that was ridiculous," says Sophie. "I asked her what she would make for herself if I weren't here?"

"Frozen dinner, a salad, and dessert is fine with me," says Edna. "Or tuna salad and a baked potato. I'm not much of a cook."

Sophie says, "I told her whatever she eats is fine with me. Stop treating me like company. We worked out the problem with the evening meal.

"I had to remind Edna to stop treating me like her baby sister. I

247

had been married 41 years and she'd remind me to shake a bottle before I poured something out of it.

"She'd worry because I'd be up late in my room watching television and I had to be at work the next day. I knew she was looking out for my best interests, but I told her that no one told me when to go to bed since I was a kid.

"She's never poked her head in my room and asked, 'Are you still up?' since."

"I was so used to being the big sister," says Edna, "it was hard to remember not to tell Sophie what to do."

Though the sisters joined furniture to create a sunny, cheerful apartment, they make it clear to friends that they lead separate lives.

"My daughter-in-law's father called and asked to take me to dinner," says Sophie. "I told him up front he didn't have to ask Edna now that we were living together. He had never asked her to join us before.

"I knew he couldn't afford to pay for the two of us every time he asked me. I didn't want other people to feel that way. We got that straight with everyone right from the start."

Material things aren't important to Sophie or Edna. They held a garage sale to get rid of duplicates they couldn't use.

"Who needs two ironing boards and all those pots and pans?" laughs Sophie. "We laid everything out and went over every piece. We decided which stayed and which went. What we didn't need, we got rid of.

"I had a good marriage," Sophie reflects. "When I lost my husband, the things I had accumulated didn't seem very important any more. They did when I was younger, but not now."

Since Edna has more income, she pays a larger percentage of the rent, utilities, and groceries. Sophie's savings were eaten up by her husband's illness and funeral expenses. For the amount of money she can afford to pay for rent, she would probably have to live in a more modest apartment in a less desirable location or in a federally subsidized building. In the city in which she lives, there is a long wait for these apartments to become available.

Edna, older and not feeling as well as she did, is glad not to be alone anymore. Sophie is comforted by being with Edna.

"It's a good arrangement for both of us," says Sophie. "We make it work by agreeing to disagree on issues we can't solve. But they are funny ones.

"We each like scrambled eggs. I like mine soft; Edna likes hers hard. Instead of one eating eggs she doesn't like, we fix them for ourselves.

"When we go to the laundromat, we each do our own laundry. Edna folds her sheets her way. I've been folding sheets a different way all these years. Why should we fight about something like that?"

• • •

One of the most creative sharers I met during the research on this book is Herbert, well into his 80s, who was a professor of education at a Midwest college before he retired.

Doctors did not want Herbert to live alone after his series of operations and his wife's death. He tried having a housekeeper for a while and didn't like being an employer. He didn't want to be a landlord. He hated the idea of being an eternal host. He feared being placed in an institution.

To ease his situation, he created a unique plan for helping others while keeping his life joyful and his mind alert.

Settled in an easy chair in his tastefully furnished, contemporary home, Herbert held forth on the premise that so strongly influences the way he lives.

"The greatest advances in society are made by people who share experiences," he says. "To put a satellite into orbit requires the knowledge of thousands of people. A scientist who shares information when he gets to a certain stage in his work gets more information back. Someone else's knowledge will then advance him. I feel you must do this with everyday life as well."

This was the springboard for Herbert's desire to share his home. But there were other incentives as well. He was lonely, and he wanted someone to share meals with. Herbert had more space than he needed in his house; he wanted to share it with someone who needed a place to live.

Most of Herbert's professional associates were dead. He had always gained much from the young people he taught; he wanted to keep in touch with the world through them.

To get a glimpse of life through each succeeding generation, to find out what it is like growing up today from young people themselves, Herbert decided he would share his home with college students. He felt those in their early 20s would be most compatible. At this stage in life, youth was moving to maturity. Adolescents were out—for him.

Herbert even narrowed down his choice to a female for a first sharing partner, though he later rented to both women and men.

"I overintellectualize life," he tells me. "My wife always said that, too. I analyze everything. I think women solve problems more intuitively—at least my wife did—and I wanted to understand this quality better."

249

After establishing these prerequisites, Herbert advertised space in his house in the college newspaper and posted notices on college bulletin boards.

"I told people who came here that I wanted to barter their use of the house for jobs I expected them to do. I have always felt it makes someone feel small to give him something if he has no way to give you something back.

"I told prospective sharers the rent would be one-tenth of the utility bill plus $15 a week, which I would match, to pay for food. They were to spend 30 hours a week with me, which would include our preparing and eating an evening meal together each day.

"While we discussed these things, I watched how the young woman reacted to the things in my house.

"I had put in a greenhouse. Did this woman like plants? Did she like birds? Did she say anything about the weaving loom my wife had used? Was she interested in the magazines I have piled on the coffee table? Did she like classical music?

"I wanted to get a sense of what we could talk about, whether our companionship was viable. I want intelligent people around me.

"In some instances, I frankly told the student our relationship couldn't work. I interviewed four students to find the first one to live here. I've had half a dozen students in residence over the past three years.

"I tell them they can live here for three months, which coincides with the college calendar. If our experimental time works, we can renew. I didn't want my house to be just a cheap place for someone to live. I wanted our association to be meaningful for both of us. If it was too long, or too easy, it would grow flat."

His ultimate goal was to have the student feel she was a family member, with the input and responsibilities any member of any family would have.

"The meal we eat together each day, we cook together. We decide what we would enjoy and prepare simple things. Other meals we fix on our own and groceries are bought out of our joint kitty. I always discuss food preferences in my initial interview. Once a vegetarian student lived here. I thought it would be fun to try that. After a while, I felt I needed meat in my diet, so she didn't object to helping me cook it.

"I take out the garbage, help empty the dishwasher, do whatever jobs I can. I want to keep as active as my health permits; I don't want to become a drone."

Other rules Herbert made clear are these.

• Common space is to be kept presentable (a cleaning woman comes in several times a week to do serious work); the student's own room is hers alone. She must clean it, but no one will invade her solitude.

• The shared bathroom is tidied after each use but is cleaned thoroughly by the cleaning woman. The student sleeps in a nearby room in case Herbert calls for help during the night.

• He provides towels and bedding if the student wishes. No pets are allowed—especially cats; wild birds have priority here. No drugs of any kind are to be taken on the premises; drunkenness will not be tolerated. Wine with dinner (furnished by the student) is fine.

• The student uses Herbert's car to do the shopping or other errands for him. She must provide her own transportation (school is an easy walk or bike ride away) for her own needs. She is free to use the washer and dryer.

• Students' friends are welcome, even an occasional overnight one, but a live-in boyfriend is out of the question.

Herbert says, "In an arrangement of this kind, you must be careful not to give too much because it demeans the other person. If you give too little, it demeans you.

"One student left a metal twister on something she put in the microwave oven. It cost $53 to repair it. Another burned out the bottom of an aluminum pan. I've made both of these kinds of mistakes myself, so I pay for these expenses. Any family member could have this kind of accident. I wouldn't fight over the expense. The human relationship is more important.

"The 30 hours a week we spend together may be spent watching the news on television and discussing what we saw, talking about books we're reading, or articles we've picked up. Thirty hours is just right to spend together; each of us also wants our own peace. We don't keep a time clock on these 'together' hours. We just use it as a rule of thumb and it works out to about that many.

"Allison, the biology student who lives here now, is a tremendous source of information I knew nothing about.

"Doug, who lives downstairs, is a genetic engineer. His field is fascinating. We put in a garden together which we both take care of. We eat from the garden and freeze vegetables. I pay for the seeds and for renting the Rototiller. The yardwork is done by a boy I hire.

"I had a married couple live downstairs for a while, but they excluded me from their conversations. They were supposed to finish the part of the downstairs that needed work as part of the 60 hours a week they owed me. They never did, and they didn't cook, and they were behind in their money.

"I asked them to leave and I haven't invited another couple since. Singles work out much better and I often have two here at a time, as I do now."

If Herbert prefers to be neither a landlord nor a host, he also does not want to be a father.

"This is the stage in a person's life when he has to learn things for himself. I don't tell him what to do or how to behave because it would ruin our relationship.

"If someone is in a bad mood and doesn't feel like talking, I don't confront him. One day Allison sulked, didn't help with the evening meal, and stayed in her room. The next day she apologized and we talked it over.

"This is a hard period to go through in life. There is a generation gap. Unless someone is willing to go more than halfway, a situation like mine wouldn't work.

"I feel strongly that home is an attitude more than a place, and students need a place where attitudes can be expressed freely. I wanted my home to be a sanctuary where they can be themselves, try out new ideas. I want to foster that kind of atmosphere.

"If you're a host or landlord, you have a role to play and the expectations that go along with it. I don't want any of that. I want the people who live here to feel so free they will express thoughts I otherwise wouldn't be exposed to. That's the excitement of this arrangement to me.

"If I make you smile, I will have given you something to make you smile. What price can you put on that?"

THE PARTNERSHIP PACT

No matter what the reason, those who share homes on a less permanent basis than co-ownership still have to go into a partnership with their eyes wide open. Desperation regrettably often causes people to throw caution to the winds. Just because you rent space to someone (or from someone) and the arrangement isn't forever doesn't mean that someone can be just anyone.

When you're stuck with a $300 phone bill after your renter has hurriedly moved out; when you suddenly realize the nice motherly woman who rented you her attic apartment so cheaply also expects you to take her grocery shopping, wash the windows, and do all of the yardwork—you'll wish you had asked more questions and protected yourself, before you got into such a fix.

This is a good time to take a look at the questions Leah Dobkin of the Shared Housing Resource Center asks when she helps make matches between people who wish to share their home and those who need a place to live. They will help crystallize your thinking—whether you are the one offering space or the one seeking it.

CONSIDERATIONS IN HOME SHARING
(A Questionnaire for the Homeowner)

House

Is my home suitable for sharing? Would any alterations be necessary to my house in order to accommodate homesharers? How much would such alterations cost? Can I afford it?

How many homesharers would I like to have?

Cost

How much income do I need in order to reduce my housing cost burdens to the point I need to? Would the income make the remodeling expenses worthwhile?

Lifestyle

What kind of homesharing relationship do I want?

Do I want to rent a room (or rooms) to a stranger, or do I want a companion with whom to share my life?

To what degree do I want to share my kitchen, living room, and other common spaces?

Does this potential homesharer have similar values and needs?

What needs would homesharing with this person meet?

What do I not like about this person?

CONSIDERATIONS IN HOME SHARING
(A Questionnaire for the Tenant)

Location

Will I be happy living in this location?

Is it close to work? To my friends?

Near public transportation, stores, services?

Cost

Can I afford to live here comfortably?

(Total housing costs—rent *and* utilities—generally should not be more than 25% of my income.)

Lifestyle

Is this the way I want to live?

Am I compatible with this (these) home-sharing companion(s)?

To what extent will we share our lives? Will I have the degree of privacy I want? And sociability?

What is essential for me in a homesharing situation?
>   For example: quiet street
>   room for my family heirloom furniture

Which needs does this situation meet?

What do I *not* like about this situation?

(*Note:* The condition of the house will tell you a great deal about your prospective landlord. Is it a mess, or does it look comfortable? Check the kitchen and bath facilities. Are they adequate? Are they clean? How much closet space is there? Can you hang up your own posters? Are there children and animals around? Is the ceiling or walls cracked? Does the roof leak? This will tell you whether your landlord is good about making repairs. Take stock of the place you're considering as well as the person who owns it.)

In the Appendix you will find a home-sharing agreement used by the Shared Housing Resource Center. Whether you actually use a written agreement or not, this one is a good model for yours.

Note particularly the clause that refers to a security deposit. Those who rent out space in homes feel this is extremely important. Should your judgment have been poor in selecting a housemate, you will be protected since you are holding some of his money.

Long-distance phone bills you are stuck with or abuse of your property can be deducted from this amount.

• • •

Some parting words of wisdom from veteran house sharer Pat Mazagatti, who also owned a matching service in Ft. Lauderdale, Florida.

"If you don't ask for a deposit from people who share your home, you're asking to be taken. If there is no money involved, the renter may not care if he messes up your house or runs up phone bills. If you are charging, say, $300 for rent, ask for a $200 deposit. If the person moves out, do not refund the deposit until you have the last utility or phone bill in your hands."

(Others advise even more money up front—as much as the first and last month's rent—so you will have 30 days' notice if a tenant vacates the premises as well as a damage deposit of at least three-quarters of a month's rent.)

"Be clear about the arrangement you want to have and don't try to be instant friends. Let that come gradually."

It's easier to add than to subtract favors. Hold off, because you may set yourself up as the person who is constantly giving.

"Also, make sure you have enough space to feel comfortable. What is adequate for one person may be claustrophobic for another, so there is no general rule. You and your tenants should be able to lead your own lives with a minimum of interference. Understand that poking into rooms you have rented is taboo. That space belongs to the people who share your house, and you must respect their privacy. Hands off."

Describe, clearly, who is entitled to use which rooms. Besides space, what else do you want to share, or not? This includes food, furniture—whatever.

For example, pin up a note that says, "The top two shelves of the refrigerator are mine; the bottom two are yours. Or, "All food inside a bag in the refrigerator with our names written on the outside is not to be shared. Tenants are welcome to use everything else."

"Even though my fruit juicer is in the kitchen, I do not wish to share its use. I have exclusive use of the third-floor bedroom and bath plus the bedroom on the second floor I use as a study; you have the two bedrooms on the second floor connected by a bath as a private space. The kitchen, living room, downstairs, bath and all other rooms are to be used in common."

Renters Should Make Agreements, Too

Two parties sharing rental space can also draw up an agreement. (The home-sharing agreement in the Appendix should give you some ideas on points to include.) It should clearly state that co-renters are both responsible for abiding by the lease, if there is one; specify what share of the rent and security deposit each is responsible for paying and whether each pays his share to the landlord or one to the other; who will pay the landlord; what areas are to be shared and which are to be private; how utilities and phone bills are to be divided, how property insurance (if they want it) will be handled; what will happen if one wants to move out; and any other important issues, from food to guests.

How about the question of subletting? It should be dealt with by apartment sharers as well as dual home owners. What happens if a partner is transferred out of town to do a special assignment for six months? He needs to pay rent in another city and finds it hard to come up with the cash for both residences. Will he be allowed to find someone to move in and pick up his share of the rent?

Does the remaining partner have the right to approve the tenant so all stays harmonious? Work it out.

·15·
How to Buy a House with Someone

"Every month, when I paid my rent, I felt like I was kissing money goodbye." says Maria. "I wanted to invest in a house; it didn't have to be an expensive one. But I wanted to put my money into something tangible, something I could see. I longed to own my own home."

Maria's feelings are echoed throughout the country as single people search for ways to do something better with their dollars than pay rent for an apartment. They want to build equity. They want the tax breaks mortgage payments can provide. Since many remain single longer these days as they build independent lives and careers, they do, indeed, have a chance to build a cash reserve to use as capital but often not enough for the initial down payment. And their incomes won't cover monthly expenses without tightening belts too much. That's why many singles are pooling resources to buy homes together.

A new housing trend is sweeping the country: Builders are constructing condominiums with two master bedroom suites in response to this increasing need. Whether it's called the mingles market or tandem living—it's been called a variety of names—builders now feel joint home ownership (for business, not romance) will account for a significant percentage of the housing in the 1980s.

Not just modest homes are being shared, either. Some, equipped with trimmings such as "entertainment centers" with every possible electronic video and stereo device, to saunas and hot tubs, cost several hundred thousand dollars or more.

It's a great way to afford "glitz." You have all the luxuries you crave by pooling resources with like-minded partners. You also have privacy because these homes have bedroom suites for each owner. For people who love to entertain at home in style, this is definitely the way to do it.

From houses and condos made for the dual market to traditional one-family homes and condominiums, modest or extravagant—those seeking to own homes are seeking each other to be able to afford what they like.

BREAKING GROUND

Back to Maria. She lived in a variety of apartments for 11 years. Her last as an apartment dweller she shared with Leslie, a fellow recreational therapist at the senior citizens' center where both worked. Leslie had been staying in a friend's apartment until the friend came back to town. When she was left apartmentless, she moved in with Maria.

They painted and fixed up the apartment they lived in together, but all the while talked about wanting to be able to own their own home. They knew they had rehabbing skills because that's what they were doing with their apartment. Maria had $5,000 saved—enough for a modest down payment. Leslie had no cash in the bank. On the other hand, Maria didn't have an income large enough to handle mortgage payments on her own. She didn't feel capable of tackling the amount of physical labor (and the expense of the major improvements) a house she could afford would demand.

They made a deal. Maria would make the down payment on a house she and Leslie both selected, and the title would be in her name. All other expenses, including capital ones, would be split down the middle. Records of who spent what would be immaculately kept. If the partnership dissolved, each woman would know what percentage of the house equity had accrued to her, for a fair split with no hard feelings.

That step out of the way, house hunting began in earnest.

"Whether we loved or hated a house wasn't the criterion," laughs Maria. "How bad the condition of the house was and whether we could fix it up was. We both wanted to continue to live in the same area of the city and we wanted an older home with character. That's what we got—a house in terrible shape with gorgeous stained glass windows we fell in love with. Those got stolen shortly after we bought the house.

"Let that be a lesson to other inner-city rehabbers. Sleep in the house, no matter what, after you buy it. Leaving it vacant while you do the work is an open invitation to get ripped off."

These two didn't need to draw up a list of priorities for what they wanted to do to their house; they fixed whatever was in worst shape first.

Their furniture is a conglomeration from past apartments plus donations from relatives; they did buy a new sofa and refrigerator. Neither is materialistic, and a *House Beautiful* house is not their style. Comfort is important, but wall-to-wall carpeting is not what Maria and Leslie need to feel comfortable.

While plastering, painting, and other heavy-duty jobs are shared equally, house-cleaning chores are done on a more casual basis.

"I think we're sensitive to each other's feelings," says Leslie. "We share a bathroom upstairs, and we leave it clean out of respect for each other. It would be offensive to me if Maria left her makeup all over the counter and her clothes on the floor. I wouldn't do that to her either.

"I'm a fanatic about garbage," laughs Leslie. "It has to go out every day. Maria hates to see dishes sitting around, so she usually does them. She likes to cook, too, but tells me if she gets tired of it.

"I do the same if I find I'm the one who's cleaning out the kitty litter box most of the time. One of us says, 'It would be nice if you'd share this responsibility. I feel I've been doing it too often.' "

"I'm blunt. Maybe that's one of my downfalls," says Maria. "But I think it's better to speak up before everyone gets too angry."

"I think you have to be a good listener to be a good partner," says Leslie. "You have to try to pick up what the other person is trying to say, because she may not want to hurt your feelings by being too direct. You also have to tell a person why you feel a certain way about something—even if it's as minor as how the bathtub should be scrubbed. If it means a lot to you, and your partner understands why, she'll try to please you."

Meals are cooked and eaten together. Food costs are split, though each puts on the shopping list those items she likes. The list is conservative, because house costs overshadow gourmet groceries.

"We don't worry about one person's groceries being more than the other's," says Leslie. "It comes out even in the end. But if one of us wants to buy a bottle of wine or a box of crackers, and the other doesn't, we buy it on our own. Of course, that person is welcome to some of it—as long as she doesn't eat or drink it all."

This partnership works because partners are easy-going but frank.

"If I'm going to bring a man home one night," says Leslie, "I'd say, 'I'm coming home with Roy tonight.' I wouldn't ask Maria's permission. This is just how it will be.

"We did have the advantage of living with each other for a year in an apartment before we bought this house. We know each other's behavior and we're comfortable with it."

Friends are shared, or not, as partners please. Maria says, "If I have friends over I think Leslie would like, I ask her to join us. If I'd prefer to spend time alone with someone, I tell her that, too. When you share a house, you can't take this personally. Otherwise, you'd be paranoid. You just say how you feel.

"That's what saved us when Leslie's younger sister moved into our house for awhile," continues Maria. "Leslie asked if it was all right with me and I agreed. She was one messy and irresponsible kid. We'd come home from work and all the lights in the house and every television set would be on. She didn't pay rent and she caused a lot of tension. It was like raising a teenage daughter.

"Leslie never said, 'Like me; like my sister.' We talked the situation over and decided to ask her to leave. Having her there wasn't worth disrupting our partnership.

"We're both commonsense people," says Maria. "Even if one of us left on negative terms, we wouldn't leave the other holding the bag to make mortgage payments. We'd pay our share until the remaining partner found a new one. We'd work out the payout even if it had to be over a period of time. We'd never say, 'Give me my money in two weeks—or else.' We gave our word to each other and we'll stand by it."

• • •

Sheila, a clinical psychologist, and Anna, a high school teacher, have shared a spacious apartment for three years. Good friends before they moved in together, each lived in smaller, efficiency-type apartments. When they saw an ad for a flat that took up half a floor in what was once an old hotel, they decided it would be grand. Neither could afford to rent it on her own. Now, after three years of apartment co-dwelling, they have just purchased a home—the first for both of them.

It's a three-story house with six bedrooms in a transitional neighborhood. At this point, the transition is upward because people like Sheila and Anna are realizing their money will buy more space and grace if they are willing to gamble a bit with safety. Seedy streets are undergoing facelifts as once-gracious homes are steadily scrubbed, painted, and plastered back to life.

Sheila says, "We picked a large apartment to share so each of us would always have enough private space. We used the same criterion in our house selection. We haven't moved in yet, we've just finalized the deal. We have great plans for our house. All we have to do is furnish and decorate it since it's already been completely remodeled by a contractor.

"The top story will be my office space. That's where I'll see private patients (she works at a clinic that treats children) and do paperwork. Anna will have a darkroom and a place for her photography equipment on the second floor.

"Right now, we're working out all the legal and financial wrinkles with an attorney and a CPA so everything is equitable. We're also making sure we get every tax benefit we're entitled to. All details will be tidily wrapped up and put on paper."

As Sheila talks of her three years with Anna, it is clear that a great deal of negotiation, of "working things out," has strengthened their trust in each other. Hurt feelings and misunderstandings they have been able to resolve make them believe they basically have each other's best interests at heart.

"We have different schedules," says Sheila. "Anna gets up at 5:30 each morning for school and goes to bed at 9:00. I get home sometimes just as she's going to bed and am asleep when she leaves in the morning. I don't have to be at work until 10:00.

"Because of our schedules, we weren't seeing much of each other. We were living parallel lives. We seldom ate meals together; we just weren't talking. Anna felt she was getting stuck with most of the house responsibilities because I was never home. She's more compulsive about cleaning than I am anyway.

"Finally, we realized what was happening and we made time to talk. I explained that I was seeing private patients after clinic work because I was trying to earn as much extra money as I could to be able to afford a house. We both wanted one!

"After working so many hours during the week, I hated spending all day, every Saturday, cleaning. So that Anna wouldn't feel resentful being stuck with the job, I suggested hiring a cleaning woman to come in once a week. I could see one extra patient to pay for it. That decision saved a mountain of hassles and was a great solution for both of us."

All apartment expenses are divided evenly; in addition, each payday Sheila and Anna put $40 into a kitty which is used for groceries, *The New York Times*, and other sundries. Since partners get paid on opposite weeks, someone is always able to put up some cash.

"We don't count nickels," says Sheila. "If there's $10 left in the kitty one week and we decide to go out to dinner, we use the leftover money. No one worries over who has dessert or who ate how much of the groceries.

"We're going to have to be much more careful, once we move into the house," she muses. "We're going to be more strapped for money. Now, if we want to eat out, we do. Our lifestyles are free. We are very aware of how much each of us will have to contribute to keep ahead of our bills and we will sacrifice what we have to, to make it work.

"We're both in our mid-30s. Anna and I have been through long relationships with men. We're not trying to find ourselves at this point. I couldn't imagine buying a house with someone who said, 'I don't know where I'll be a year from now.'

"We know ourselves and each other. For mature reasons, we decided to live in an apartment together—and now a house. But you have to be careful partners don't get too dependent on each other; that they don't merge and become one person. If they break up, they'd lose their sense of self.

"I'd grieve if our partnership ended, because our lives are intertwined. But I wouldn't lose who I am." (This is an important thought to keep in mind in house partnering. Those who share living space also share each other's lives—sometimes too closely. If a break in the alliance occurs, the emotional disruption is huge. Though it is natural for people to live together to become deeply attached to one another, it is important that they keep a strong bead on who they are. No one person should feel smothered by another, lost in the tide of two personalities becoming one. A partnership thrives because strong individuals support one another, give to one another without burdening the other with emotional demands.)

Because Sheila and Anna are partners for the long haul, they don't let little things get them down—angry, yes, and angry enough to fight. But not fights destructive enough to tear apart what they've built.

"I like to straighten," says Sheila. "Anna likes to clean. I like reruns on television; Anna watches the news—which I watch with her when I'm home. If I'm alone, I go back to reruns.

"When Anna's sister and her 2-year-old son stayed with us one weekend, the kid crayoned all over our kitchen wall. Sure, it made me mad. But I trusted Anna to take care of it.

"Our talents also balance out. I could play with figures all night long. I'm handling the house finances because I love to. When we move, though, we have to break our apartment lease. Anna is going to talk to the landlord. I feel as if she is taking the weight of the world off my shoulders because I hate those kinds of confrontations. We complement each other.

"Our values are the same. When we looked at houses, we both liked old woodwork and high ceilings. We chose an area of town convenient to both our jobs. We both work with children.

"When two people join together, the world expands so much. And it's not just money I'm talking about, though one person can only afford so much on one salary. It's having a diverse group of friends, someone to talk to when you need company. It's sharing the excitement of being able to buy your first home.

"Neither of us can guarantee we'll never get married, but neither of us feels we're biding our time until 'the right man' comes along. Our house is not going to be a way station. Though this decision has really thrown our parents for a loop because they're fearful for us, we've made a very measured decision."

FROST WARNINGS

So far, it might sound like buying a home in partnership is a piece of cake. Well, as you can see, it is easier when people like Maria and Leslie and Sheila and Anna have a chance to live together and learn a great deal about each other before they plunge in and make the purchase.

You've also been given a glimpse of people who are skilled "talkers," who value each other more than things. Who may care whether or not there are fingerprints on the refrigerator, but would not blow up over it. They have faith that neither is going to cheat with money. These are optimum partnership conditions, because even when winds whip up, roots are deep enough to weather the storm.

Though some partners feel the sun will always shine on them, others overestimate their alliance in the face of frost warnings.

Nan is one of them. A head nurse in a hospital intensive care unit, in her late 30s, part of a group of about twenty friends strongly committed to supporting each other, she felt buying a home with a man she had known for two years, who was also a member of this group, would be a natural success.

Though they didn't know each other well, they knew each other through this community of people. All were ex-commune types, still active in politics and social causes. Now, holding mainstream jobs and making good money, they continued to consider shared property and shared lives a plus.

Living in the same neighborhood in rented apartments, friends bought houses on the same street as they could afford them and as they became available. When one couple decided to sell their house in order to buy a larger one, Nan and Rudy felt it was fate.

They didn't have to run around looking for a home they both wanted to own. They knew the sellers and trusted them. There was no romance between Nan and Rudy; they simply felt buying this house together would make economic sense.

"We felt the house, a big old two-story built in 1906, was roomy enough to give us both the privacy we needed," remembers Nan. "And we had faith that we would always be fair with one another. Neither of us was comfortable with rules, so we didn't discuss do's and don't's before we moved in together. We felt we could negotiate any difference we would have, and we were overwhelmed by the thought of working out everything that could conceivably come up on paper."

Even so, to appease the bankers and lawyers who felt they were being unrealistic in assuming that co-owning a house could be done with such a relaxed structure, Nan and Rudy drew up their agreement (without the help of an attorney, another rash move, their friends thought) and had it notarized.

1. If one partner died, the other would have the first option to buy his shares. Otherwise, they would go to his heirs or estate.
2. If one person wanted to dissolve the partnership, the other partner had first option to buy his shares.
3. If one partner wanted to move out of the house and rent his portion, the remaining partner would have the right to find a renter he could get along with, even though the exiting partner would be paid the rent.
4. The partners were to keep the house, according to these rules, for two years. After that, renegotiation or change could take place.
5. If the partners got into trouble and could not come to a resolution, before either went to a lawyer or through the court system, they would go to other people in the community who would act as mediators. Nan and Rudy agreed to abide by their decision.

Nan took the master bedroom on the second floor and the sunporch; Rudy took the two smaller bedrooms. They shared a bath. Nan worked a 3:00-11:00 shift; Rudy worked as manager of a garden store from 8:30 to 4:00. Both were gone a lot.

But in the beginning, they also made sure they talked a lot. They dealt quite well with what they were comfortable and uncomfortable with.

So Rudy wasn't fastidious about the bathroom. When Nan complained too much, he hired someone to clean the entire house to make up for it.

He became more aware of house responsibilities; Nan became more flexible.

They were cordial to each other's guests but respected each other's use of the living room space. They ate meals apart but kept food, bought separately, in the refrigerator.

"His groceries were mostly on the left side," Nan remembers. "Mine were on the right, but we did a lot of borrowing without problems."

It all started to crumble when Rudy's 11-year-old son came to stay with his father. He started to eat everything Nan baked (for fun and "therapy") every weekend.

"I knew he was going to live with us half-time when we bought the house," Nan says. "I have always liked kids. I looked forward to Rudy's son being with us. I never knew a kid I didn't like—until this one. He was obnoxious.

"At first I baked brownies for him so he would have snacks to eat. But that wasn't enough. He ate everything I cooked.

"When I finally told Rudy I wasn't going to put up with this any more, he said he would make sure to stock up on enough food for the whole neighborhood. He wanted to smooth out the difficulty. The only problem was, the kid wasn't good at sticking to his father's rules and his father didn't press him to do so.

"Next came Rudy's girl friend. When she first began to spend nights there, her father would call her every morning at six. It drove me nuts. Rudy finally got a separate phone so it would only ring in his room and not wake me up.

"When she became a permanent fixture. I felt I was being outnumbered in my own house."

Nan and Rudy tried to work this out peacefully by Rudy contributing an extra $25 a month for house payments and also assuming two-thirds of the utility bill. Previously, all house-related expenses had been divided equally. As they had hoped, they were working out problems as they came up. But not well enough.

"Roxanne was a taker," says Nan. "She didn't cook or clean. I hadn't bargained on living with Rudy and a girl friend, anyway.

"It all came to a head when I saw her wearing my sweater. She had picked up one I left in the bathroom and wore it two weeks. When I saw that she had it on, I said, 'Gee, that sweater is like the one I lost.'

"She said, 'I'm so spaced out, I don't even think about things like that. You mean, this sweater isn't mine?'

"I blew up."

Conditions at that point—a year and a half into the two-year agreement—declined. Rudy felt Nan was trying to damage his relationship with Roxanne.

Nan wanted to split the house into two apartments. She would put a kitchen upstairs and a bath downstairs; she could have the upstairs and Rudy and Roxanne could live downstairs.

Rudy refused. He felt that Nan was trying to stop him from doing what he pleased in his own home and tempers boiled. Small angers, underground all along, came to the surface. Negotiation became impossible. Rudy had grown away from the community as he grew closer to Roxanne. He refused mediation.

He moved out. He didn't care if the bank foreclosed on Nan if she couldn't come up with enough money for the mortgage payments. He figured if that happened, he'd get back some of the money he had invested anyway.

Frantic, Nan was able to take out a new loan (but at a higher rate) to pay off Rudy's share. They reached a price that was fair to both of them with great difficulty, and if Nan's parents hadn't helped her financially, she would have lost everything.

"Obviously we were too loose," says Nan. "If I had it to do over again, I would have made a more detailed contract between the two of us. Our agreement for a two-year commitment didn't mean anything. I sure would have talked about a lot of things we didn't and would have wanted to work them out in a way that was right for both of us."

• • •

Just to reaffirm how powerful other people can be to a partnership, let's take a look at what happened to Pete and Marty.

Pete rented the top half of a townhouse after his divorce and became friendly with Marty, who lived on the first floor. Marty had also been married and was now alone.

Both were executives with large corporations. They traveled extensively in their jobs, but when they were home they loved to attend sports events, liked to share meals, and were delighted to find they had each worked at construction trades during college days.

They both wanted to buy a house, and Pete proposed they buy one together. Marty thought it was a fine idea, so they engaged a realtor to show them urban houses they could rehab. They bought the first one they looked at.

"We wanted a place that needed fixing up so we could use our construction skills," says Pete. "We wanted to live in the same area of town where we had rented apartments, and we didn't want to spend so much money that if we messed up the house while we were working on it, it would be a big deal.

"We were both making between $40,000 and $50,000 a year. The home we bought cost $30,000."

Pete knew he didn't want to go from living alone to constantly being with someone else. He also knew that if he continued to live alone, it would be hard to keep a home because he was away so much. This arrangement seemed perfect.

"I had the house to myself about 25% of the time," Pete remembers. "About 50% of the time we were home together. The other 25% of the time neither of us was there. It was a fine balance.

"Marty and I are both high-energy people. We loved getting into house projects. We installed skylights on the whole third floor. We found a guy who was a good carpenter to help us. That way Marty and I were not totally dependent on each other's skills. And when either of us went out of town, the man we hired provided continuity.

"We never disagreed over the cost of materials. We shopped for major purchases together, such as the Ben Franklin-type stove we wanted to install. But we never even questioned each other over minor acquisitions. We just split them."

The three-bedroom house had a kitchen, solarium, dining and living room, full basement, and garage. There was enough space for Pete's 13-year-old daughter when she came to visit and for women friends of both who occasionally spent the night. Pete and Marty's style was confrontive. If something was going on they didn't like, they said so. They never put the lid on feelings and stewed.

Expenses were shared equally. So were meals. Both loved to cook and would eat all kinds of food.

"When I shopped, I might buy Chenin Blanc wine," says Pete. "Marty might buy Chablis. Each time we went to the store, we bought what we liked so each of us would feel in charge. We kept the grocery receipts and once a month we sat down and split the cost.

"Whoever got home first started dinner. If one guy was held up, no one got upset."

Cleanliness was not an issue either; and though both liked each other's friends, each knew when it was time to split.

After two years together, Pete and Marty decided to buy a bigger house. They called in the same realtor who had sold them the first one, but during the time they were searching for a grander model, Marty fell in love. Within six weeks he married the woman, who had a 5-year-old daughter, in the courtyard of the new home he and Pete purchased.

"All of us looked at the new house and approved of it before we bought it," says Pete. "My daughter was visiting from out of state, so the four of us picked it out.

"Marty and I would have bought the house whether or not he got married. We agreed it would take two incomes to manage the mortgage. It was a much bigger home, big enough for everyone—we thought.

"I took the third floor, which had a bedroom and bath. Marty and his wife took the master bedroom and bath on the second floor; her daughter had a second-floor bedroom; I had a den on the second floor; the extra bath on th .t floor was communal. First-floor space including the solarium and numerous other nooks and crannies belonged to everyone."

Mortgage payments, and gas, electric, and water expenses were split equally by the two men; how many meals each person ate at home per month was recorded. Where groceries were concerned each partner was a unit; Pete was considered a third of the whole. After food costs were totaled, he generally paid a third of the sum.

"Though our partnership was based on economics, Marty and I always had fun together," remembers Pete. "Our partnership began to deteriorate as our relationship with each other went downhill.

"Marty thought he could go to the hockey game with me after being away all week just as we always had. His wife got angry. Before he got married, I'd ask Marty on the spur of the moment whether he wanted to go to a basketball game. He'd accept at the drop of a hat. Now he asked his wife if she'd mind if he went with me. He had to deal with two relationships under the same roof and it was just too much.

"Marty thought it would all be fine. We had faith we could work it out, but it just started to go stale.

"Marty's wife did the grocery shopping and the cooking because she wanted to. I cleaned the third floor, they cleaned the second, everyone cleaned the first. We alternated cutting grass and other chores like that. Since Marty was away a good deal of the time, his wife was happy to have someone else in the house, but we didn't have much in common. It was Marty I liked. Not that I disliked his wife, we just didn't share many interests.

"I liked her daughter a lot. She was the same age my daughter was when I got a divorce. It was fun having her around because I missed that period with my own child. I even babysat for her while Marty's wife studied (she was taking college courses) or had to go out. She was very careful not to take advantage of this, too. I can see why Marty loved her. I just wasn't interested in her life. There was no real dialogue between us. Our conversations were forced.

"We each began to spend more and more time on our own floors. Before, Marty and I would immediately face each other with a problem and make history of any issue that came up. Now, I dealt with him, he dealt with her, she dealt with him, he dealt with me. It was a mess.

"When she became pregnant, it was the perfect time to dissolve the partnership. I had lived in the house a year. We each had the first option to buy each other out at the appraised value plus 10%.

"So that Marty wouldn't have to refinance the house at a higher interest rate, we agreed that during the next year he would give me $5,000, then another $5,000 later to reimburse me for my half of the down payment.

"I didn't lose any biggies in the deal. I didn't want half of the $20 shovel or $10 hammer we had bought together. I left all that behind. I had already been through one divorce and that was enough."

• • •

A few years out of graduate school, Catherine, a newspaper reporter, started to feel the itch to own a house. Her friend Elena, an art director with a publishing company, had had the urge a bit longer; it was she who proposed the idea of a joint purchase. When Catherine became enthusiastic about the plan, they began house hunting in earnest.

Catherine and Elena had known each other enough years to feel their personal preferences and living habits were compatible. Since they had spent a lot of time with each other and in each other's apartments, smoking, cleanliness, music, and matters of that sort would hold no surprises. They felt they had a lot in common.

Catherine and Elena were both involved with men they felt they were going to marry. They liked each other's fiances, too, so they decided to buy a multiple-family dwelling. The women could live in one unit and rent the other apartment (or apartments) depending on the kind of house they could find. Then when they married, the couples could move to separate units. Everyone would have a place to live— neat and tidy planning, they thought.

The 60-year-old duplex they found in a neighborhood with a fine view of the city seemed like a perfect choice. Actually, it was two side-by-side, two-story houses which were connected. Each had an attic, three bedrooms, and a bath on the second floor and a living room, dining room, and kitchen on the first.

Catherine and Elena decided (as per their original plan) to live in one house together and allow the present renters to remain in the other unit until they needed it for themselves. They agreed that if neither decided to live in the units after she married, both could move where they pleased and keep the duplex as an investment.

Catherine and Elena each took one bedroom on the second floor

269

and shared a bath. Elena moved her paints and easel into the third bedroom; Catherine stored her camping equipment in the attic. All other rooms were used by both.

"Though we divided cleaning chores by floors," Catherine remembers, "we didn't do much of that until after we had lived in the house a year. The place was such a mess, it wasn't a question of dusting. We had to do a huge amount of remodeling.

"We were naive about the amount of work the house required. For instance, we thought all we needed to do to the bathroom was wallpaper. When we removed the old wallpaper, we found out we had to put up new sheet rock. Then we had to fix the toilet and replace a pipe in the floor.

"We had an idea of what we wanted to spend on the house. The house just didn't cooperate. Finally we took out a home improvement loan to cover the major jobs. When it got down to the smaller ones, we just put them off."

That's when trouble began. Catherine was more willing to put things off than Elena.

"When we were working on the house, I wanted to stop and have lunch, sit for awhile and talk," says Catherine. Elena wanted to run out and bring back some fast food to eat while we were painting. She wanted to get things done the fastest way—and I could understand that. But as time passed, I felt I was continually conceding to Elena, always compromising instead of cooperating. One of us was always giving in to the other and grumbling rather than feeling good about what we were doing together.

"Elena took a real estate investment course after we moved into the house and she got caught up in housing as a way to make money. Her friends were older than mine and had arrived professionally. I didn't want all those material things she began to think were important. I just wanted a decent place to live and some good times with friends."

When they bought the house, both worked from 9:00 to 5:00 at their respective jobs. Then Elena left the publishing company to start her own agency.

"She came home exhausted in the evenings," remembers Catherine. "She wouldn't finish work until 10:00 some nights. After putting in that many hours, the only thing she wanted to do when she got home was go to her room and be alone. I had already been by myself for a few hours. I was unwound, feeling good, ready for company.

"For a while, it was hard for Elena to tell me she needed to be by herself after work. It was hard for me to understand that. We didn't do a good job of reading each other's feelings."

Other issues, once considered unimportant, began to take on significance. Though Elena knew Catherine's habit of letting a day's worth of plates accumulate before she washed them, she suddenly became angry when she saw a dirty breakfast bowl sitting around until dinner.

Their habits didn't change. Their feelings about each other did. Idiosyncrasies, previously overlooked, became sore points. Partners fought about those instead of what was really bothering them.

"When Elena told me my dirty dishes bothered her, I tried to remember to do them right away," says Catherine. "Sometimes I just left them in the sink to get back at her because she made me so furious.

"I know I made her angry, too, when I began working part-time booking folk singing groups. Some of the performers who came to town stayed with us—maybe one weekend a month. If the singer was a woman, she slept in my room. If the singer was a male, I camped out on the couch in the living room while he used my room. People moving in and out became a big issue.

"We did handle finances pretty well, and I think we worked out a good system. We kept a joint bank account at the same savings and loan that held our mortgage. We charged ourselves rent each month to cover maintenance and improvements, and we deposited that amount plus our tenants' rent to our account. The savings and loan automatically withdrew the mortgage amount each month and it all worked smoothly.

"We bought food separately because we rarely ate meals together, but we bought cleansers for the house together. Whoever went shopping replenished these as needed. We kept receipts and split the cost.

"We took turns keeping books on a monthly basis. In retrospect, it would have been better to establish a house checking account than use personal checks. We had to get copies of receipts from each other at tax time, which was a bother. Our bookkeeping became sloppy as it became another one of those 'I'll get to it sometime' chores. We should have been more businesslike."

Catherine's relationship with her fiance dissolved. Elena's continued, though her romancing took place mostly at his apartment on weekends.

But as Catherine's life became more free, she involved herself in new activities to fill the void. Too many, Elena thought, because she felt Catherine was letting her house responsibilities slide.

Catherine would say, "Let's make out a plan for what needs to be done, divide the jobs, and we'll get to them."

Elena would say, "You're never here anyway. No matter what you

271

say, I wind up doing all the work. I had to leave my office to meet the storm window man at the house today. You wouldn't have done it."

Catherine would say, "It didn't have to be done today."

Their sense of urgency just didn't jibe.

"The consistent problem was, I wanted a partnership for company, for a human relationship as well as economics," says Catherine. "It seemed that all Elena cared about was money. I was tired of being pushed to work on house projects all the time. Elena was angry because she felt she had all the responsibilities, but she was the one who kept taking on more because she was intent on getting things done."

The agreement Catherine and Elena had their attorney draw up had a clause that specified the following: During the first two years of joint ownership, in the event of the death of either party or should either wish to sell her share, the remaining partner would have the option to buy it for the original purchase price, without interest, plus half the dollars spent on improvements. A 30-day written notice must be given.

After two years, the buyout price would be the fair market value of the house (at least two professional appraisals must be secured) or the amount of money spent to purchase and improve it, without interest—whichever was higher.

Initially, neither woman had the money to buy out the other. That's why this clause was written—to discourage splitting up. They paid a low price for the house, but during the two years they owned it the value soared.

After two years and 10 days, Elena served Catherine notice that she wanted to sell her half of the house.

"Suddenly it dawned on me why Elena pushed for all the improvements," says Catherine, "why her timetable was so much more rushed than mine. She wanted to increase the value of the house as much as she could during that two-year period and then sell it at a profit.

"She had already bought a three-family home with another partner when she gave me notice she wanted to sell her share of our house. She moved out within two weeks. One day I came home and found she had hired a truck and moved all her furniture. The house looked awful."

Because of high interest rates at the time all this happened, Catherine wasn't able to afford the payments on the longer loan she would have to assume alone. In arranging for a new mortgage, she would have lost the house if her parents hadn't been able to bail her out. She was ready to sell to pay Elena.

Though Catherine thought she had a contract that covered everything, she realized how much just one more clause could have helped her—one that would have given her a reasonable period of time to come up with the money to buy out her partner after Elena served notice she wanted to sell. It's especially important for people with shoestring budgets; less necessary if partners have healthier cash reserves as a backup.

"I learned a lot from that partnership," says Catherine. "I thought Elena and I knew each other so well we wouldn't have any problems. We liked each other. We wanted to own a house. It never occurred to me that *why* we wanted to own a house was chasms apart."

A MODEL HOUSE

Paula and Betty became acquainted in veterinary school. Their friendship continued after they went into private practice. When Paula was going through a divorce and began looking for a multiple-family house to buy, it seemed natural for Betty to become her partner. They both had the same value system; they both loved big old homes.

Not only did they find just the right house to convert into gracious apartments, they went to an attorney who drew up a partnership agreement that clearly covered all the points that could cause them hardship.

Perhaps one of the reasons this joint venture has done so well is because each woman has her own separate living space. The other reason is how they approach obstacles.

For instance, Betty and her live-in friend, Glen, each own 25% of the building and Paula owns 50%. Maintenance, however, is split in thirds. Paula didn't consider a 50-50 job split between her alone and Betty and Glen as a team quite fair. They agreed. This is an important point to consider when a couple and a single person become house partners.

Betty kept the financial books on a permanent basis. Other jobs, such as lawn work, snow shoveling, taking out the garbage, renting apartments, and tracking down and pricing rehab materials are done by all three with no regular assignments.

A work notebook is kept and partners write in the hours they spend on house projects. If the hours don't come out even, the one who does the overload is paid $5 an hour out of the house account.

Paula insisted on three bids for all work done on the house, though the others were not so particular.

"I kept an eye on everything we put into the house in terms of its resale value," says Paula. "When Betty wanted more frivolous things installed, she paid for them herself.

"To redo the rooms we made into my apartment didn't call for much money, but we had to invest $30,000 in Betty and Glen's apartment. I paid half of that amount because it contributed to the overall value of the house. Still, I insisted on three bids for everything.

"Though this partnership is an economic boost and I am living in a much nicer place than I could have afforded on my own, plus gaining equity and tax benefits, it helped having Betty around for support while I went through my divorce. Working full-time, renovating, and renting apartments in a house is quite a chunk to do by yourself. I just couldn't have managed it on my own."

Blueprint for Success

Though your agreement will be shaped by the kind of property you purchase and by the needs of the people involved in the partnership, Paula and Betty's contract is reproduced on pages 339-342 of the Appendix as an example of how specific issues were dealt with—precisely and well. It covers many points you will need to think about and is a good illustration of what you and your partners will need to cover when you consult your attorney.

DYNAMIC DOUBLE DUOS

Though it is common for a parent whose mate has died to share a home with grown children, just as commonly a lot of grief is woven into the arrangement. Whose home is it? Who really lives with whom? Who feels put upon, at a disadvantage, on someone else's turf? Lots of feelings are swallowed to make this kind of necessary alliance plod along as best it can.

A mother-daughter (and the daughter's family) wanted to share a home; they needed to. The system they created should give encouragement to many who have been fearful of even thinking in such terms.

Inga says, "It was always understood that when Mom couldn't live alone any longer, we would live together. We have always been close. My husband and three children love her.

"I would advise anyone who wants to try what we did to not even think about it unless the group is basically harmonious. If your relationship isn't good to start with, it's sure not going to get any better after you live in the same house.

274

"Anyway, Mom got sick one night while she was still in her own home. She was dizzy and she couldn't call for help. It scared her and us enough that we knew the time had come to make our move."

Inga and her family had a small house in the suburbs. Her mother owned one in a different part of town. They decided to buy a larger house in partnership so neither would feel they "lived" with the other. They would share equally. Mom was adamant on that point.

Inga's mother had loaned her and her husband the money to buy their first home. They paid her back with interest lower than that a bank would charge. With the sale of their house, they would have the money to finance half of the new one. They would still be paying interest to Mom. Mom had the money from the sale of her home to buy—outright—her part of the new house. No bank loans of any kind were to be involved, but a good attorney was. Everyone's investments and legal obligations were spelled out in detail.

Meanwhile, the search for the new house began. Inga wanted to stay in the same school district, and that was fine with her mother. But her mother made clear what she needed in a home as well.

Mom wanted a bedroom with an adjoining bath so she wouldn't have to share bath facilities with the kids. She wanted the lefthand side of a garage if there was a two-car garage; the whole garage if it accommodated only one car. She was used to pulling her car in from the left and felt comfortable that way. Inga laughed and agreed.

Mom wanted a home big enough so everyone could go off into separate rooms and have privacy. A living room plus a family room was essential.

They all looked at homes and eliminated those they found fault with. They seemed to like and dislike the same things, so they settled happily on one with four bedrooms (a master with an adjoining bath for Mom; Inga and James were satisfied with the large room with a bath across the hall), a family and living room, dining area, large basement, nice-sized yard—in the right school district. It was little more expensive than they had planned, but they were able to work it out.

More arrangements:

Any large improvements that would add to the saleability of the home were to be divided evenly. If one partner wanted to do something the other felt was not necessary, he would pay for it alone. Joint improvement examples are a covered patio and storm windows. Inga and her husband footed the bill for the little covered front porch they wanted.

Mom paid a fixed monthly amount toward expenses—food, utilities, the works. If prices rose, Inga had to absorb it. They felt this was fair because Mom didn't raise her interest rates, as a bank would. She could pay more each month for expenses if her money was earning more. Instead, she used her capital to finance Inga's home. Everyone is satisfied.

Mom pays half of the house insurance and taxes. All other expenses are Inga and James's.

But Inga and James's dollar investment in the house is protected in their legal agreement. They keep track of improvements they make, so that their value can be added to their equity.

Further, when Mom dies, one-fourth of her estate will be Inga's. They figure this will probably be equal to what Inga and James will owe on their share of the house. They will also have first option to buy Mom's share and a reasonable length of time to finance a bank loan to pay for it.

Mom's will also states that the furniture in the house belongs to Inga. This is a lifesaver because furniture from both households was blended to fill the new one. Everyone talked over whose fit best in each room and gave away the overflow. If relatives could claim favorite pieces after Mom's death, Inga and her husband would be in sorry shape.

"Mom made it clear, at the beginning, she didn't want us to tell the kids to be quiet all the time because of her," says Inga. "She didn't want the children to resent her. At the same time, they know that if she goes into her room and closes the door (there is a television set and desk in there), they are not to bother her. They can make noise, have friends over, but not charge into her room. She had a real concern that our life and the children's lives not be inhibited by her presence. But the children have learned a lot from her. They love to talk to her about 'old times.'

"She babysits my kids a lot. She did that before we moved in together, but she doesn't like to have that taken for granted.

"When I know which days in the week I'm going to work [Inga has a part-time sales job, but the days she works vary], I ask Mom if she'll be home after school or whether I should make other arrangements. She's usually there, but wants us to respect her time if she's busy.

"Mom dusts, shares in the cooking chores, takes care of her room, and waters the plants."

Inga does the harder jobs, such as vacuuming and mopping. The yard and garden are her domain.

Laundry is done separately, though Inga and her mother throw in each other's dirty clothes if they don't have a full load.

"Mom pitches in whenever she sees I'm really pushed," says Inga. "On the days I work, she always fixes dinner. If I'm out in the yard, she'll yell out that there's a sandwich ready for lunch. She does all the mending for the kids. She's willing to do a lot, she just likes it to be noticed.

"She's more particular than I am in cleaning, so James and I try to keep the house more straightened than we would if we lived alone. Sometimes she'll say, 'It's a good thing this dirty stove bothers me, because it sure doesn't bother you.' "

Yes, there are strains in this house, on occasion. Inga doesn't like it when Mom corrects the kids or tells her she's being too hard on them. She doesn't like it when she has a phone conversation with someone and Mom asks who called.

"When I get aggravated, I clam up," says Inga. "That makes Mom feel bad. Often James comes to the rescue and we talk about it. He tells me to go talk it out with Mom. Sometimes I do. Sometimes it just goes away.

"If either of us has bad moments, we stop and think about how much better off we all are. James and I have a house, in a neighborhood we could never afford ourselves. Mom knows we'll be here to take care of her. She has asked specifically that we never take her to a nursing home if her health fails. Some way or another we'd manage if she couldn't take care of herself. She has health insurance that would help in getting someone to assist us if she became bedridden.

"It works both ways, you know. Mom is a very patient, loving person. When I'm sick, she takes care of me."

• • •

Howard and Victoria wanted to put down roots. They had been married 10 years and had lived in apartments in various cities throughout the country.

Although Howard was making a career change from government employee to establishing his own fledgling building business, and Victoria was just recently made the paid director of a community day care center instead of a volunteer, buying a house at this time seemed right. They figured that even with their lean budget, they could afford a $20,000-$30,000 home.

In 1978, when Victoria and Howard did their scouting, that amount of money led them to rundown houses in poor urban neighborhoods.

"It's not that we didn't plan to do a lot of work on the house we would buy," says Howard, "we wanted to feel that we lived in a part of the world that had some zip to it. We wanted to have a good feeling about the neighborhood. We yearned for trees, for a yard. In our search, we began to notice some houses that were big enough, had enough character, were just plain powerful enough, to be shared.

"When we found this house [where they have lived since 1978], we loved it immediately. We bought it from the owner and we didn't know how in the world we were going to manage it. But somehow, whether we would share it or rent part of it, we knew we would have to come up with a creative solution."

The house Howard and Victoria fell in love with is a genteel white frame farmhouse built in 1856 in a part of the city that today is close to everything.

The house, which at one time was turned into a private school and later into a sanitarium, is on the fringe of a modern hospital grounds. There are large old trees in the front yard and the back. Rolling lawns that separate the house from the hospital make you forget you're not out in the country when you plunk down on the back porch. The house has history and charm. It's easy to see why Howard and Victoria succumbed.

"We couldn't qualify for this kind of purchase ($50,000) with the official folks," remembers Howard. "Our income was too small for the size of the loan we needed. We had the $5,000 down payment. We were able to get a $25,000 loan and luckily our parents came up with the difference. That's how we bought the house.

"Then we went about trying to find a way to afford living in it. We talked to my brother and his wife about becoming partners in the house, but they weren't too keen on the idea. We spoke to a woman we know who had a daughter the same age as ours, and another who was divorced with several children. But by this time, my brother, Greg, and his wife Mary had seen the house and fallen in love with it, too. Their interest in sharing it perked up.

"When we all sat down together and talked over how we could live in the house and make the partnership work, it took away a great deal of anxiety. We set up a structure and bylaws. We decided how we were going to run the house, and then we went ahead with it.

"Many of our friends thought what we wanted to do was pretty strange since we were so middle class and straight," says Howard. "We wanted a sound partnership based on economic realities. We wanted to own our own property. We viewed our partnership as a way to build equity that was out of our reach.

"Because the house had so much life to it, because we all loved it, we could get over the hurdles of not owning it exclusively, of not having full control. We knew there would be trade-offs, but we knew it felt good. We all had the house we wanted; we also had the determination to make it work."

To make the arrangement succeed, the couples felt it was mandatory that both have their own bedroom and bath. This was easy to accommodate because the house was so spacious. The couple at one end would never know what was going on at the other. No one was foregoing much privacy.

Victoria says, "I felt that buying a home with Greg and Mary was a blessing. Because we all had jobs we were so involved with, the amount of work it would take to clean the house would be overwhelming. Coming from an apartment to this kind of responsibility would have been too much."

A work schedule of seven hours a week per person was established to maintain the house. Whether each person works one hour a day or seven on the weekend or more than seven hours, is up to him. Though specific jobs are assigned, everyone winds up doing a little bit of everything.

Each couple takes care of their private space, which is a bedroom and a study; communal space is the responsibility of all.

Food is another issue the partners dealt with head on to keep it from becoming an issue. Two refrigerators—one for each couple—were installed in the kitchen; each couple uses separate sets of cupboards in which they keep their respective food and pots and pans.

"This way," Howard says, "everyone can eat what they please when they feel like it. There are no arguments about tofu versus potato chips or who ate the last chocolate chip cookie. We use the same stove and sink and often wind up cooking our meals at the same time and sitting down together to eat what we've each cooked. We all had utensils from our own apartments before we bought the house and keeping things separate in the kitchen has been extremely successful."

Though the couples buy their own food, cleansers, detergents, and dog food (for the jointly loved Golden Retriever) are bought in common. Whoever goes to the store buys what is running low and then circles the item on the grocery list.

Howard, who acts as the house business manager, keeps the receipts and tallies them every two months. Expenses are totaled and divided.

"We were more uptight about who owed who what at the beginning of our partnership," says Howard. "We split expenses more often. As our partnership has progressed, we let these expenses ride longer before we divvy them up."

Howard and Victoria, Greg, and Mary came up with an ingenious solution for decorating the house that took the heat off everyone.

At first, the house was furnished with the best of what both couples had accumulated. Greg and Mary's dining room set was nicest, so Howard and Victoria's made a one-way trip to the Salvation Army. But their living room furniture was in better shape, so Mary and Greg's was sold at the yard sale they held to get rid of overflow.

When the two couples were in good enough financial shape to purchase new furniture, they hired a decorator, one who had worked with the people next door and whose taste they all admired.

"It's hard enough for one couple to decide on what wallpaper they want, and what color couch will go with it," says Howard. "When two couples have to decide, it can be inflammatory. The decorator brought swatch books and fabric samples for all of us to see. If somebody didn't like something she recommended, it was the decorator who was being rejected, not one of us criticizing the other.

"No one said, 'Do you know how long it's taken me to find this fabric?' or 'I searched all week for this arm chair and now you don't like it.' We could afford to hire a decorator because four people split the cost. It was one of the best things we did for each other."

"There is a price to pay in negotiating all these decisions," cautions Victoria. "For instance, if three people want to hang a picture in the stairway and the fourth doesn't, the outnumbered one will have to be generous. When our gas and electric bill comes in the mail and we divide it in half, I feel much more flexible about where we're going to hang a picture. It puts small disagreements back into perspective."

At first, house meetings were held once a week to discuss problems. They were a good forum to head off out-and-out arguments, which did happen on occasion.

As the partnership has matured, bits and pieces of house business are interspersed in daily conversations. If resentment flares into harsh words, there is a chill in the air for a while, but after a few days it wears off.

Televisions are kept in private spaces because the common living areas are meant to be places you can relax in peace.

"We regard television as an intrusion in our lives, anyway," says Victoria. "We figure that if we keep televisions in our bedrooms, we'll watch it, if we do, at the end of the day instead of making it a big part of our evening."

Howard and Victoria feel their ten-year-old daughter, Evelyn, is a benefactor of the shared living arrangement. Since Uncle Greg is a great gardener and keeps bees, Evelyn learns much from him she wouldn't from her parents.

"It's an extended family kind of feeling," says Victoria. "Or perhaps like a small village. We share a house, but we all share each others' lives, ideas, and dreams."

That's true. But it isn't always a benefit. When Greg and Mary's marriage fell apart, the entire household went through a divorce. Mary wasn't as committed to the living arrangement as the rest of them (and apparently not to Greg either).

Though Howard and Victoria are sad about the split, they feel the marriage was in trouble before the partnership was formed, not because of it.

"There was a lot of tension when Greg and Mary were deciding to divorce," recalls Howard. "It also made Victoria and me reexamine our own marriage. We began to take less for granted and our relationship got better. We felt like survivors."

Greg now has a new female friend, one who sometimes comes to the house to spend the weekend. Howard and Victoria like her and feel she might make a better partner than Mary. But explaining Uncle Greg's weekend friend to Evelyn was tricky.

"I told her that Uncle Greg's living with someone on the weekends he's not married to was all right with him, but wasn't what we necessarily approved of," says Victoria. "Evelyn just laughed and said, 'Oh Mom, I know all about that kind of stuff. I know what you mean,' and shrugged it off." Victoria shakes her head. "Kids know everything these days."

In retrospect, Victoria says, "When I get mad, I rant and rave. There's a big storm and then it's over. Howard and Greg are also confrontive. Mary would hold her anger in. The rest of us locking horns and doing battle must have been hard on her.

"Now, I've learned to try to hold some of my feelings inside. I try to be more sensitive—then I explode.

"I guess the main advice I can give to people who want to co-own a house is to be as clear as you can about who you are and what makes you feel comfortable. You must communicate this regularly before you become partners and during your partnership. At the same time, you must be flexible and willing to compromise. You must tell yourself, 'It really doesn't matter if Greg and Mary's mail is stacked up all over the kitchen counter. It's their side of the kitchen and it's not my problem. I have this whole house to enjoy and I wouldn't have it without them.'"

Howard feels that house co-ownership is an adventure and people who want to try it must be risk takers. At the same time, those who do must be willing to draw up a detailed map to keep the expedition on course.

"Structure is like a safety net for a trapeze artist," says Howard. "You don't miss it until you fall, and then it saves your life."

The day-to-day operational house rules Howard and Victoria, Greg, and Mary put down on paper are copious. They show the depth of thinking that went into the partnership. Here are a few examples:

- We are determined to help each other, especially in illness and when "blue" spirits abound.
- Stop drippy faucets whenever spotted.
- Turn lights out when leaving rooms. Keep lights off in unoccupied rooms.
- Wash and dry full loads of clothes.
- Mark clothes to help identify them when washing mixed clothes.
- Within reason, try to keep heat around 65 degrees.
- For viewing special television shows, share one set rather than operating two sets.
- Try to keep phone conversations relatively short, especially during busy times.
- Take phone messages for others carefully and leave them in the agreed-upon place.
- Last person leaving the house should make sure all the doors of the house are locked and, if rain seems likely, close all windows.
- Responsibility for the care of individual houseplants should be carefully defined among household members. Everyone should be careful that water damage does not occur.

Their Agreement

The agreement of this partnership, which was named "Home Made Enterprise," is lengthy. It is reproduced in its entirety on pages 343-349 of the Appendix, not as a legal model (some of the terms in it are not consistent in the legal sense), but because it's a good example of an agreement that codifies *intent* as well as specifics. It expresses the spirit in which the partnership was formed and the feelings the partners wish to nurture. It deals not only with partnership business affairs but with the goals and objectives that underlie the venture.

You will find topics in this agreement familiar to you from other parts of the book, but here you can see exactly how these principles are put in practice.

Pay particular attention to the buy-sell agreement. It protected all couples when Greg's divorce could have threatened home ownership. Also note that couples can announce to one another they want to sell their shares only in January of each year; if they do, the other partners have first option to buy or elect to sell the house.

Howard feels this gives everyone fair notice and makes the partnership less rigid. Each year it is reviewed and renewed. Partners can elect to go on another year or dissolve the agreement.

"It's like an anniversary each January," says Howard. "It invigorates our relationship and our commitment."

A FRIEND IN DEED IS A FRIEND, INDEED

Making your house partnership into a legal entity that serves your best interests—and those of your partners—needs your full attention. Find an attorney you have confidence in who does a lot of real estate work, tell him what you want your partnership to do for you, and let him work it out. There is no one right way to go about it. Agreements can be written any way you wish (as long as they're clear, they don't have to be in forbidding legalese) in any spirit that suits you. Find the right way—for you.

Mark Berliant, a Cincinnati attorney specializing in real estate taxation, is currently serving as chairman of the Committee on Real Estate Tax Problems, Section of Taxation, American Bar Association.

"Seek both real estate *and* tax advice when you're considering joint property purchases," urges Mark. "An attorney specializing in real estate may not necessarily be up on the latest tax breaks, which change constantly. Arm yourself with the facts you need—from the experts—to put together the most advantageous partnership for everyone involved."

Yes, an attorney's time costs money. And you are partnering to save dollars. Don't scrimp in this category. Too many people I talked to say, shaking their heads, "I wish I had put *that* on paper." Seek sound advice.

Mark says, "When I advise people who wish to form property partnerships, I follow this agenda for discussion":

1. *Basics.* The partners have decided to go in on a deal together. They must agree on the general nature of their joint venture at this stage. Then they must consider whether they are getting the property at the best price, also considering additional costs such as improvements that need to be made and required furnishings. Can they afford to pay for it outright, or will they need a loan? What is the most advantageous kind of financing, and is financing available?

2. *Mechanics.* Who will be in charge of bringing the concept to life? Who will negotiate for the property? Who will handle the closing? Who will obtain needed financing? All the details that go along with acquiring property must be tended to by the partners. Who will do what?

3. *Capital Contributions.* How much money is each partner going to put up to cover the purchase price? Will it be equal, or will the partnership be 40-60, 75-25, whatever? Will partnership privileges be apportioned in accord with the amount of each partner's equity?

4. *Assessments.* What about additional capital if and when it is needed? Who is going to put up the money? Will it be contributed in accordance with partnership shares?

5. *Default.* What if your partner is a little short this month and can't pay his share of the mortgage payment? What do you do? Mark says, "This issue can really hurt, especially if you yourself are in a bind and can't lay out your partner's share of the money as well as your own.

"Most large business partnerships keep money in a bank account equivalent to two or three months' mortgage payments and upkeep costs as a cushion for this very reason."

Mark advises houses partners to do the same. This way you have breathing time so your partner can raise money, or if he can't, you have enough lead time to take legal steps to save your property before you run out of funds.

6. *Split.* What happens when the partnership doesn't work, or when it simply is time to end it? Mark says, "I can give you fifteen different ways to write a buy-sell agreement. When I speak to prospective partners, I suggest a variety of ways it can be done and I tell them to pick which they prefer."

Buy-Sell Variations

Probably the most effective buy-sell agreement is to require the party who wishes to sell or terminate (and thus causes the problem), to name a price at which he will either buy or sell. The remaining partner, who did not seek the division, has then the option to either sell at the named price or buy out the departing partner at that price. This puts real pressure upon the terminating party, which is usually fair under the circumstances.

A variation is when the remaining partner has the option to buy out the departing partner, but the value is set by others. You can write: "At any time, I can give you notice that I want to end the partnership. You then get 60 to 90 days to buy me out. I name an appraiser. You name an appraiser. If they cannot reconcile, they agree on a third appraiser, or a single disinterested party to evaluate the house to come up with a fair price."

Still another variation has the remaining partner with the option not only to buy or sell his partial interest, but to cause a sale of the entire property. It may be that the non-terminating party just can't pull off full ownership.

In any case, partners must think out at the beginning, not at the end, what they will do, want to do, and be financially able to do when a partner has had enough or wants to cash in his chips.

What if one partner has just overreached himself financially?

Mark says, "Maybe the answer should be that if one partner defaults, the other has the right to buy his share at the original price without any markup at all. Even though the house and consequently his share is worth more, there should be a dollar penalty for one partner not carrying his load."

A provision can also be written that states if partners don't get along, one can give the other a list of complaints that must be responded to in a specific number of days. If there is no response, the partnership is off.

Mark feels strongly that partners should make sure they write into their buy-sell agreement that there is at least a 90-day period (even conceivably longer) to come up with money in case their partner wants to sell.

"Partners should also decide whether the payout will be expected in one lump sum or over a period of time," emphasizes Mark. "This is often determined by how much money is involved.

"If each partner has put up $10,000 in cash and together they borrow $100,000, and the property is only worth the same, then one partner may be able to pay the other $5,000 right away or may be able to pay $1,000 a month for 5 months—or even $500 a month for 10 months.

"On the other hand, if the partners paid $100,000 for a house that is now worth $200,000 and one wants his $50,000 profit out of the deal, the other may need as much as five years to come up with the money and may need a second mortgage from the selling partner. He needs a reasonable length of time which both partners must decide in advance.

"The key factor in all this is the terms of the underlying first mortgage on the house. If both partners have signed for the loan and one wants to leave the partnership, the remaining partner may have to re-negotiate the mortgage at a higher rate. There should be a penalty for this because there is a severe and tangible change whose consequences the remaining partner has to suffer.

"The party who doesn't want to be in the partnership any longer should not have the right to just turn around one day and tell his partner that he now has to be a buyer without having some discomfort. The buyer should get some sort of dollar discount.

"Yet another way to unwind: The person who wants to sell should agree to have a third party appraiser come in and set a price on the property. The remaining partner buys his share at half the appraised price minus a percentage they've agreed to in advance. If the exiting partner turns down the appraised price, the property is put on the market but the dollar penalty stands."

There are, as Mark declares, a million ways to write a partnering agreement. Bring a list of the issues important to you and your partner to an expert, and based on your monetary situation and the type of agreement you want to build, construct one to keep your joint venture rolling smoothly along.

Insurance

Up to this point, the only insurance we've talked about covers the risks of co-owning vehicles. Certainly, when you purchase a home in partnership you'll need insurance to protect your property. You'll also need insurance to protect yourself if a catastrophe strikes your partner.

Chances are, if you're just starting out and have split the purchase of a first home, you couldn't afford to buy it alone. If something happened to your partner, could you manage the mortgage payments out of your own budget? Many of the partners you've just been introduced to would have lost their homes if relatives hadn't come to their financial rescue. This is why life insurance is an issue to consider.

If your partner dies and his portion of the house goes to Uncle Bruce, who wants to sell his shares, he's selling half of your home. Uncle Bruce may offer you first option to buy, but where are you going to get the money?

Experts suggest that joint home purchasers buy life insurance policies listing their partners as beneficiaries. The policy should be commensurate with the amount of money the partners have invested together, not necessarily the total value of the house. In other words, buy insurance on the amount of money you think you may not be able to pay—usually the amount of your loan.

In any event, you will have to buy a policy that is realistic. If you have a $50,000 home, you won't be able to justify to many agencies why you need a half-million dollar policy on your life.

In addition to naming your partner as the beneficiary, you may want to consider transferring ownership of the policy on your life to him. In this way, your partner is assured the policy will not be borrowed against, nor will the beneficiary be changed. Of course, both should do this for peace of mind.

Although you could name your partner as beneficiary of a portion of an insurance policy you already own (and vice versa), you would still be the owner. Since our goal in partnering is to always allay suspicion by being aboveboard, buying a separate policy naming your partner as the beneficiary and transferring ownership to him is the cleanest method.

Seriously—think about what you don't like to think about and provide for the calamities that can happen. It's one thing to give your partner first option to buy out your shares, but if you die suddenly and your estate takes over, how is he going to come up with the money to exercise that option on such short notice?

Evaluate whether disability insurance would also be worthwhile if you own a house in partnership—that is, if you are not covered in some way by the company you work for.

If you cannot work, how are you going to pay your half of the bills? How long will you or your partner be able to carry each other before your house is in jeopardy?

Seek out an insurance agent to help you set up a program to take care of you—and your partner.

House Meetings

A regular time to talk over house business is essential to successful partnering. This should be when you discuss day-to-day matters that come up, make future plans, talk about what pleases you, and unload what is on your mind.

It's a good idea to do all this with Jane Engeman's positive problem-solving approach in mind. (See her step-by-step method in Chapter Six). This way, discussions are constructive and feelings are not kept inside to fester.

It's easy for two people to set up a convenient meeting time. Group households may post a notice of an impending gathering on a bulletin board and ask for attendance. People may also write on a blackboard those issues they want to place on the agenda.

However you wish to call the meeting to order, have a definite schedule. Dispatch issues, point by point, so no one gets off the track. Groups may need a leader, chairman, facilitator—whatever you wish to call him—to keep discussions on course and flowing. It's easy for a lot of people who are hot on a subject to get bogged down in trivia. It's also a good idea to limit the time you'll spend at a meeting in advance to keep business moving along.

Start on an encouraging note—things you've done right—to set a positive tone. Then deal with gripes—but again, do this constructively, without attack. Don't just vent anger. Try to come up with solutions to please everyone. (Again, refer to Jane Engeman's approach.)

People may vote on issues or use consensus to settle how they will act on a matter. If there is an impasse between two people, or a group is divided, mediation or third-party advice can help.

Consensus

You have heard the word "consensus" frequently on previous pages. So you can employ it if it suits your needs, this is how consensus works.

Consensus is the most nonviolent method a group can use to make a decision. It can be used effectively when there is a high level of homogeneity and commitment. The feeling of well-being among members must be more important than any one decision.

For instance, in a group meeting, when a proposal is brought up you do not agree with, you state your concern about it. Someone else may say, "I hadn't thought of that." Everyone's point of view is taken into consideration. One person's concern may point out issues that will influence the whole group.

Because everyone participates fully in the decision-making process, everyone feels responsible. You don't just hold up your hand and vote "yay" or "nay." You have had to say, "Yes, I do agree" or "I don't agree"—and *why.*

If everyone in the group agrees to a proposal except you, do not block the group. You may say, "I'm not happy with what you are going to do, but go ahead with it." You may not want to be involved in the action that follows the decision, and that's all right. Step aside. Don't let your personal feelings get in the way of the group decision.

With consensus, no one wins and no one loses. No one votes, but everyone contributes. The system gives everyone a chance to speak.

Everyone's ideas and viewpoints are taken into consideration and then synthesized. Based on everyone's input, the group is able to choose the right way to progress.

A facilitator is needed to keep this process orderly, the agenda adhered to, and issues from being overhashed. As you may have imagined by now, getting a group to make a decision through persuasion rather than coercion feels wonderful, but it can take a while.

If the atmosphere in your group is one in which people's feelings and thinking are affirmed and respected, if everyone tries to deal with conflicts in a sensitive manner, if no one tries to overpower others because they are more forceful, richer, or better-looking, consensus may be for you.

If it sounds exhilarating, it is. It is also exhausting. You will need a step-by-step guide to help you get used to settling matters this way and to explain exactly how meetings should be run. Such a guide is *Building Social Change Communities.* It is available from the Philadelphia Movement for a New Society, 4722 Baltimore Avenue, Philadelphia, PA 19143.

·16·
Urban Nerve and Intentional Communities

Rescuing a once grand house from ruin and restoring it to a livable state is an adventure that can take a giant dollop of nerve. Architectural gems are often uncovered in fearsome settings.

Sure, you can go it alone. A "first-on-the-block" outpost can start a chain reaction that brings whole neighborhoods to life. Not all of us, however, have the heart (and guts) to be streetwise pioneers. Not everyone is willing to take chances. And it's not always safe to take chances alone. Followers, however, pay a price for letting others blaze the trail.

Real estate speculators, spotting boarded-up windows giving way to new panes framed with wooden shutters, recognize a weary neighborhood starting to lift its head. Latecomers to the area pay dearly for their caution. That's why a group effort to buy a down-at-the-heels block makes so much sense.

The territory is still virginal. The prices remain low. Going into adjoining homes in concert provides security for each individual family and stability to the area. Here is how one group went about it.

URBAN NERVE

In a small southern city bordering the Mississippi River, street after

291

street is lined with century-old row houses exuding antebellum charm. Until 15 years ago, most were owned by absentee landlords who chopped them into apartments and rented them to whoever would live in the state of disrepair into which the buildings had fallen.

A real estate developer who owned eight houses on one particular block contacted the priest of the Catholic Church in the midst of this area. He wondered if the Father knew of someone in the parish who would be interested in buying the property.

The developer was having financial problems, and since he was holding the houses as an investment, he needed to dump them. He had always felt that one day he'd fix them up, but he never did. Forget about the historic value of these circa 1850 houses; $60,000 was left on the mortgage, and he needed his money. The priest said he would try to help.

Father Mendez hated to see the neighborhood around the church so decrepit. He was also interested in historic preservation. Throughout the summer and early fall of 1972, he contacted people in the parish he thought might be interested in buying the houses. He finally came up with a core group of 13 activists.

They all wanted to own their own homes, and these were to be their first. Most were people in their late 20s and early 30s—some married; three were priests. Everyone knew each other directly or indirectly through the church.

For the young people with little cash, buying a home on this street as a group was the only way they would be able to afford one. For the three priests, these houses, once restored, would be a place for them to live when they retired. (Do note, these priests are members of an order that does not ask for a vow of poverty; they are allowed to own property. Since the church did not ask them to divest themselves of personal property acquired before they became priests, they used their modest savings for the purchase.)

Though economics brought everyone together, there were other mutual interests. All participants wanted to live in the inner city and restore old homes; all wanted to be owner-occupants; no one was involved in the deal to do a quick fix-up to turn over some dollars.

To make it happen, they approached a friendly bank, which was willing to issue one mortgage. With the purchase of another house on the block owned by an elderly woman willing to sell to the group, a partnership was formed which assumed the $70,000 mortgage on the total of nine houses involved in the group purchase.

This agreement, drawn up by an attorney, stated that partners had to maintain the original character of the houses, named a managing partner, specified when meetings would be held, and clearly defined the financial obligations as well as buy-sell arrangements of all involved. The partnership was also to be used as a vehicle to purchase other houses on the street (there are two dozen) as they came on the market and resell them to people who would be owner-occupants and promise to restore them. The idea was to branch out on all sides to create a stable neighborhood.

Each person or couple was committed to buying one house from the partnership on a land contract.

Who got which house?

Norman, one of the most outspoken of the partners, says, "One person wouldn't have entered into the partnership unless he was promised a particular house. It was in such terrible shape nobody else wanted it. Others also had special choices. People worked things out if there was a conflict.

"You have to understand that all the houses were in awful shape. One house had been divided into a bunch of apartments that had to be torn apart. Another building needed all new wiring and insulation in the kitchen. Another needed a third of it rebuilt as a result of a fire.

"There was no way we could value one house more or less than another. Each had so many good and bad points it was impossible. After everyone was satisfied with his choice, we divided the mortgage evenly. Everyone paid $7,600 for his house and would make payments of $76 a month for 13 years. We put $510 down in cash for closing costs and taxes and to pay the attorney, who charged us $2,500 for the legal work.

"Everyone signed personally on the mortgage, but the three middle-aged partners were the heavyweights. Their balance sheets looked a whole lot better to the bank than the younger partners who really didn't have anything.

"But once we were able to convince the bank we were all going to do something really positive to bring back a residential neighborhood, once the bank made the first move, they were behind us every step of the way."

Though the bank provided money for a collective mortgage, each partner had to find cash for restoration any way he could. Some borrowed money from relatives; a few borrowed on life insurance policies; others took out home improvement loans.

"We got money in whatever way we could manage," says Norman, "so we could make these places habitable. Since we were all living in apartments, we moved into our homes right away. We fixed up a couple of rooms and lived in them while we did the major tearing out work in the rest of the house. From 1973 to 1975 people were literally rebuilding structures around themselves.

293

"So many people, in the same fix, helping each other couldn't help becoming involved in each other's lives. There was a lot of caring."

"When I bought my house, it was so torn up I couldn't move in," says Martha. "I had to live at a neighbor's for a month because I had to get out of my apartment."

"When my kitchen was being worked on," says Charles, "I went to other people's houses for meals until I could use mine again.

"We shared names of contractors, gave each other do-it-yourself tips, cried on each other's shoulders. We were all risk takers and more than a little crazy to take on houses with very little money."

In 1974, the city introduced a community development program that gave a tremendous boost to the residents of Columbia Street. The terms of the program were that those who invested $9,000 in the interior of houses they were renovating would get a grant of $3,500 to fix up the exterior.

City officials knew full well people had to make the inside of run-down homes livable first. At the same time, they wanted renovation fever to spread. If the outsides of the homes looked splendid, others would be attracted to the area.

Since Columbia Street and some of the neighboring streets had become a beehive of activity, these were selected as the city's pilot project.

The lending bank looked at the $3,500 grant as additional down payment money and was then willing to lend Columbia Street residents whatever they needed to bring house interiors up to city code specifications. Most people estimated they invested $15,000 to $20,000 or more in their homes.

If this sounds like a Cinderella story and you feel it happens only to other people, think again. Columbia Street residents are industrious. They are liberal thinkers, politically and socially, but they don't just think about what they want to happen. They work for it.

Some are volunteers on political campaigns, even go door to door spreading the word for politicians sympathetic to their views. They attend city council meetings and make themselves heard on issues that affect them and their neighborhood. They support local art and cultural organizations.

A healthy percentage of the residents of Columbia Street were in college in the 1960s; a few lived on communes. They still believe in alternatives or they wouldn't have had the pluck to take on a street of houses with no cash and find a way to remain solvent. They have learned to work through the system and make the system work for them. They hold responsible jobs. There are several attorneys; one partner is a heating and cooling repairman. He is probably the most popular resident on the block.

In accord with the original partnership agreement, other houses on the street were bought from absentee landlords as they became available. The bank loaned the residents the money to buy them, and the partnership made the mortgage payments until residents found buyers they felt would be committed to the area. Houses held by the partnership were sold for what was still owed on the property; the partnership did not make a profit. If it took a few months to find a good prospective resident, the partnership made mortgage payments. These expenses were taken as individual tax deductions by Columbia Street residents. No matter what, they wanted to sell only to people who would live on the premises and upgrade the neighborhood.

"I know it all sounds too good to be true," says Norman. "And there was a lot of suspicion about what we were doing. People can't easily accept that a group like ours isn't buying property with an immediate profit motive.

"In the last six years our group has owned and sold 28 houses in the vicinity. Collectively, we've lost about $1,500. Most people just can't understand that what we're doing is stabilizing a neighborhood. We've gained immensely by creating places to live we could have never even thought of by ourselves."

The street began to look like it stepped out of a historical photograph, complete with cobblestones. To further that effect, the group wanted it free of cars. They went to the city council and negotiated to have one end of the street closed off, making it a dead end to cut down on traffic. Norman found some great-looking iron gates at a junkyard and had them installed at the closed end.

Then a few of the more solvent residents bought a vacant lot at the end of the street with the intention of making it into a parking lot so that cars wouldn't line the curbs. The same day they signed for the loan, they sold it for the same price, to the Columbia Street partnership. Enough money was included in the loan to grade the lot, put down gravel, and fence the perimeter. After a year, all chipped in to raise the money to have it blacktopped.

Whoever uses the lot pays $20 a month per parking place, and after 14 years, street residents will own it outright.

Norman says, "When someone runs into the gates at the end of the street, we pass the hat for money to get them repaired.

"When we decided to plant flowering crab apple trees along the sidewalk, we didn't have enough money to put one in front of everyone's house, but no one fought over their placement because they made the whole street look good. We try to avoid pettiness.

"We look out for each other on this street. Everyone knows everyone else. We're careful to respect each other's privacy, but we know each other's habits. We'd certainly notice strange people if they appeared in the neighborhood.

"If someone screamed, there would probably be a dozen people outside their houses within 30 seconds.

"I remember a few years ago, some teenagers stole an aluminum ladder leaning against my house and dropped it in the middle of the street. That made a huge amount of noise. People ran out of their house; *everyone* called the police—which drove them nuts—Nick's dog went after them; there were police cars everywhere. Those kids didn't have a chance. In retrospect, it was kind of funny."

If someone has a roof problem, one person helps another. Nick, the heating man, works out furnace problems. People exchange books, flower bulbs, help plant trees. If someone is going to buy a load of mulch, he'll ask others if they need some, too.

"We have cooperation and assistance if we need it," says Norman. "But we have our own lives as well.

"We're generous people, but no one has to contribute the same amount of time and energy to what goes on here. Not everyone can. But we want like-minded people to live here.

"If we have a house to sell and we show someone around who has a 'this is my house, don't step in my yard' kind of attitude, we know he won't work out in our neighborhood.

"We don't care about lifestyles. We're tolerant of any belief or taste. But if you don't take care of your house or yard, we'll all hate you for that."

(A footnote: Though gains on Columbia Street are more than monetary, wise investing always pays off. One house that was put on the market by a person who had invested $22,000 rehabbing it sold for $44,000 in 1981.)

The legal work on all these properties is fully detailed and solid. From setting up day-to-day operating procedures to buy-sell agreements, documents are well thought out and in order.

Any group attempting to emulate such a venture as Columbia Street should expect to spend time and money working out the technicalities with experts.

• • •

Tackling Manhattan alone is tough. Group synergy can soften the blows this city dishes out. Just barely making it becomes making it big.

Dave, an architect, renovated many old buildings into livable apartments for others. He wanted a building of his own. He kept his eyes open for any with interesting possibilities, approached owners about the availability of some he spotted, maintained close contacts with real estate people.

In 1976, he found one he knew was right. The five-story loft building with a business on the first floor was in a part of the city called TriBeCa (the triangle beneath the canal). At the time of Dave's discovery, this area had not yet been caught up in the real estate frenzy that started just a short time later. In 1976, the action was in SoHo, where prices for loft space were being driven past the point of affordability for most of the people who had originally settled there.

TriBeCa was to be the next place New Yorkers could find commercial buildings that were still cheap. When Dave learned the sale price of "his" building was $100,000, he knew he had a great deal.

Dave wanted to establish a cooperative venture with three other partners. He also wanted to set up the structure before he approached anyone else.

He'd seen situations fall apart when friends got together to decide whether or not they wanted to buy a particular building, what they were willing to pay for it, and dozens of other details. He didn't want that to happen.

Dave met with an attorney and formalized a structure. They decided how much partners would have to pay, how the building would be financed, and other specifics.

Then he offered his closest friends the chance to buy into the building. It was such a fantastic opportunity, Dave knew there wouldn't be a chance of a refusal.

Each person picked the floor he liked—and every floor had advantages to please someone. The first floor was rented to a business. The prime concern of all partners was rehabbing the building and getting the financing to do it so the structure could be declared a legal residence. By the book, it was still considered commercial. To get a certificate of occupancy, they had to bring the building up to code.

"Everyone wanted the partnership to work," says Dave. "Everyone was willing to give time and energy to it. But I was the leader in cutting red tape to get the certificate of occupancy and plowing through the paperwork. My wife, Renee, takes care of the books, for which she gets a salary each month. Everyone pays a monthly maintenance charge and her fee is deducted from that."

Each partner has about 900 square feet of living space on his floor. There is an additional apartment one-third that size on every floor as well. Each owner has plenty of room, plus incremental income from "his" rental apartment and 25% of the rent from the business on the first floor. All this helps defray expenses.

Not only are the partners friends, they try to rent to people who are also congenial. Everyone wants to live with people they like.

All partners have round-robin jobs in the maintenance of the building. Keeping the stairs and sidewalk clean, replacing light bulbs in the stairway—all chores are clearly defined. If a partner wants to hire someone to do his job for him, that's fine with everyone else, as long as it gets done—because if it doesn't, he is fined. The accumulated penalty money is used to buy trees for the garden that is being built on the roof.

Renters do not have building maintenance responsibilities, nor can they make improvements without the permission of the owners.

As per their formal agreement, partners must use specified grades of materials for building projects; plumbing and electrical work has to be performed by licensed professionals. There are no rules about what each floor should look like, but the quality of construction must be uniform.

"People look after each other in the building," says Renee. "If I hear someone coming down the steps at an odd time when I know the people on that floor are at work, I stick my head out the door to see what's going on. We water each other's plants when we're out of town. We all realize how lucky we are to have found this building when we did. We want it to be a success."

Within five years of Dave's discovery of TriBeCa, the neighborhood has become residential. Rents for spaces like the one he lives in are $2,000 a month or more. In 1977, just a year after Dave's group purchased their building, the owner of the one next door turned down a $450,000 cash offer. In 1983, it would be painful to price anything in the area.

"The only way you can get something for yourself is to get a group of friends together and buy a building," says Dave. "If you own it yourself, you won't be forced out by high rents. This place is so fashionable now, so lucrative for big developers, it would be hard for people to do what we did now.

"I get calls all the time from real estate agents who want to buy our building. But where would we go? Prices to live in this area are out of the range of the original people—like us—who developed it."

It pays to have foresight, but to live in a peripheral area—especially in a big city—it also pays to have friends nearby. These friends, together, were willing to forego the comforts of an established neighborhood. The nearest grocery was nine blocks away. Garbage had to be hauled to the corner since there were no pickups at "unestablished residences."

In the long run, disadvantages like these seem small in light of the financial windfall.

Dave's group was smart enough to anticipate that when conveniences come on the scene, rents zoom. Quietly, they chiseled out a small piece of the city for themselves and created a home.

INTENTIONAL COMMUNITIES

People who choose to become each other's neighbors form intentional communities, and there are as many reasons why people decide to cluster as the differences in people themselves. Among the most common are religious, social, and political beliefs.

Environmentally concerned citizens like to share land they treat in the same manner. Others who eschew a "buy more" society retreat to establish their own, based on less materialistic values. Nonviolent, antimilitary, solar versus nuclear energy, nutritional and health, back-to-the-land, sexual, and political preferences—these are just a few examples of the energies that draw people to live together.

I'll talk about group houses in a later chapter. Here, we're talking about people who buy land and/or houses, in close proximity, as a joint venture because they believe that together they can do better than alone.

In an undertaking of this nature, it does help if economics is not the only reason people share. A common commitment·to God can help smooth over some pretty earthly squabbles. But not always.

Many residents of intentional communities I talked to created detailed written agreements based on their knowledge of the hard work it takes to make sharing successful. Knowing how difficult it is, regardless of what they hold dear in common—save-the-country or save-the-whales—they spell out in concrete terms who owns what and who does what.

Though you may not believe in an ideal strongly enough to create your own mini-world, intentional communities are an admirable and innovative solution to consider.

• • •

A group of Mennonite doctors, on graduation from medical school, decided they would set up practice together in the part of their state with the lowest income and the least amount of medical facilities. This was to be both a religious and a social commitment.

But in making such a move, the doctors and their families knew they would need each other for support. Recognizing that the schools would offer fewer educational advantages than they wanted for their children, that the values of many of the people they would serve would be quite different from theirs, they needed to build an atmosphere in which they felt they could thrive.

In a county where rusting, junked cars out front are as common as a few pigs rooting out back, these highly educated professional types might have a rough time if they tried to make it on their own. It's lonely being different, even if you think your kind of different is right.

The group bought 75 hilly, wooded acres in partnership. Each took three-quarters of an acre to build rustic, contemporary houses (each was built to individual tastes with individual dollars but subject to everyone's approval) nestled amidst the trees. They all shared the rest of the acreage, a pond, a tennis court they had built, a playground, a ball field, a barn, a tractor, dozens of other tools—and each other.

These people had more than "the things money can buy" in mind when they made this land purchase. Yet, they have an inordinate amount of privacy, comforts, and pleasures none of them could have afforded alone.

When a land purchase comes out of many pockets, you can buy more. If you've always wanted to have space around you and the only piece you can afford is a half-acre carved out of a raw development named something like Timber Trails (why that name after every tree has been bulldozed down?), you can do better if you make your purchase in conjunction with others.

If you want neighbors you can share your life with, or just neighbors you respect and who will respect you and your values, this is the way to achieve that kind of lifestyle. It's an alternative to backyards stamped out of the earth and separated by fences. And to people who feel the best kind of neighbors are those who mind their own business.

Intentional communities work, but only because of the efforts of their inhabitants.

Is it worth it? Only you can decide that. And only you know whether you can assemble a group close enough to make the idea feasible. To demonstrate what's involved, let's examine the doctors' arrangement.

Within this community of the original families plus two other families who joined them, there is an enormous amount of give and take. Also, since one of the cornerstones of the community is Christian commitment, there is abiding faith that partners will always try to work things out with each other.

Hannah, a nurse, and her husband, Barry, a physical therapist, say, "This is the glue that holds everyone together. There is a commitment to find solutions and not write someone off because of a disagreement."

This theory was sorely tested when one of the partners produced plans for his home that shocked everyone else.

"In our agreement," says Lucy, "houses were to be compatible with the natural surroundings. Blueprints had to be okayed by the group, which reserved the right to reject house plans it found offensive. We couldn't believe it when Len and Eve decided to build a flashy colonial with big white pillars in front.

"Frank, the psychiatrist in our group, is good at confronting people in a kind way. He led the discussion with Len and Eve which convinced them their plans wouldn't fit in. They agreed to go back to the drawing board and come up with an alternative more consistent with our original plan."

The families decided that the clearing in the woods is where the playground for the children, the ball field, and the vegetable garden would be.

The first house was built just off the clearing; the second on top of a hill nearby. The rest are scattered throughout the tree-filled property, though not in the area kept wild. Each member's house has the privacy the family desires but is close enough to others to provide the security they feel is important.

One rule of the group is that any tree over 10 inches in diameter cannot be taken down without everyone's permission, even if it's on a member's own three-quarter-acre plot.

"We felt strongly that if you don't want to live in the woods, don't build a house here," says Hannah. "We all heat with wood, but we only cut what is already on the ground."

Community-owned property is paid for by family assessment. This includes the ball field, playground equipment, barn, tools, even the tennis court—although there was a lot of discussion about that particular project.

"Several people in our group are avid tennis players," says Hannah. "They really wanted a tennis court and the suggestion was made that since we had sold some timber, we could use money from the sale to pay for it.

"Barry and I never played much tennis. But we didn't feel we should block the majority of the people who did want it. Since it hurt me to see the woods after some of the timber was taken out, before we ever agree to do that again, the rest would really listen to me on that point."

"We use consensus to make decisions here. Everyone must have his opinion heard and must listen to other people's concerns. All must agree before an issue is okayed or dismissed.

"I asked what the benefits of the tennis court would be, whether we'd have high electricity bills if we put in lights. Though Barry and I were fairly sure we'd rarely use it, we didn't stand in the way of the rest. We all went ahead, feeling good about it.

"Those who wanted to put in a basketball backboard and hoop adjacent to the court at the same time the tennis court was built paid for it themselves. We just couldn't afford to go in on that one and didn't want to."

Tools owned by the community are treated respectfully, and whoever breaks one gets it repaired, though the cost comes out of the general fund. If someone was continually negligent, he would feel the disgruntlement of his neighbors. Common courtesy to each other—and the tools—is the hoped-for plateau. If the plateau isn't reached, people talk about it.

What implements are to be purchased is decided on at community meetings. It usually works out that the person most interested in buying a certain appliance is the one most diligent in maintaining it.

Who uses what gadget when? That was answered the day I visited. Barry had been using the Rototiller when I arrived. He left it sitting out in the yard when we went inside to have a cup of coffee. As we were talking, Cliff walked over, waved to Barry, and wheeled the Rototiller over to his yard.

"Tools are generally kept in the shed near the clearing," says Barry with a smile. "But if they're not there, we go looking for them. People use them when they need them, but if someone wants to make sure a specific piece of equipment is free on a certain day, he'd make arrangements to have it in advance.

"This summer is the first the group worked out a mowing schedule for the clearing. We share the work on that area, using the tractor we bought in common. People use a small push mower to take care of their own yards.

"One partner would rather keep our gravel roads graded, so he doesn't mow the clearing. Whoever is free right after it snows, or has the next day off, runs the plow to dig us out of here. Jobs are not specifically assigned."

This form of equipment use and maintenance works for this group. Other intentional communities find that assigning one person to be in charge of a specific piece of equipment or a group of them is better. One captain in charge of a car, woodworking equipment, or a lawn mower simplifies the question of who is supposed to keep it scheduled, clean, oiled, repaired, and in the garage.

With all the Christian commitment in the world, a common garden didn't work out. When I was there, I saw a large area that had been tilled, with each family's individual plot neatly marked off.

"Our gardening systems were different," says Hannah. "We were all using organic methods, but we had our own idea about putting them into practice. Some people felt others did more harvesting of crops than anything else. The solution was for each family to take care of their own garden. This has kept the peace."

As for finances, Barry is the community treasurer. He keeps track of the bank account and pays the bills. Families are responsible for financing their own houses and keeping up their own mortgage payments. All pay assessments to keep up community holdings.

"Kids monitor kids here," says Hannah. "They know they're not allowed to ride their bikes on the playing surface of the tennis court. If we catch one child who is old enough to know better doing this, then none of the kids can ride where they *are* allowed to for a week. That helps other kids tell the erring one to keep off. His mistake takes everyone's privileges away. That rule goes for most things around here.

"A couple of kids ran the mower into the woods one day. They didn't really know how to use it and they didn't do it on purpose. We made a new rule: You can't use the mower without adult supervision. The damage to the mower was paid out of a community account because it was an accident. No one says to anyone else, 'If you're negligent, you have to pay.'

"Children are not to run into other people's homes or ride each other's bikes without permission, though we all borrow things from each other. We watch each other's children, drive after-school car pools, are always available in case of an emergency, but we're very careful not to overuse our neighbors. We don't assume others will do things. We ask. We respect each other's privacy."

"We don't have relatives nearby," says Lucy. "There are no aunts and uncles and grandparents in the vicinity. The families here are our brothers and sisters and cousins. We share holidays and, on occasion, meals.

"When Barry was laying stone one day, someone came along and pitched in. When Len was building a deck on his house, others helped who weren't busy with their own projects. We have a strong sense of community."

The community also provides a barn with a fence around it for those people who want to raise animals. The interested parties pay for their livestock and feed and take care of them. Not everyone is committed to caring for a goat or feeding a steer, though those that want to are welcome to try.

The doctors set their own salaries at a third less than what most physicians in the area charge and put any extra money the joint practice brings in to build up an assistance program for patients. However, Barry and Hannah make somewhat less than the others. Differing income levels can cause problems which people interested in establishing communities of this sort should consider.

"When the other families wanted to blacktop our roads, I thought it was extravagant," says Barry. "The rest had the money for it. We didn't. We asked, at a meeting, if everyone felt this was really the best way to use our resources even if there was money to go ahead. We all sat down and talked it over and decided it wasn't as important to asphalt roads as most people thought. Hannah and I could just have stepped aside and let the others go ahead and pay for it. And they would have. But this was an issue we just had to stand up and be heard about. Other times, when the majority wants to spend money on a project we can't afford, we go along with it. Some live on a higher scale than we do, though our social commitment keeps life relatively simple.

"Some families having more money than others can cause jealousy, even in a place like this. Kids feel it and it's hard."

Like values, similar needs, how much money you feel is necessary to live comfortably—these are dynamic points people who choose to live together must get clear.

A walk through the area revealed a house of interesting design. It is actually a double house. Built for two families to live in definite separation, the lower level contains a shared recreation area, laundry and guest room. How sensible!

Hannah and Barry, however, went one step further. Their house was originally designed for the two of them and another family, though they are now the only occupants.

"We didn't want our house to look like a condo," says Hannah. "We wanted it to look like a one-family dwelling."

It does, too, with sloping ceilings and exposed wood beams, wide-plank wood floors, open fireplaces, but with an upstairs and downstairs built for two separate families. The kitchen, on the middle, common-area floor, is big enough to accommodate lots of people cooking at the same time, though there is one set of appliances.

There are, however, two dining areas, which can be closed off if families wanted to eat separately. If one group wanted to entertain, the other would still have a place of their own to eat quietly. If one family was having discipline problems with a small child at mealtime, they could mercifully excuse themselves.

"We chose the upstairs area because it was light and airy and we love the open feel," says Hannah. "The other couple liked the snug atmosphere downstairs. It was a perfect match.

"We built the house ourselves with the help of a local contractor and thought it was a lifetime arrangement.

"We set up a house account, with Barry as treasurer, and averaged out monthly house mortgage payments, electric bills, groceries, and all the rest. We each contributed half the money needed every other week.

"We all ate the same kind of food, cooked the same way—that was no problem. No one smoked. No one approved of very much television. Mona and I both worked part-time and alternated our work schedules so one of us would be here to watch the children.

"We even had the same values for our children. A house rule was: Don't reprimand a child unless you love him. Also children were not to run into each other's areas without permission—especially when any of us wanted to sleep late in the morning.

"We held weekly meetings and worked out any problems that came up."

What proved to be the biggest problem was one Barry and Hannah never dreamed of.

"When we built this house, we committed ourselves to this area forever. Vince and Mona were committed to their jobs. And they were upwardly mobile. The jobs they wanted to move up to are just not available in this rural area.

"When a position Vince wanted opened up somewhere else, he took it. Vince and Mona didn't have the deep attachment to the community we did. We never knew that. Our lives were much alike, but obviously not our goals.

"Vince and Mona moved quickly after he changed jobs, though they still paid their half of the monthly expenses for awhile. We finally borrowed money to pay them for their share of the house.

"We had no buy-sell agreement. We always thought we'd be able to work anything out that would occur. We learned a lot from that experience. We learned to ask better questions."

The partnership agreement of this intentional community reflects its feelings and concerns. It also covers, very specifically, how partnership business should be conducted. It is included on pages 350-353 of the Appendix for you to consider as an example of how an intentional community became a legal entity.

·17·
Group Houses

Tough times change perceptions of shared housing. While many still view a group of people living in one home a holdover from commune life '60s style, a growing number are finding that this arrangement serves today's needs quite well.

This book's primary focus is on more permanent living arrangements—those where partners have an equal responsibility for where they live, and ultimately for ownership. Nine times out of ten, funds come from partners, not outside sources. Partners sink or swim on their own, without a hired arbitrator to smooth problems.

Group houses are a world unto themselves, and the details of group house living have filled whole books—and should. Two good ones are Eric Raimy's *Shared Houses, Shared Lives* (Los Angeles: J.P. Tarcher, Inc., 1979) and Nancy Brandwein's, Jill MacNeice's, and Peter Spiers's *The Group House Handbook* (Washington, D.C.: Acropolis Books, Ltd., 1982). They are filled with valuable and detailed information to help make your experience a positive one, should you decide that group living is for you.

The information here will give you a good idea of how group houses operate, so you will know if you should consider this option further.

The whole idea of group houses is to give people independence through interdependence. Giving support to each other, individuals live better collectively than they could alone.

Group houses have become a successful way for the elderly to support one another. Intergenerational homes, filled with active people of all ages, have outmoded "old folks' homes." Older residents feel secure with stronger people in the house to assume chores that would be too much for them. Younger residents learn skills from older ones and benefit from their experience and wisdom. The atmosphere is electric with the mix.

For example, Maggie Kuhn, well-known founder of the Gray Panthers, has filled her Philadelphia home with social activists of all ages. Although residents have demanding and erratic schedules, when an occasional meal is shared, one inhabitant describes the atmosphere as a "yeast factory" of ideas.

In some ways, group houses take the most energy and commitment because given the number of people involved, jobs must be more clearly spelled out; meetings are more essential to keep the air cleared; and common versus private space and property must be more specifically defined.

On the other hand, group houses may have a mobile population. There is an owner or core group that stays put, but some residents tend to move in and out yearly.

The Boston Shared Living House

The Boston Shared Living House is a pioneer in the intergenerational concept. For 14 adults between the ages of 24 and 84, a Victorian row house in Boston's historic Back Bay area is home.

And as collective lifestyles become increasingly popular, to their amazement, this home and its residents have become downright famous. Television cameras, newspaper reporters, magazine writers (and I) have trooped through this delightful old mansion to ask inhabitants, "How come it works so well?"

One big answer comes from Kay Thomas, the house facilitator (she and her husband are paid, live-in "smoother-overs").

"The idea for the house was born in 1976 over the concern for the sparsity of housing for the elderly and their isolation," she says. "The inflated cost of utilities, housing, and food, the scarcity of rental housing, the disappearance of extended families, the fact that people are living longer caused activists to search for options for older adults other than living alone—often poorly, in nursing homes, or moving in with families not enthusiastic to have them around.

"The local chapter of the Gray Panthers and the Back Bay Aging Concerns Committee (a network of church, community, professional, and corporate groups working together to serve older people in the area) co-sponsored the development of the shared household and in 1977 received a $15,000 federal grant through the Commission on the Affairs of the Elderly.

"This enabled groundwork to be laid and a staff person to be hired. The steering committee and volunteers pushed the idea, until, in 1978, the Back Bay Aging Concerns Committee purchased a house and became primarily responsible for its management, though the Gray Panthers have remained committed and are on the steering committee. Residents finally moved into the house in July of 1979, and the house is run by an administrative committee made up mostly of the people who live there.

"The job of the house facilitators is to provide low-key leadership, aid the decision-making process, convene weekly meetings, and work with residents to increase their involvement in managing the house."

Residents who wish to live here must agree to assume a house job, come to a weekly meeting, and participate in a weekly meal (these are minimum requirements). Of those who inhabit the house, 70% must be over 55; 70% must be under what the Department of Housing and Urban Development calls a low to moderate income level.

Applicants who wish to live in The Boston Shared Living House must go through a series of interviews with residents, have their references checked, and then, by consensus, be approved by everyone. Criteria often are weighted to the need to fill a vacancy with a person of a specific age and income level. But newcomers and veteran residents must, at all times, expect to be held accountable for their commitment to keeping the house running.

For instance, an older resident broke her hip, and when she returned from nursing facilities where she did her initial recuperating, house residents agreed to pitch in and take on her jobs until she was able to assume them. The key word is agree. Everyone has to be in favor of the action.

Residents must be able to fulfill their house duties, but that doesn't mean others won't help out. They do. There are few house rules other than promising to shoulder your share of responsibilities. Residents may have guests whenever they please—overnight or not; smoke or not; use the kitchen facilities as it suits them.

The day I was there, four people had returned from work and the kitchen was a beehive of activity. Each was preparing his own meal, in harmony. House food is bought in bulk and residents pay $8 per week toward its purchase.

Mostly basics are stocked, such as breakfast cereal, milk, eggs, cheese, coffee, tea, sugar, flour, rice, pasta, tuna, potatoes, onions, and fruit. These can be the backbone of meals for residents—especially breakfast and lunch. Extra food must be purchased individually and residents must chip in $2 apiece for the weekly shared dinner.

Jobs generally fall into the categories of management and housekeeping. Management means being responsible for something like paying the phone bill; a housekeeping job would be to take out the trash. The ideal is for residents to pull their weight in both areas.

Most people work according to their capabilities, and age is a factor. If one person complains that another does a terrible job of wiping the kitchen counter, it might turn out that the erring person wasn't able to see the crumbs very well. More people might then be put in kitchen rotation. Residents help each other to be self-reliant.

Everyone who lives here knows exactly what he is supposed to do—and he better do it. Peer pressure is subtle, but you have to have a pretty thick hide not to feel the disapproval if you become lax.

House meetings are the key. Held after the communal Monday night meal residents prepare and eat together (this is solidifying, everyone feels), this is where problems are dealt with. Since there are no specific rules on "how to live here," any issue of concern is brought up at house meetings.

For instance, one resident had a friend visit on a regular basis. To ward off hard feelings she suspected were about to erupt, she declared, "You may have a concern about Fred being here a lot, and I don't want you to think he's eating your share of house food. We've been supplementing it." Everyone felt better.

Repairs are done by professionals if house members can't coax an appliance back to health. No one is judgmental about who breaks what, and the issue of negligence is handled at house meetings.

Smaller issues may not be brought up at meetings if people can work them out for themselves. For instance, if people who share a bathroom feel one person isn't cleaning it sufficiently, they tell him about it. If a satisfactory conclusion isn't reached, the facilitator helps solve it.

Only four violations are considered serious: (1) nonpayment of rent, (2) not meeting a house commitment, (3) disruptive behavior or misuse of alcohol or other substances, and (4) dangerous behavior toward another resident.

Rooms in the Shared Living House cost anywhere from $135 to $275 per month. Some are lovely and even have fireplaces; others are more modest. Some are furnished completely with resident's property, making them homey; others are stocked with "house" property and have a less personal feel.

"Financially, you can't beat living here," a vivacious woman in her mid-20s declares. "Every time I get sick of all the work it takes to live in this house, I look at what I get for what I'm paying. For a second floor apartment with a bath, fireplace, and balcony like this one that costs $275, you'd pay twice that much if you could even find a place like this in the neighborhood."

Another resident has lived in boarding houses in this same area.

"They're not safe," she says. "People break in and it can get pretty scary. Yes, I get aggravated with some of the petty squabbles that can go on in the house, but it's worth it to feel secure."

A thoughtful woman in her mid-40s says why she likes it at the Shared Living House.

"I see my mother living all alone and I don't want to live that way. My children are grown and I'm divorced. I'm used to having people around.

"Sharing with people of all ages gives me insight. When I look at someone here who is in her 50s, I see myself 10 years from now—and it's not so bad. Aging can be frightening, but if you see older people still vital, it's reassuring."

One of the older residents says, "I wouldn't live in a house without younger people. I love the vitality. It's stimulating."

The brew of ages, talents, temperaments, and ideas percolates within the walls of this place. An old house has been physically uplifted; it's also enjoying a true renaissance.

338 Harvard Street

On the other side of Boston, an equally exciting project—a private congregate residence for elders—has begun to blossom. Product of a marriage between architect Gwen Rono and the firm with which she is associated, Unihab, and CLOE (Cambridge Living Options for Elders), a 10-unit condominium has been fashioned from an old rectory at 338 Harvard Street. Eight units are to be inhabited by those over 62 years of age; two are for younger residents. (At the time I visited, the house was still under construction.)

A tour of the converted house shows exquisitely designed living units of about 900 square feet. Each condominium has sunny rooms, generous closets, all new plumbing and wiring, fully equipped kitchens—but also grab bars in tubs, nonslip floor surfaces, no thresholds at doors to trip over, smoke detectors, and alarm bells owners can sound to call for help.

Gwen Rono has preserved the details of the original house with architectural integrity in her clean design.

While Unihab is promoting the sale of the condominium units, CLOE is assisting in setting up a sharing structure and supplying support services. Representatives will interview prospective condominium buyers and choose the mix of people who will ultimately live here. Health is a concern; the person's desire to foster cooperative living is another.

Condominiums sell for $95,000-$120,000, certainly an upscale figure. The residence hopes to fill the housing needs of people who wish to lead an active, dignified life in high-quality individual units—but with sharing and support from others.

"Big old houses in Cambridge sell for hundreds of thousands of dollars," says Gwen. "Any older person who has been living alone in one of those too-big-for-him homes and sells it could certainly afford one of these condominiums. Living well doesn't have to mean living alone or with paid companionship."

Facilities that have been built into the house for residents to enjoy in common are a dining room, kitchen, social area with a fireplace, guest room, laundry, porches, and landscaped garden. These are inviting areas where people can gather when they wish.

Residents have the best of many worlds. They have delightful places to live on their own, balanced with activities within the house they can share as much as they please. The structural provisions that have been built into the house help maintain their well-being; there are also others nearby for aid.

"We're providing older people with mind-opening possibilities," says Gwen, who is an active member of CLOE. "We feel we're on the cutting edge of a new idea. There are big old homes in every city in the United States where an arrangement like this one could be created."

Once the household is formed, members can option—as a group—anything they think is important. For example, they can contract for outside services such as cleaning, laundry, bookkeeping, or transportation.

A basic agreement was created so that condominium buyers will know exactly what is expected of them. It is a promise to give the project time, thought, and energy.

Residents must participate in a minimum of one house meeting weekly, which will address topics such as how building security will be maintained, the procedures for guest room use, and how condominium appraisers will be chosen.

Residents agree to share at least one meal weekly. They understand that misuse of alcohol, drugs, and tobacco is prohibited for the sake of everyone's safety and that they are to exercise reasonable judg-ment in these areas. If not, they could be asked to leave. Then the con-dominium association would be obligated to repurchase the unit at the appraised price.

As for the buy-sell agreement, the condominium association has first right to buy out the exiting resident within 30 days of when he gives written notice of intent to sell. Again, one or more approved ap-praisers selected by the condominium association will set the resale price.

Finally, residents are asked to give candid responses to questions about their health and produce a written statement from their physi-cian. They are asked to have a guarantor who can take over payments in case they become very ill and cannot make decisions.

For more information on this project, write to Unihab/Cam-bridge, Inc., 14 Arrow St., Cambridge, MA 02138; phone (617) 868-8572.

Partnership for Living

Besides group houses, intergenerational or otherwise, that have come into existence with the aid of organizations, staff, and/or fund-ing, there are group houses put together by private individuals.

Northern Lights is a fairly typical example. It was founded in 1972 by four people who interested four others in joining them. Most were anti-war; some were pacifists and vegetarians. All of these men and women were feminists who agreed that there needed to be a radi-cal change in the way men and women related to each other. They felt women needed to have more power in society.

House members were teachers, social workers, artists, nurses, and some who hadn't found a vocation yet, but all were interested in social change through progressive politics. Most had lived in coopera-tive or communal groups before Northern Lights, and they wanted this roomy but faded Tudor house to be a place where cooperation and sharing would be nurtured.

They took over the mortgage from a collective group that had owned the house and then set up a nonprofit corporation. It was agreed that if the group broke up, the house would be turned over to another nonprofit group which would take over the mortgage; or, if the house had to be sold, any profit would be given to a worthwhile nonprofit organization.

Residents were required to pay a set amount into a house ac-count each month that would cover all expenses—from mortgage to food—except personal long-distance phone calls. A rotating treasurer paid the bills.

Sean, a former Northern Lights resident, says, "One treasurer felt it wasn't his business to inform house members if someone fell behind in payment and let one resident pile up a $500 debt.

"After that, we all agreed the treasurer must give a financial statement on members' accounts at the house meeting once a month. If someone was more than a month behind, he had to explain why to all of us and get permission to continue living there."

Jobs were listed on a chart. People wrote their names next to the chores they would do for a given week. They were generally allowed to do those they liked best, but everyone was expected to cook one dinner a week.

All were expected to let the cook know if they would not be at home for dinner or whether there would be guests. There was a place on the sign-up chart for this information.

"Jobs were well defined," says Sean. "Someone was expected to put garbage on the compost pile, take cans and bottles to the recycling center. Cleaning was divided by space. One job would be to vacuum and clean the first floor; another person took care of the second floor, and so on. Someone was expected to clean the kitchen once a week."

Job descriptions defined what was supposed to happen. People did, within that outline, what seemed to be necessary for that week and what they had time for. Generally a half-hour to two hours a week was spent on jobs.

"Cleanliness," says Sean, "was not a preoccupation. Mostly we cared about keeping the kitchen in good shape."

Eating dinner together was an important and even ritual event in this house. Members felt it was a time to relax and keep in touch with one another. Someone with an erratic schedule would have had trouble living here.

House meetings were held once or twice a month. There was a chalkboard in the kitchen so people could list agenda items.

"At a meeting," says Sean, "if the condition the living room was left in was an issue with someone, he'd state his grievance. He might say, 'My understanding of our agreement was that after you had guests over, you cleaned up—and it's not getting done. Let's either renegotiate this or recommit.' It usually helped to talk over points like this."

Three or four times a year, house workdays would be held for repairs and painting. Furniture was minimal and of thrift shop origin, so its maintenance was not a major concern. If someone caused damage and felt guilty about it, he replaced the object. Otherwise, the house paid for it.

Personal property was kept in a member's room. If he wanted to keep it private, it stayed there. If anything was out in common space, it was everybody's.

"If we were looking for a new member," says Sean (those who were accepted committed themselves to a year), " we posted notices at the recycling center. Whoever answered the phone at the house interviewed him. If the person seemed like a good possibility, we invited him to dinner.

"Everyone was expected to spend some time with the prospect, and if we all liked him, he was invited over a second time. Then we'd have a more formal meeting and talk about what we all thought would be beneficial and difficult about living together. By the time the person got to the final meeting, we were all reasonably sure we wanted him to move in. However, a single house member could veto his entrance.

"We were clear from the beginning what our house was about. Our notice stated we were a no-smoking, vegetarian, feminist, cooperative, conservation-conscious household. We weren't just looking for a new roommate."

Day-to-day details in this house worked. Relationships that developed among members didn't. When lovers changed, emotions flared. There were jealousies. That's why many group houses promote celibacy among housemates.

Northern Lights tried to salvage feelings. Everyone in the house—even lovers—had to keep their own separate rooms, so that if a couple broke up and one person left the house, there would be no disruption. The house refused to deal with people as couples. It was considered important for individuals to be treated as individuals and to function as individuals.

But, oh, the power of romance. There were alignments and realignments. According to Sean, it all got pretty confusing. There was tension. There were fights. Love flowered. The house folded.

• • •

For this reason, Barbara's house banned sex among members, and if a member was romantically involved with someone outside the house, the involvement had to be consummated on the outsider's turf. Part of the decision for this rule was to keep peace. The other part was that this house had a Christian commitment and residents felt loose sexual attachments didn't fit the lifestyle they had in mind.

Though Barbara's parents helped her buy the house and the deed was in her name, two other residents formed a sharing community. There are more than three people living here at times and most are Mennonites and Catholics. All are devoted to living simply, recycling waste, and not eating much meat. They're generally teachers or social workers or have other jobs related to "doing for others." They find communal Bible study once a week a consolidating experience.

Though schedules are hectic, members make sure they know what's going on with each other at house meetings. And community members are responsible for recruiting new ones who, they hope, will commit to stay at least a year.

Expenses are split, but not evenly, since Barbara owns the house. Of the $500 a month it takes to keep it running, Barbara pays $300. The two other members pay $150 each. (Additional members are being solicited so that individual expenses can be reduced.) Gas and electric, telephone and water bills, and the cost of groceries are equally divided. A treasurer keeps track of the books. Jobs are rotated and listed on a chart tacked up in the kitchen.

The theme of this house is simple living. All residents pledge to use less processed foods and eat less meat, conserve energy as much as possible by foregoing many appliances, turning down the heat (they mean hovering around 60 degrees), and being aware of how items they consume affect the environment. Milk is bought in glass bottles or waxed cardboard containers rather than plastic ones, and detergents must be low- or no-phosphate.

Residents recycle jars, cans, newspaper, and magazines, have a compost pile, use public transportation as much as possible, and buy nothing unless it's really necessary.

Barbara says, "We define simple lifestyle in detail to people who are interested in living here so they know what they can expect."

She's right. Someone who feels "doing without" is having his electric toothbrush go on the blink would flip when he discovers that he'll have to do his wash in the basement in a machine with a hand wringer and then hang clothes on a line to dry.

Make the philosophy of your group clear to newcomers—in advance.

·18·
Vacation Homes

A place in the country, a house near the ocean, a condo where it's warm in winter, or right smack in the middle of a choice place to ski—pipe dreams or possibilities?

For many, buying one house is such a major production that even thinking of another, tucked away somewhere special, would be pie in the sky. But some can afford a second spot, to hang their bathing suits or park their hiking boots. And more people could if they bought a vacation home in partnership with others.

If a second-home partnering does take place—and joint purchases account for a respectable percentage of this category—the scenario is something like this.

Leonard and Jill go to their favorite spot on Martha's Vineyard five summers in a row. The fifth summer they are there, they begin to look at houses. Wouldn't it be wonderful to have a place of their own?

It would. And there are a couple for sale right in the area they consider prime. Everything is prime—especially the price. Would they use the house enough to justify the expense? Could the cost of upkeep become a burden?

They go back home and talk to their best friends, Marge and Don, about the place—or Jill's cousin Alan and his wife Sarah, or Leonard's sister Minnie and her husband Maury (however you want to write the

317

script), and the second couple gets excited about the project, too.

They fly to Martha's Vineyard and take a look at the house, fall in love with the place (maybe they're even familiar with the area), and a partnership is born.

In a goodly number of vacation home partnerships, one party finds the residence and starts seeking a partner among friends and acquaintances. It is rare (at least I found it so) for these partnerships to take place among strangers.

Doubling up on vacation home purchases enables people to stretch their buying dollar, which, in turn, enables them to stretch out on a nice beach somewhere—sometimes in bliss, sometimes with knots in their stomach because, for the second time in a row, the house was a mess when they arrived.

These partnerships demand courtesy (leave the place for others as you would expect it to be left for you) and mutual financial responsibility. If anyone has troubles, a vacation home is the first thing to be axed from a budget. You must make sure you're joining up with someone who's not going in over his head. You must also provide—legally—for the possibility that your partner may come on hard times and default. You don't want to be left holding the bag.

Those I interviewed who bought second homes in cooperation with others have come up with some enviable arrangements, as well as some pretty sobering stories. Before you slip off to a place in the sun—in partnership—read on.

No Man Is an Island

Boris and his wife and children rented a house on a small island off Vancouver and fell in love with its pristine beauty. Since Boris is a social scientist at a northwestern university and doesn't teach classes in the summer, the thought of having his own home in this area—where he could write, sail, and just plain relax in peace—was enticing. His family agreed.

A group of five couples who owned 900 acres of land including four miles of shoreline in this part of Canada asked Boris and another person who also vacationed there to buy into the deal so yearly payments would be brought to a reasonable level. He jumped at the chance—too fast.

"This core group," says Boris "was made up of people who had been going to this area for 30 years. They had grown up vacationing here as children. None had houses there, but rented from friends or relatives. Two were cousins; two were roommates in college; two were business partners. The sixth couple asked into the 'in group' was a close friend. I was the outsider.

"My advice to anyone invited to join a group like this is to stay out. Everyone else had longstanding emotional attachments to this vacation spot. With emotional attachments comes craziness. People tell you they want to do what they want to do, and it doesn't make sense. It does to them, but not to anyone else.

"I was asked into the group because they thought I'd be valuable in helping people work with each other. I was totally ineffective."

The most undermining factor in the partnership was the difference in income levels between Boris and his partners. He had the least amount of money and because of it felt considerable pressure.

"When we bought the property," says Boris, "a trusteeship was formed. Each of us owned one-seventh of every fraction of a square inch of the land. Our goal was to provide summer homes for all. Each of us was to get four waterfront lots. We could build our own house on one of them and sell the rest to whom we pleased. Each of us also owned part of the interior 800 acres which many felt should remain wild.

"Sounds simple enough, doesn't it? Well, it was six years before anyone could agree which 500 feet of frontage they wanted to build a cottage on. If a couple picked one spot, then they couldn't have another. It was like getting married. If you pick a mate, you can't play the field anymore. There were so many exciting places on the island, each with its own unique features, people couldn't make decisions until they walked over the land three dozen times.

"I went into this deal so I could have land to build a summer home. Every summer I couldn't build because of everyone's indecision, I had to spend money to rent a cottage. And I couldn't afford to rent a cottage for my entire summer vacation—only a few weeks.

"The rest of my partners kept telling me not to worry about not being able to build because the land was increasing in value. That's true and they could afford to hold onto it with no strain.

"I couldn't. And as each summer passed, the cost of construction rose. If I could have built the cottage the first summer I owned the land, it would have cost half as much as it did. I was really in a bind.

"Finally, after six years of fighting over who would build a house on what part of the island, we drew straws."

Since partners lived in cities scattered all over the country, meetings to discuss the jointly held property were difficult to arrange. It was hard to settle business by phone, and when they did get together, they found they couldn't agree even then.

Boris remembers, "There was a lot of carrying on at meetings, but no face-to-face fights. Most issues were dealt with behind people's backs. Two weeks after a meeting, partners would still be phoning each other to discuss what wasn't said at the meeting."

Boris advises any group to have a concrete timetable of what will happen when. Partners should have common goals. His bitter lesson came when partners were locked somewhere between their desire to make a profit on the land and keeping it wild, between holding lots for family and friends or selling them to outsiders and making more money. Because no one could agree, nothing moved forward.

"Some partners held up land choices because they were afraid others, after choosing their own home plot, would sell land to people they didn't know and they'd end up with neighbors they didn't like living too close to them. Others who didn't want 'outside' neighbors picked land close together so they would be each other's neighbors. They wound up closer together than they intended. As I say, it was craziness."

Boris also suggests that the written partnership agreement mandate regular meetings. In his group, a subgroup that wanted to hold onto the land and not build dragged their feet setting up meetings. No meetings, no building discussions. Feelings smoldered.

Boris feels a third party, a strong manager to run the whole enterprise, would have helped. Their manager was a member of the faction who didn't want to move matters along. He did his job well.

Finally, 15 years after the partnership was begun, the land was divided up. There are no more partners. Boris owns 125 acres and a vacation home he loves. Everyone else owns a similar piece.

"In the long run, I've come out ahead," reflects Boris. "I have a gorgeous place to go to in the summer, some lots to sell or to hold onto for my children. If I sold them now, I could probably break even. But for the first time in my career, I was completely helpless in getting anyone to make up his mind in a rational manner. No one could deal rationally with 'our island.'

"I came into the group knowing what I wanted. The others said that was what they wanted. Then everything got hazy. If I had insisted, at the beginning, that all of these contingencies be written into an agreement, they wouldn't have let me join the group. I wanted a home in that area more than anything. I overlooked what I knew would cause problems and thought I would be able to deal with them. I keep saying it over and over—craziness!"

A Place in the Country

One hundred acres that include a lake, a swimming pool, nature walks, and plenty of spots to sit quietly and just listen to the birds sounds utopian. Add the fact that it's a two-hour drive from New York City and that a piece of it costs only $10,000-$20,000 and it sounds almost unbelievable.

But it's happening—as a cooperative community in New York State. Our farsighted friend, Dave, the smart Manhattan architect who nabbed the TriBeCa loft before market values skyrocketed, put together a joint country venture as successful as his city dwelling.

It all started in the Catskills in the 1940s. Sullivan County was populated by dairy and egg farmers whose city relatives came to visit. As more people flocked there for a breath of fresh air and respite from the city in the summer, Sullivan County became a place for tourists to vacation. All the relatives brought friends! To accommodate vacationers, farmers built rows of white clapboard bungalows, often with pine-paneled interiors, near the farmhouse. Bungalow colonies, they were called.

They were popular for about 30 years, then fell on hard times. The children of the original bungalow dwellers wanted more glamorous vacations. At resorts like the Concord and Grossinger's, indoor swimming pools, endless-course dinners, and dancing seemed more alluring than country quiet. Most bungalow colonies were left vacant and deteriorated; a few were taken over by religious groups such as Hasidic Jews and followers of Hare Krishna.

In 1981, Dave and a partner purchased one with the intention of selling shares to create a cooperatively owned community. Other developers woke up to the possibilities of bungalow colonies and began buying, too.

But Dave was already a veteran bungalow colony resident. Ten years before he struck out with a single partner to buy one he named Lake Nekoma Vacation Community, he and 12 friends had bought Maple Tree, a 12-acre bungalow colony.

For a $35,000 mortgage (the property was valued at about $50,000) partners got vacation homes for between $1,000 and $1,500 each.

"We were all young artists, writers, directors just starting out," remembers Dave. "We were delighted to have an affordable way to get out of the city for vacations. We fixed up the bungalows as best we could; people did most of the keeping up of the area themselves. There was a minimum of rules because no one wanted them.

"We were all friends, all people who appreciated nature. We were idealistic, altruistic, more socialistic than capitalistic—appropriate for who we all were in the early '70s. In spite of how loose we were in setting up Maple Tree, it has survived.

"But in 1981, I decided with a partner to buy a bungalow colony with more acreage and more amenities and set it up as a cooperative venture. By establishing structure, by becoming the moving force and strong manager of the development, I wanted to create the same community átmosphere as Maple Tree, while avoiding some of the problems that arose from its live-and-let-live governing style." (You hear that, Boris?)

The offering plan for Lake Nekoma Vacation Homes is book-length. It was set up according to what the attorney general of New York State demands for properties to be legally offered to the public to establish cooperative ownership. The law says the sponsor (Dave and his partner) must disclose all specifics about the property in the prospectus, including the minimum and maximum number of shares that must be sold before the sponsorship can pass to cooperative ownership.

"I became a legal expert as this venture progressed," says Dave. "Anyone wanting to spearhead a similar project must seek an attorney experienced in setting up co-ops."

Whatever it took to start Lake Nekoma was worth it. It's hard to imagine that this idyllic retreat is even in the same world as New York City. There are fish in the lake. Birds sing. It's a joy to walk the land.

The major drawback of a bungalow colony is how close together the cottages—whatever their charm—were built. They were usually placed in rows a handshake apart, so that plumbing and electrical wiring could be installed economically. Some bungalows housed two families; there are two bedrooms in the front of the house with kitchens, two bathrooms in the middle, and two bedrooms in the rear. Overall they're about 600 square feet, not counting the porch out front.

These are being converted by owners into single-family dwellings. (Some have been extraordinarily revamped, complete with skylights.) All at Lake Nekoma preserve their original aura even though they are updated. The asking price is about $20,000. Smaller, one-family cottages are $15,000; apartments in the original rooming house (there were eight, which Dave converted to four larger ones), with 750 square feet and private entrances, cost $10,000.

"Sure, you might be able to afford a house of your own with a small piece of land in the area," says Dave, "but nothing with nearly 100 acres and all the facilities we have. You couldn't touch this kind of privacy."

To make the bungalows more appealing, Dave has painted each one a different color to give it individuality, but in complementary hues so all are part of a whole. The interiors remain untouched so owners can do what they please according to their needs. If they wish to hire Dave to do architectural drawings and oversee construction, his services are available. Some bungalows have also been moved to fringe areas to give the other units more elbow room.

Each shareholder pays a specified amount per month for maintenance (to keep up the grounds, repair the swimming pool, taxes, etc.) commensurate with the number of shares he purchased. Dave manages the project; his wife keeps the books. They are paid a fee for this out of the monthly charge.

A board of directors consisting of five shareholders was elected by the group to make decisions on expenditures up to $1,000. Anything over that amount must be brought before the cooperative community for approval at a twice-yearly meeting.

"Everyone has a strong desire to enjoy the country and not infringe on anyone else's pleasure," says Dave. "No one has television sets here or dishwashers and disposals. You never hear a radio blasting.

"It's very important to have copacetic people in a community like this. When you sit around the swimming pool, you want to be with people you like.

"When I showed interested buyers around the property, I made sure I sold shares only to those who would be tolerant of people's differences, who wanted a simple lifestyle and who could be respectful of privacy [all age groups and income levels are represented]. They promised to maintain or enhance the present ecology. It took two years to sell all the shares.

"Though everyone loves this place, I was the one who set down the guidelines in the beginning. Prospective buyers could take or leave my deal. There needs to be a strong leader in the embryonic stages of a venture like this one until a governing body takes over. If it's totally democratic from the start, a partnership among so many people can disintegrate because everyone wants to implement his own ideas. I set up Lake Nekoma in the way it was most likely to work."

"We even have an unwritten rule here that owners can't sublet their places for a week at a time. We don't want people with different outlooks on what 'the country' is to disrupt our enjoyment."

"If an owner is going to be away for a summer, he tries to rent to friends, or he'll ask other owners if they have friends who want to rent a place. We feel the more inbred we keep Lake Nekoma, the more successful it will be."

Even if owners want to sell their bungalows, new buyers must be approved by the board of directors. What they sell them for, however, is determined by what the market will bear.

"We've created a village," says Dave. "Everyone knows everyone else. We've all winterized our cottages so we can use them year round. Even when most of us are in the city, we rest easy because there's always someone or other here, which prevents vandalism—a big problem to vacation home owners. People help each other out here. Parents trade off babysitting. If someone is going into the city, he lets others know and asks if he can pick up groceries or run errands.

"The group is an '80s montage of a family structure. There are couples with children, couples on their second marriage with his and her children, gays, older couples, singles, divorced people. All have many friends in New York scattered all over the city.

"In New York, a person goes into his own apartment in a city of a million apartments. People have a mental community of friends, but I feel they also have an inherent need for a physical one."

A Cabin in the Woods

Two couples who felt stifled in the city wanted a place in the country they could use as a weekend retreat. These good friends decided to look for land they could afford—together.

Marv and Lynn, Dick and Claudia had been friends for years. Their children—all in high school—were friends as well. Though Marv, as a professor, makes less than Dick, who is vice president of a company (both wives were in graduate school at the time of the proposed purchase), values matched. Everyone wanted to spend the same amount of money for undeveloped land where they could enjoy the quiet and feel free.

"We quickly found we had to get outside the area close to the city where speculators drive up prices," remembers Marv. "We weren't looking to buy property for profit, just beauty and trees. The search was half the fun. We spent a lot of time exploring the countryside together. Finally we settled on 50 hilly acres that even had a gurgling creek. We bought the land for $25,000—the amount we had agreed on in advance.

"No one wanted to take out a loan to buy this land. We used money we had available and split the cost down the middle.

"What we had in mind was a place we could use on weekends, not for the whole summer. What we found was perfect."

Their buy-sell agreement is one familiar to us by now. If one doesn't want to buy out the other, the property will be sold.

How the couples divided the cost of taxes is unique. Since the land falls in two counties, two different tax bills have to be reckoned with. Each couple pays one bill. The shares are not always equal but they balance out in the long run.

"We used the land for camping, often together, for awhile," says Marv. "Or we'd go there to spend the day since it was just an hour and a half drive away. But it was uncanny. We'd leave home and it would be sunny. When we got to our land, it started to rain. We started to think about building a cabin."

All were interested in the building process and got together on weekends to design cabins.

"Comparing our designs was wonderful fun," says Marv. "I even made some models. Finally we decided to build a prefab cabin from a kit made in New England. All materials were packaged by the company so they could be carried to any spot people chose to erect it. Since we picked the top of a hill to place our cabin, we knew we'd need help. We also knew if we didn't make fairly rapid progress, we'd get discouraged."

Everyone took a week's vacation from work and school to erect the cabin when the kit arrived. Children and relatives were pressed into service. They rented a truck to haul everything as far as they could drive to get to the cabin site; the rest of the way, they carried supplies piggyback.

"We constructed a 12-by-9-foot module with a porch," says Marv. "We could use the place alone or together with the other family. We put in a floor but there's no plumbing. We have some furniture, but no beds. We use sleeping bags. Believe me, the place has no decorating scheme. It's filled with odds and ends, but we love it.

"Building the cabin was an exciting experience. Expenses were not a problem because we knew, in advance, what we were going to spend. We each bought the necessary extras to put the kit together. We stapled the receipts into a notebook and split the cost at the end. All of us brought our own tools and used everyone's.

"I hated sticking tar on the roof when we were finished," says Marv. "I don't know why, but it made me nervous having that gooey stuff all over me. Dick, happily, took over the job. But he couldn't stand taking care of the chemical toilet, so I always emptied it. We never created a formal list of jobs to do; we just sensed each other's feelings and equaled out the nasty ones. We were grateful to each other for it.

"We wanted our children to be able to use the cabin for camping on their own. They were teenagers, and they did.

"Dick and Claudia's kids didn't dry a skillet they used very well and it rusted. It aggravated them as much as it did Lynn and me. We all talked to the kids about how the cabin should be used. But after all we went through to build it, we're not going to break up a partnership over pots and pans."

Co-Condos

People own vacation homes to relax and to leave worries behind. After their energy refueling weeks are over, they want to leave and forget about the place until the next time.

That just isn't realistic. Dishwashers in condominiums in Hawaii break just as they do at homes in Toledo. So do television sets, washing machines, and all the other motorized conveniences we take for granted until they stop working and aggravate us.

When vacation home partners make no rules for how the place should be left for one another, when everyone treats it like a rented hotel room and none of them is particularly responsible, they're in for trouble.

Trouble is exactly what plagued Art's group.

"Six couples—all friends—bought a condominium in Aspen," says Art. "Our initial investment was $4,000 apiece; the monthly payments were $650, which we divided by six.

"It was no big financial deal for any of us. Everyone involved went into the partnership with the assumption that if he lost everything he put into it, it wouldn't hurt him. The property was appreciating anyway, so no one was afraid he'd lose money.

"We figured in the price of decorating the condo at the beginning. Two of the men's wives went to Aspen and picked out everything. What they chose was a little loud for my taste, but I didn't really care. I don't like the furnishings in all the places I rent either. For the few weeks a year I intended to spend there, it didn't matter."

A lot of things didn't matter to this group. There was no agreement on how the place should be maintained and how many people could use it at one time, although Art's secretary did keep track of who wanted to use the condo, when, on a first-come, first-served basis.

"The condo had two floors," explains Art, "and when people carried their suitcases up the stairs, they always banged the wall. It began to look awful."

A window cracked and the person who was staying there at the time put a piece of tape over it instead of getting it fixed. The next person who arrived was furious.

"One time, on the last day I was there, the washer and dryer went out. The repair service couldn't come right away and I wasn't going to extend my vacation to wait for them, so I left. The washer and dryer were broken when the next couple came to use the condo. They weren't too happy with me.

"One partner spent the first day and a half of every vacation cleaning the place before he felt comfortable. The rest of us thought he was just a fussbudget.

"People carried dishes and silverware and glasses out to the pool and forgot them there. Supplies started running down to nothing.

"One partner's 17-year-old son used the condo for a week—with 26 friends. It was one long, wild party. The condominium association was up in arms. We didn't know anything about what the kid was doing until the manager called us.

"People left food in the refrigerator for those who would be arriving, but the ones who came didn't know how long the food had been there. Some of it was rotten.

"Finally we made rules. People were to throw all leftover food away and just leave unopened bottles and cans. We posted signs over the light switch in the kitchen to define what keeping the condo clean meant. Then we hired a cleaning service to come in and go over the place thoroughly after each person used it. We split the cost.

"What broke up the group was one person insisting we rent the condo. The rest of us didn't want to do that. When the guy who wanted to rent the place asked to be bought out, the whole group disbanded. One partner bought the condo for its appraised value. We were all glad to be out of it."

• • •

Pat and Jerry, Ginger and Nate were close friends for years before they bought a condo in Hilton Head together. They shared many vacations—from swanky cruises to renting rustic cabins in a state park—with all their kids.

Pat and Jerry loved Hilton Head more each time they rented a place there. When they decided to buy a condominium but didn't want to assume the expense alone, it was natural that Ginger and Nate became their partners.

"I hadn't even seen the condominium," says Ginger, "when we bought it with Pat and Jerry. They thought it was terrific. We trusted their judgment. Jerry buys and sells real estate; we trusted his business acumen as much as both of their tastes. If he felt this was an appreciating property and a good investment, we'd go ahead with the purchase in good faith."

The purchase of the condominium was not a financial burden for either couple. But they agreed, in advance, that the money they invested would not interfere with their lifestyles. They wanted the condominium, but they didn't want to be overpowered by its upkeep.

The cost of decorating the condo was figured into the overall expense. They flew to Hilton Head to meet with the decorator who would help them make fabric and furniture selections.

"You'd see that we have completely different tastes if you'd visit our city houses," says Ginger. "Furnishing the condo, we picked pieces we both agreed on. Though we love the place, none of us feels that personally involved with it as a home. Everything is pretty, but there's nothing there I'd be upset over if renters ruined.

"We buy things on our own, too, if we feel we need them. If we're low on towels, I buy a dozen when I'm down there. The partnership pays for it.

"If Pat and Jerry feel we need new glasses, they buy them. We agree on what's needed to stock the condominium and trust each other's purchases.

"I know Pat isn't going to go out and buy a $1,000 painting for the condo. She knows I'm not going to bring in dimestore glasses."

The condo is used separately by the couples and together. Jerry is the manager of the operation, and all partners are happy about his role. He places advertisements for renters, pays the bills, keeps the books and is glad to do it.

The owners schedule use in the prime vacation months and rent the condo for as much of the remaining time as possible. After each renter leaves, a cleaning service goes through the place. Broken appliances are repaired under their auspices.

Although both couples love the condo, they strongly feel it is always for sale. It's not actively on the market, but Jerry is called frequently by people interested in making purchases in the area.

"If the right price was offered, we'd take it," says Ginger. "We'd trust Jerry's instinct on this. We love this place but we can always buy another one—in partnership."

HOW TO GET AWAY FROM IT ALL (TROUBLE)

The legal points attorney Mark Berliant noted in Chapter Fifteen as important to joint homeowners are just as pertinent to vacation home partners. He offers some additional advice for those who plan to purchase recreational properties:

"Try to have the vacation home you buy titled in all partners' names, if you can," he cautions. "This is difficult because, for instance, many condominiums in Florida have stringent rules for a single owner-occupant. Partners who want to buy into one of the places get around this rule by one actually taking legal ownership and the other becoming 'the cousin who uses it all the time.' This may work if the partners get along, but if there's a falling out and only one partner's name is on the title, there can be real problems."

Another veteran condominium partner says that year-round residents don't like co-owners who hold condominiums strictly for vacation use, because they're likely to rent the place as often as they can, have friends and relatives use it, and the natives don't like the noise and disruption of so many people constantly moving in and out. So the association of condominium owners may pass a regulation that prohibits owners from renting.

Those who form condominium partnerships with an eye to making the mortgage payments with rent money are going to be in trouble. Make sure you can pay the bank out of your own pocket or you run the risk of losing your place in the sun.

Mark says, "Money problems split vacation home partnerships more than people not getting along. When a person runs into hard financial times, luxuries are eliminated. A vacation home is like membership in a country club, it's one of the first items to be dropped.

"It's important to join up with someone you feel is financially sound. For instance, if you and your partner are investigating the purchase of a condominium and he seems to be having difficulty putting up his half of the down payment, be cautious about proceeding. It may be very likely he'll also have trouble coming up with monthly payments."

Who uses a vacation home and when can also cause arguments if a schedule is not worked out in advance. This is especially important if everyone wants prime time. Mark advises clients to set ground rules in this manner.

"Let's use the example, once again, of a condominium in Florida," he says. "Many of my clients want to use it during Christmas and spring vacation because they can be with their school-age children. Partners sit down with a calendar and one may take spring vacation one year and Christmas the next. They alternate these two holidays annually.

"After that, the months of January and February are considered most desirable. Each partner agrees to take four weeks during that period. The weeks can be consecutive or not—whatever the partners agree to.

"Next best months are November and December, March and April. The same use pattern is worked out. Partners concur on which weeks they would like to use the condominium and mark off that time on the calendar.

"Partners must be frank about all this at the beginning and must honor each other's usage rights. If Gene calls Henry constantly asking, 'Are you going to be using the condo the week you have marked off in March because my daughter would love to go down with her husband,' Henry is going to get aggravated.

"Some switching is fine, if it's agreeable to all the partners. One person constantly taking advantage of the other or wanting to change becomes a pest."

Who else can use the vacation home besides partners, and how many at one time, are other issues important to these kinds of partnerships. Co-owners must decide, at the outset, whether partners alone can use the place; whether use should be limited to brothers, sisters, and parents; whether it can be lent to business acquaintances or anyone a partner wants to. An absolute limit to the number of people who may stay there at one time must be set.

Will there be charges for the use of the condo if it is lent to others by the partners? If you decide not to charge rent, will you ask friends to pay the gas, electric, and phone bills? Long-distance calls can be a real killer if owners get stuck with them.

This is why Mark emphasizes, "A partner should always be responsible for expenses incurred by his guests. Whatever they are, he should pay them promptly into the partnership account.

"It is irresponsible to say, 'I'll pay for the shower door as soon as I get the money from my aunt.' A partner should front the money and do his own collecting."

Vacation homes can be a pleasure, but they can also be a long-distance headache. It's bad enough when a pipe bursts in the house you consider your permanent residence, but when it happens in an A-frame in Fond du Lac and you have to deal with it from your command post in Pittsburgh, it can be frustrating. Especially when you have to pay bills, arrange for the rental of the place when you and your partner aren't using it, and tend to dozens of other details.

Mark says, "Many partners divide these responsibilities so they don't become too much of a burden for one. One partner may become Mr. Outside and take charge of renting the place, collecting money for it, paying the bills, taking care of the insurance. Mr. Inside makes sure the dishwasher works, the maid service is doing a good job, the mugs get replaced when they're chipped.

"If there are three partners or more, a chairman usually takes over. He does it because he loves to take care of all these details, or has his secretary help him. He doesn't generally receive payment for his services, but he might get a special birthday gift from his partners or get treated to a nice dinner now and then."

A cleaning service should not be considered a luxury by partners who purchase a home or condominium in partnership—especially if there is one readily available. If you're racing for a plane and don't have time to straighten the condo, your partner, who is arriving tomorrow morning, is going to be angry. Chances are, if you can afford to split the price of a second home, you can afford to share the cost of having the place well cleaned after each use. These services (or the condo manager) can also arrange for repairs or any other work that needs to be done. In areas where vacation homes or condominiums abound (unless you're talking about a remote cabin in the mountains), services to keep your home in tip-top condition can be hired.

Cleaning services are just one matter you should discuss *before* you seal your partnership. If one partner feels this is something he doesn't want to pay for and the other considers him cheap for saying so, the road ahead may be rocky.

Like values are important here, as in all the other partnerships I've described, because if one partner wants to furnish the condo with bits and pieces gathered from relatives while the other wants to go first class and hire a decorator, there shouldn't be a partnership.

Mark feels trust is paramount among co-owners of a vacation home. Each must feel the other is doing right by all the rest. For instance, if one partner crams the disposal with artichoke leaves, he should be responsible for having the machine fixed and pay for it. He is clearly negligent. If it just stopped running, the partnership should assume the expense.

What happens if the partner who overloaded the disposal charged the expense to the partnership and just said it broke?

When his partner calls the same serviceman the next time because the condo dishwasher stopped running, and the repairman says, "Oh yeah, I was here the last time for the man who stuffed all the artichoke leaves down the disposal and ruined it," he's going to be upset. And lose trust.

"Disclosure is 90% of being a good partner," says Mark. "If the guy who broke the disposal told his partners what he did, they might have told him to forget about paying the bill himself. Any of them could have done the same thing. The key factor is being honest."

Draw up clear rules for the day-to-day operation of the condo or vacation home and post them where everyone can see them. They don't have to be elaborate or unpleasant, but how about . . .

"Welcome to our condominium. Here are a few things we'd like you to keep in mind while you're here:

1. Trash pickup days are Tuesday and Thursday. Please bind up refuse in plastic bags and put it in the cans located in the service area at the end of the hall.

2. When you leave, place $25 under the ashtray on the coffee table in the living room for Ace Cleaners, who will come in when you leave. Please let them know when you intend to depart. Their phone number is 921-6877.

3. Posted beside this list on the bulletin board you will find a laundry ticket from XYZ cleaners. Take the ticket to the cleaners (it's two blocks to the right out the front door); you are expected to pay for the clean sheets and towels being held there. Bring them back to the condo and make up the beds. When you leave, place the dirty linen in a laundry bag, take it to the cleaners, and pin the ticket back on the bulletin board. The next person arriving will take it from there.

4. Please do not use up tissues, napkins, dishwasher detergent, soap, etc., without replacing them. Leave these staples at the level you found them on arriving.

"It's incredible," says Mark, "how easy it is to make a partnership work when all the ground rules and instructions are agreed on in advance. Partners can write in whatever they feel is important. And 95% of the time, people will do what has been agreed on.

"It's when co-owners simply say, 'You take half; I'll take half,' and leave details up in the air that they're going to have problems."

. A Lot in Common .

So even vacation homes, pie-in-the-sky dreams, can become reality through partnering. Cabins to condos can be co-owned successfully by setting down a no-nonsense framework. But then, that's the thread woven through this book. Clear thinking, careful choosing, frank talking, generosity, and caring make joint ventures fly. It makes good sense. But instead of ending this book by making sense, however good, let's finish with a dream. One that could be yours. One you can make come true.

You want a secret place. A retreat. One no human has imprinted. One maybe no one else knows about. There are no roads, no cars, no people. Maybe it's an island. Maybe it's an inland island. Maybe it's a mountaintop. Or a gorge. Or a river bottom. However you imagine your perfect place in your mind's eye, that's what I'm describing.

You want to sit quietly and catch a glimpse of the deer that come to drink from the stream in the late afternoon. Sit on a rock overlooking the beach and watch the sun dip below the water. You want to walk through untrampled woods full of ferns and wildflowers.

You never want this place developed. No houses. No electricity. No wires or poles or pipes poked in the land. You would camp there—gently. Insiders call it "minimum impact camping." What it means is that when you leave "your place," there'd be no mark on the land, no signs you've been there. That's how much you love it. You don't want to dig into it or chop it or scar it. You want to keep it in its natural state forever.

Land. Space. Enough of it to escape from hot dog stands and knickknack shoppes, from ringing phones and big screen TVs. From other people. You'd like to look as far as you can and know that all you see will remain as it is forever.

That takes money.

But there are other people like you. Maybe you've camped with them in the past. Maybe they belong to the same environmental groups you do. Maybe they're your best friends. They'd probably have to be to share a dream like this one.

If you can partner with them, the way you want to live in peace with the ecosystem, you can buy a hideaway—together. More money means more land; more people, more energy to make hope reality. Hearts beating in the same sure rhythm can make miracles.

Appendix:
Shared Living Space
Agreements

THE SHARED HOUSING RESOURCE CENTER
HOMESHARING LEASE

1. Parties

The parties to this agreement are _____ , hereafter called the Homeowner and _____ , hereafter called the Homesharer.

2. Property

    a. The Homeowner shares the following property with the Homesharer for the term of this agreement:

        (1) Premises located at _____

        (2) The following furniture, appliances, and other items of property: _____

    b. The Homesharer shares the following furniture, appliances, and other items of property: _____

c. The following areas of the house or items of property are *not* to be shared or shared *only as specified:*

_____

_____

_____

_____

d. Other restrictions to the use of the premises are as follows [**e.g., pets, smoking, alcohol consumption, guests**]:

_____

_____

_____

_____

3. Term

This agreement is [month-to-month or year-to-year] _____ and shall begin on _____

4. Rent

a. The monthly rent shall be $ _____, due and payable by the Homesharer on the first of each month.

b. If there is a service exchange in addition to or in lieu of rent, the following activities shall be performed by the Homesharer [**be specific and include frequency**]:

_____

_____

_____

_____

c. In the case of a Homeowner who provides services to a Homesharer, the following activities shall be performed by the Homeowner in exchange for the above rent [**be specific and include frequency**]:

_____

_____

_____

_____

5. Utilities

Utilities shall be paid by the party and in the percentage indicated on the following chart:

	Homeowner	Homesharer
Electricity	_____	_____
Gas	_____	_____
Heat	_____	_____
Water	_____	_____
Garbage Collection	_____	_____
Trash Removal	_____	_____
Other: _____	_____	_____

6. Telephone

The Homeowner and Homesharer agree to the following provisions for telephone use **[whether: a) the telephone and costs are to be shared and how the costs will be divided, or, b) the Homesharer is to install his/her own telephone and pay the charges thereof]**:

_____
_____
_____
_____

7. Food Costs

The Homeowner and Homesharer agree to the following provisions for food costs **[whether: a) food costs are to be shared and how the costs will be divided, or, b) the Homesharer is to purchase his/her own food separately]**:

_____
_____
_____
_____

8. Security Deposit

    a. The Homeowner hereby acknowledges receipt of a security deposit of $_____, to be applied toward costs incurred by the Homeowner if the Homesharer violates the agreement as outlined in Section 9.

    b. The Homeowner shall keep the security deposit in the following depository: located at: _____

    c. Within 14 days after the Homesharer vacates, the Homeowner shall return the security deposit, with accrued passbook interest, less any deductions the Homeowner is entitled to make as outlined in Section 9. If any deductions are made, the Homeowner shall give the Homesharer a written, itemized statement of the deductions and an explanation of why each deduction was made. _No deductions shall be made for normal wear and tear to the premises._

9. Homesharer's Duty to Maintain Premises

The Homesharer shall keep the dwelling unit in a clean and sanitary condition. The Homesharer shall be liable for any damage to the dwelling unit (other than normal wear and tear) caused by acts of neglect of the Homesharer. The Homesharer shall also be liable for any damage to the dwelling unit which he or she permits to be caused by any member of his or her family, invitee, licensee, or any any person acting under his or her control.

10. Homeowner's Obligation to Maintain Premises

The Homeowner shall maintain the premises in a decent*, safe, and sanitary condition. **[*The Homesharer may want to define what this means to him or use different words here.]**

11. Repairs

Any repairs to the premises or personal property that become necessary due to the negligence of any party shall be the responsibility of the negligent party.

12. Alterations

No substantial alteration, addition, or improvement shall be made by the Homesharer in or to the dwelling unit without prior consent of the Homeowner in writing.

13. Noise

Both parties agree to refrain from excessive noise or any other activity which disturbs peace and quiet.

14. Notice of Termination

    a. The Homesharer may terminate this agreement by giving the Homeowner written notice at least 30 days before the end of the rental term.

    b. The Homeowner may terminate this agreement by giving the Homesharer written notice at least 30 days before the end of the rental term.

    c. Under the provision of _____**[your]**_____ State landlord-tenant code, the Homeowner may terminate this agreement in the following ways: [Note: *Since each state has provisions governing landlord-tenant relationships, it will be necessary for you to inquire into the correct provisions for your state. Provisions 1-3 below are those of the State of Washington.*]

       1. Three days' written notice if the Homesharer fails to pay/perform rent.

       2. Three days' written notice if the Homesharer destroys property or maintains any nuisance upon or about the premises.

       3. Ten days' written notice if Homesharer continues to breach any material provision of this agreement after written notice is given to Homesharer to discontinue such breach.

       4. **[And such other provisions as your state may have.]**

    d. The Homeowner may agree to provide the Homesharer with additional days' written notice for any of the terminations under Section (c) above. If the Homeowner so agrees, mark down the total number of written notice days agreed upon:

    _____ days for failure to pay or perform rent
    _____ days for destruction of property or causing a nuisance
    _____ days for material breach of agreement
    _____ days for [And such other provisions as your state may have.]

15. Disability Termination

If either party becomes substantially disabled, this Agreement will terminate on 30 days' written notice as provided for in 14 (a) and (b) and a new Agreement may be entered into if both parties agree.

WHEREFORE we, the undersigned, do hereby execute and agree to this rental agreement.

Homeowner: Homeowner:

Date: _____ Date: _____

MODEL HOUSE AGREEMENT

This Partnership Agreement made this 28th day of July, 1982, by and between Paula Hunter, Elizabeth McCarthy, and Glen Ludwig (hereinafter referred to singly as "Partner" and together as "Partners").

Witnesseth:

Whereas, the Partners have jointly purchased a residential dwelling located at _____ (the "Building"); and

Whereas, the Partners desire to form a partnership to own, manage, lease, rent, and maintain the Building; and

Whereas, each Partner intends to occupy a portion of the Building; and

Whereas, the Partners intend to rent a portion of the Building to persons who are not Partners;

Now Therefore, the Partners hereto agree as follows:

1. Ownership

The Partners hereby form a Partnership under the name of _____ to own, manage, lease, rent, and maintain the Building. The principal office of the Partnership shall be at the Building.

2. Term

The Partnership shall begin on the date thereof and shall continue until terminated as herein provided.

3. Initial Capital

Each Partner shall contribute, as initial capital of the Partnership, his or her ownership interest in the Building. For purposes of th capital accounts, the Partners' initial capital contributions shall be valued at:

Paula Hunter   _____
Elizabeth McCarthy   _____
Glen Ludwig   _____

(Hereinafter the Partners shall be deemed to have the following "Interest in the Partnership"):

Paula Hunter   50%
Elizabeth McCarthy   25%
Glen Ludwig   25%

4. Additional Capital

All Partners shall make such additional contributions to capital, in proportion to their interests in the Partnership, as shall be deemed necessary by Partners having a 75% interest in the Partnership, to make capital improvements to or to pay expenses relating to the operation of the Building. In the event the Partners are in dispute as to the necessity for any capital improvement and such dispute is submitted to arbitration in accordance with Paragraph 20 hereof, the determining factor in assessing the necessity of such capital improvements shall be whether or not the improvement will pay for itself (by increased rents or by an increase in the "fair market value" of the house) within a

339

reasonable period of time. In addition, the Partners hereby declare their intention to put and keep the Building in good condition and repair.

5. Capital Accounts

A separate capital account shall be maintained for each Partner. Except upon the written consent of all other Partners, no Partner, during the terms of this Agreement, shall withdraw any part of his or her capital account. If the capital account of a Partner becomes impaired, his or her share of subsequent partnership profits shall be first credited to his or her capital account until that account has been restored, before such profits are credited to his or her income account. Upon the demand of any of the Partners, the capital accounts of the Partners shall be maintained at all times in the proportions of the Partners' interests in the Partnership.

6. Profit and Loss

The net profits and losses of the Partnership shall be divided among the Partners in proportion to the Partners' interests in the Partnership. No additional share of profits shall inure to any of the Partners by reason of the fact that his or her capital or income account is in excess of his or her interest in the Partnership when compared to the capital or income account of another Partner.

7. Income Account

A separate income account shall be maintained for each Partner. Partnership profits and losses shall be charged or credited to the separate income account of each Partner. If a Partner has no credit balance in his or her income account, losses shall be charged to his or her capital account.

8. Drawings

Except as otherwise agreed by all the Partners, any Partner, from time to time, may withdraw the credit balance in his or her income account.

9. Salaries

The Partners shall establish, in advance, an hourly rate for work performed by Partners in connection with significant Building improvements. Thereafter, any Partner who performs work in connection with such Building improvements shall be paid a salary based on the number of hours she or he worked on such improvements and the hourly rate established by the Partners. Except as set forth above, or except as authorized in writing by all the Partners, no Partner shall receive any salary for services rendered to the Partnership.

10. Interest

No interest shall be paid on the initial or on any subsequent contributions to the capital of the Partnership.

11. Management and Duties

The Partners shall have equal rights and responsibilities with respect to the day-to-day management and operations of the Building. Except as otherwise specifically set forth in this Agreement, the Partners having a majority interest in the Partnership shall make all other decisions relating to the management and operations of the Building, including wthout limitation, the leasing of any portion of the Building to any person who is not a Partner.

12. Restrictions

No Partner shall, without the consent of the other Partners, endorse any note, or act as an accommodation party, or otherwise become surety for any person. Without the consent of the other Partners, no Partner, on behalf of the Partnership, shall borrow or lend money, or make, deliver, or accept any commercial paper, or execute any mortgage, security agreement, bond, or lease, or purchase or contract to purchase, or sell or contract to sell any property for or of the Partnership other than the type of property bought and sold in the regular course of its business. Except with the consent of the other Partners, no Partner shall assign, mortgage, grant a security interest in, or sell his or her share in the Partnership or in its capital assets or property, or enter into any agreement as a result of which any person shall become interested with him or her in the Partnership, or do any act detrimental to the best interests of the Partnership or which would make it impossible to carry on the ordinary business of the Partnership.

13. Banking

All funds of the Partnership shall be deposited in its name in such checking account or accounts as shall be designated by the Partners. All withdrawals therefrom are to be made upon checks signed by one or more Partners. During any one calendar month, any Partner may withdraw, without the prior approval of the other Partners, up to three checks of $50 or less for the payment of Partnership obligations. All other withdrawals of funds must be approved in advance by all Partners.

14. Books

The Partnership books shall be maintained at the Building by the Partner designated by the Partnership, and each Partner shall at all times have access to such books. The books shall be kept on a calendar year basis, and shall be closed and balanced at the end of each calendar year.

15. Withdrawal from Partnership

a. Any Partner (the "Withdrawing Partner"), by written notice to the other Partners (the "Remaining Partners"), may elect to withdraw from the Partnership. Within 30 days after receiving the written notice of withdrawal, the Remaining Partners shall elect (1) to continue the Partnership without the Withdrawing Partner or (2) to dissolve the Partnership.

b. In the event that the Remaining Partners elect to continue the Partnership without the Withdrawing Partner, the Remaining Partners shall pay the Withdrawing Partner, in cash, the amount specified in the Withdrawing Partner's income account plus the Withdrawing Partner's interest in the fair market value of all property of the Partnership. The fair market value of the property of the Partnership shall be determined by appraisal by a certified appraiser who is also a real estate broker. In the event that any Partner is not satisfied with the appraisal given by such appraiser, the dissenting Partner may obtain another appraisal by another certified appraiser who is also a real estate broker. The same procedure shall be followed to obtain a third appraisal if any Partner is not satisfied with the second appraisal. The fair market value shall be deemed the average of all appraisals obtained in accordance with this paragraph.

c. In the event that the Remaining Partners elect to dissolve the Partnership, the Partners shall proceed with reasonable promptness to liquidate the business of the Partnership. The assets of the Partnership business shall be used and distributed in the following order: (1) to pay or provide for the payment of all Partnership liabilities and lquidating expenses and obligations; (2) to bring the income accounts of the partners to the same proportions as the Partners' interests in the Partners' interests in the Partnership; (3) to discharge the balance of the income accounts of the Partners; (4) to bring the capital accounts of the Partners to the same proportions as the Partners' interest in the Partnership; and (5) to discharge the balance of the capital accounts of the Partners.

16. Voluntary Dissolution

The Partnership may be dissolved at any time by agreement of the Partners, in which event the Partners shall proceed as set forth in Paragraph 15 (c) above.

17. Death

The death of any Partner shall be treated as a voluntary withdrawal of the Partner upon written notice (as set forth in Paragraph 13) and the surviving Partners shall be treated as the Remaining Partners. The estate of the deceased Partner shall be entitled to obtain an appraisal of the Partnership property for the purpose of determining its fair market value.

18. Title to Property

The title to property of the Partnership may be held either in the name of all the Partners or in the Partnership name.

19. Disputes

In the event the Partners cannot resolve any dispute which may arise among them, the Partners, upon the written request of any Partner, agree to submit the dispute to nonbinding arbitration to be conducted by a mutually agreed-upon individual.

20. Amendments

This Partnership Agreement shall be amended only by the written approval of all Partners.

In Witness Whereof, the undersigned have set their names on the day and year first set forth above.

_____

Paula Hunter

_____

Elizabeth McCarthy

_____

Glen Ludwig

342

THE HOME MADE ENTERPRISE AGREEMENT

A. Name of the Partnership and Names of the Deed

For ease of reference and accounting purposes the name of the partnership will be "Home Made Enterprise."

Legally, the names on the deed will be Howard and Victoria Grant, as one side of the partnership; and Gregory and Mary Grant, as the other side of the partnership. The two partners hold the property as "tenants in common," with inheritance to their individual heirs.

B. Definition of the Partnership

This is a business partnership between two couples (Howard and Victoria Grant, hereafter called H&V in this agreement; and Gregory and Mary Grant, hereafter referred to as G&M in this agreement). Basically, this partnership is formed by a contract between the two couples in which each agrees to furnish an equal, one-half, share of the capital and labor for the property at _____[**address**]_____, and by which each couple shares in equal proportion, or one half, the profits and expenses. H&V and G&M agree to own, maintain, and improve the _____[**address**]_____ property.

Both couples agree that each owner will have an equal voice in the management and decision making of the business. Furthermore, they agree that if one member of a couple dies or separates from the other member, then the member of that couple remaining with the house acts for both of them in any business matters relating to the property.

This written agreement makes explicit the rights and duties of the partners. However, the partners reserve the right, using the decision-making process described by this agreement, to change, add, or delete from the agreement anytime in the future.

This agreement also allows the formation of a corporation in the future if both couples decide that incorporating the partnership is to their advantage.

C. Objectives of the Partnership

The partners will:

1. develop a comfortable, enjoyable place to live
2. establish a successful living and working relationship among the partners
3. establish a successful balance between property objectives and personal objectives
4. improve the quality, appearance, and thereby the resale value of the property

D. Management Techniques of "Home Made Enterprise"

The partners will:

1. actively work to maintain and improve the property rather than just waiting for problems to arise
2. efficiently and consistently use good planning for carrying out the financial business, maintenance work, and partnership responsibilities
3. set clear goals and timetables for restoration, maintenance, new projects, materials purchase, etc.
4. realize that good planning means flexibility, and the ability to change and make corrections when needed

5. use cooperation and encouragement as motivations, in place of negative pressure and antagonism
6. follow the principles of shared or rotating leadership, meaning that
    a. different tasks and demands of the household and property require different members of the partnership to hold leadership positions;
    b. in some cases these positions will be permanent and in other cases temporary, depending on the decisions of the partners working together.

E. Organizational Structure

The partnership is organized legally as an agreement between two couples (H&V and G&M) and operationally as a partnership among four individuals (Howard, Victoria, Gregory, and Mary Grant).

"Legally" refers to ownership, resale, and inheritance concerns plus financial decisions of more than $50 total. "Operationally" refers to property maintenance work, restoration work, day-to-day living, and household management.

For legal matters, each couple acts as one and has one-half share of the responsibility and profit. Operationally, each individual of the partnership acts as one and has one-fourth share of household decisions, except in the case of death or separation of his or her partner, for then the remaining spouse acts for two in the decision-making process.

1. Decision-Making Procedures

All matters requiring a decision will be discussed thoroughly, all options will be examined, and both short- and long-term considerations made before the actual decision will be reached.

In all cases the partners are obligated to make decisions considering (a) their own advantages balanced with the advantages of others; (b) the balance of business and personal advantages, and (c) the balance of fairness and maximum profit.

For legal decisions, each couple has one vote. Therefore, each couple must agree or compromise on their decision first. Then the two couples must agree or compromise on their decision together before a final decision is made. The partners state in this agreement that, as much as possible, they will avoid hard line confrontation and stalemates, opting for cooperation and compromise instead. But when obstacles are met, then they insist that, to the best of their ability, grudges and bad feelings will be minimized and not allowed to build up.

For operational decisions, each individual has one vote. Consensus is the first objective of the partnership. However, they realize that in some occasional cases three partners will consider a decision differently than the fourth partner, and they agree that in that case three out of four should carry an operational decision. Again, compromises will always be searched for, and the feelings of each person in the partnership will be considered carefully during the decision process. Also, confrontations and stalemates will be avoided whenever possible.

For operational decisions, one or more partners may not have strong opinions one way or the other about the decision and therefore decide to "pass" the vote. The majority vote of the others will carry the decision, or if the vote is tied, a decision will have to be resolved by compromise or a new alternative.

Emergency decisions may be necessary because of unusual circumstances such as accident or national emergency, etc. If both partners are available, they will make the appropriate decisions together in response to the particular emergency. If one partner or couple is not available because of vacation, or other reasons, then the partner who is available is entrusted to make the emergency decision that is best, in his or her opinion, for the partnership as a whole and the well-being and protection of the property.

2. Partnership Meetings and Procedures

The primary end-of-year, beginning-of-year meeting will occur in the month of January. The specific date of the meeting in January will be determined by mutual agreement. The purpose of the meeting will be to review the past year's progress, make general plans for the upcoming year, and, beginning with the January meeting in 19 _____, determine whether one or both couples plan on selling the property, or their share of the property. Income tax matters will also be reviewed at this time and decisions made if needed.

In addition to January, the partners will also meet each month to work on the issues and concerns of the partnership. The time of these monthly meetings will be set by mutual agreement of the partners. The goals of these monthly meetings are to (a) resolve issues before they become problems, (b) evaluate operations for the last month, (c) plan new projects and maintenance programs, and (d) resolve food preparation and food-buying concerns.

When one or more partners considers that a issue should be presented to the others without waiting for a monthly meeting, then that person can call a meeting for a time convenient to the others. As always, each partner will try to be as cooperative and understanding as possible, even for issues that, on the surface, seem insignificant or unwise to consider.

Of course, it is understood that many or most of the issues and concerns of the household and property will be resolved by day-to-day conversations and agreements among the partners. The formal monthly meetings might be deemed unnecessary for some months, and if all four partners are in agreement about this, then the meeting may be canceled for that particular month.

The partners agree that to help the meetings flow more easily, the following methods will be used: setting an agenda; setting time limits for discussions of individual items and overall length of meeting; using a chairperson to keep the meeting on target; inviting experts or advisors (for example, an interior decorator) to provide ideas; requesting individual partners to do research for making final decisions.

Also, to help keep the partnership records accurate, one person in the group will take notes of each meeting in a ledger. Therefore, a short synopsis of each item discussed and decisions made will be on record for future reference. This task can be rotated between partners or held permanently by one person, depending on the decision of the group.

All members of the partnership must be present to make the legal and operational decisions that affect everyone.

3. Organizational Timetable

An important part of the decision-making process will be the establishment of a timetable setting forth in clear terms the goals and projects for the household management, maintenance, and restoration. This timetable, of course, can be adjusted from month to month. Possibly the timetable will be broken down into various segments: day-to-day, long term, outdoor, indoor, maintenance, and restoration. This is dependent on the decisions made by the partners. A record of timetables and successful completion of individual projects will be kept with the notes recorded from the monthly meetings.

F. Accounting Procedures

Another outcome of this partnership agreement is the necessity for accurate and strict accounting of all financial matters concerning the partnership. The partners will decide which person or persons will serve as treasurer and accountant for the partnership. This person will be responsible for all accounting work, issuing checks, collecting rents, etc. Financial reports will be a major part of the monthly meetings and especially the yearly meeting in January.

As a minimum requirement the accounting procedure will include:

1. an Expense Ledger: tallying both cash and checks disbursed
2. an Income Ledger: itemizing the "paid in" capital including income from rent or sale of items, and partner's investments in the "business"
3. a Balance Sheet: balancing assets and liabilities.

Additional accounting measures to be followed are:

1. all receipts will be retained
2. a "partnership business" bank account will be established, and the partners are responsible for fixing the amount to be reserved as working capital
3. all items that possibly serve as an Income Tax Deduction will be recorded in a separate file and be made available at the January meeting.
4. all accounting and financial decisions are the responsibility of the partners through the decision-making process outlined in this agreement.

Occasionally a partner may make a loan to the partnership in general or to another partner. In such instances, the loan and its terms will be put in writing and signed by both partners. If a loan is not repaid at the time of resale, then the final sharing of money after resale will take that loan amount into account and the debt plus accrued interest will be erased in that way.

G. Procedures for Terminating the Partnership

Basically the partnership between H&V and G&M will end when one or both of the couples sells the property. There is a selling timetable the partners will follow and a particular procedure to use in going through that process. These items are detailed below.

1. Selling Timetable

The decision of whether one couple or both wishes to sell the property will first be raised officially, by agreement, at the January, 19 _____ partnership meeting. After that the next time to consider the resale question is January 19 _____ and then every January thereafter.

If the decision is to resell, then the following steps will be taken during the months of January through March: prepare the house for optimum resale appeal and profit; determine through comparable market value and two professional appraisals the maximum asking price and lowest acceptable price the partnership will settle for; and determine the strategy for advertising and selling, especially the question of whether or not to contract with a realty company. The timetable ends with the months of April through June, for then the house is publically advertised and sold.

If the property is not sold by the end of June, then the partners are required to work out a revised strategy and timetable.

3. Only One Couple Wishes to Sell the Property

When this occurs, again, everyone will work together to successfully prepare the house and property to make the sale. The January timetable will be followed, and the couples are required to work out a fair and reasonable resale for both parties.

Two options can be pursued:

a. one couple buys out the other's share or

b. a one-half share of the property is sold to a third party.

If neither option is successful after five months from the January decision, then both couples agree that they will sell the house together, as a whole, neither of them retaining ownership.

Both couples must agree on the price for selling through any method. Differences will be worked out in a spirit of compromise and fairness. The process for setting the price to sell one-half the property is the same as for selling the complete property: The figure will be derived from the current market value as compared to other similar houses in the area and from two professional appraisals.

Any new co-owners of the property must be approved and agreed upon by the owners remaining. A new "Contract of Agreement" must be worked out and signed between the new owners before resale takes place.

H. Inheritance Provision

Both H&V and G&M will have their names on the deed. With each couple, inheritance goes to the individual's spouse first and to the couple's child, or other beneficiary, second. Each couple determines its own inheritance. One couple does not inherit the other's share.

If both members of a couple should die, then the "Provisions for Terminating the Partnership" would go into effect with the Executor of the deceased couple acting in their place.

If one member of a couple should die, then the remaining member would retain and exercise all the rights and duties of the couple for one-half the partnership.

I. Delegation of Work Procedures

It is understood that the work for maintaining, operating, and restoring the property both inside and outside the building will be approximately shared by the partners. Individual initiative and voluntary "picking up" of duties will be an important aspect of working together. Some jobs will be regarded, naturally, as undesirable by each partner and will have to be rotated among the partners by their mutual decision.

Identification, delegation, and evaluation of work responsibilities will be an important part of the monthly business meetings of the partnership. Fairness, reasonable expectations, and personal preferences will be followed as much as possible. The partners agree that they will try their best to be generous, supportive, and encouraging about work, rather than selfish, competitive, and critical. Much of the work will be attempted in the spirit of contributing to the good of the household. Each person's skill and energy level with particular chores will be respected. Looking over the other's shoulder and criticizing negatively will be minimized.

Not everyone will be able to do the same work or do the same work equally well, but there will be enough work for everyone and for a wide range of abilities.

J. Methods to Handle Disagreements

It is agreed between the partners that cooperation and compromise will be the goals of all interpersonal and business matters, but when and if disagreements arise, the following methods will be used to help resolve the impasse:

1. determine a cooling-off period of one day, one week, one month, or more before making a final decision
2. look for alternatives or new compromises that possibly have not yet been recognized as possible
3. ask for an outside opinion from a person or persons mutually agreeable to all partners
4. review the advantages of the property and partnership, so that the individual negative aspect is seen in proper perspective
5. basically search out, no matter how difficult, mutual advantages rather than individual advancement at the expense of the other partners.

K. Procedures for Renting to a Third Person or Persons

The decision to rent a portion of the house to a third party is exclusively and mutually the decision of the partners.

The amount of rent and portion of utilities to be paid for by the renters will be determined by H&V and G&M. A guideline to follow for rent between August and December 19 _____ is: 1 person, $125; 2 persons $155.

Income from renters will be equally divided between the two couples or deposited in the Partnership Bank Account and used later at the discretion of the partners.

The interpersonal and household agreements among the partners and renters will be documented in general terms in a booklet of "House Bylaws" so that partners and renters know what to expect from one another.

L. Use of Rooms in the House and Use of Garage

H&V and G&M will have complete, private control of at least two rooms in the house. They may use these rooms for bedrooms or a bedroom and a study. Another room or rooms may be set aside for the complete and private use of a renter or renters. The remainder of the house is to be shared by the partners and renters, if any. In all areas, however, privacy and the rights of others will be respected at all times. For example, a closed door means that a person should knock and ask permission to enter.

The kitchen in particular will require sensitivity and careful sharing from all persons to make its common use move smoothly and easily.

Each couple is entitled to one garage unless they mutually agree to rotate the use of the garage with a renter on a week-to-week basis or whatever the partners decide.

The owners have the right to limit the number of cars that a renter may bring onto the property. Each individual owner is entitled to one parking space on the property.

M. Furnishings

Outside their private rooms the partners will share and blend their furniture and belongings except for those items that have been clearly identified to the others as not for common use. Ownership and resale profit of furniture and belongings will be retained by the original owner unless the item has been bought or attained in partnership, in which case the ownership will be held by both, or eventually one partner will buy out the other's share, or the income derived from resale to a third party will be divided equally.

As of June 19 _____, the partners' common property includes a freezer, a Rototiller, and all of the items left with the property by the former owner.

N. Insurance Claims

If there is damage to the house and property in which the owners must pay the $100 or $200 deduction, then the owners will divide the cost.

If the damage is caused by direct and obvious negligence of one owner, then that owner is responsible for paying the insurance deduction.

If extra insurance is required for personal belongings of extremely high value or special significance, then the owner of that property pays the extra premium.

Renters are required to provide their own tenant insurance.

O. Taxes

Property taxes will be paid in equal, one-half shares, by each partner couple.

Personal income tax is an individual concern of each couple. The couples retain the right to decide between themselves whether the mortgage interest deduction should be shared equally between the two partners on their individual IRS returns or placed entirely on the return of one partner with a subsequent sharing of the tax savings that result. Both couples must agree on using this second procedure and agree on a fair and reasonable sharing of the savings before the procedure can be used.

P. Pets

Both couples will agree before pets become a part of the household or property. Before a pet arrives, partners must determine whether they will share expenses or not and who will keep the pet if the partnership is ended in the future.

Q. Provision for Adding, Changing, or Deleting from This Agreement

Both couples agree that any additions, deletions, and changes in this agreement will be negotiated and settled by mutual consent in a spirit of openness, friendliness, and cooperation.

Any major changes in the agreement (other than language adjustment or simple reinterpretations) will be signed by the partners to show common agreement.

This agreement will be periodically reviewed by the partners to keep it up to date and fresh in everyone's mind. A minimum review period would be every six months. The same for the "House Bylaws," which will be kept consistent with the agreement.

H&V's signatures _____ Date _____

_____ Date _____

G&M's signatures _____ Date _____

_____ Date _____

INTENTIONAL COMMUNITY AGREEMENT

This Agreement, entered into this _____ day of _____, by and among

_____

Witnesseth:

That the parties agree to become equal members of the organization known as _____ Property Owners Association in the County of _____, State of _____. Said organization shall have its principal place of business at such place or places as designated by the joint consensus of the partners.

1. Purpose

The partnership is formed for the purpose of owning and managing property, hereinafter described, for a place to live which shall include, but not be limited to, residential areas and common recreational areas for the benefit of the members of this partnership agreement.

2. Commencement Date

That the partnership shall commence on the _____ day of _____, 19 _____, and shall continue until terminated by the joint assention of all the parties hereto or as otherwise herein provided.

3. Property Subject to Agreement

The real property which shall be subject to this agreement is located in the County of _____, State of _____, and is more particularly described as follows:

[Here the legal description of the property is entered.]

4. Membership Defined

The term "membership" shall be defined as the partners set forth in this agreement as well as any subsequent partners.

5. New Members

New members may be added to the membership if they shall be approved by the consensus of the members as well as pay their entrance fee, as hereinafter provided for, and assume the responsibilities of the membership.

6. Rights of Membership

Membership in this partnership agreement shall give each family unit the following rights:

    a. The right to have individually titled to him a three-quarter ($3/4$) acre plot of land subject to restrictions as to use, lease, sublease, and sale as set forth hereinafter in this agreement.

    b. Right to the use of the common area of the above described property, which is not individually titled to any other member of this partnership, subject to the restrictions as hereinafter stated.

    c. The right of the individual member and any individual in his family unit who has attained the age of 18 years to participate in the meetings of this association by discussion as well as by vote.

7. Responsibility of Membership

The members of this partnership shall have the following specified responsibilities; however, the designation of same shall not relieve the member of any other responsibilities as provided in this agreement:

 a. Each family unit shall pay an entrance fee in the sum of Three Thousand Dollars ($3,000.00), which may be paid in regular payments if said payment plan is approved by the consensus of the membership.

 b. Each family unit shall share equally in the expenses of the partnership which shall include, but not be limited to, payment on the partnership indebtedness, improvements to the property and maintenance of the property. The foregoing expenses set forth as a responsibility of the member shall be determined at a semiannual meeting as provided for hereinafter.

 c. Each member shall have the responsibility of using his three-quarter ($3/4$) acre plot of land for ecologically sound purposes as well as doing the same for the common area.

 d. Design of individual residential property shall be submitted to the membership for review and comment prior to actual construction.

 e. Any and all additions to the residential property shall be submitted to the membership for review and comment prior to actual construction of same.

 f. No member shall commit waste upon his individual three-quarter ($3/4$) acre plot or allow any activity which would decrease the value of the real estate.

8. Conduct of Partnership Business

The partnership shall conduct its business by semiannual meetings. The purpose of said meetings shall be as follows:

 a. To determine the semiannual assessment for association expenses.

 b. To conduct the normal business of the partnership, which shall include, but not be limited to, the election of officers to preside over the business of the association. Said officers shall be a President and a Secretary-Treasurer. Further, said officers shall be elected by a majority vote of the members for a two-year term.

9. Semiannual Assessment

The semiannual assessment as provided for herein shall be as stated above, based on the interest owed by the partnership as well as the principal amount of the partnership's obligations as well as the amount it requires to pay for improvements and maintenance of the common property of the partnership. In reaching said semiannual assessment, not only shall the past six months' record of payments and expenses be considered, but in addition, the future six months of anticipated payments and expenses shall be considered. Upon the determination of the semiannual assessment each family unit will be notified of same and upon such notification shall pay this assessment within a six-month period thereafter.

10. Termination of Individual's Membership

An individual member of this partnership may terminate his membership by serving written notice upon the other members at least ninety (90) days in advance of his expected termination. In addition, an individual membership may be terminated by the death of the member. Further, an individual membership may be terminated by the consensus of the remaining members upon a showing of a violation of the terms of this agreement. The procedure for termination shall be as follows:

The individual member(s) shall appoint an appraiser to appraise his individual residential three-quarter (3/4) acre property, and the remaining members shall appoint an appraiser of their own choosing to do likewise. The average of both appraisals shall be the price at which the remaining members may purchase said residential property. If the remaining members fail to purchase said residential property, then the individual member, after a lapse of four (4) months after appraisal, may sell his residential property to the highest bidder.

11. Sale, Lease, or Sublease of Residential Property

The individual member shall not have the right without the consensus of the other members to lease or sublease his property to anyone outside of the membership of this partnership.

12. Acquisition of Additional Property or New Indebtedness

The partnership may not acquire any new or additional indebtedness or real property without the consensus of the members of the partnership.

13. Termination of Partnership

This partnership may be terminated upon the consensus of the members hereof. Upon such a consensus the partnership property shall be sold and the proceeds of said sale shall go to pay the expenses and indebtedness of the partnership; and the balance shall be distributed equally among the members.

In Witness Whereof, the parties hereto have hereunto affixed their signatures on the date first mentioned in this agreement.

_____

_____

I asked attorney Gloria Haffer to take a look at this contract, since she has advised many business and house partners in her practice.

She took exception to the wisdom of paragraph 6c and said particular attention to its impact should be given.

"Throughout the agreement," says Gloria, "parties are referred to as a "family unit." Paragraph 6c grants voting privileges to individuals 18 years of age or older. Clearly, a family unit with many members age 18 and over can have a great deal of influence in voting matters—more than a family unit with few or no 18-year-olds. This creates an unfair advantage which could disrupt the harmony of living in community."

Gloria suggests paragraph 6c be modified to provide equal voting power for each family unit as follows:

"The right of each family unit to participate in the meetings of the association and to have one vote on matters."

Hannah, however, sticks with the wisdom of the clause as it is written. She says, "Children in our community, especially when they reach the age of 18, will be treated as individuals. When they vote on matters, they will not be expected to automatically agree with their parents. They have a right to their own opinions.

"Of course, with voting privileges comes financial responsibility. Eighteen-year-olds will also be expected to help finance the issues they favor. We've left this issue wide open on purpose. When the time comes to face it, we feel we can handle it well."

Perhaps they can. But for your information, these are the two sides of that particular coin.

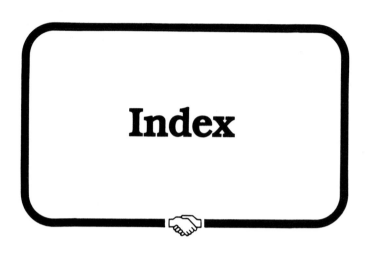

Index